THE OTHER SIDE OF SAN DIEGO

THE OTHER SIDE OF SAN DIEGO

PHOTOGRAPHS BY MIGUEL VALENCIA

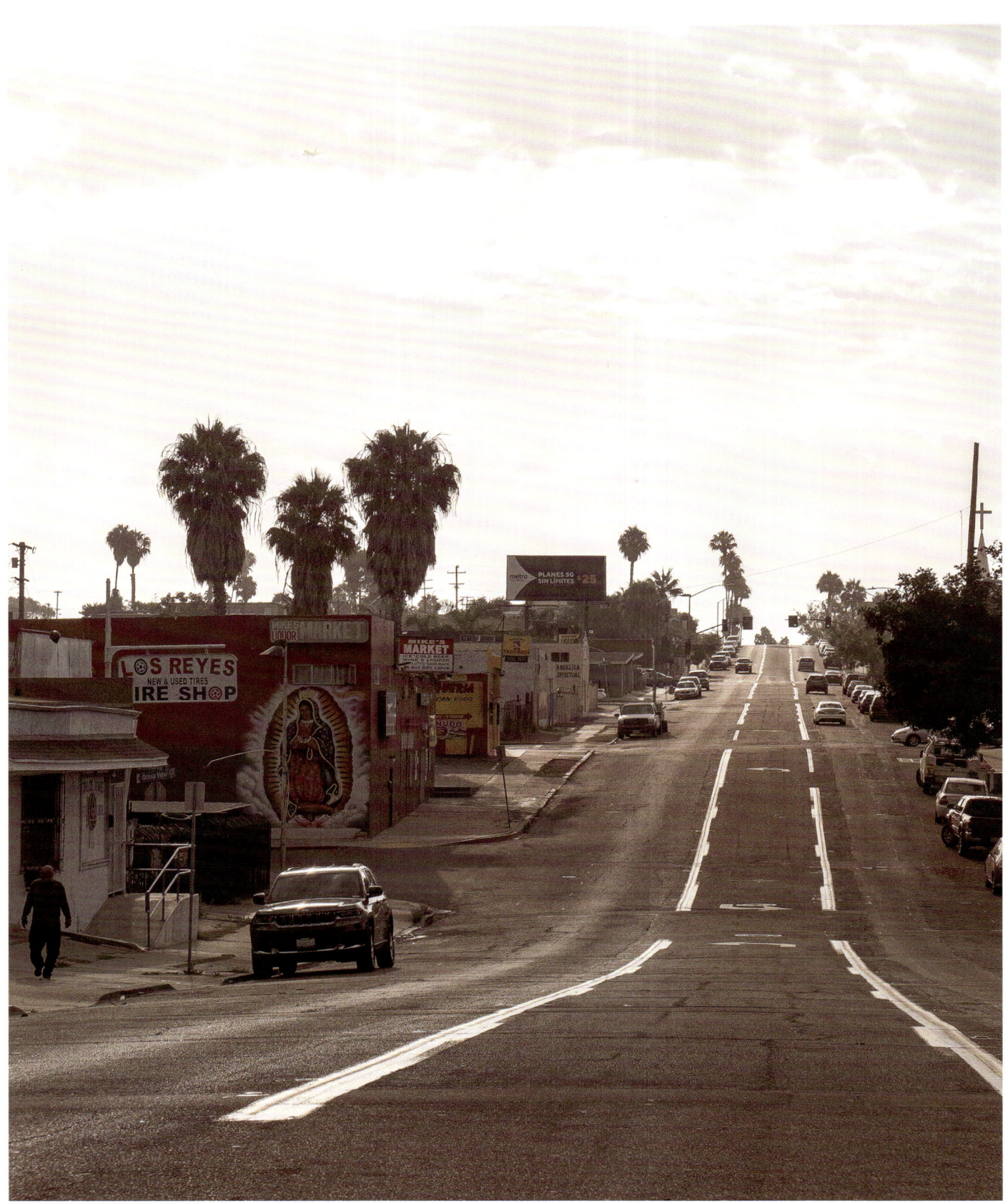

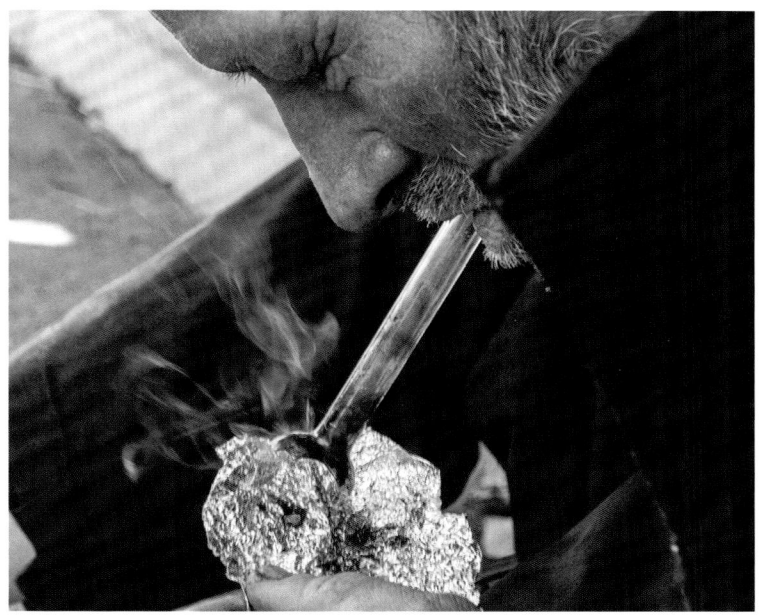

When I was a little kid, the things I watched through screen doors and the steps I took on those sidewalks, they did something to me. The drug presence, the sounds of screeching shopping carts being pushed, and the people that are with that "business" of pushing the line. It represented something to me—but it always has.

For whatever reason, I've always done dangerous stuff in my life. Taking chances for what I want or believe in, ro matter what it took from me. I am not just like everybody else, my lifestyle is very different. So this subject that I photograph, that I affiliate with, the hands that I shake, are no different from what I am accustomed to. From the dope fiends slumped over from the heroin and meth to the sounds of 808 bass that rattle windows along the neighborhood blocks, to the names hit up blasted over alley walls.

The people: the homeboys I fuck with, the lifestyle they come from, and those communities that I represent, and why I went about shooting such material—they are "the other side of San Diego." Monochromatic tones of how I see life defy the reality of what these sidewalks could turn into or what they have always been about. Another type of personality kept away from the mainstream. A lot of times, people unfamiliar with San Diego get on our trolley line and they become confused.

—MIGUEL VALENCIA, 2024

SHELL

TOWN

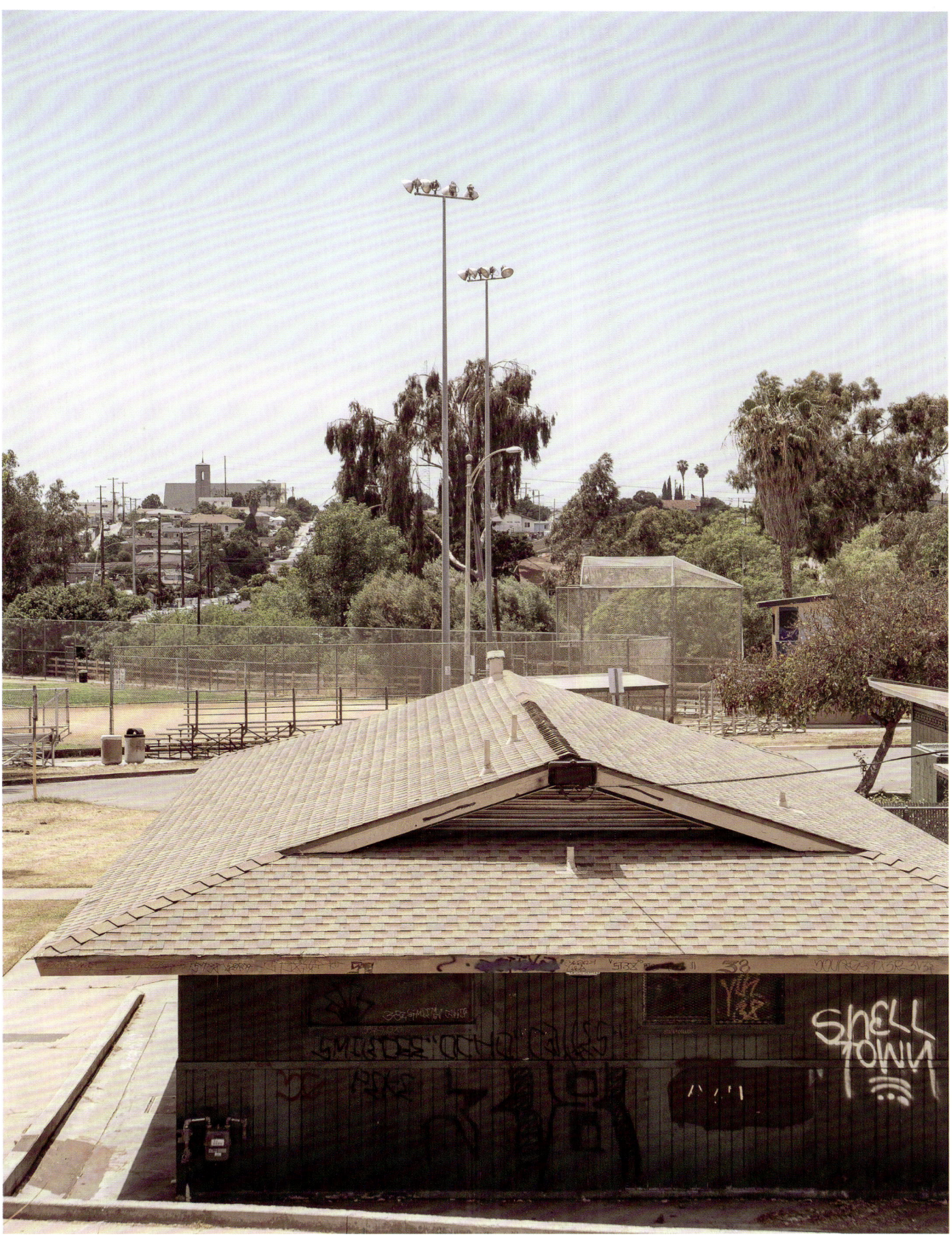

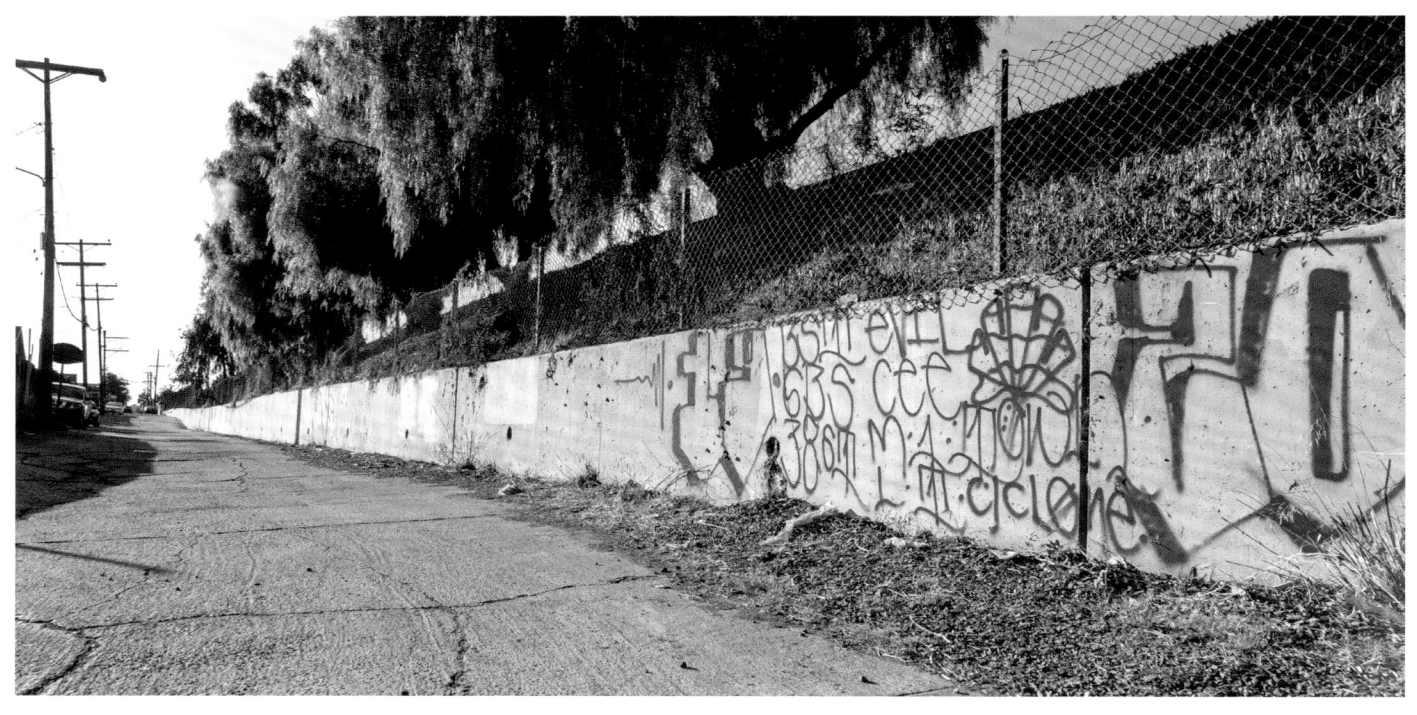

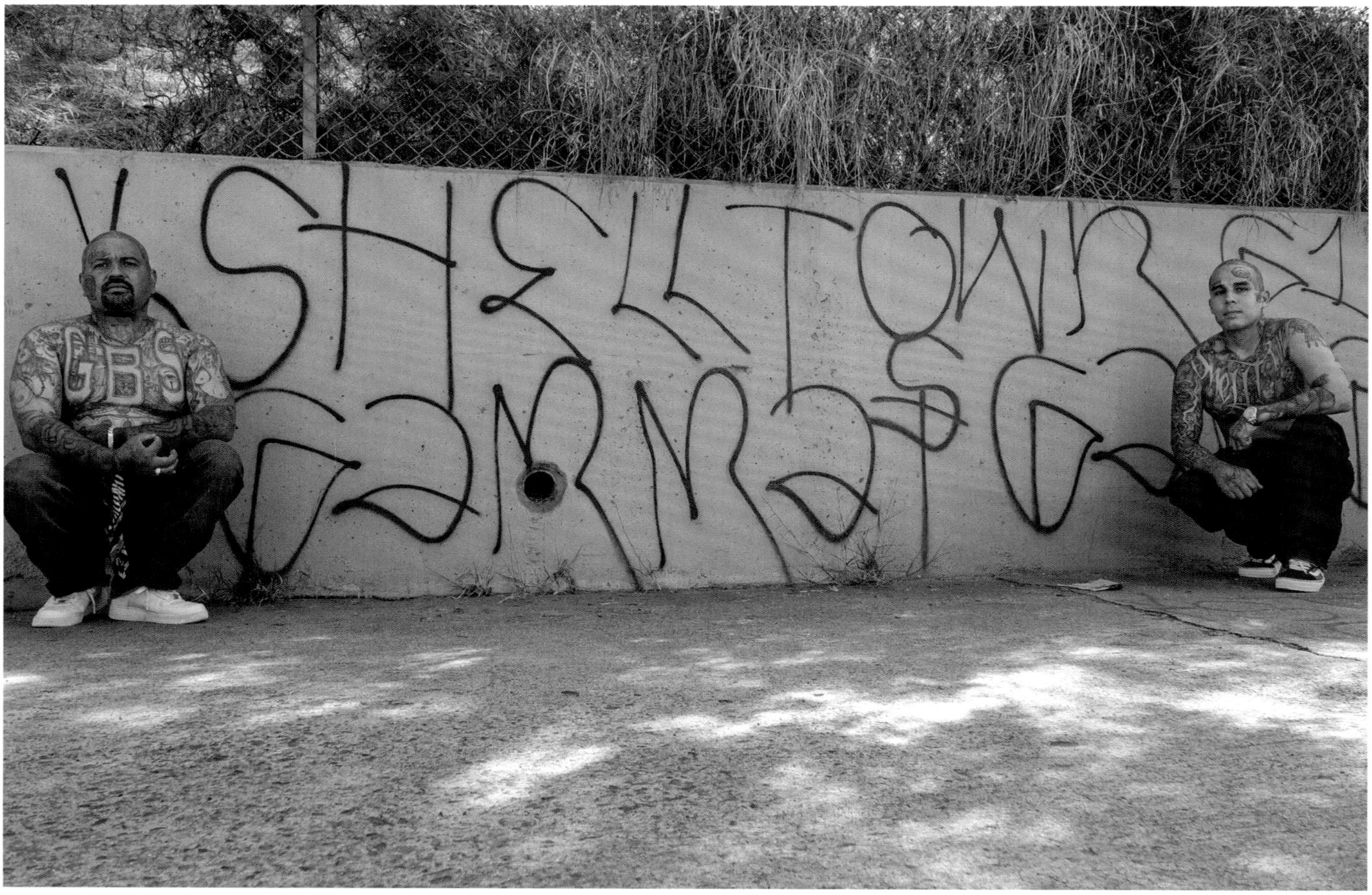

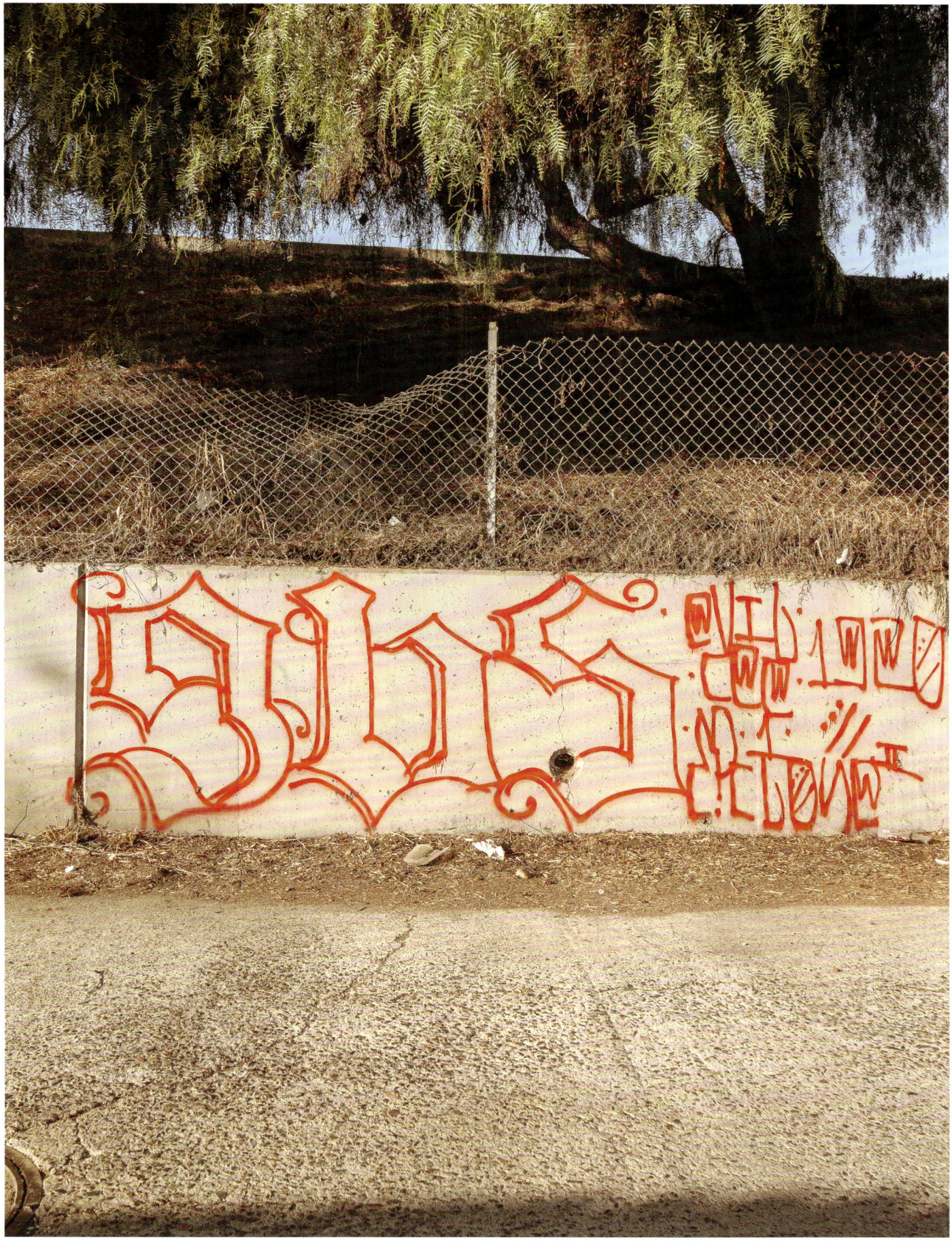

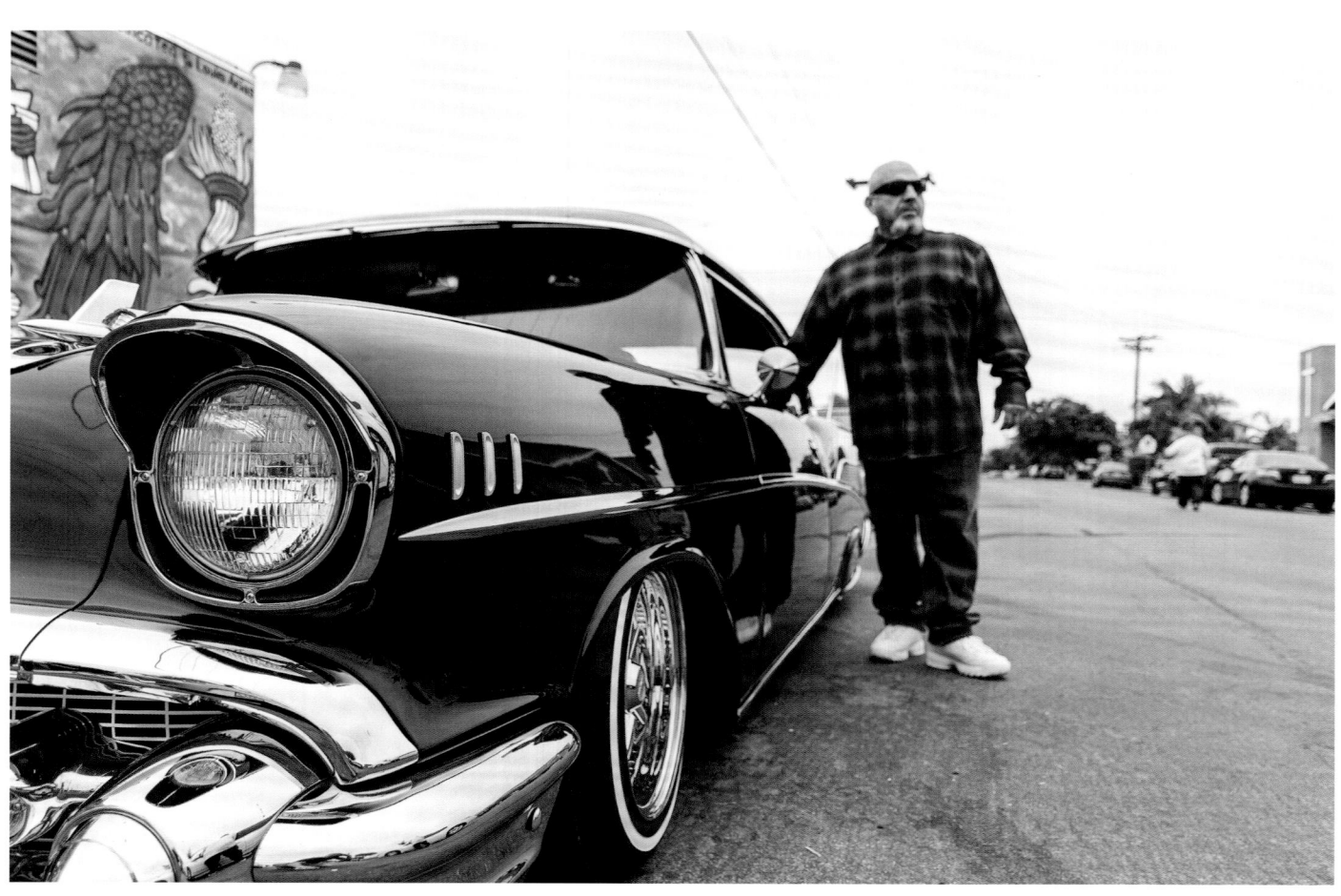

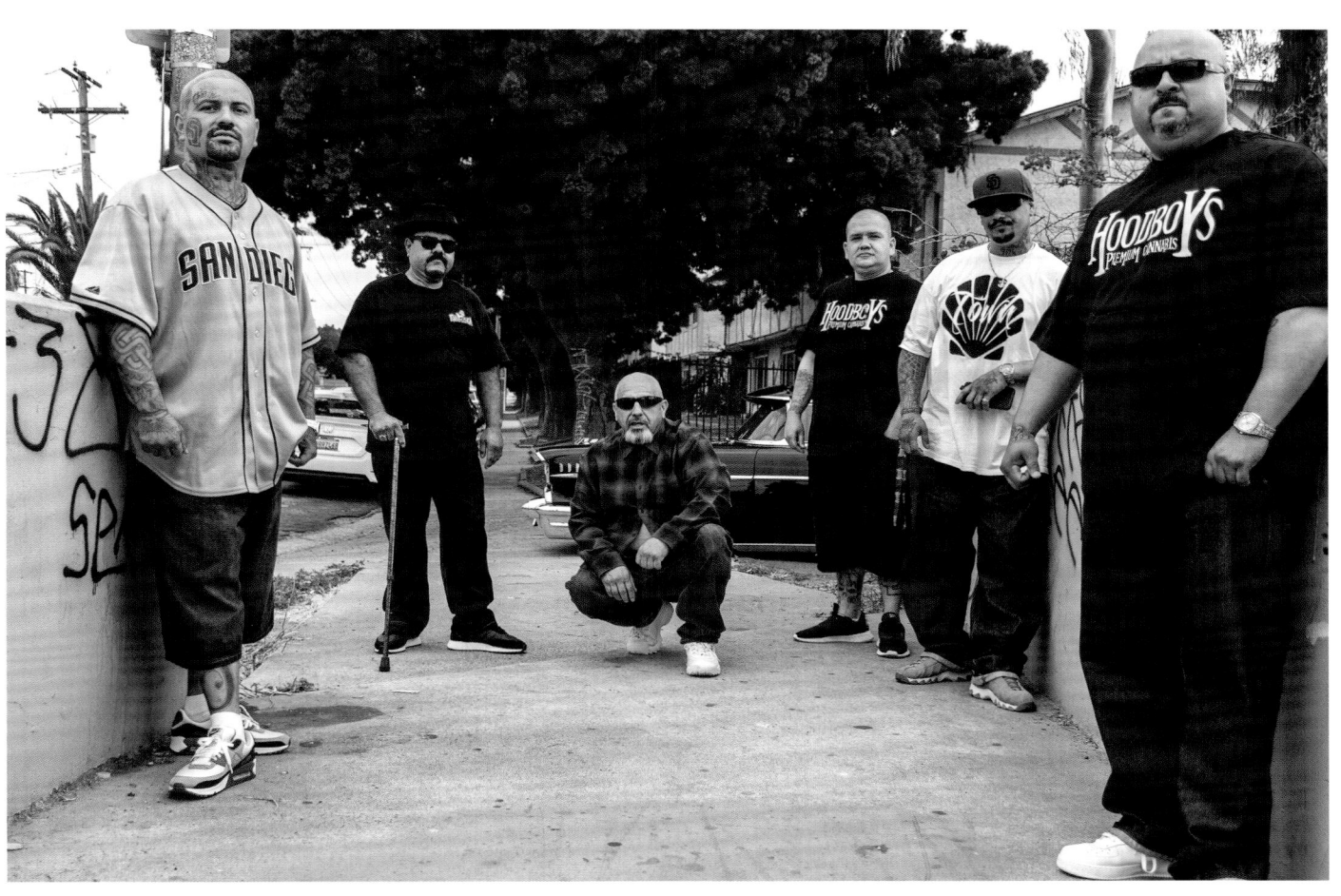

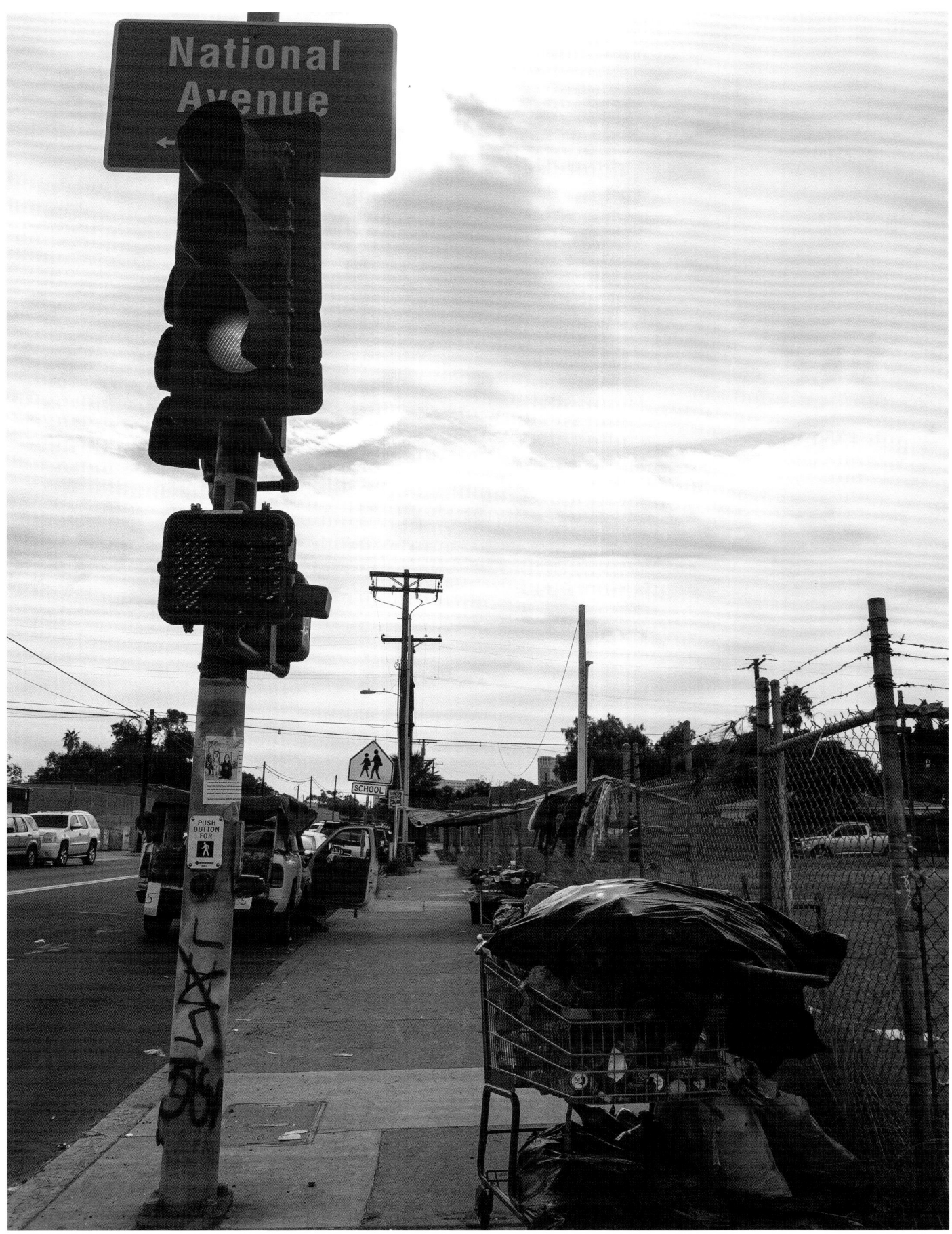

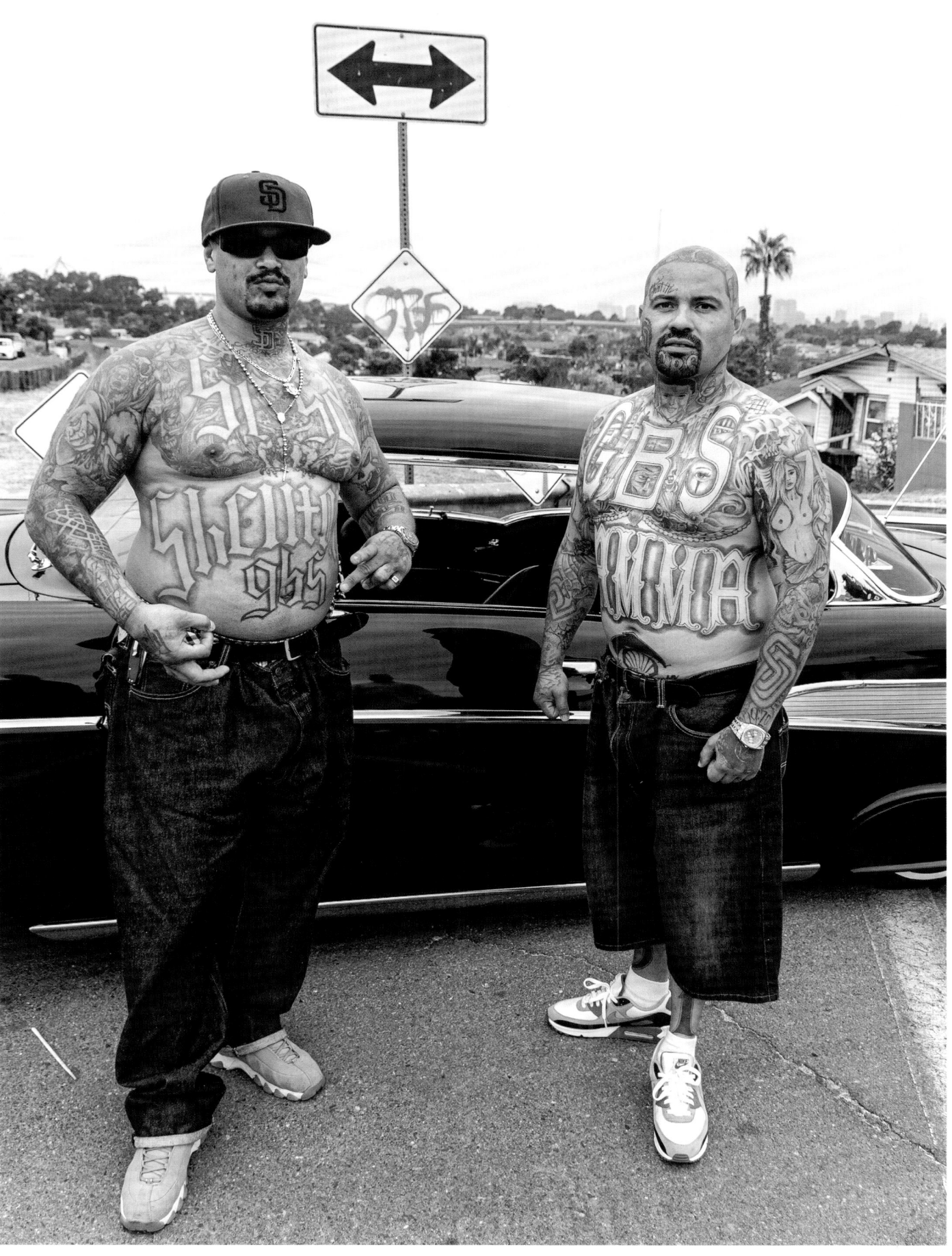

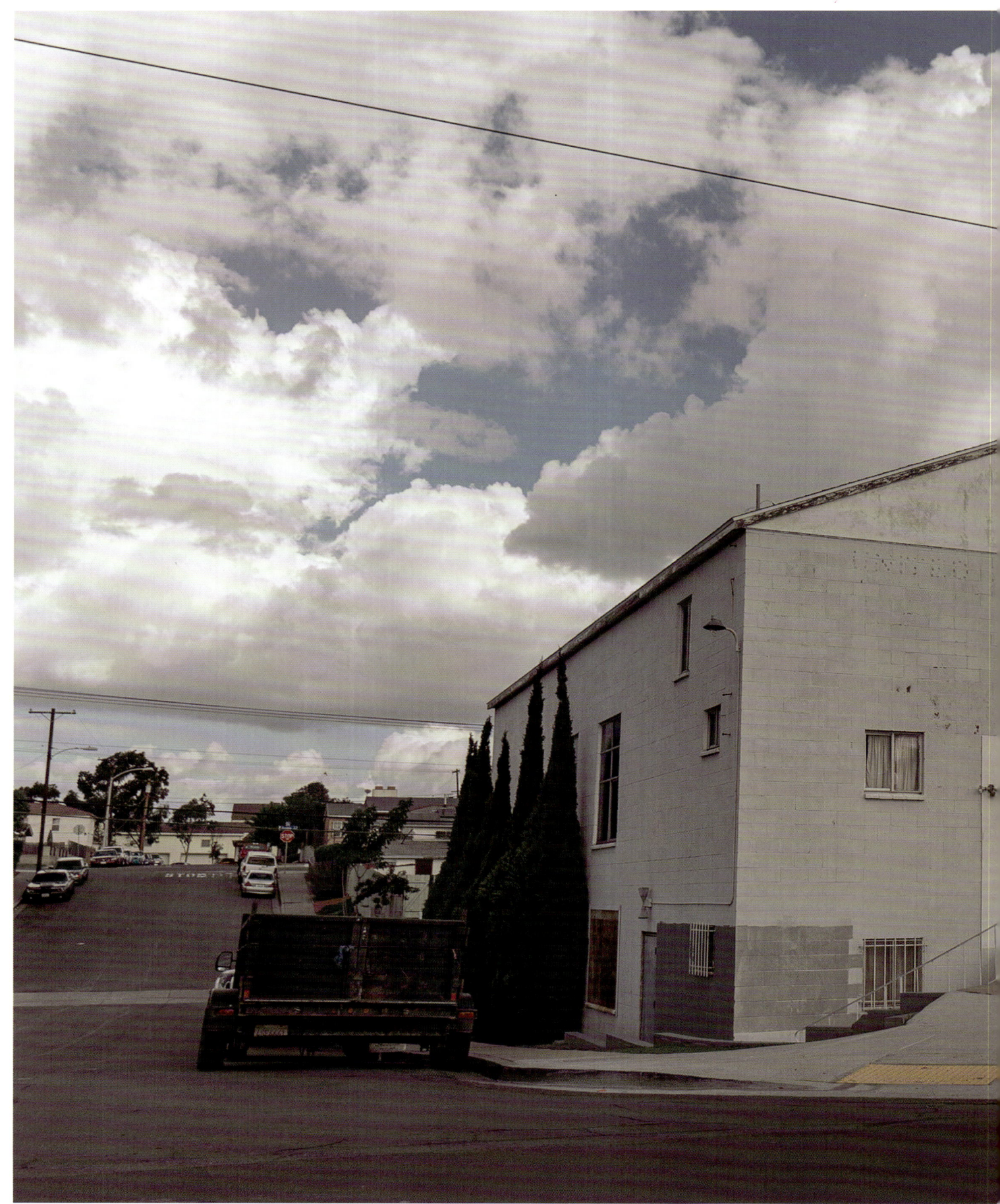

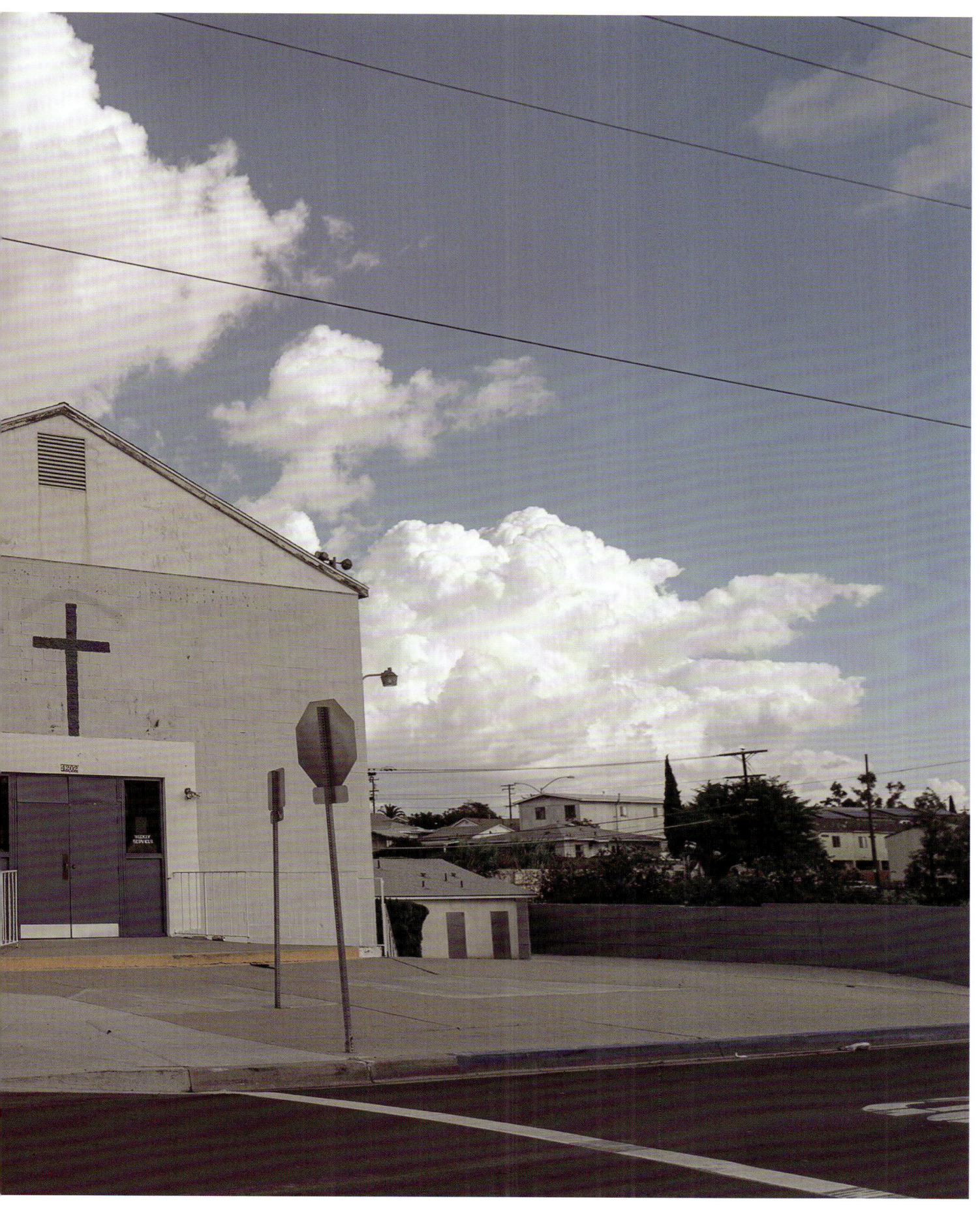

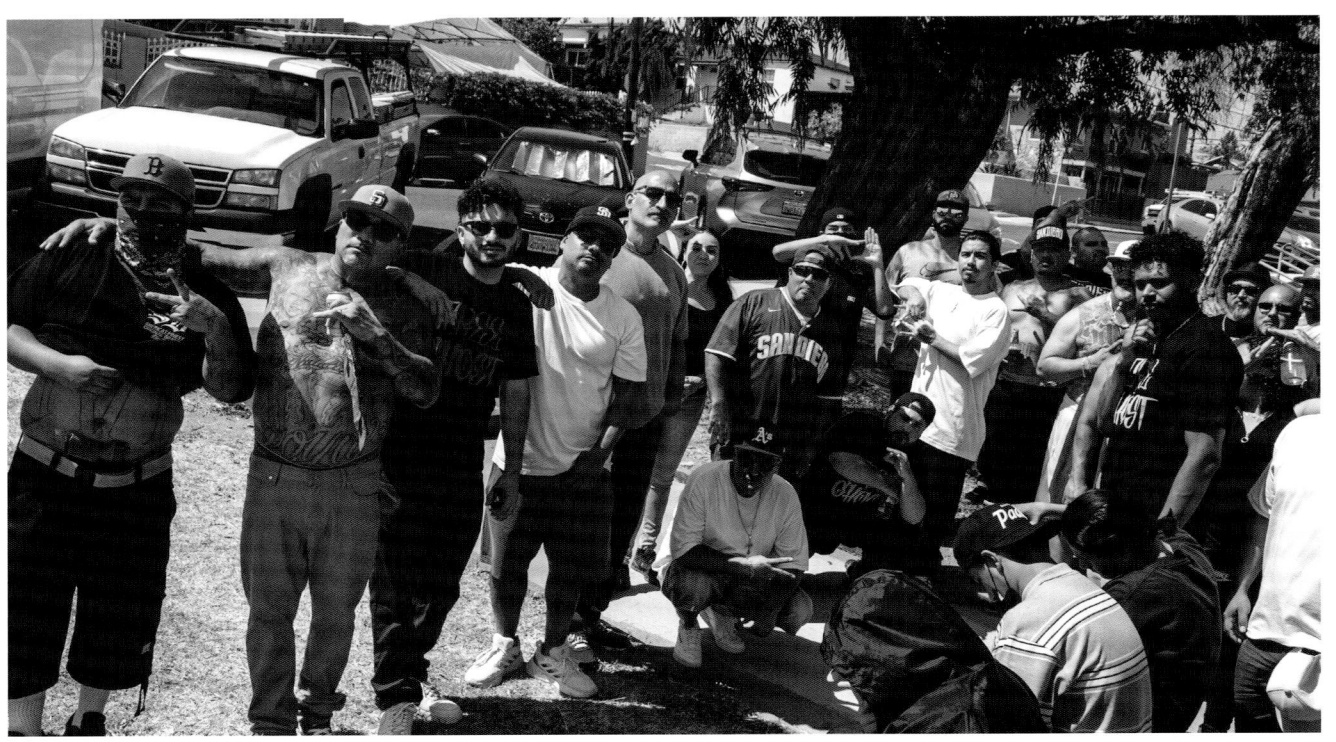

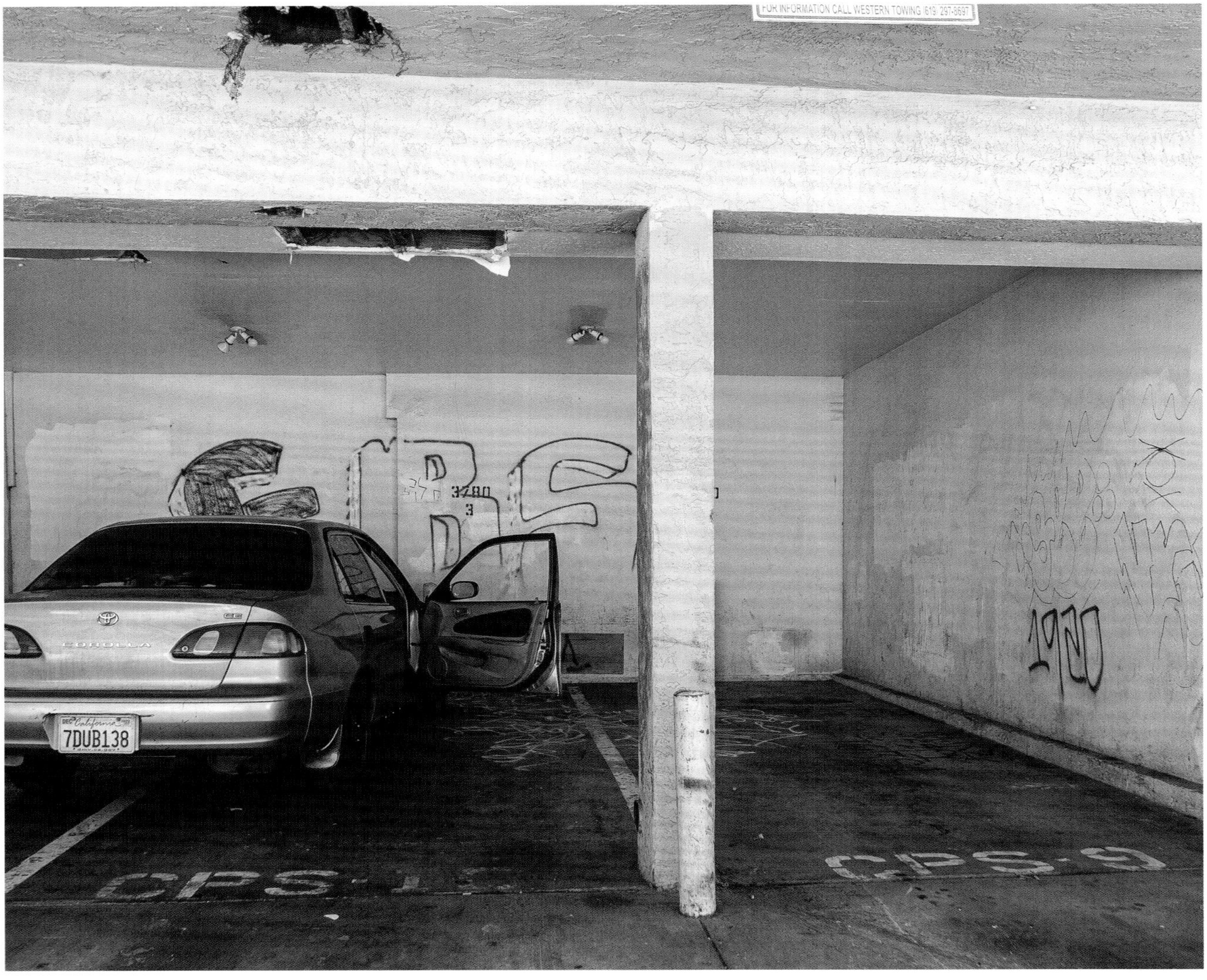

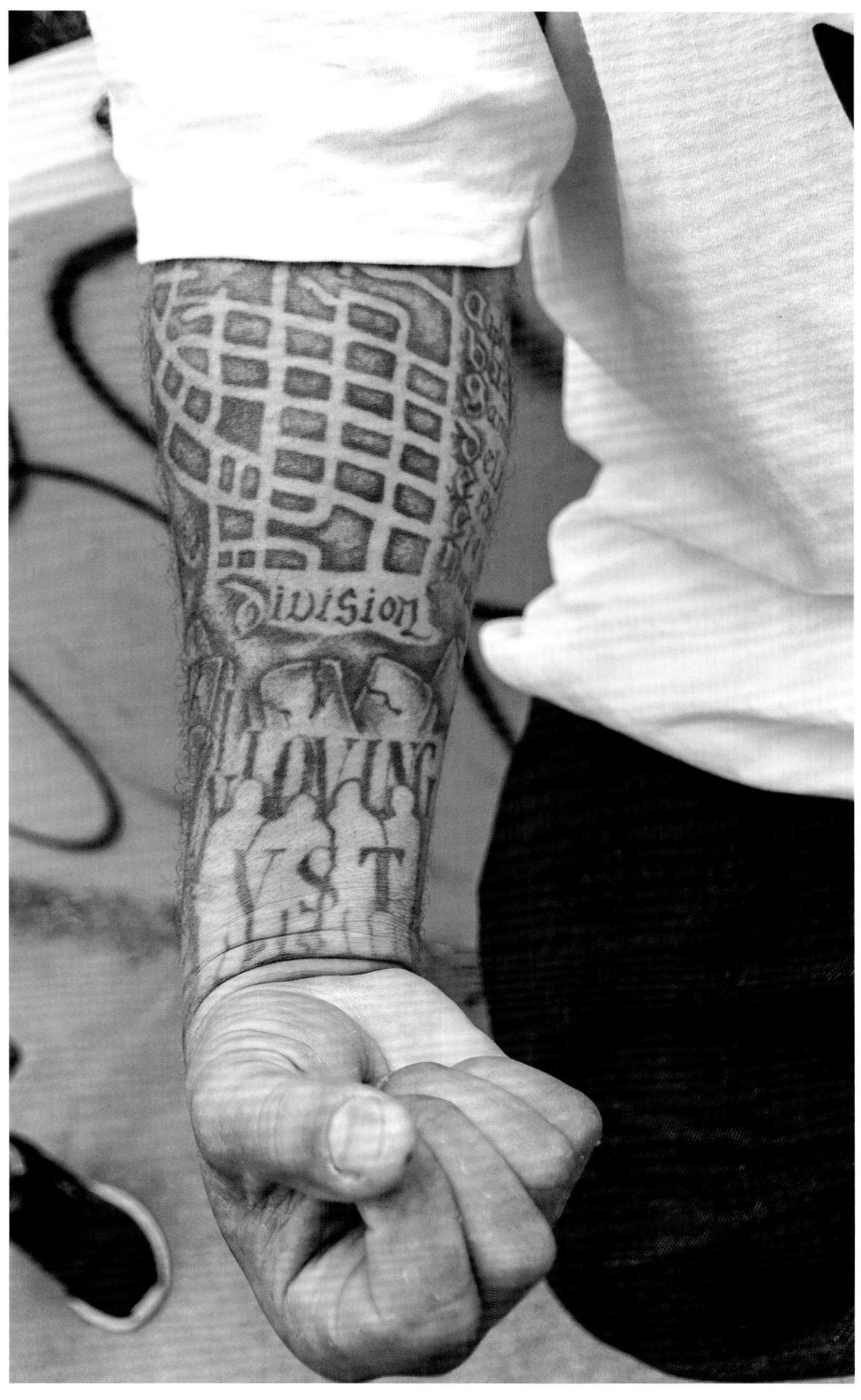

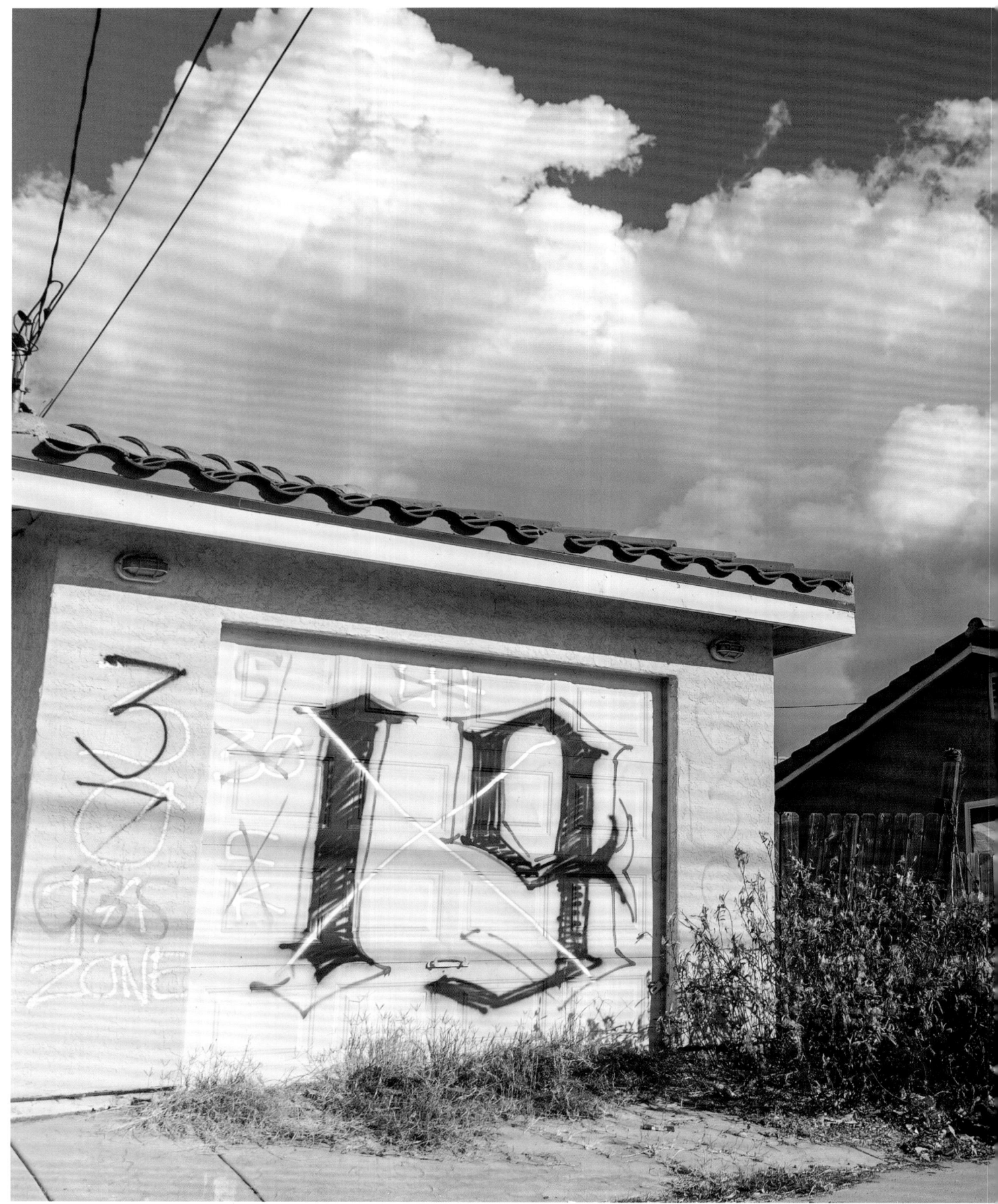

18

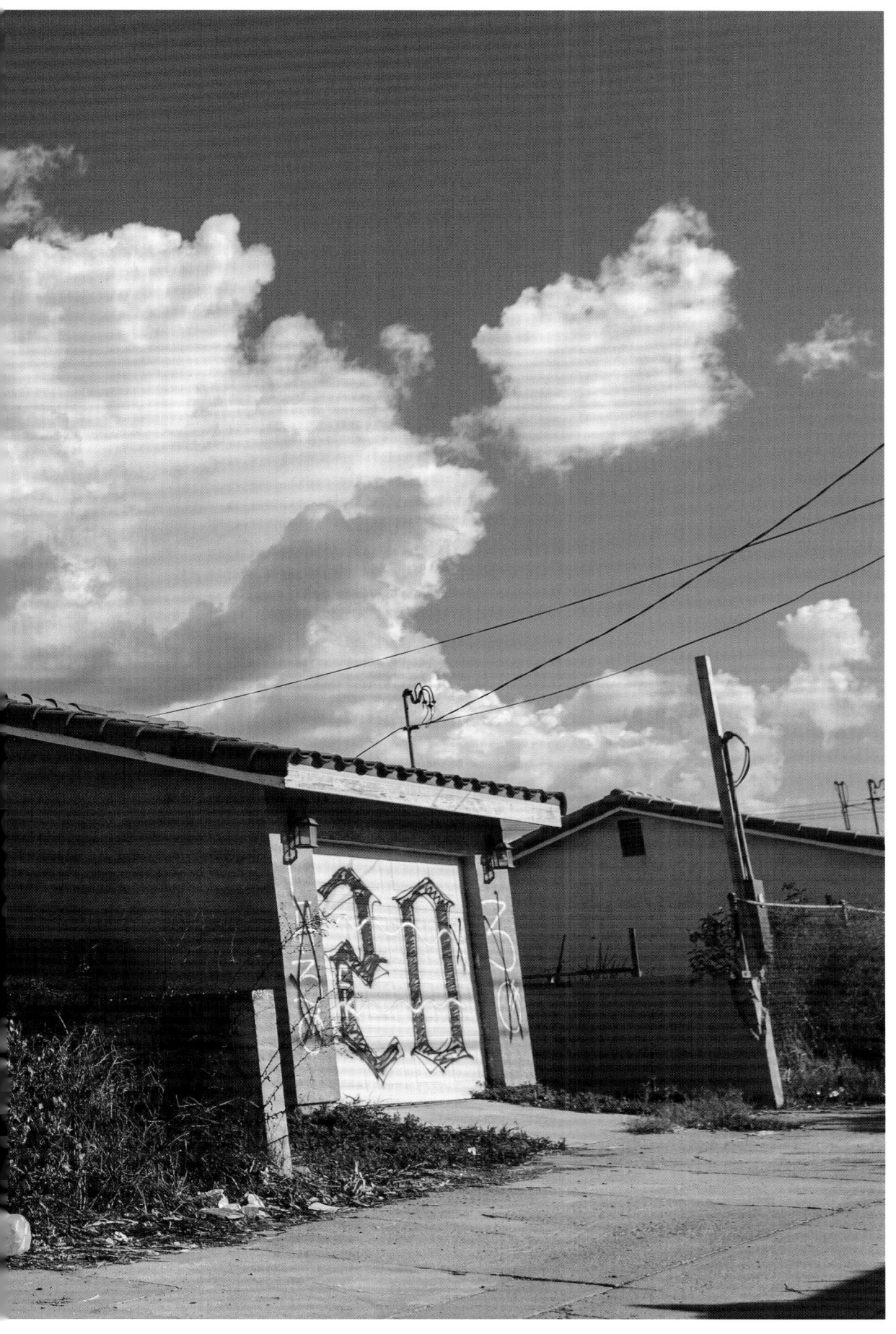

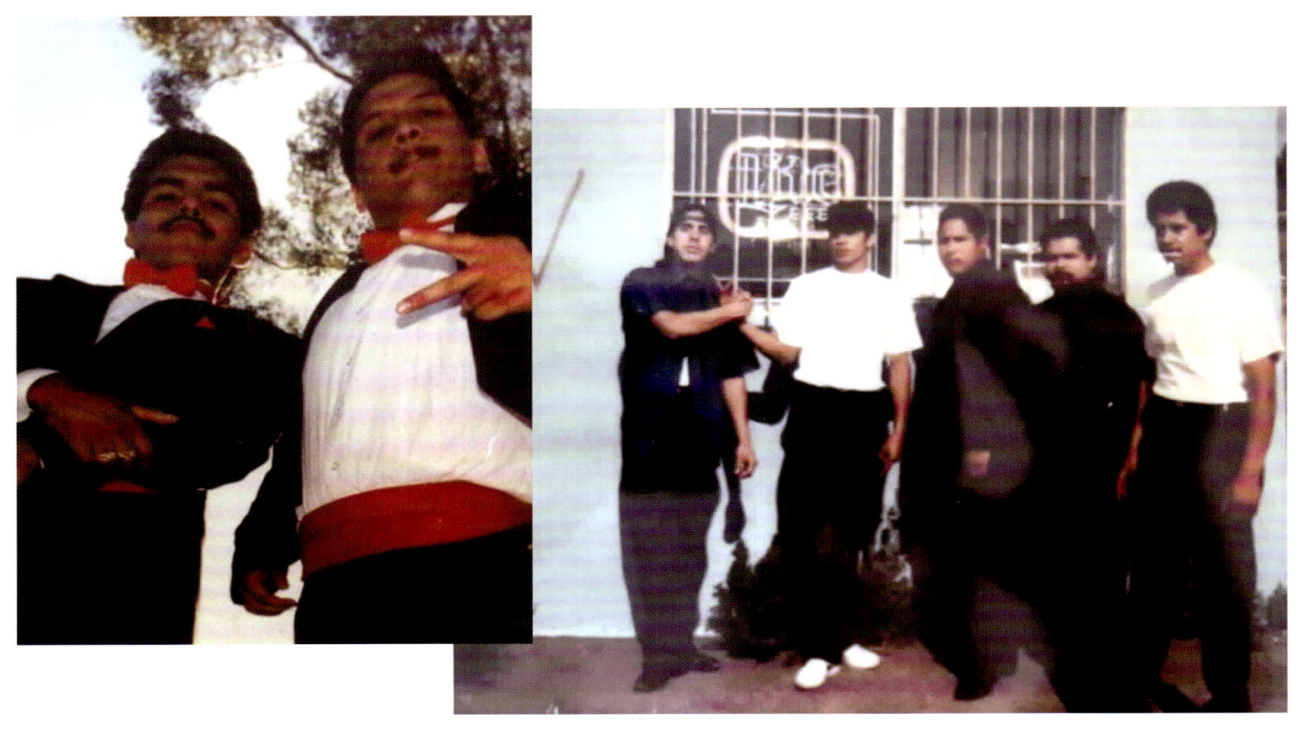

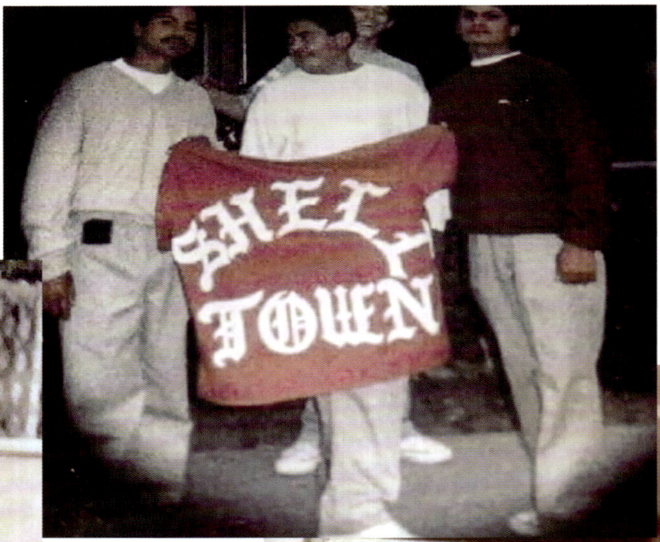

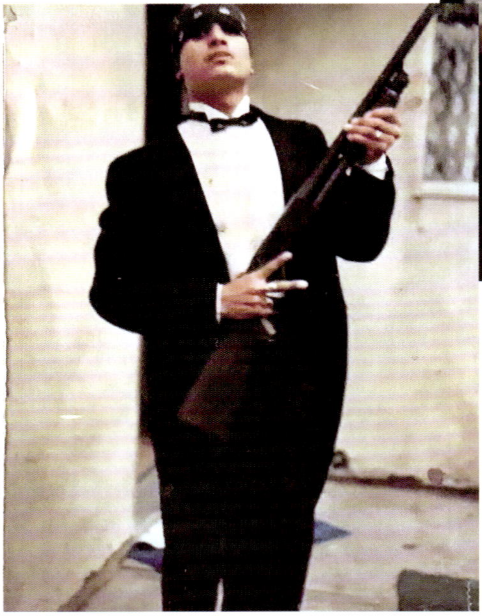

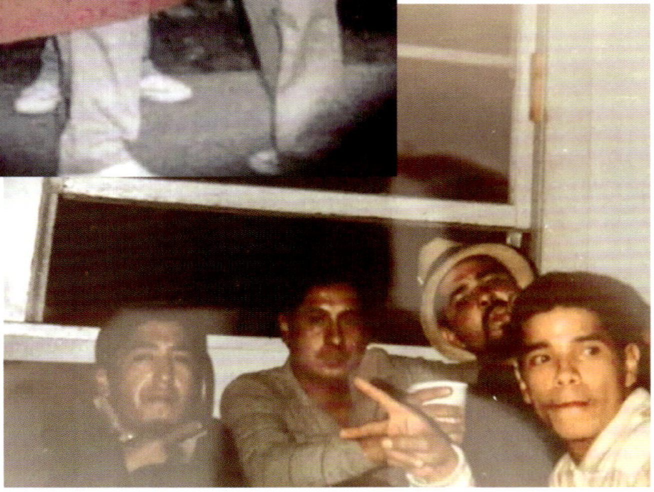

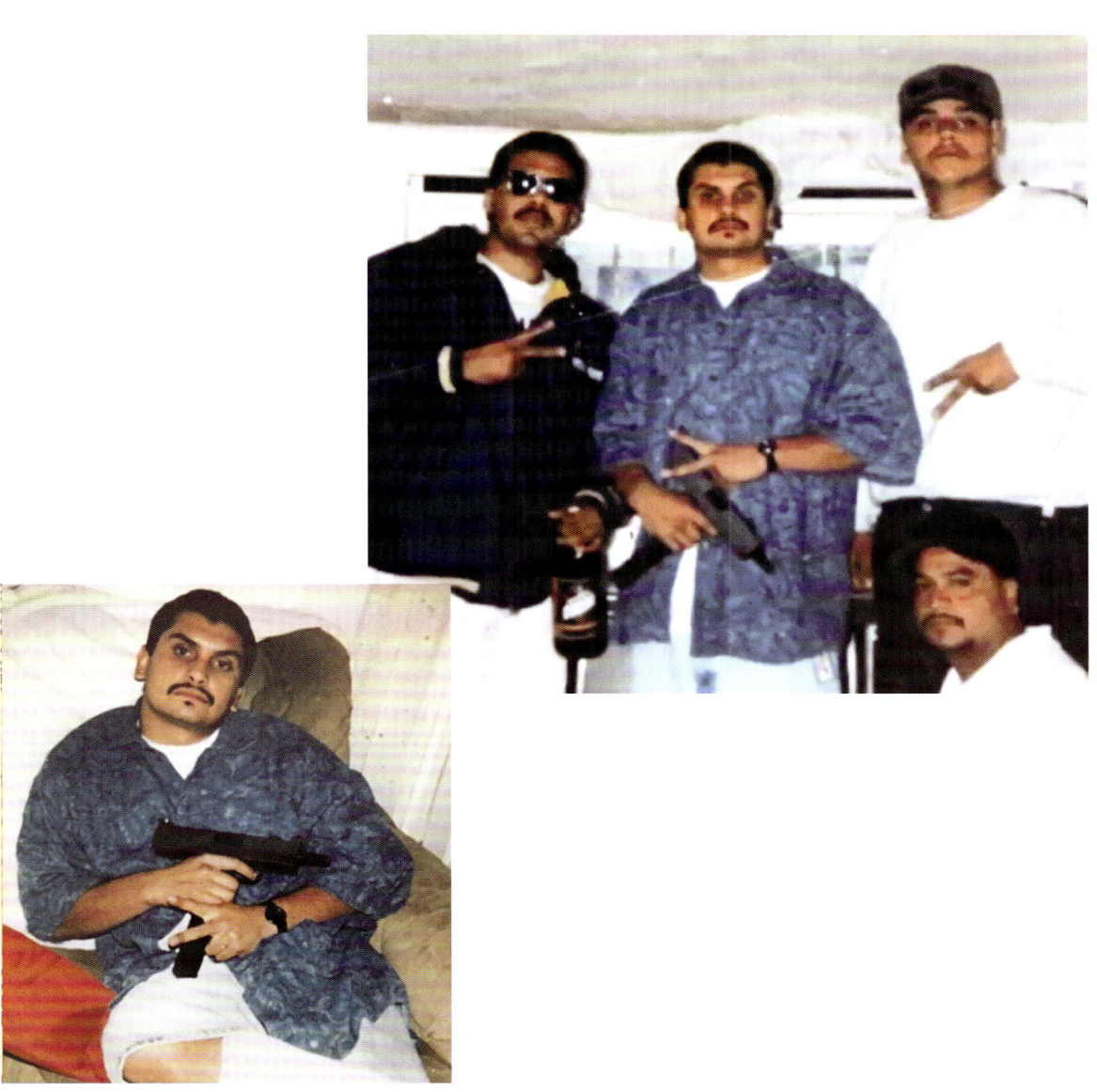

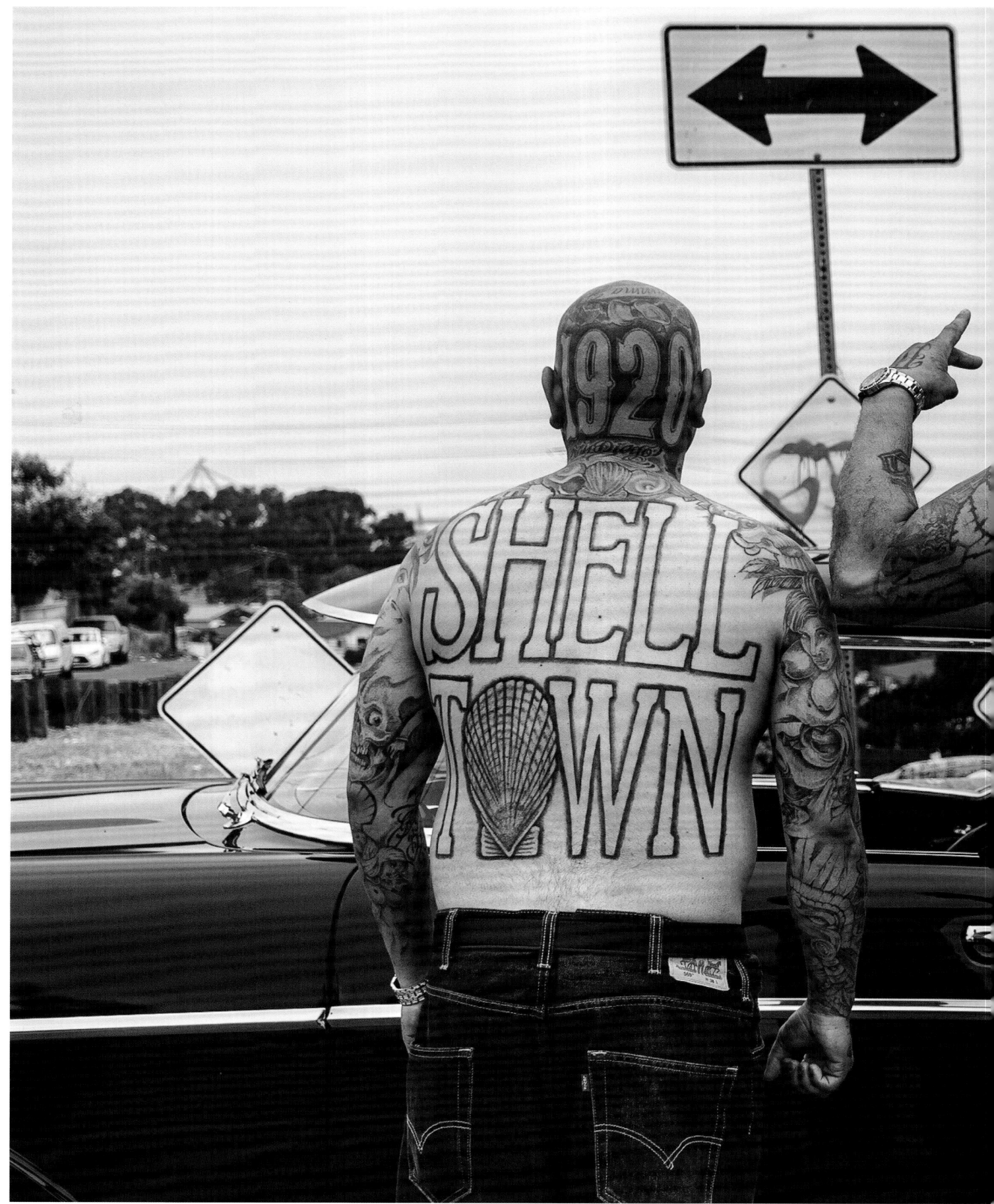

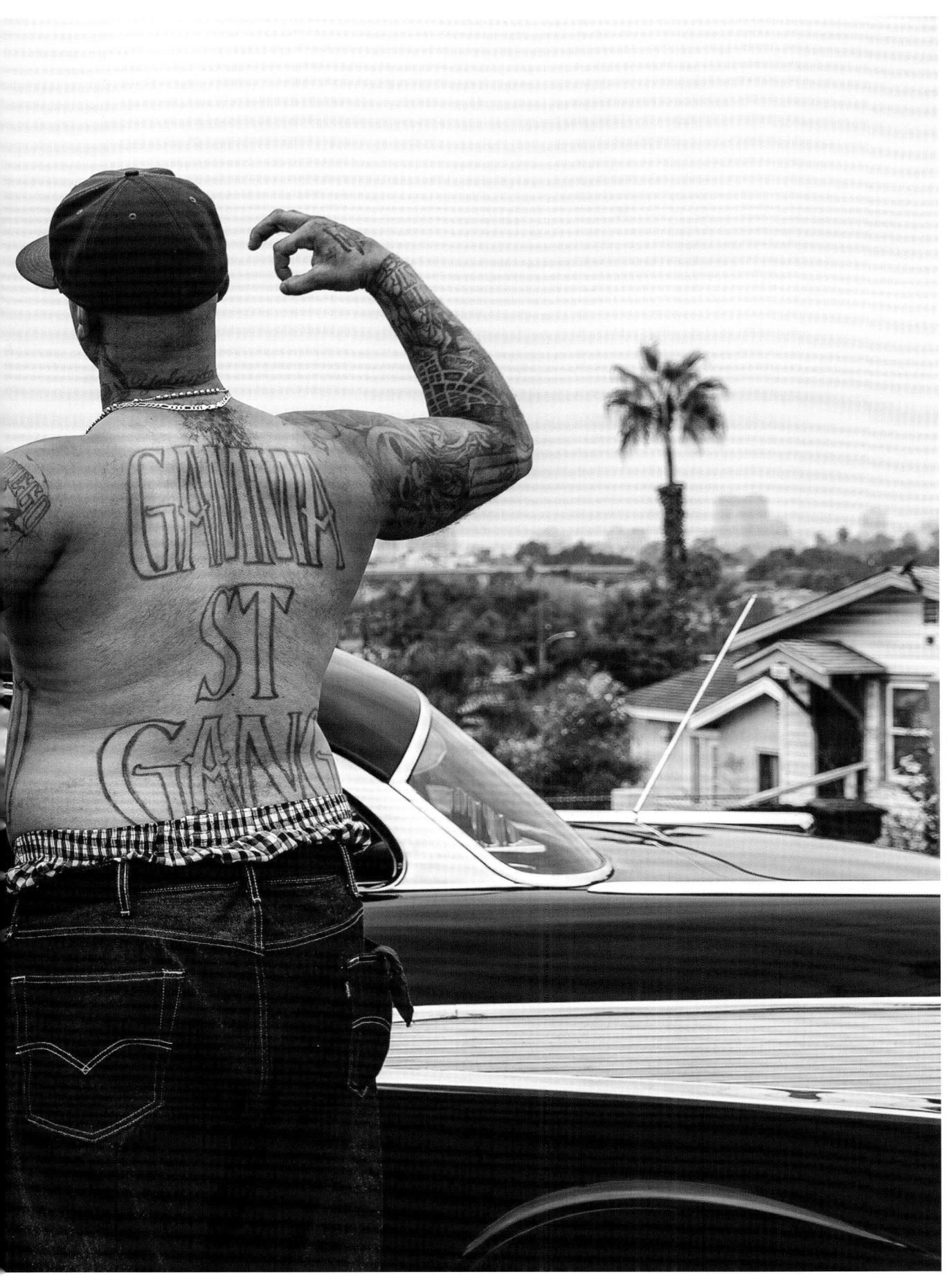

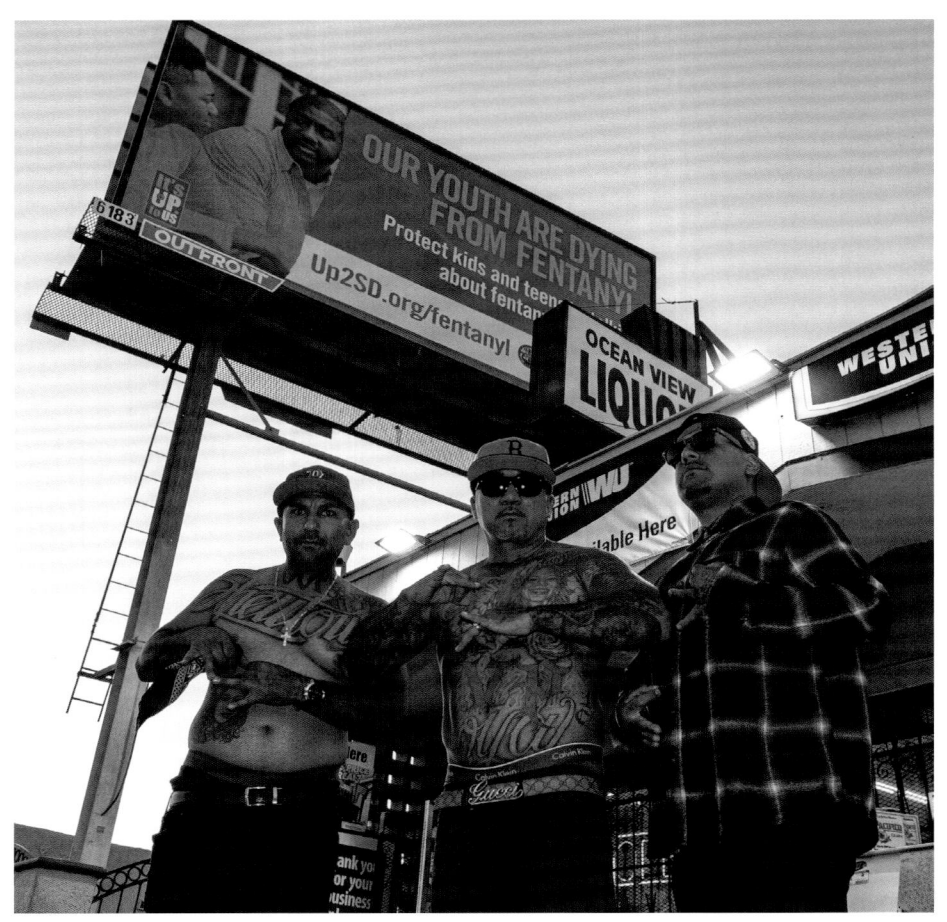

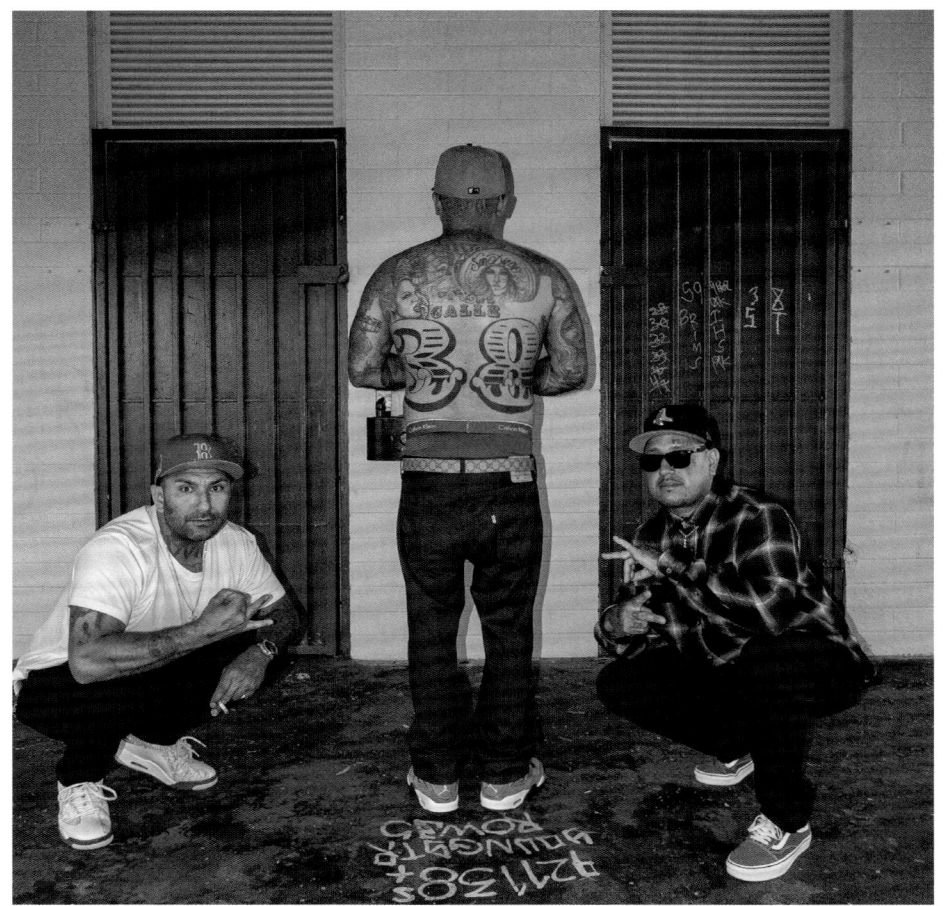

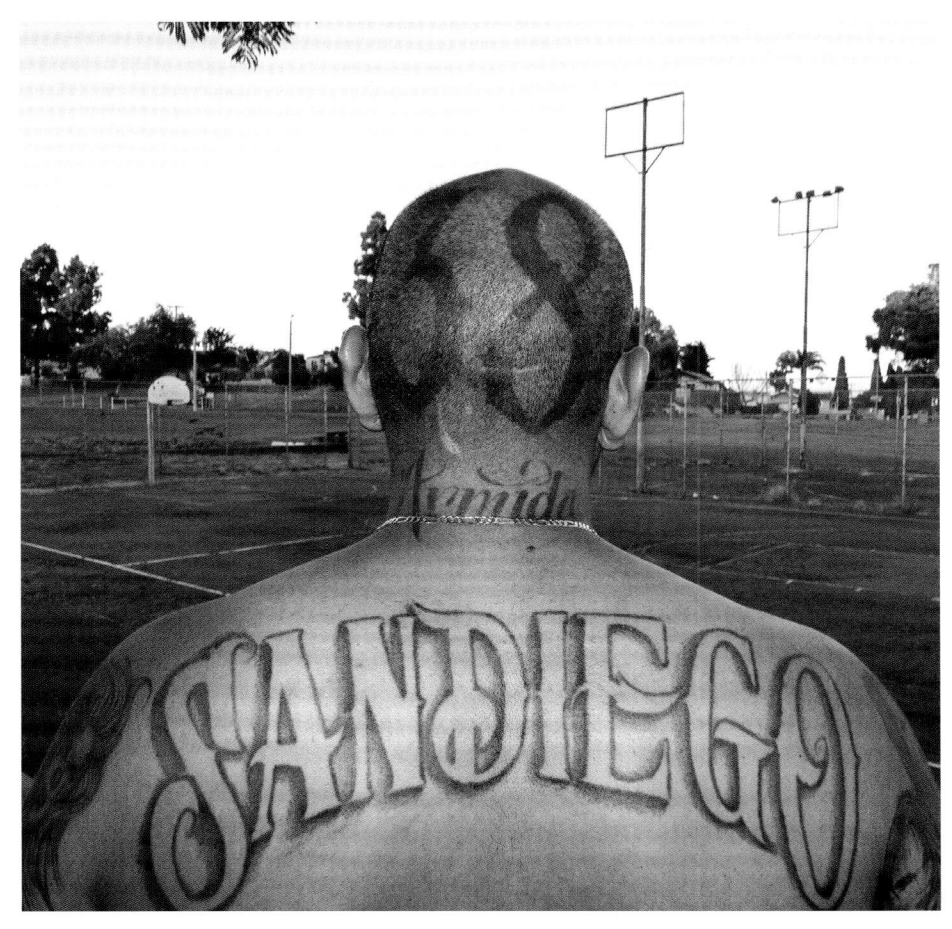

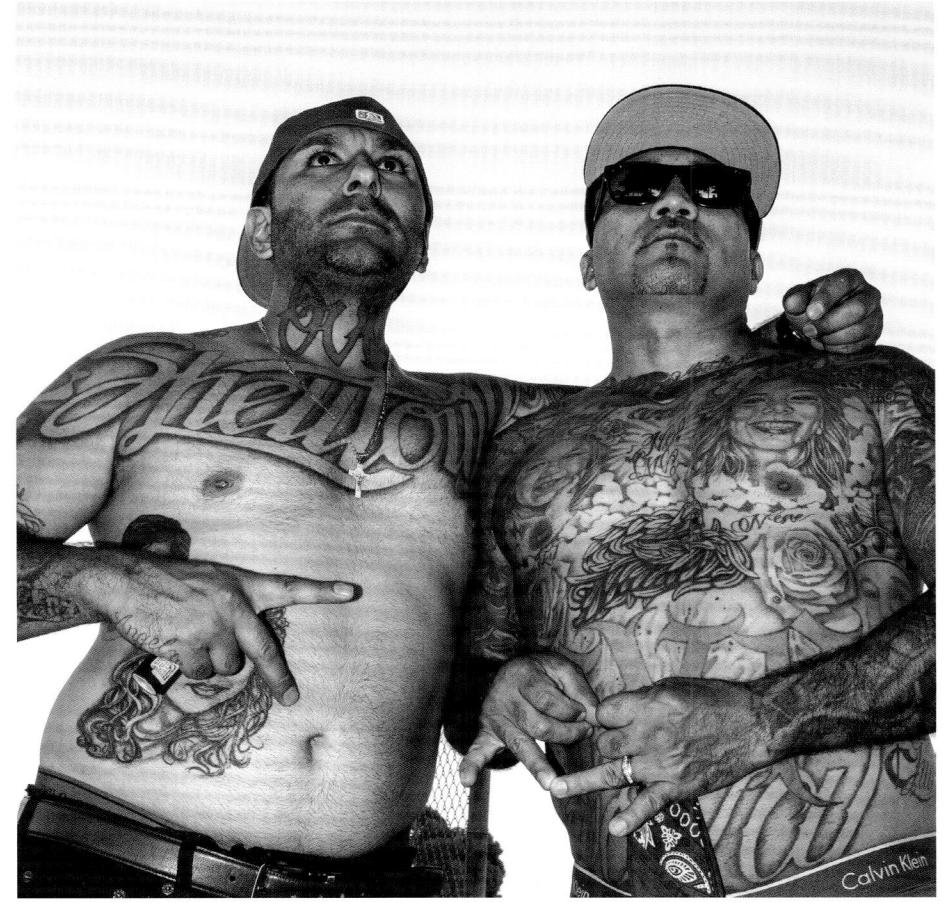

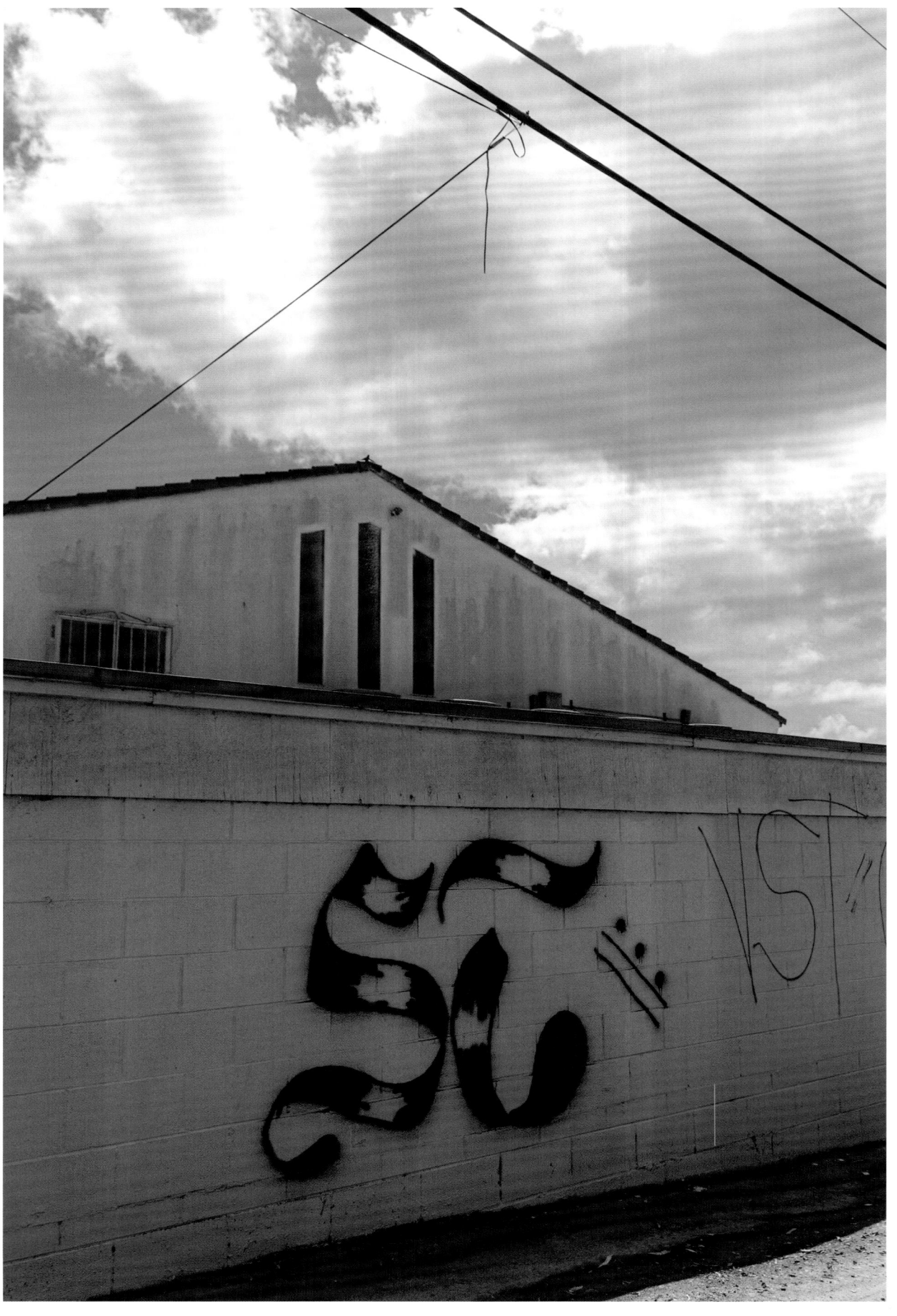

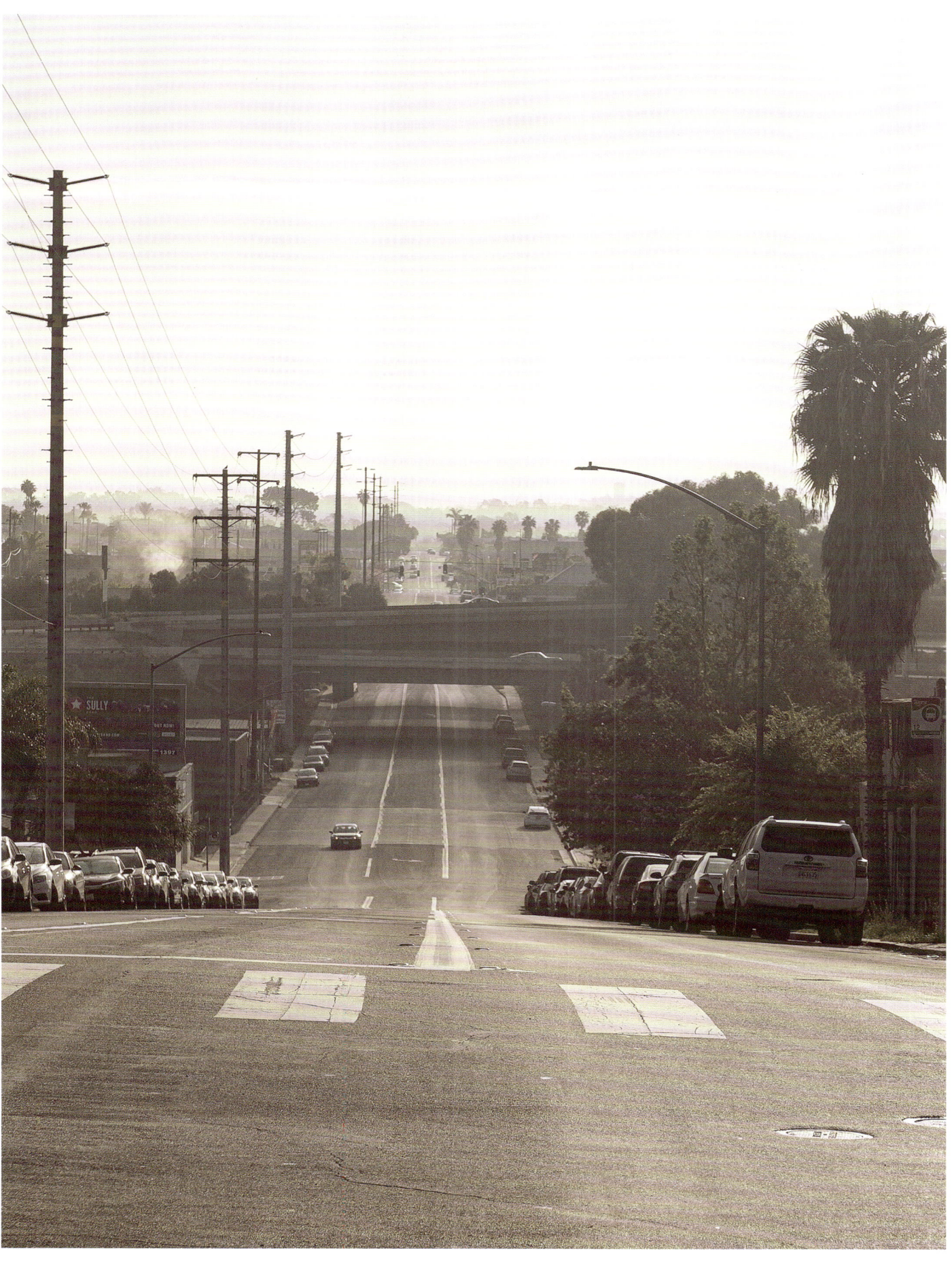

NATIONAL

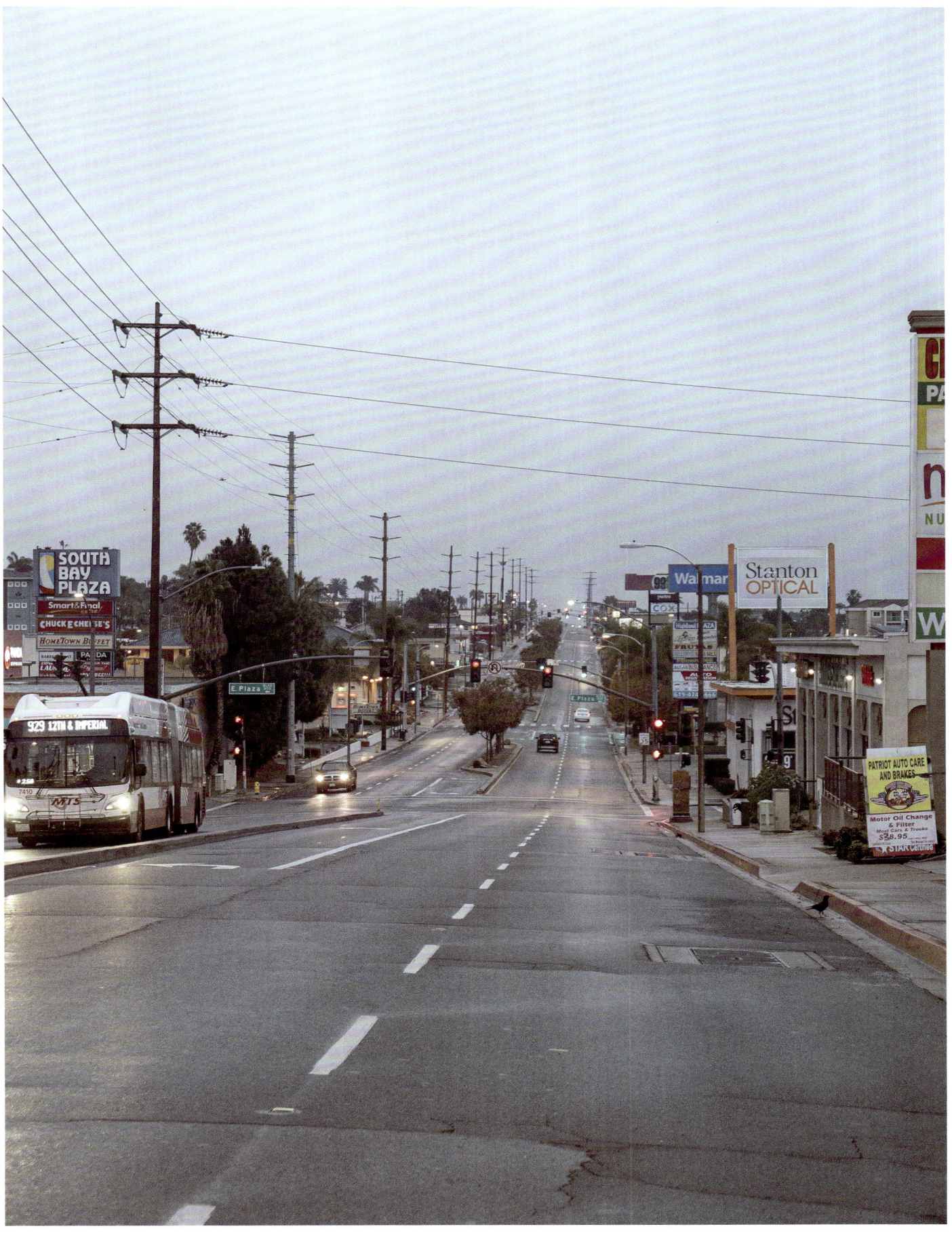

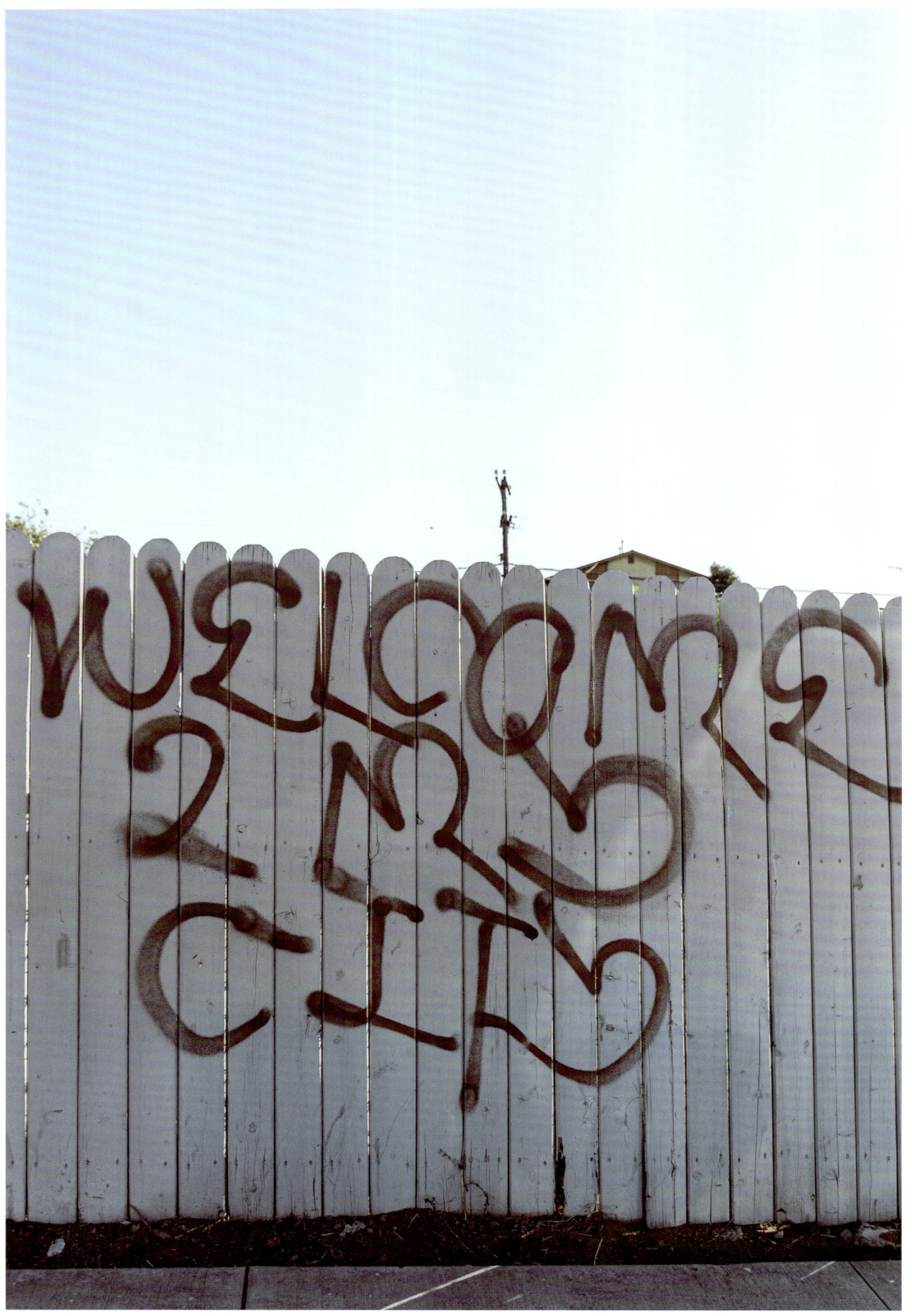

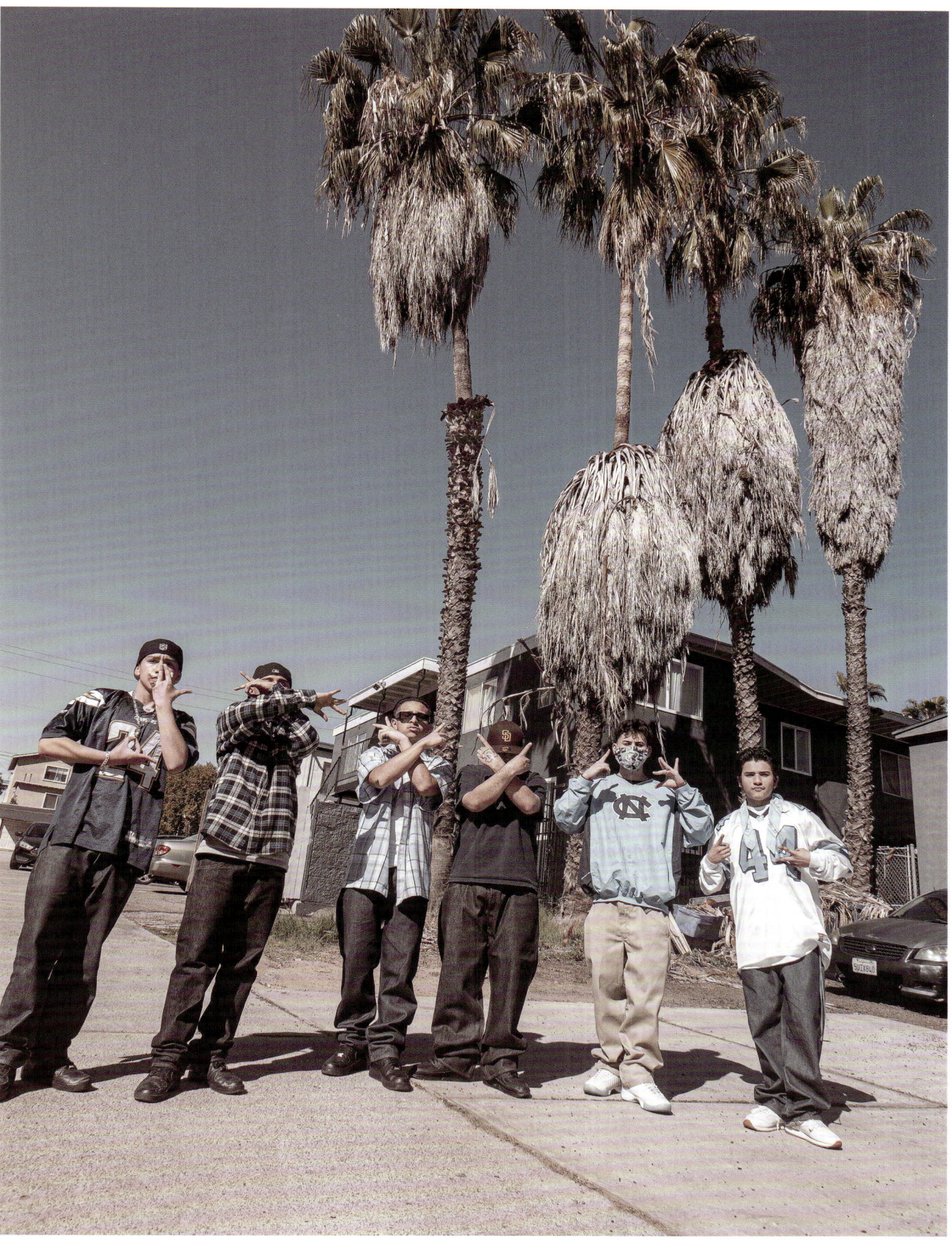

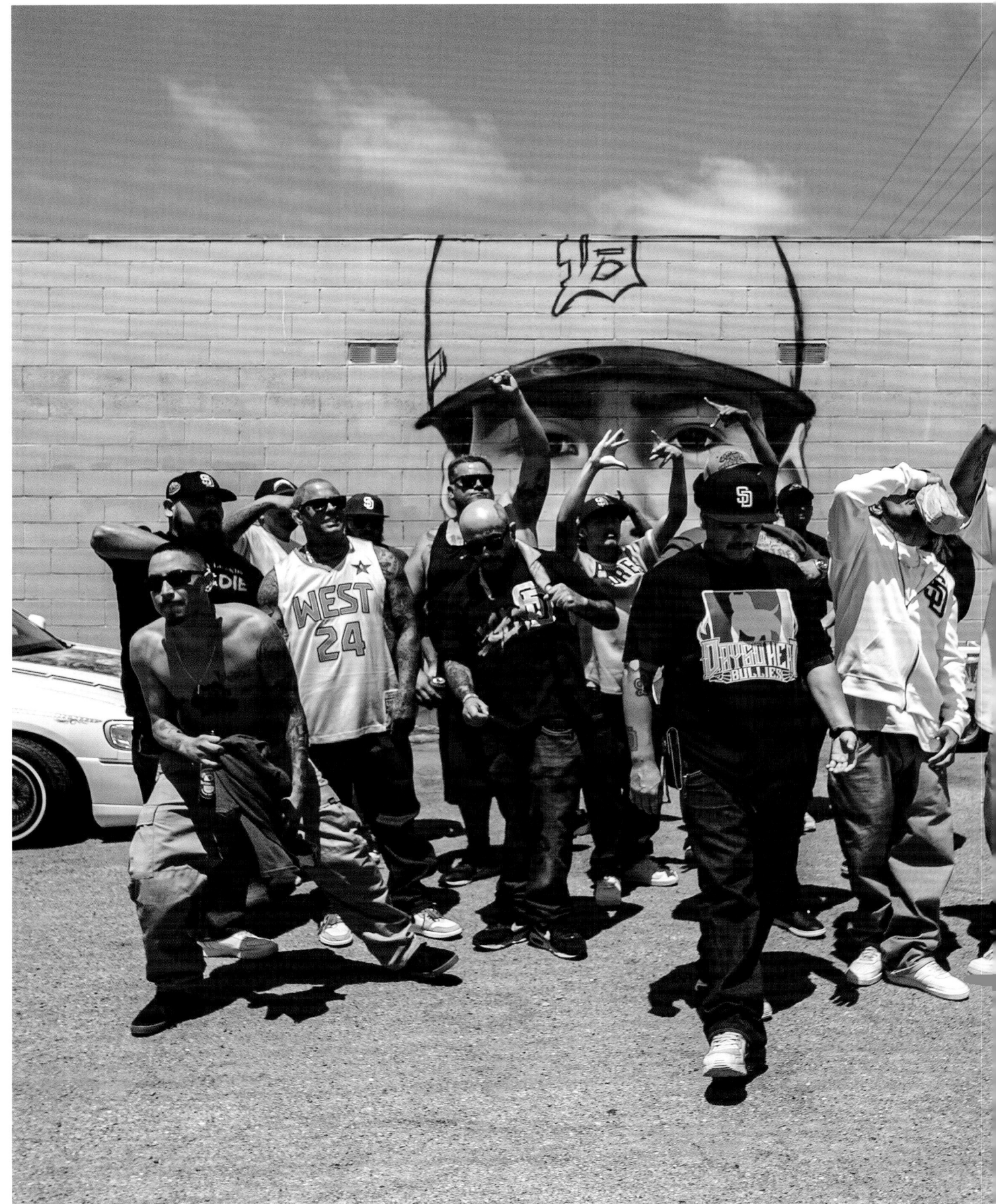

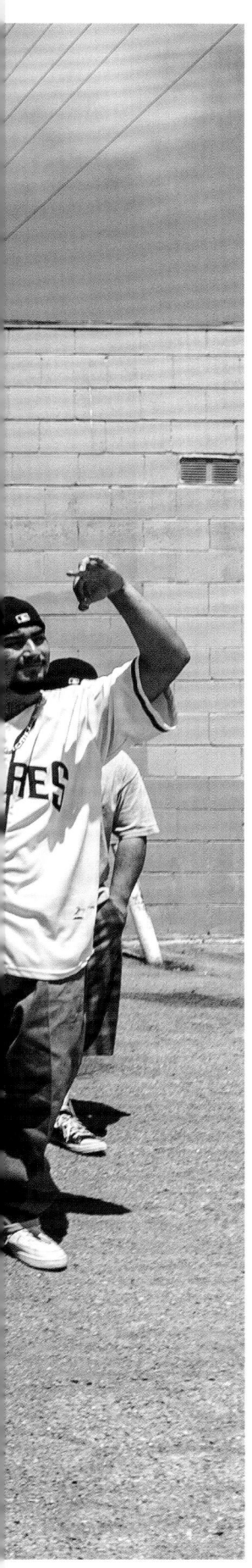

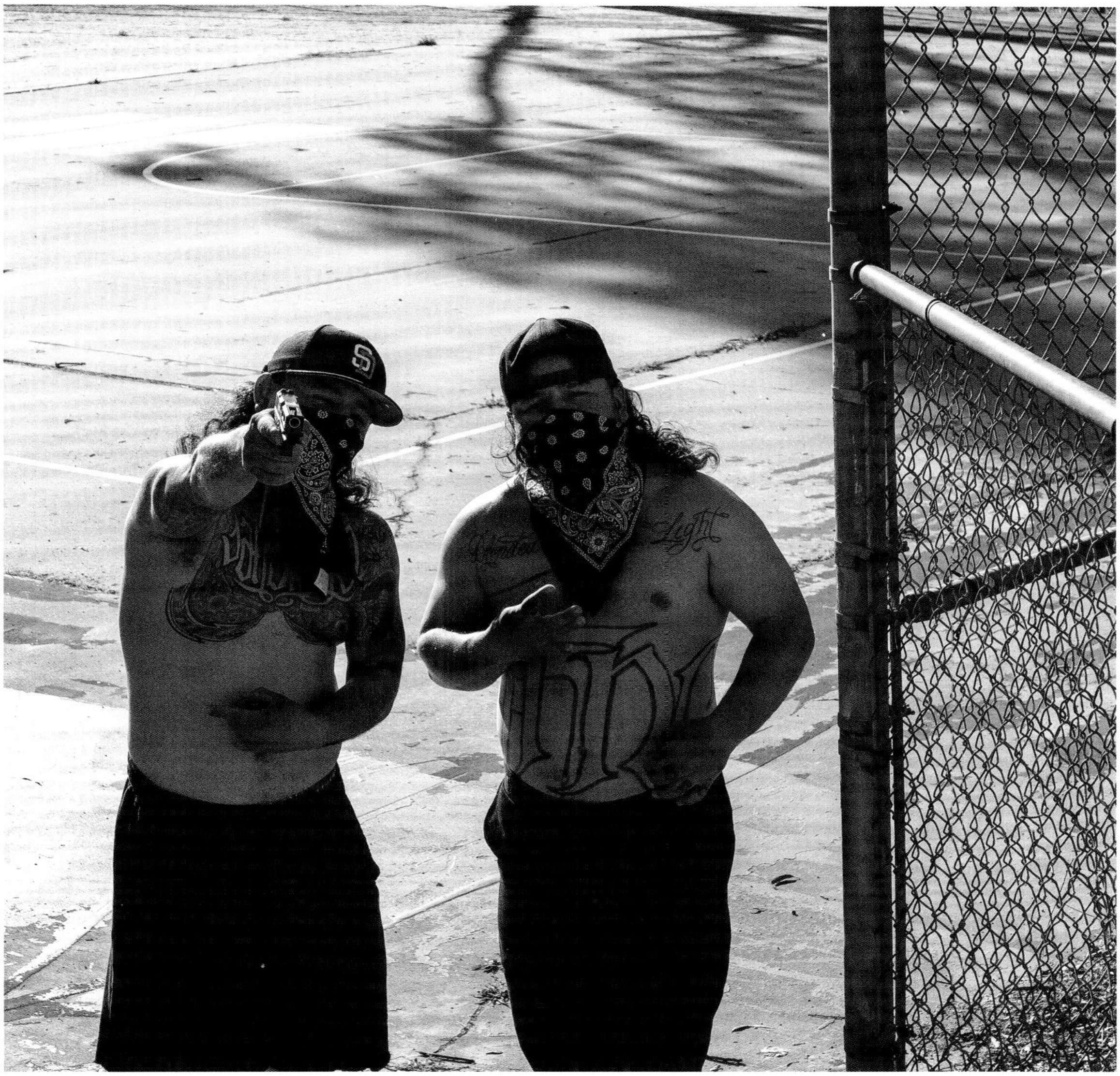

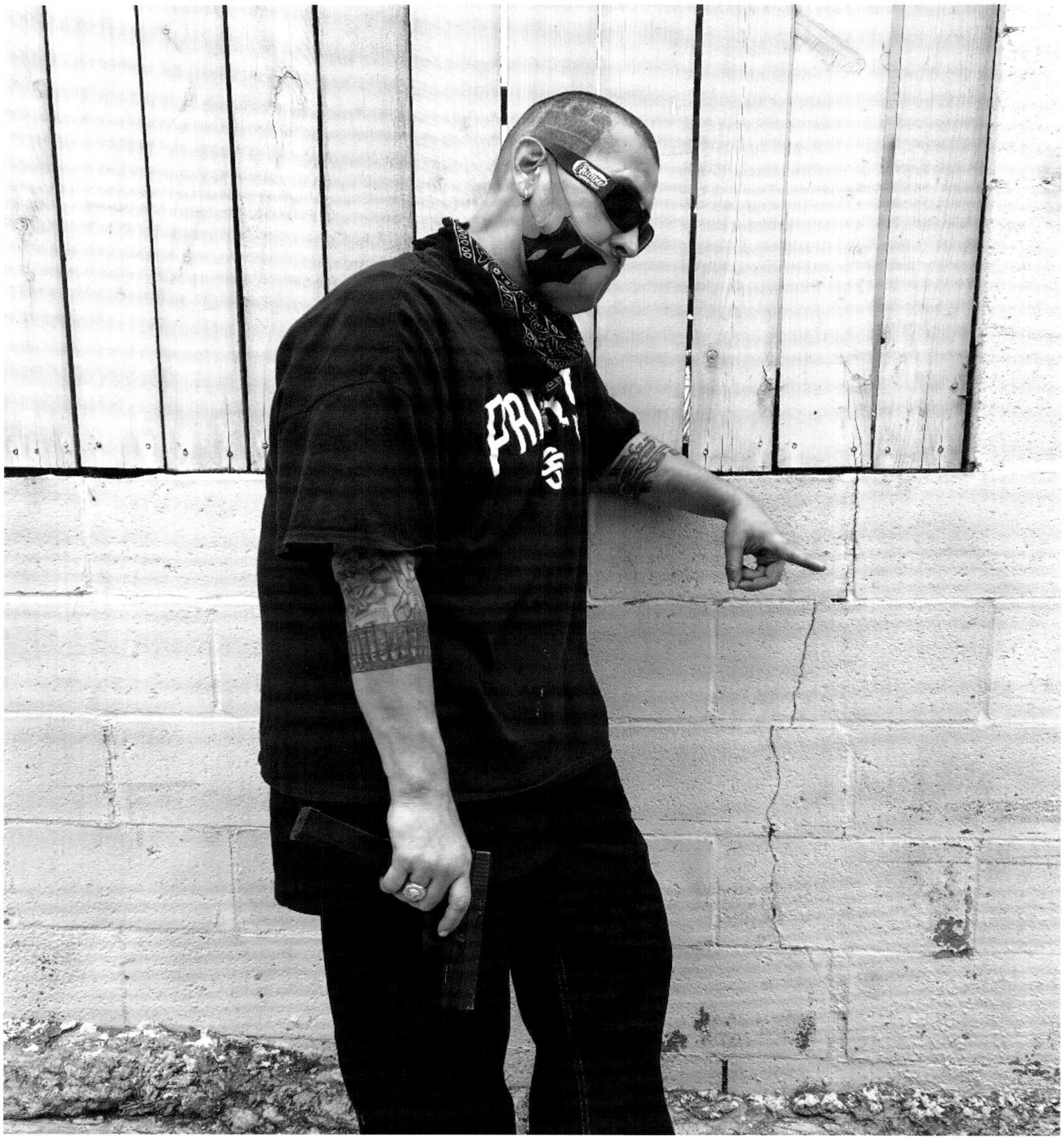

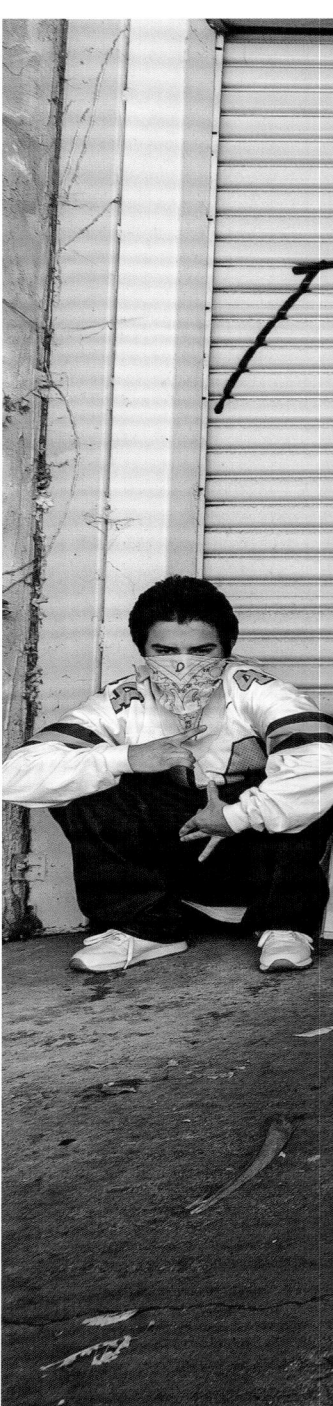

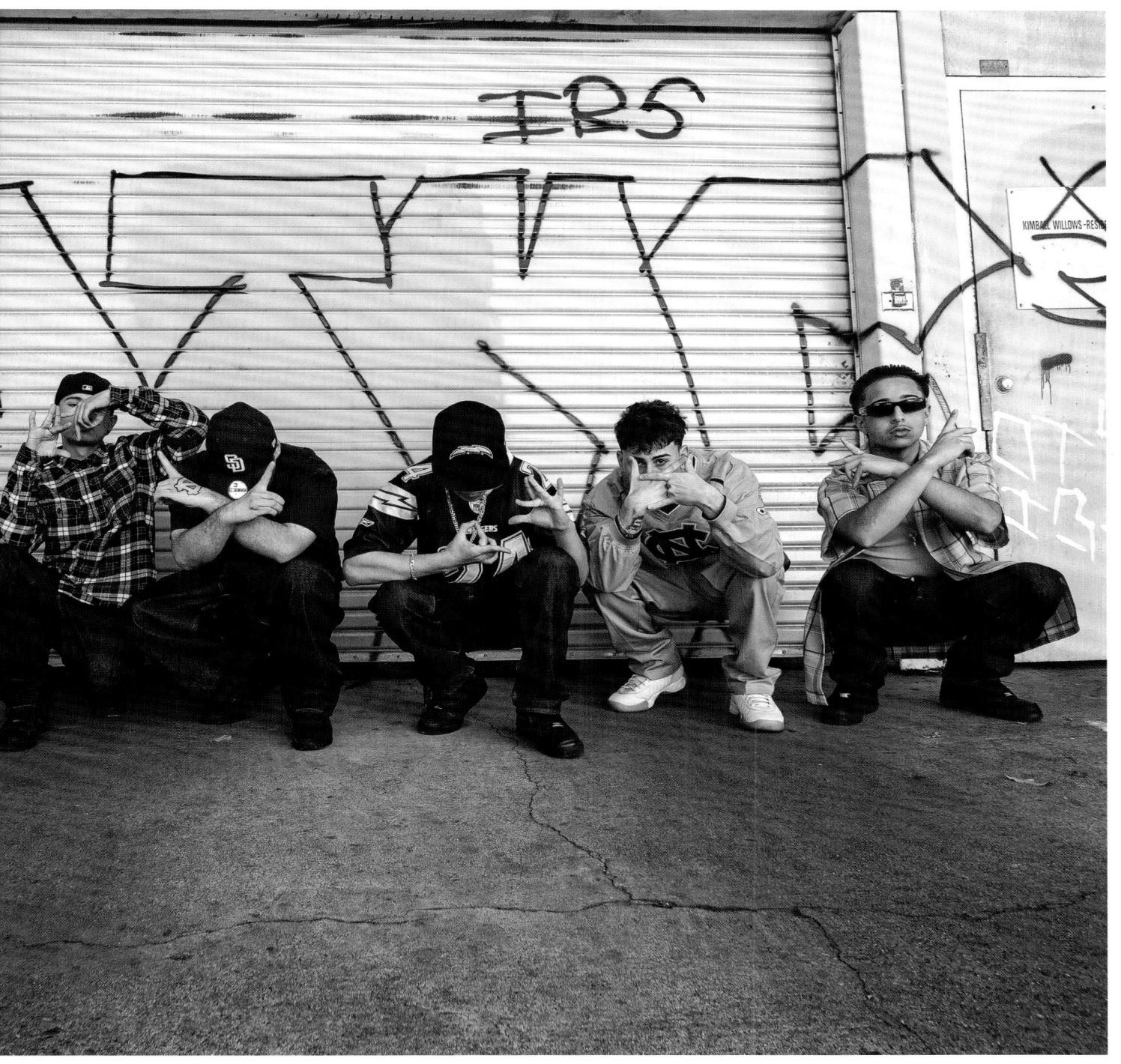

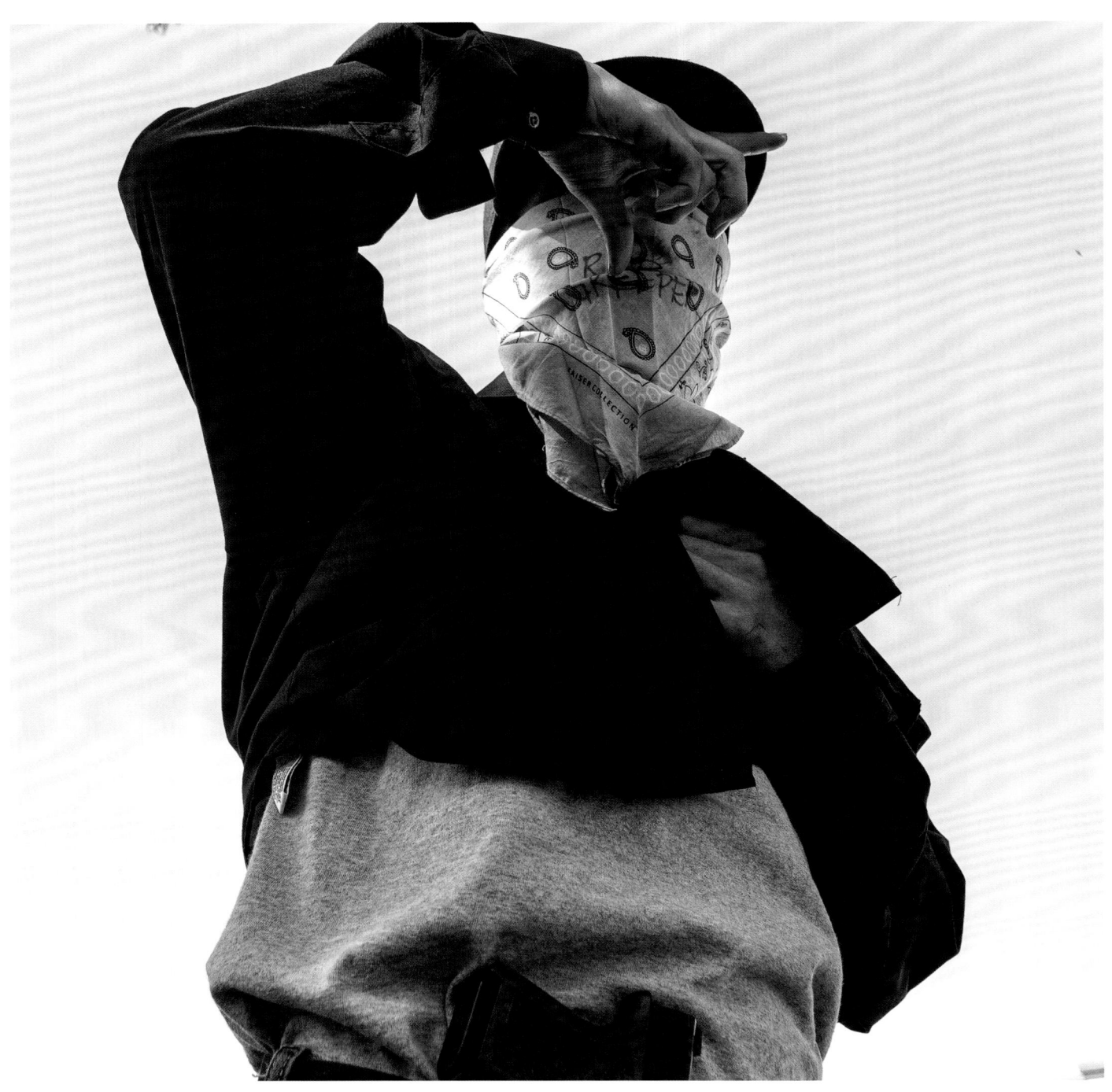

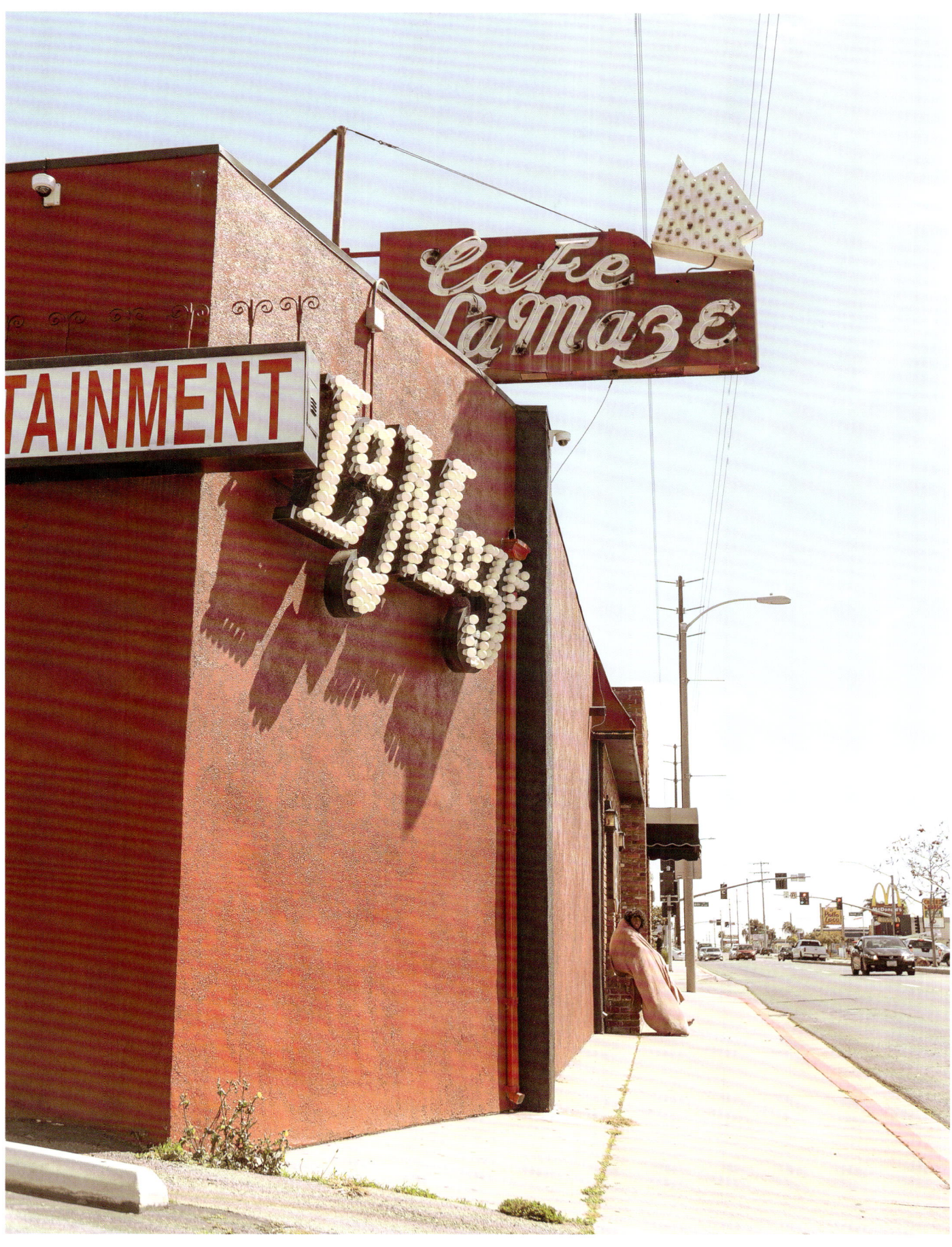

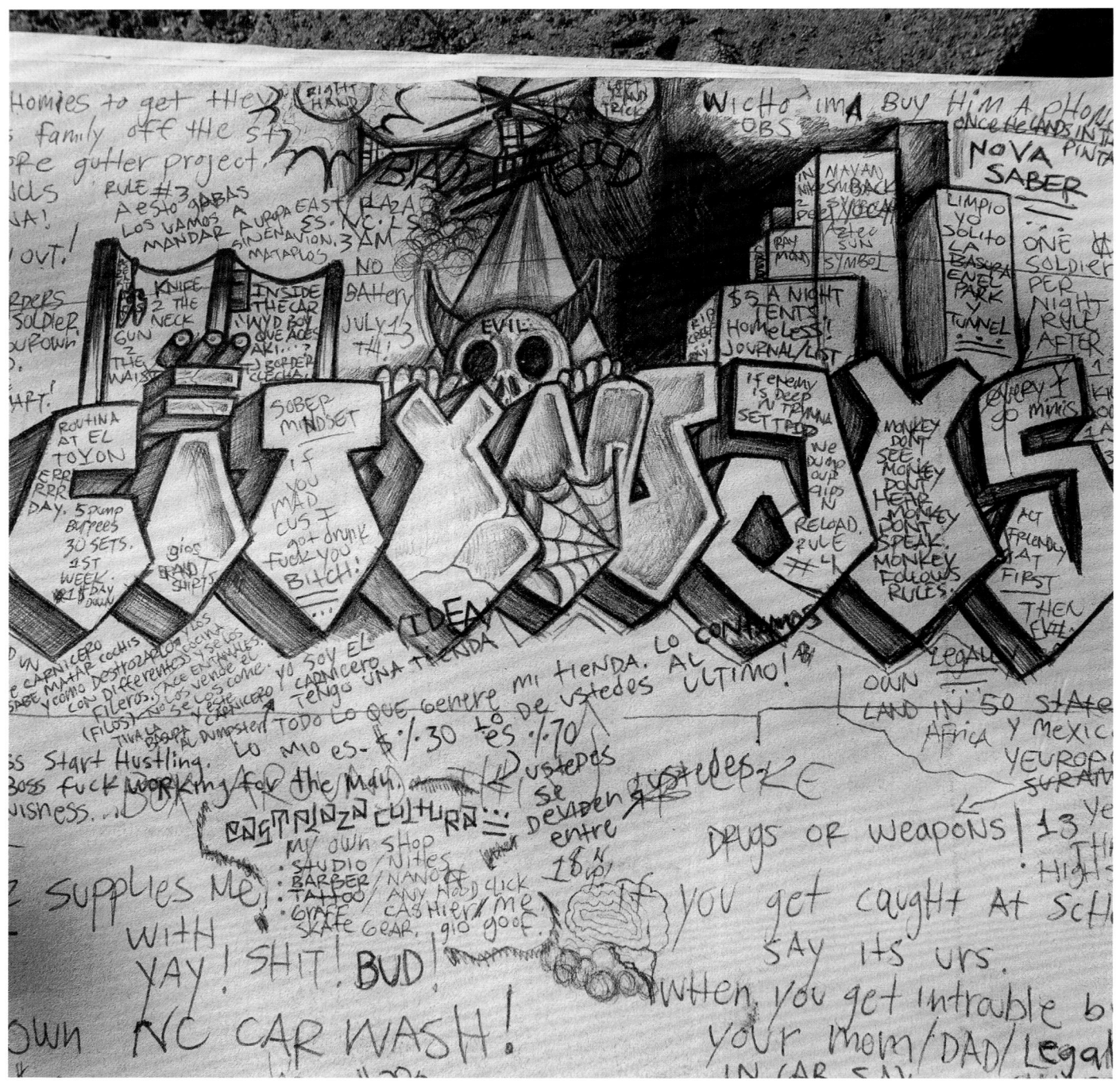

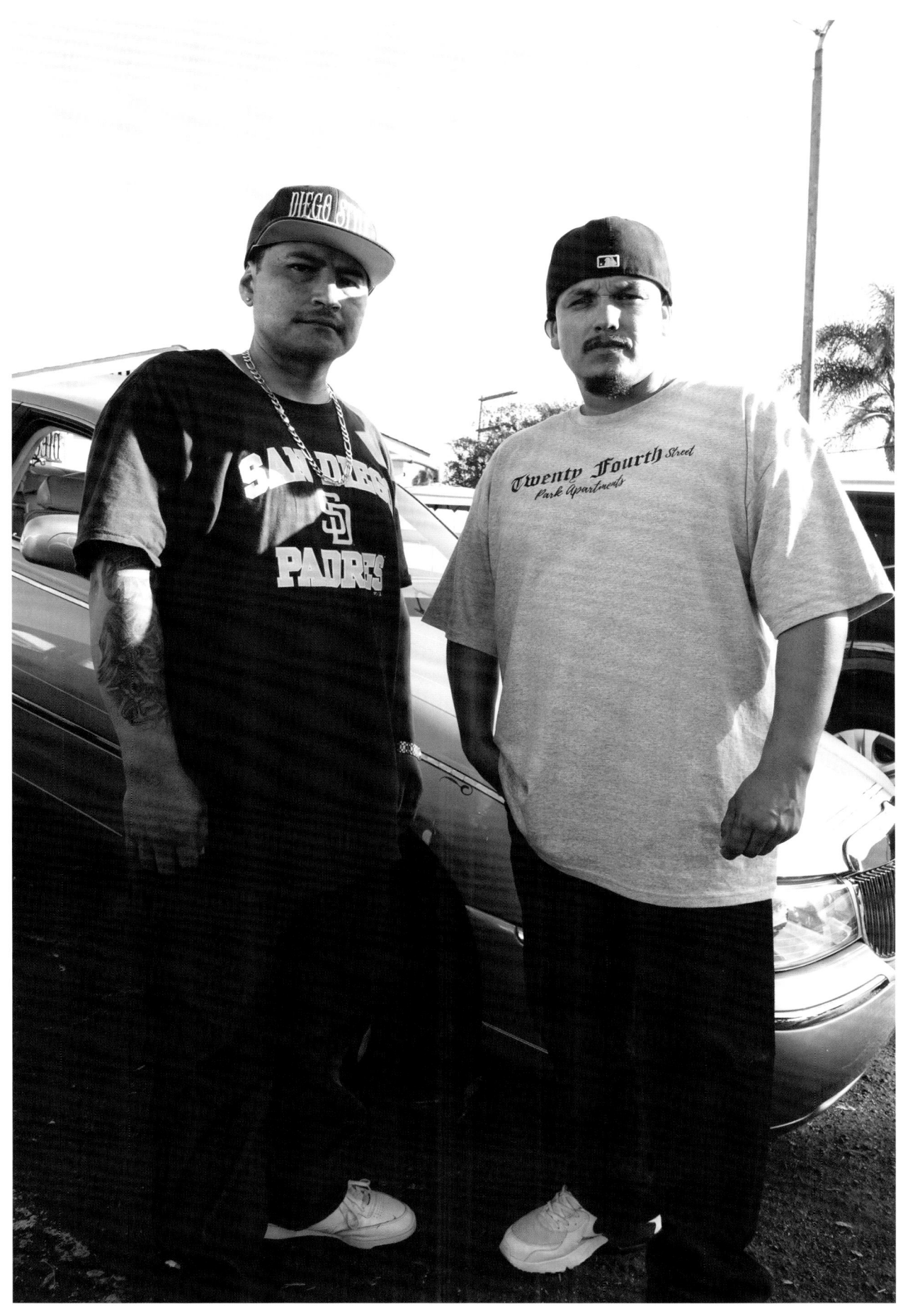

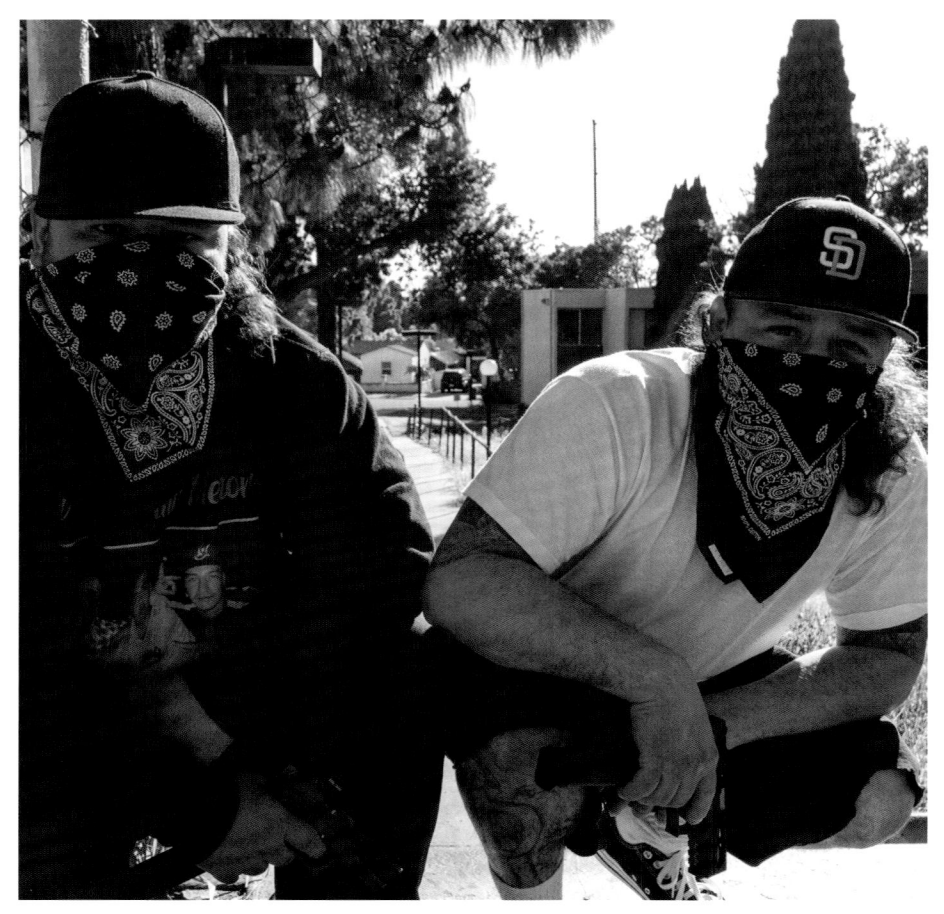

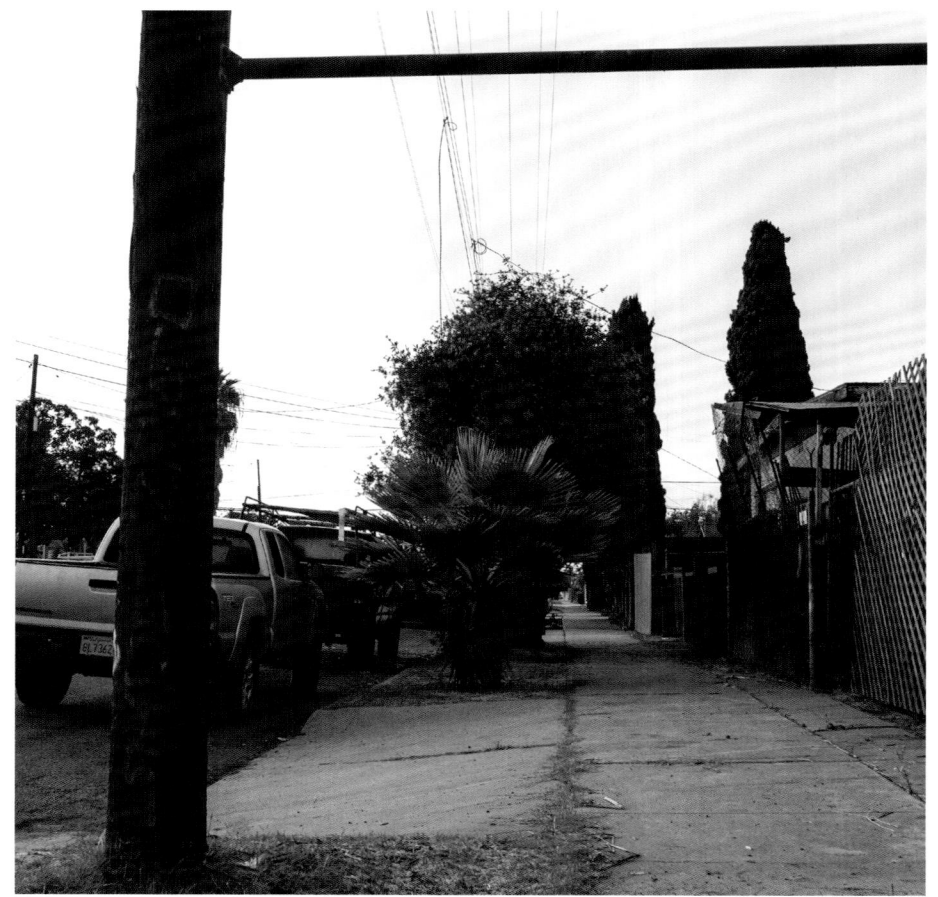

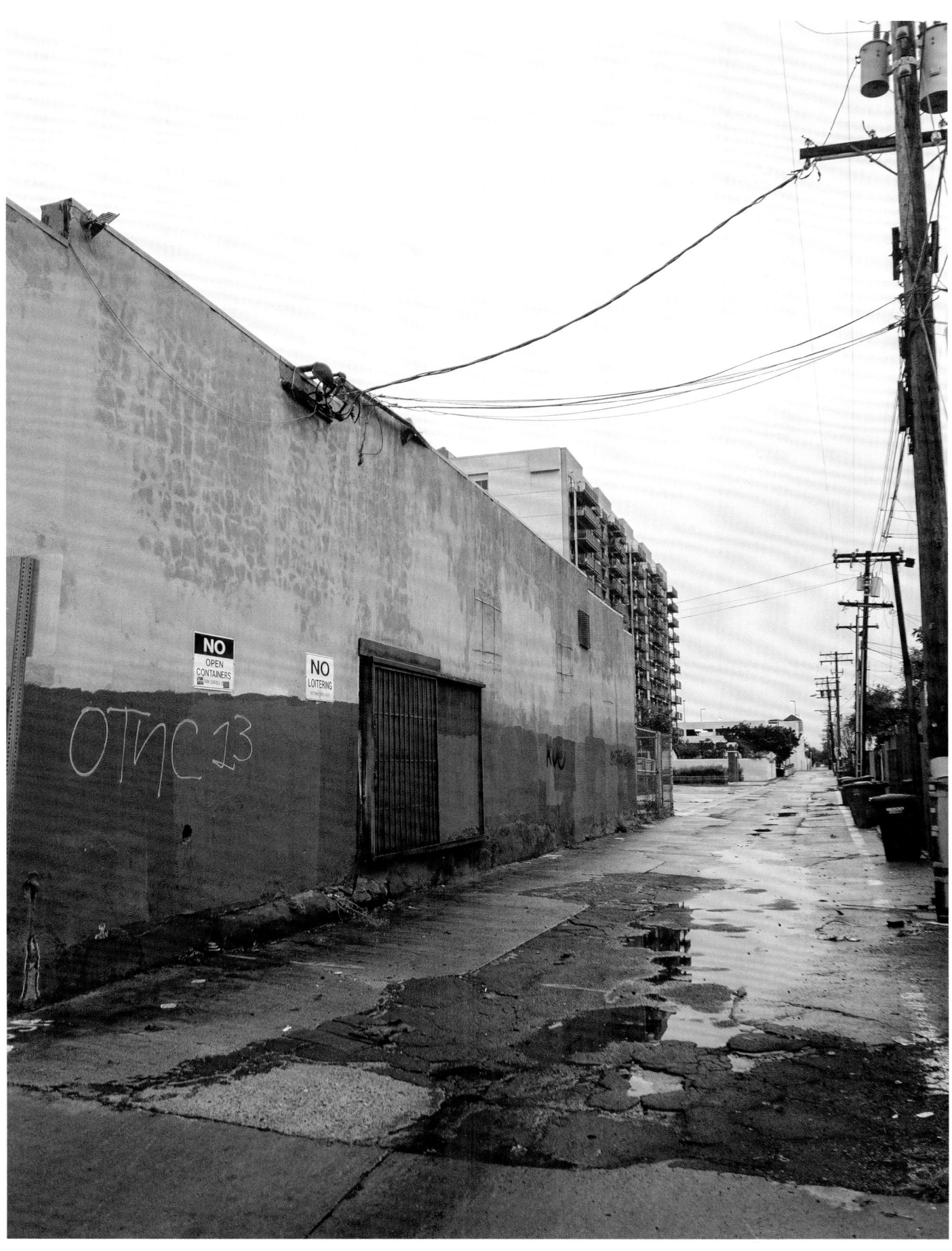

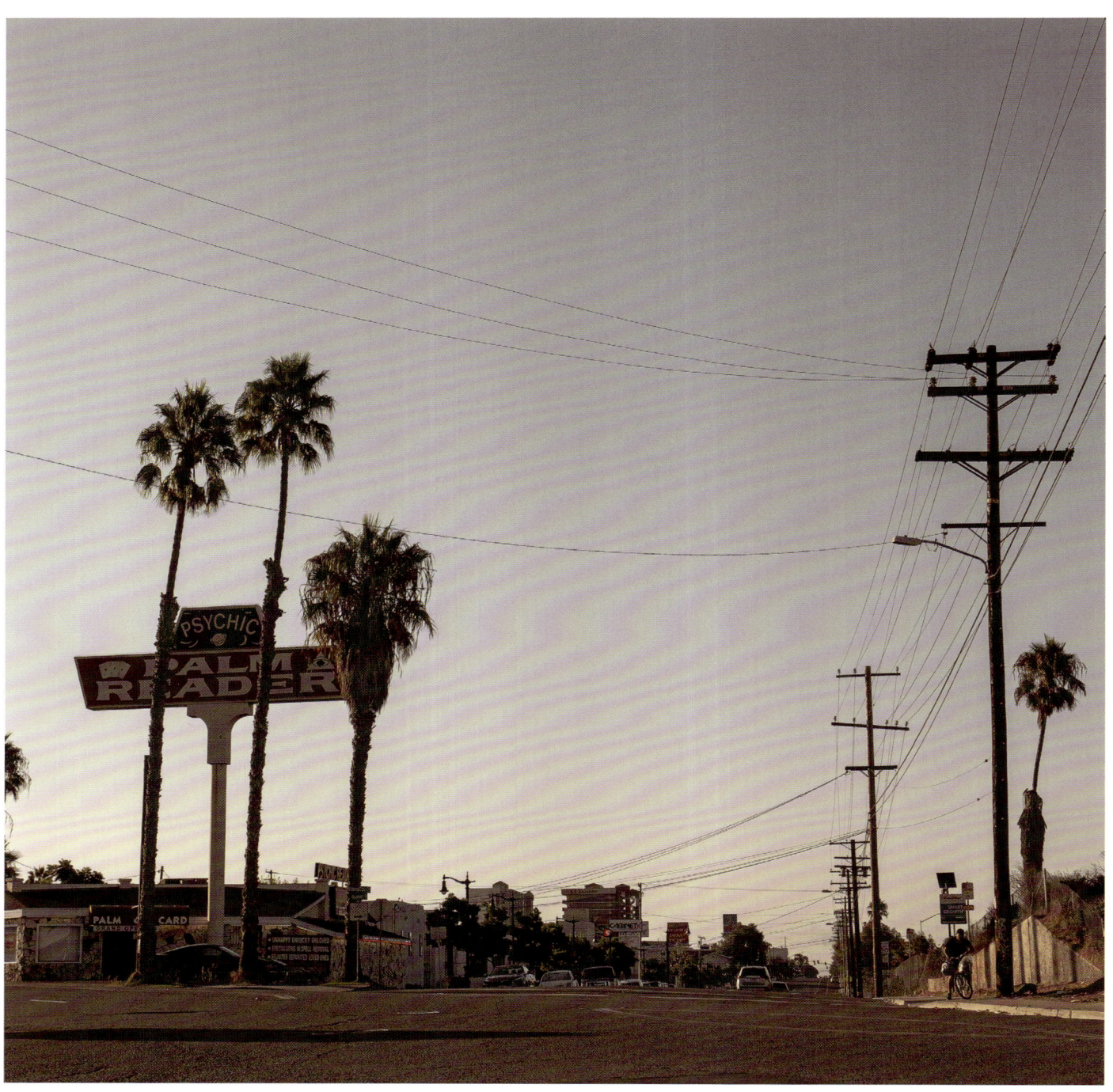

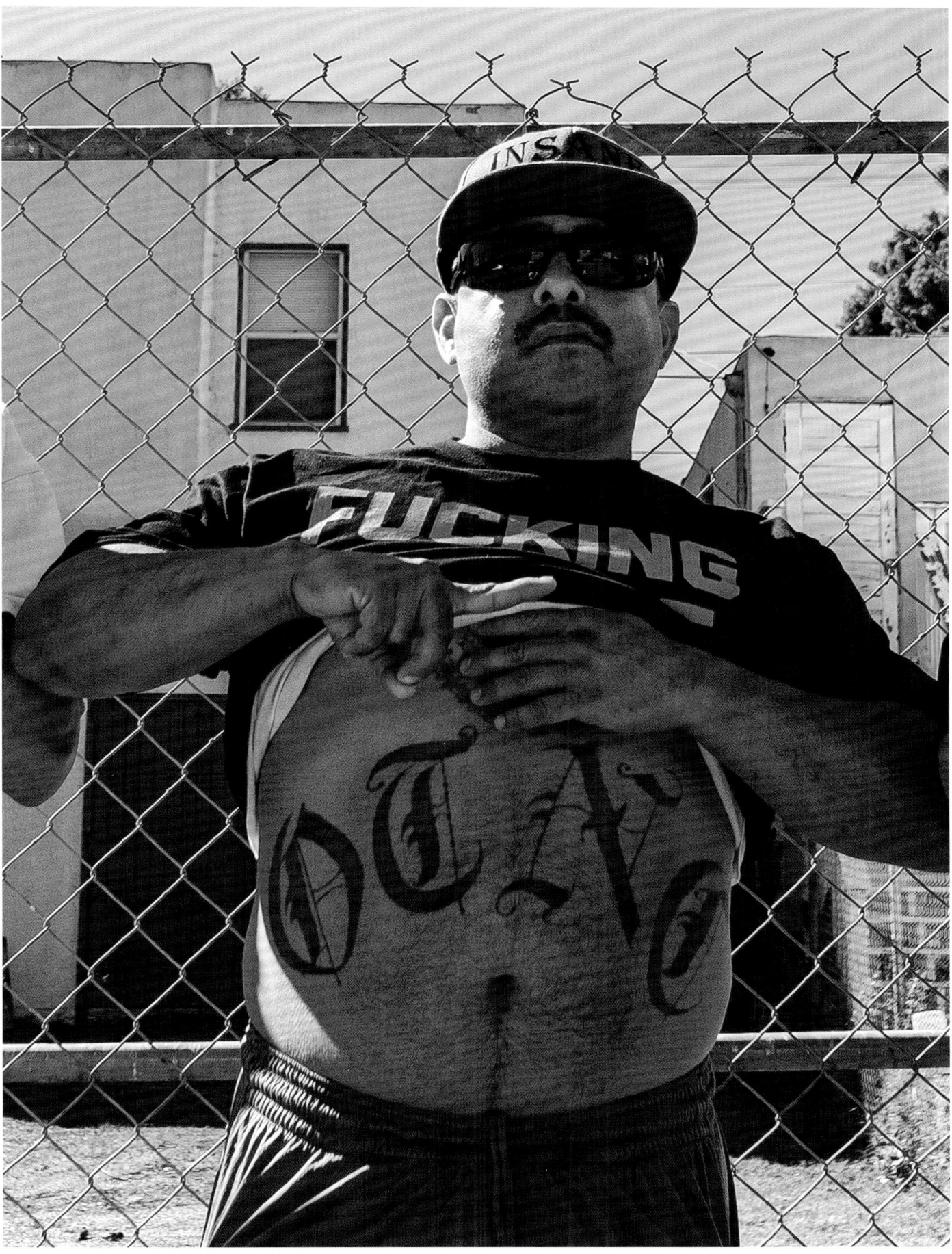

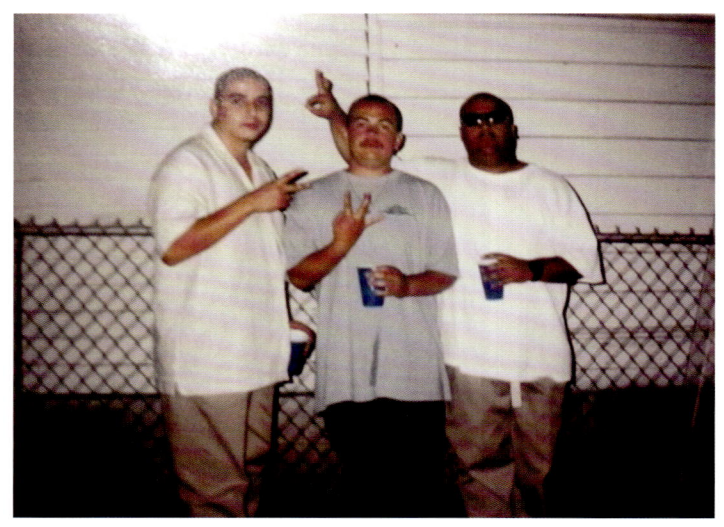

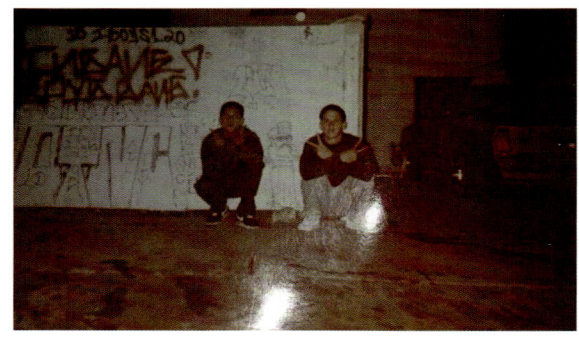

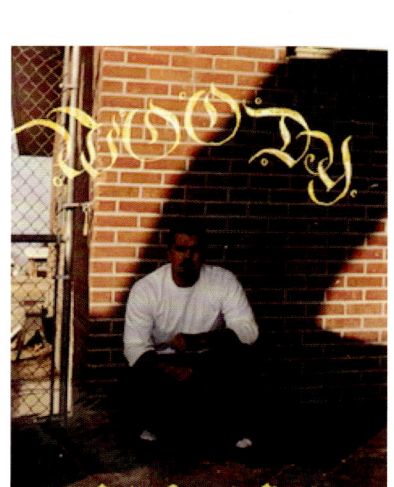

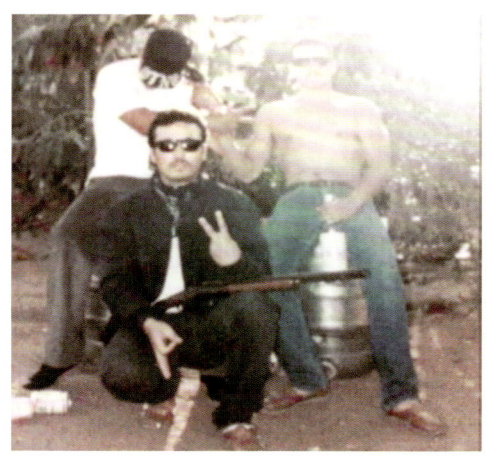

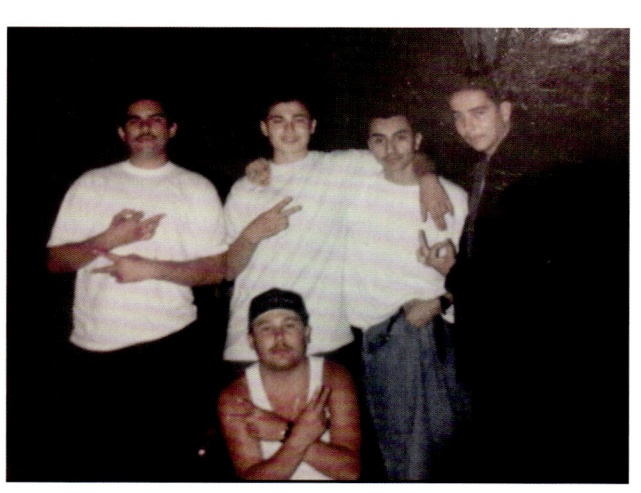

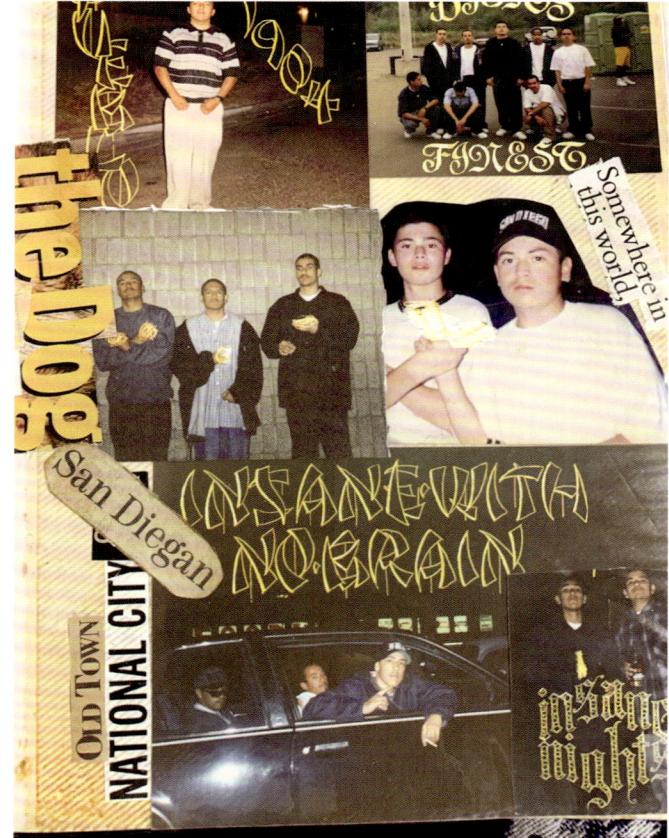

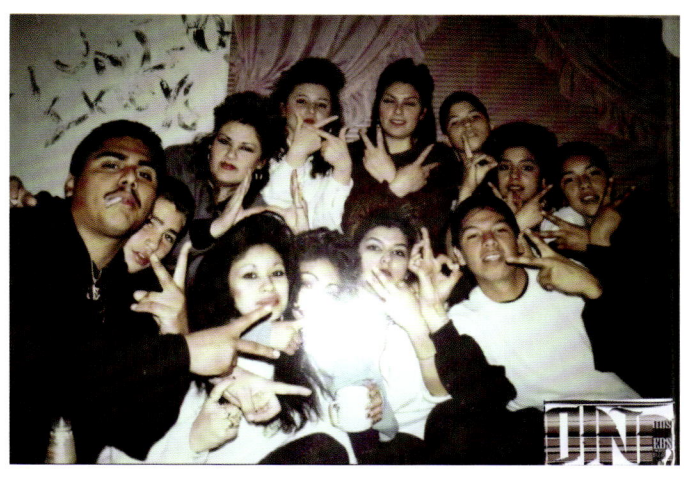

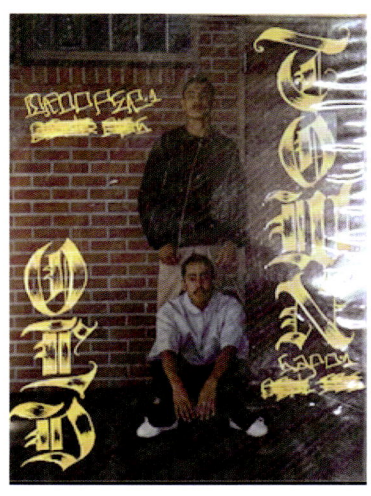

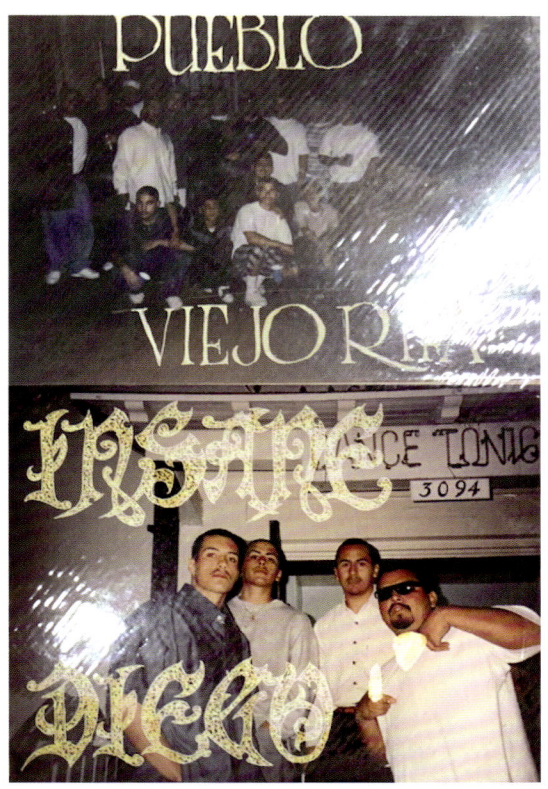

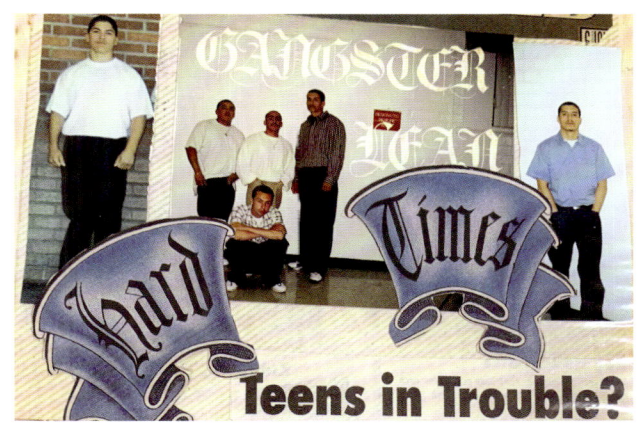

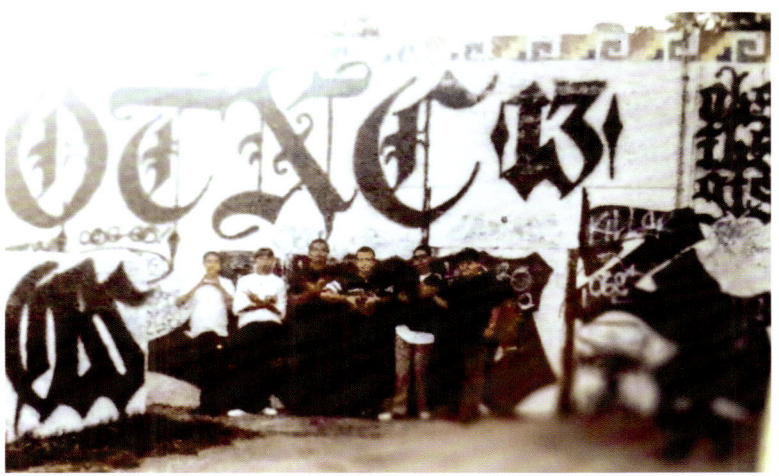

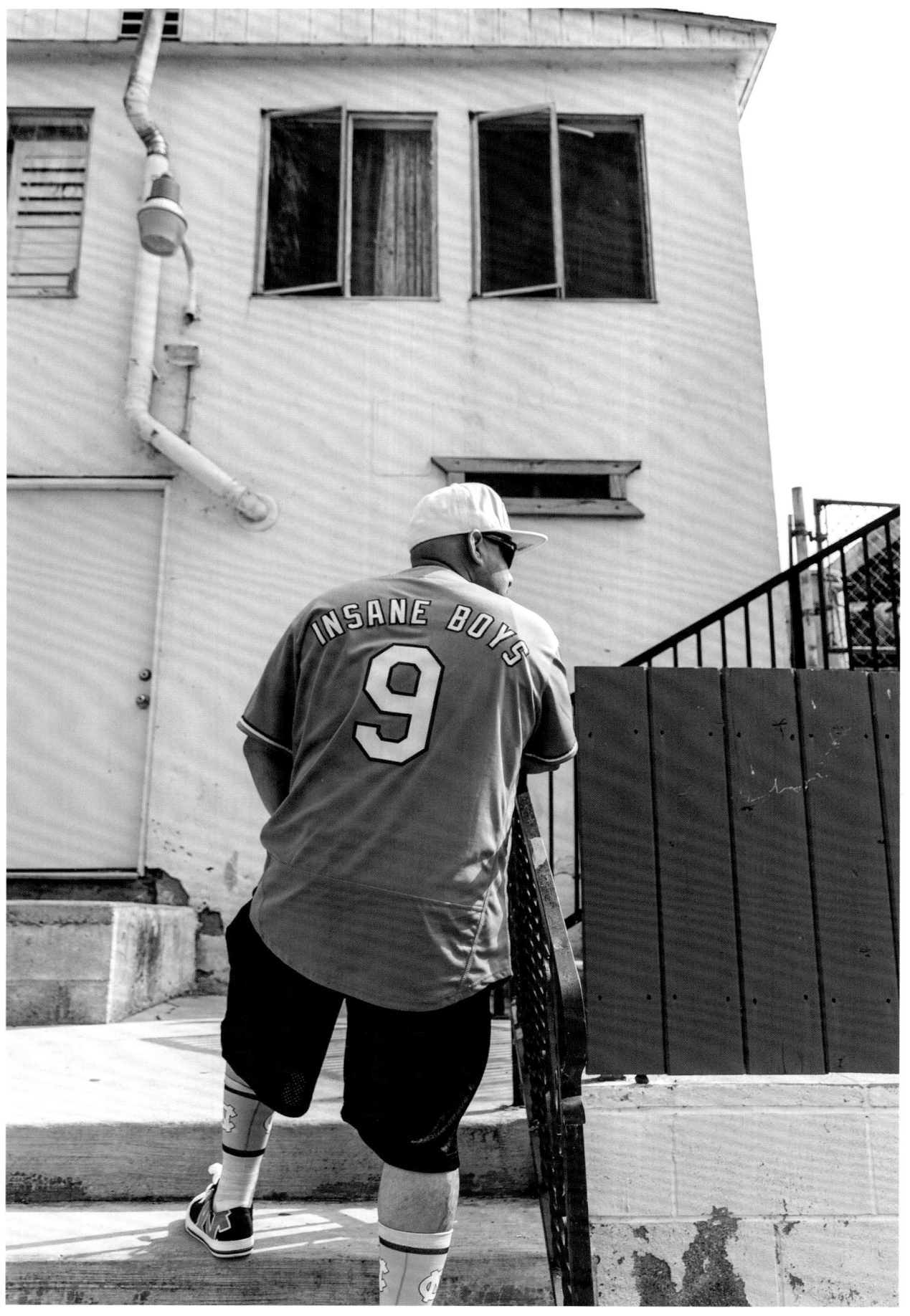

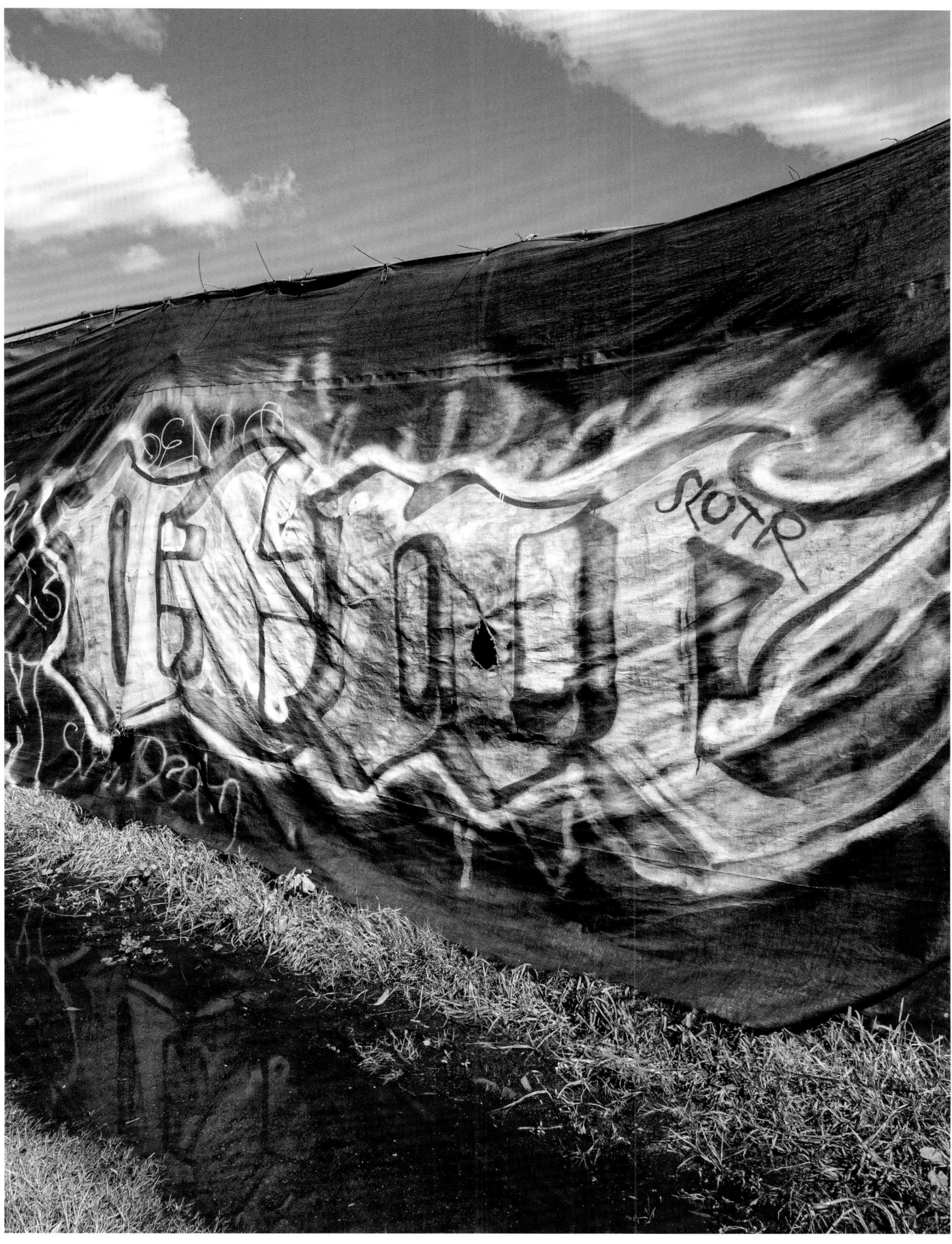

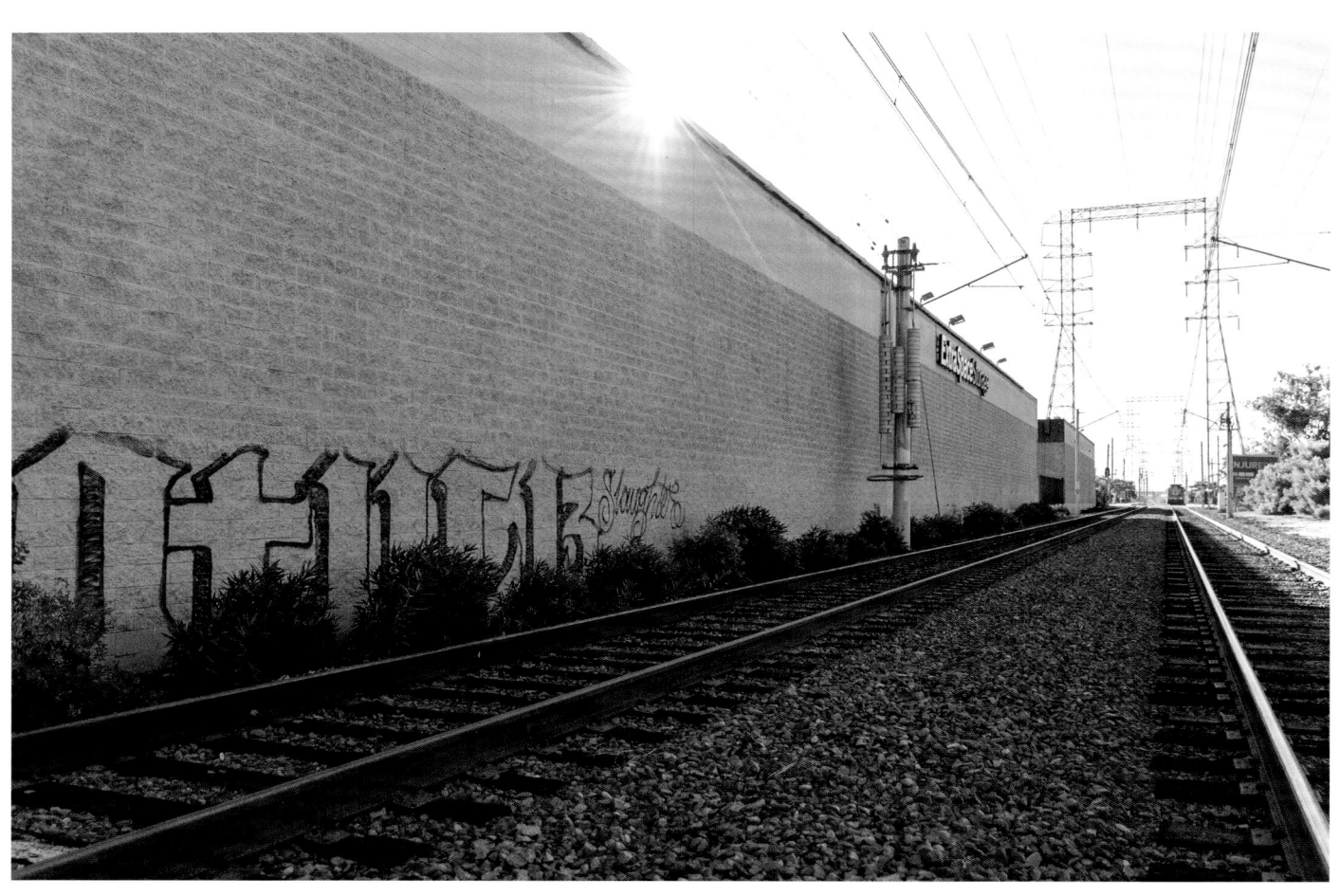

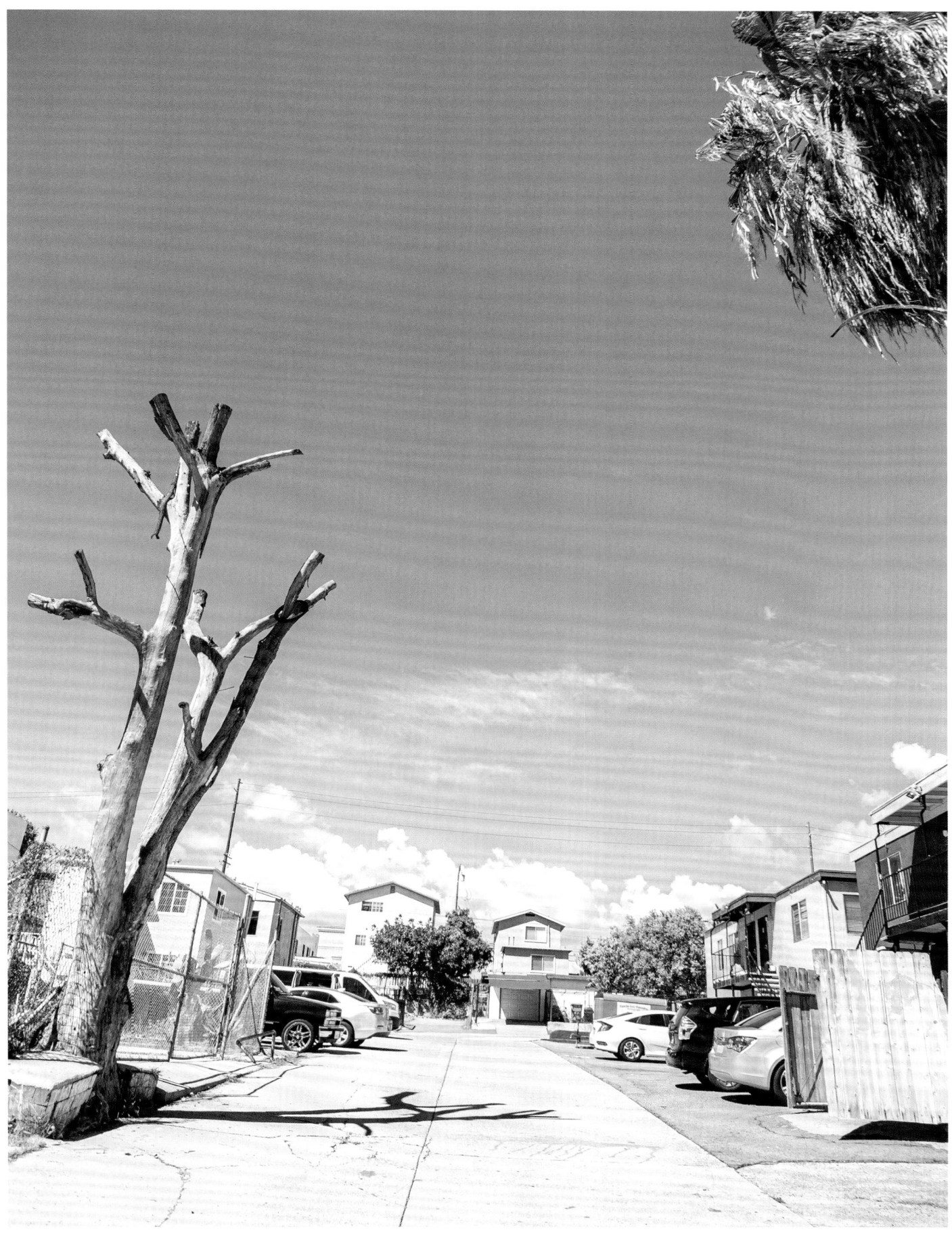

LOGAN

HEIGHTS

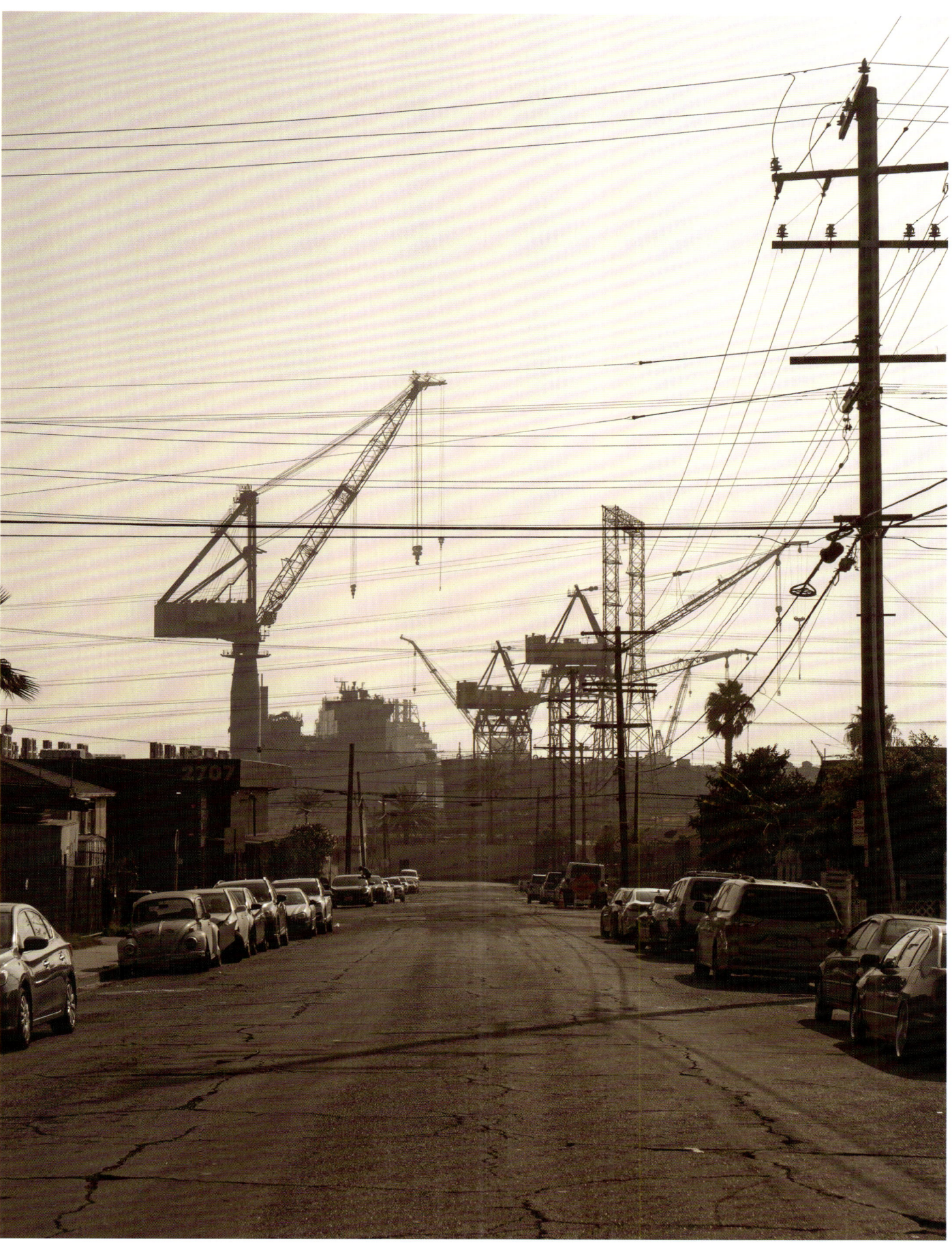

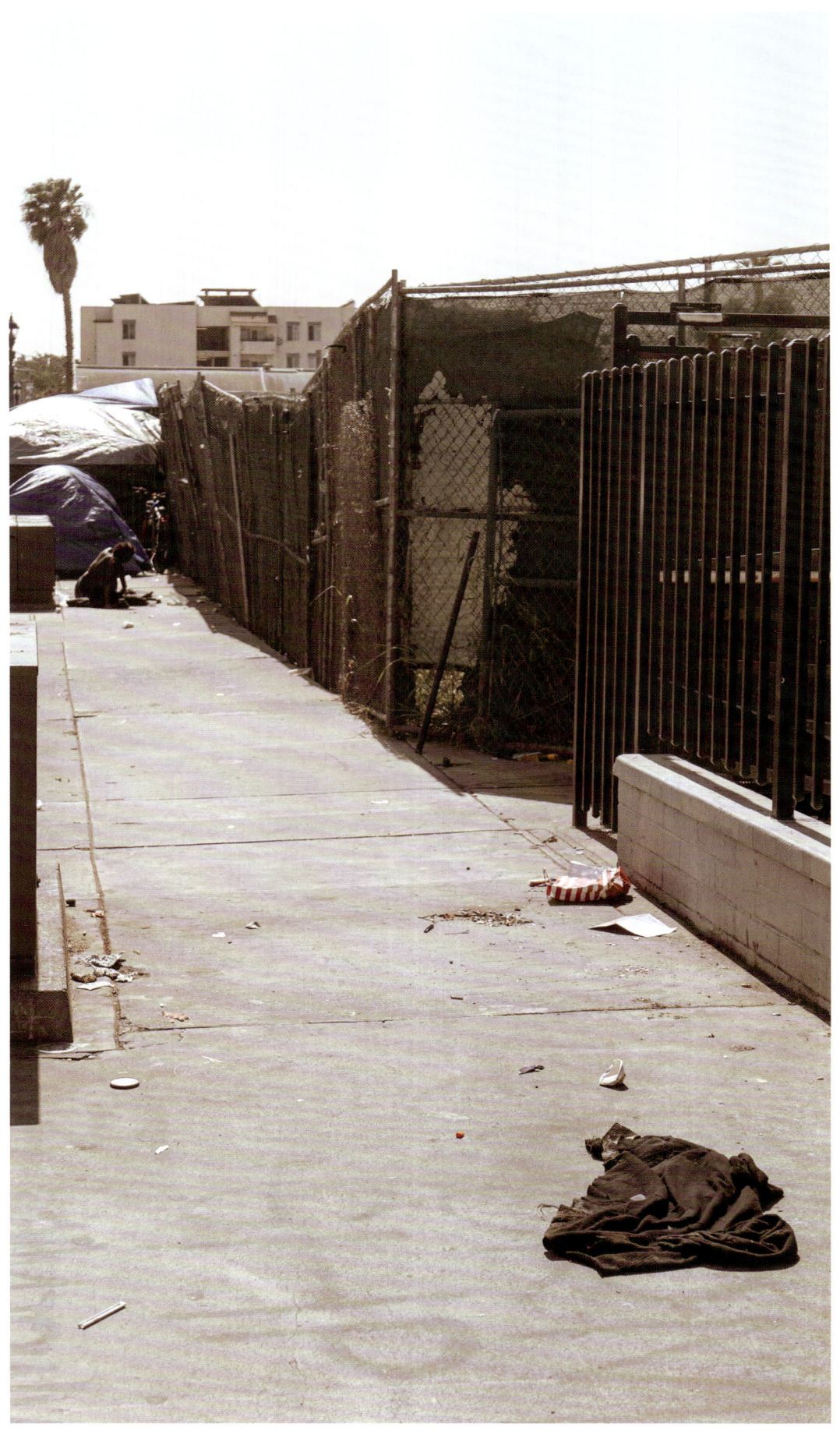

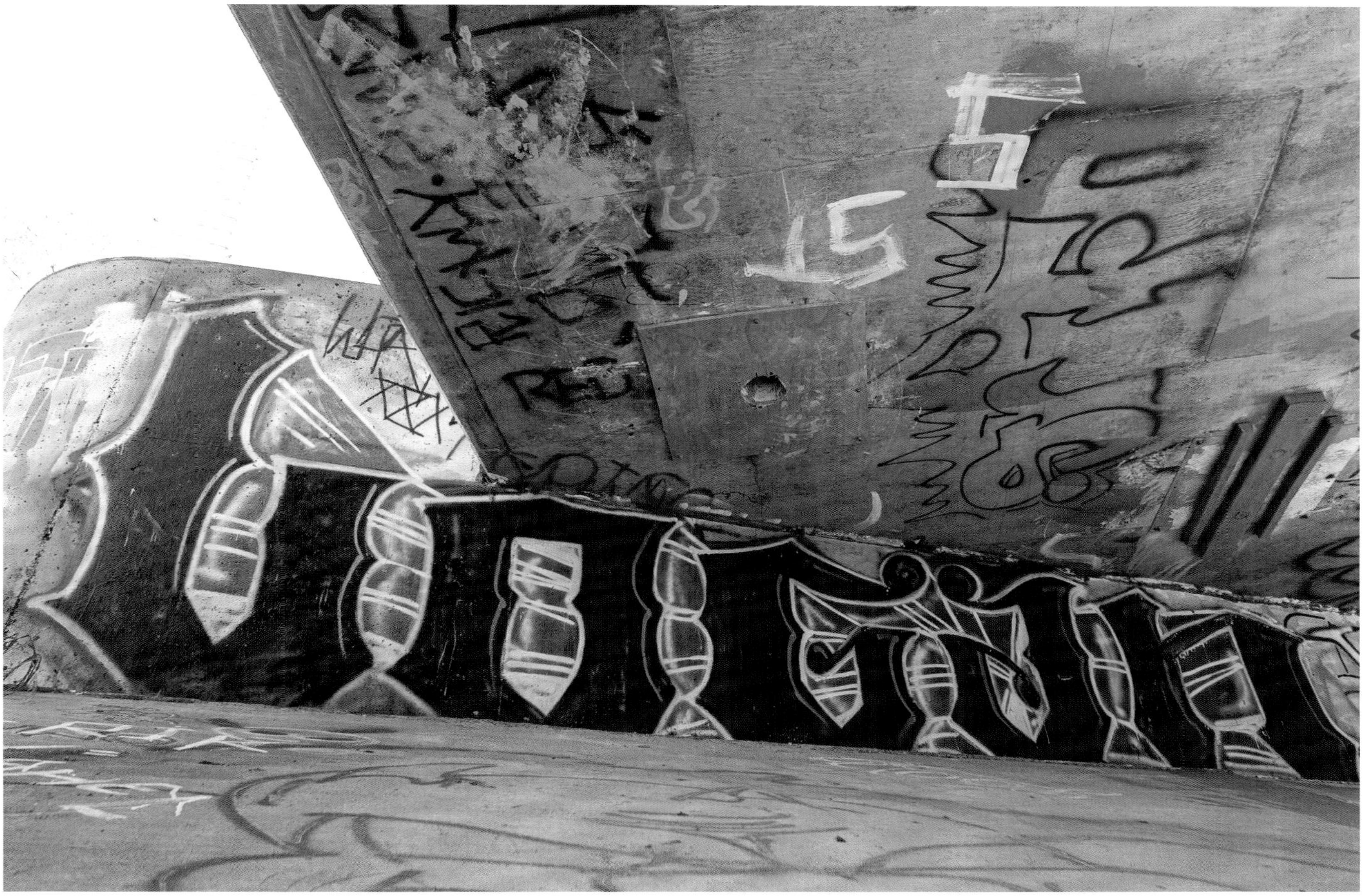

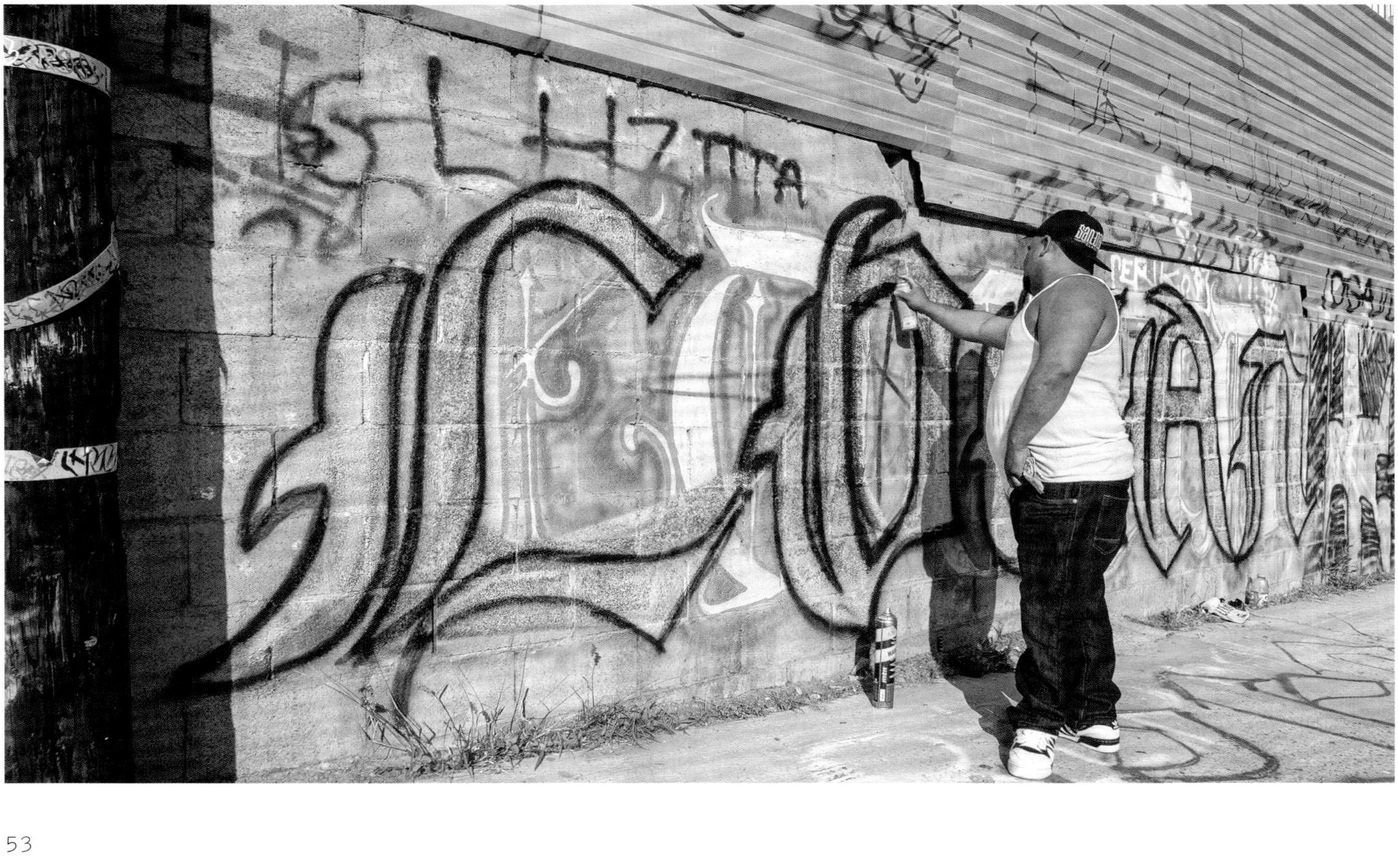

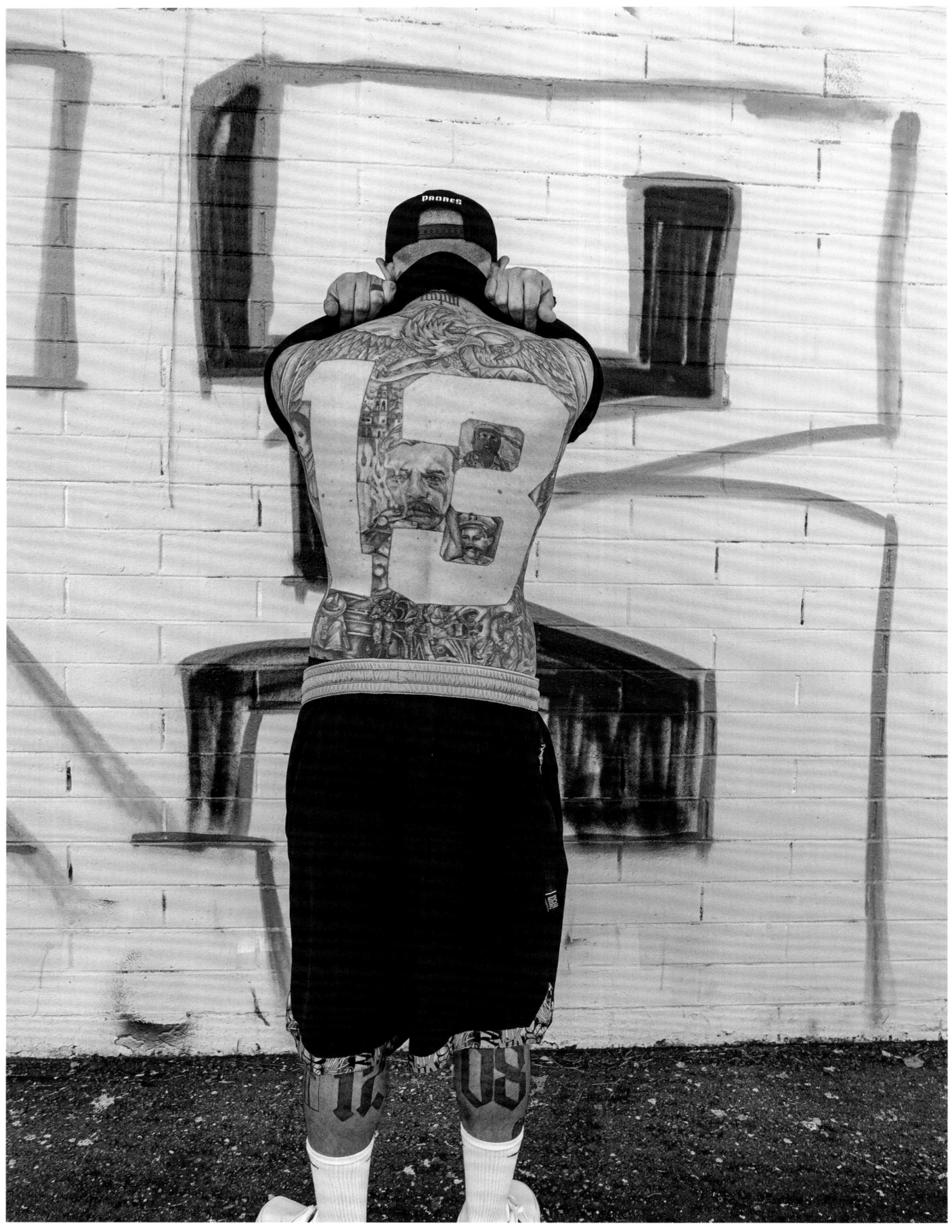

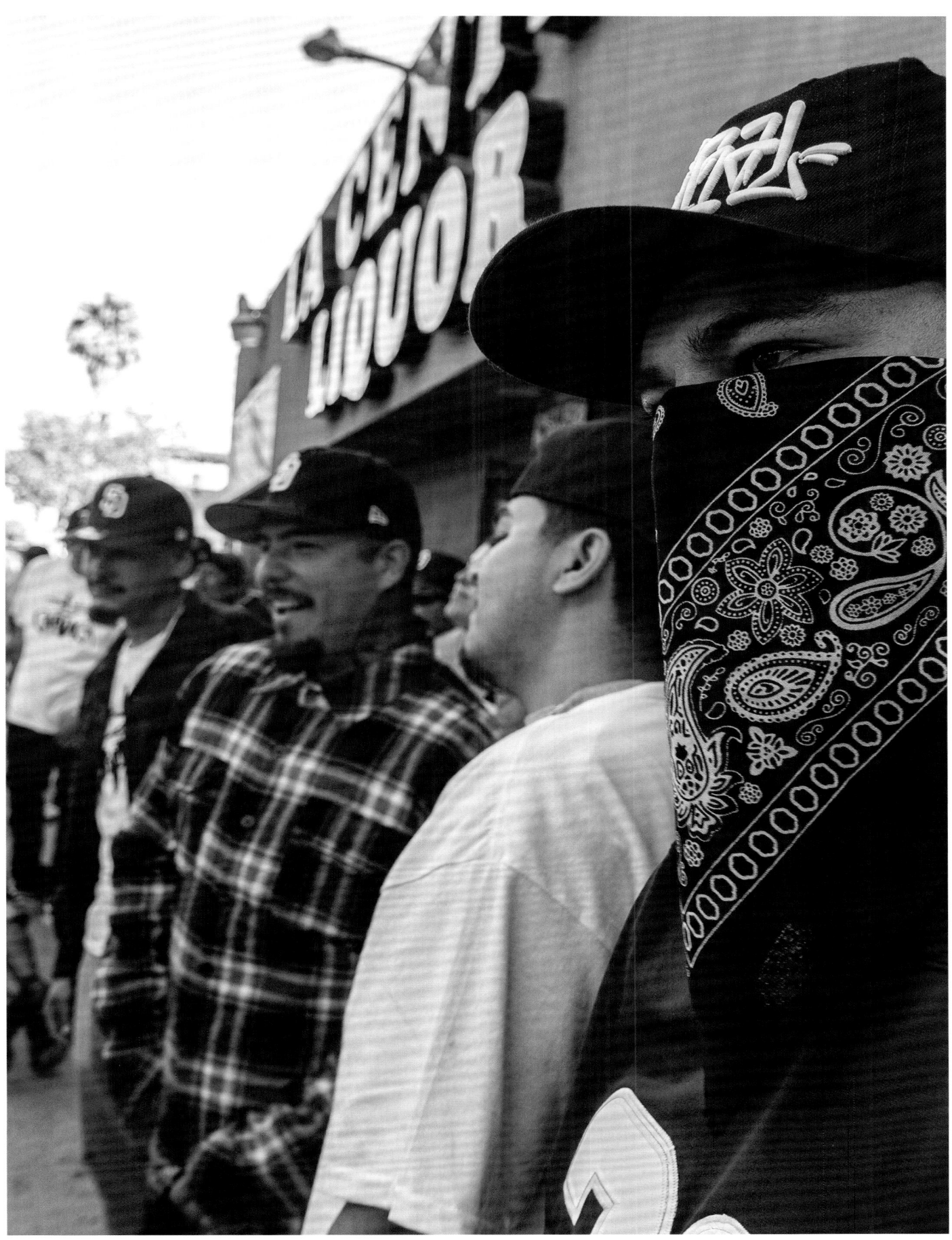

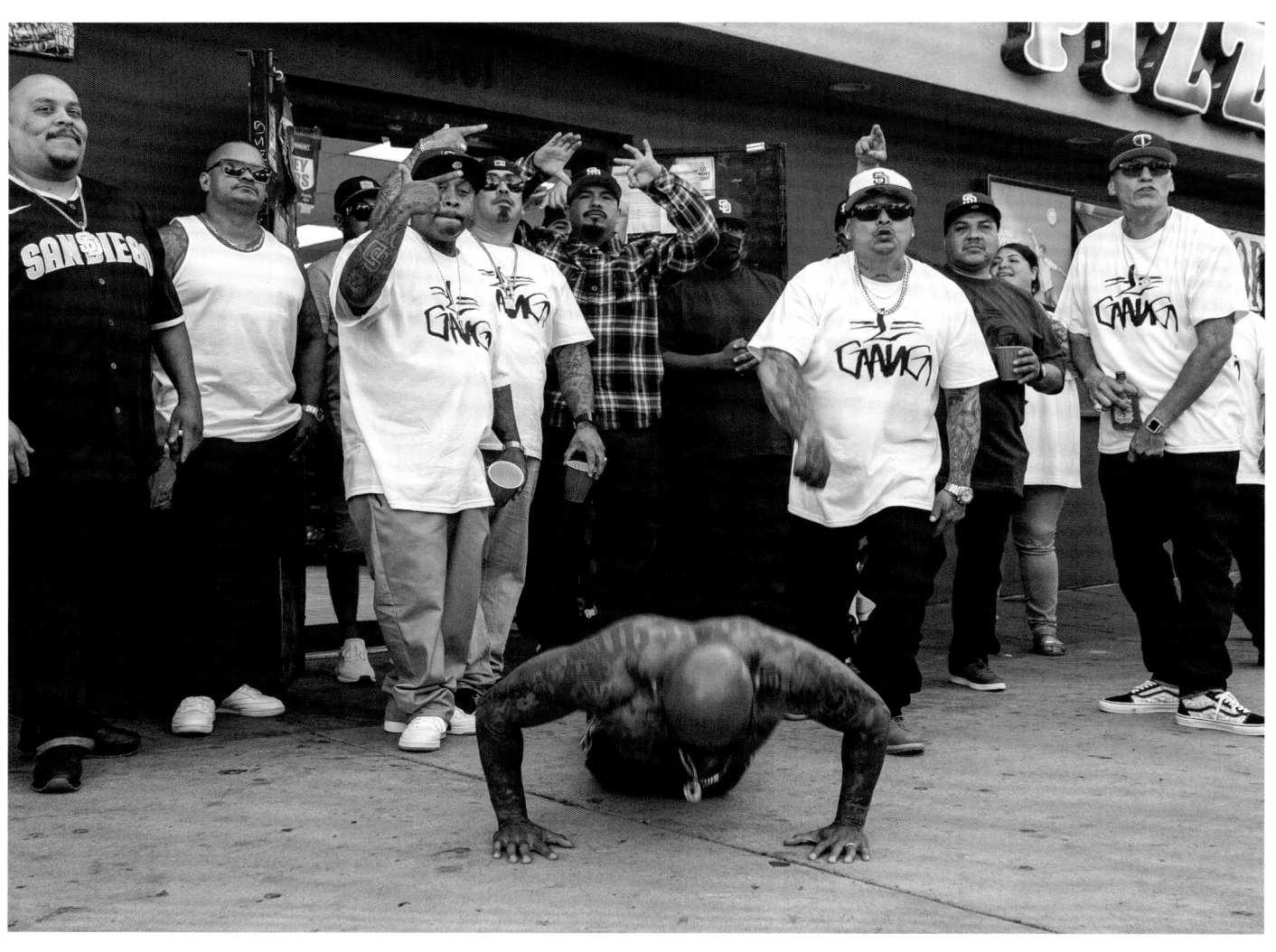

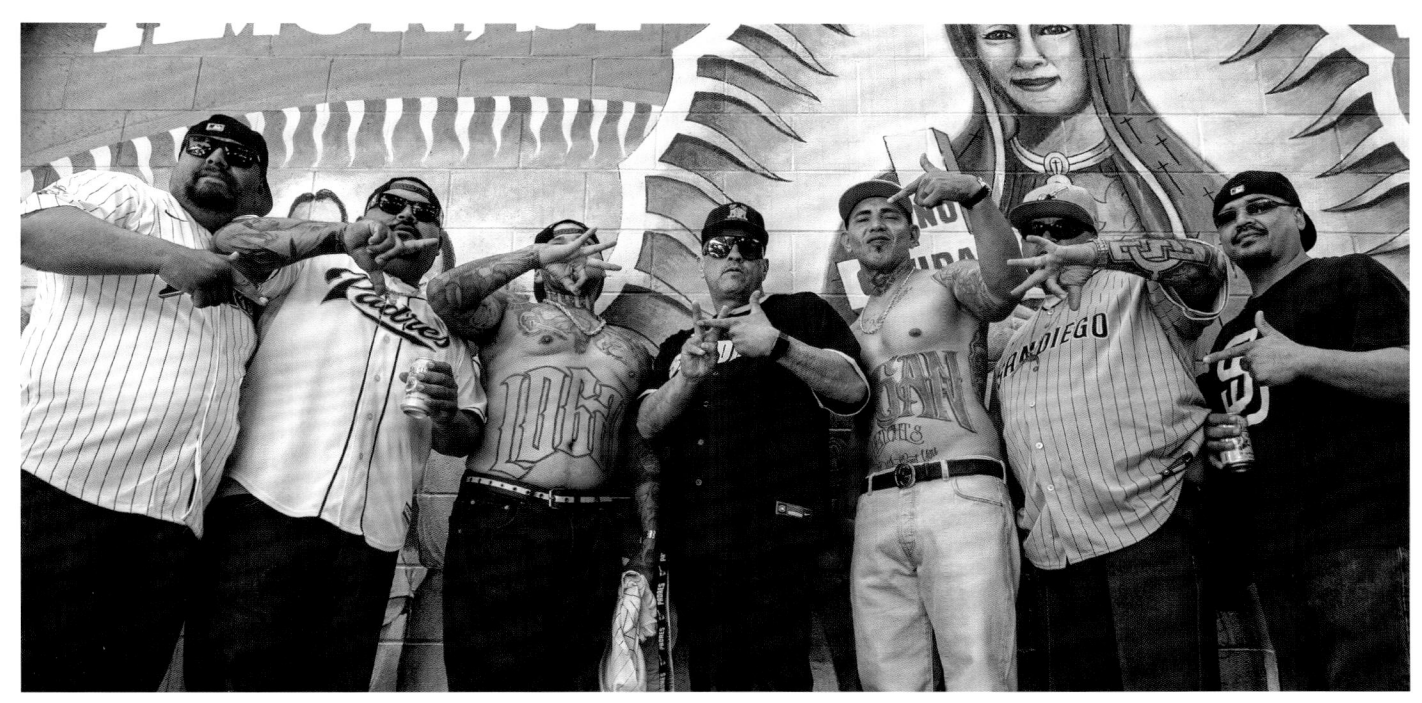

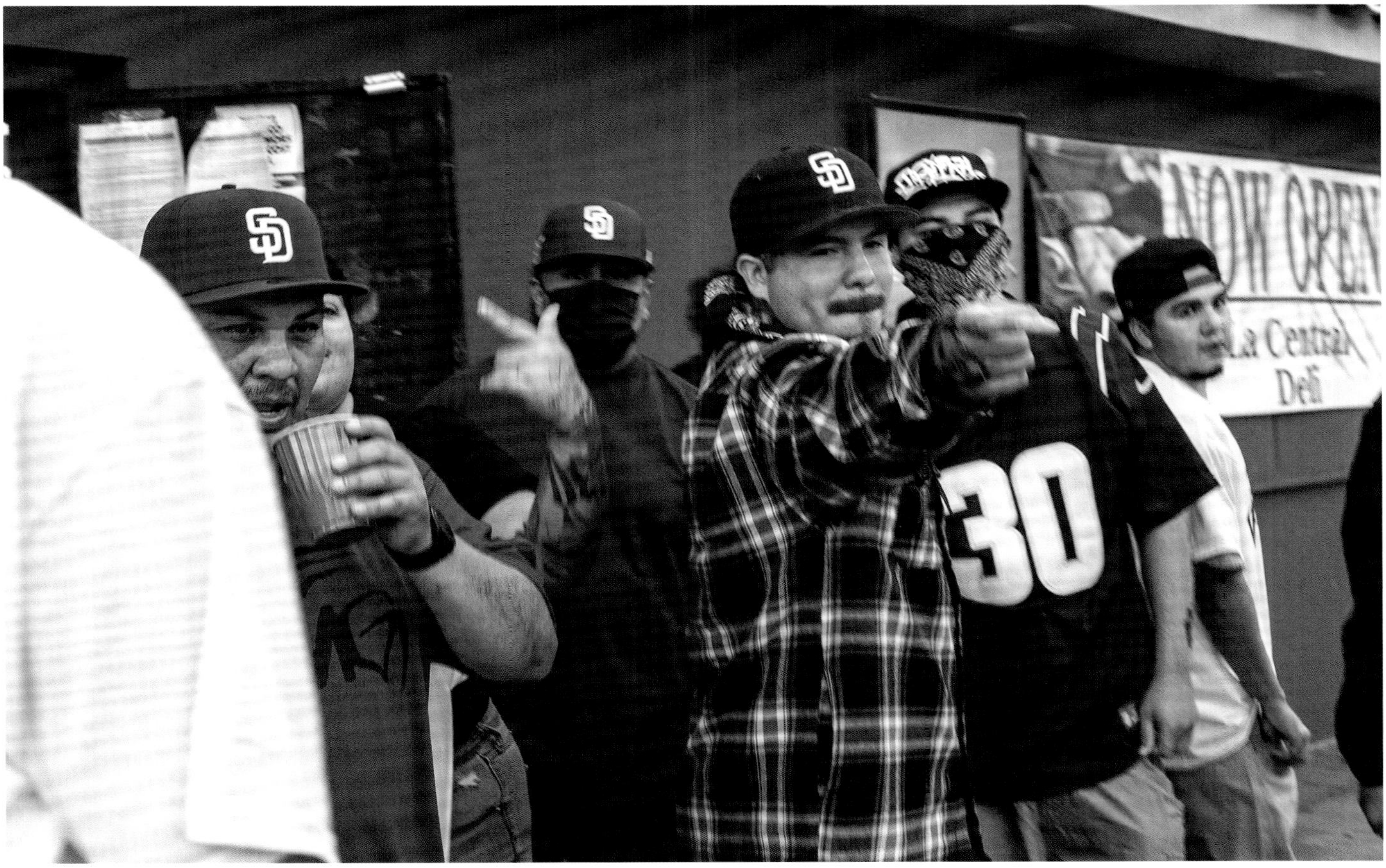

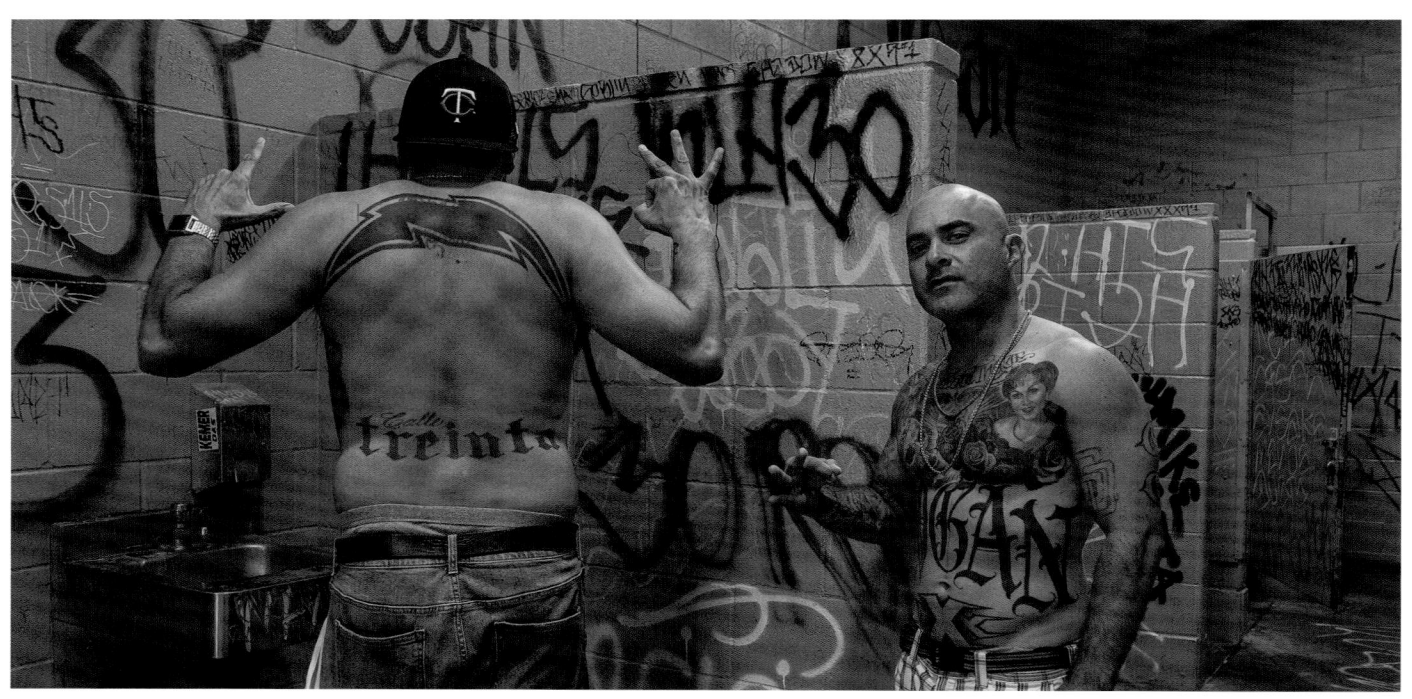

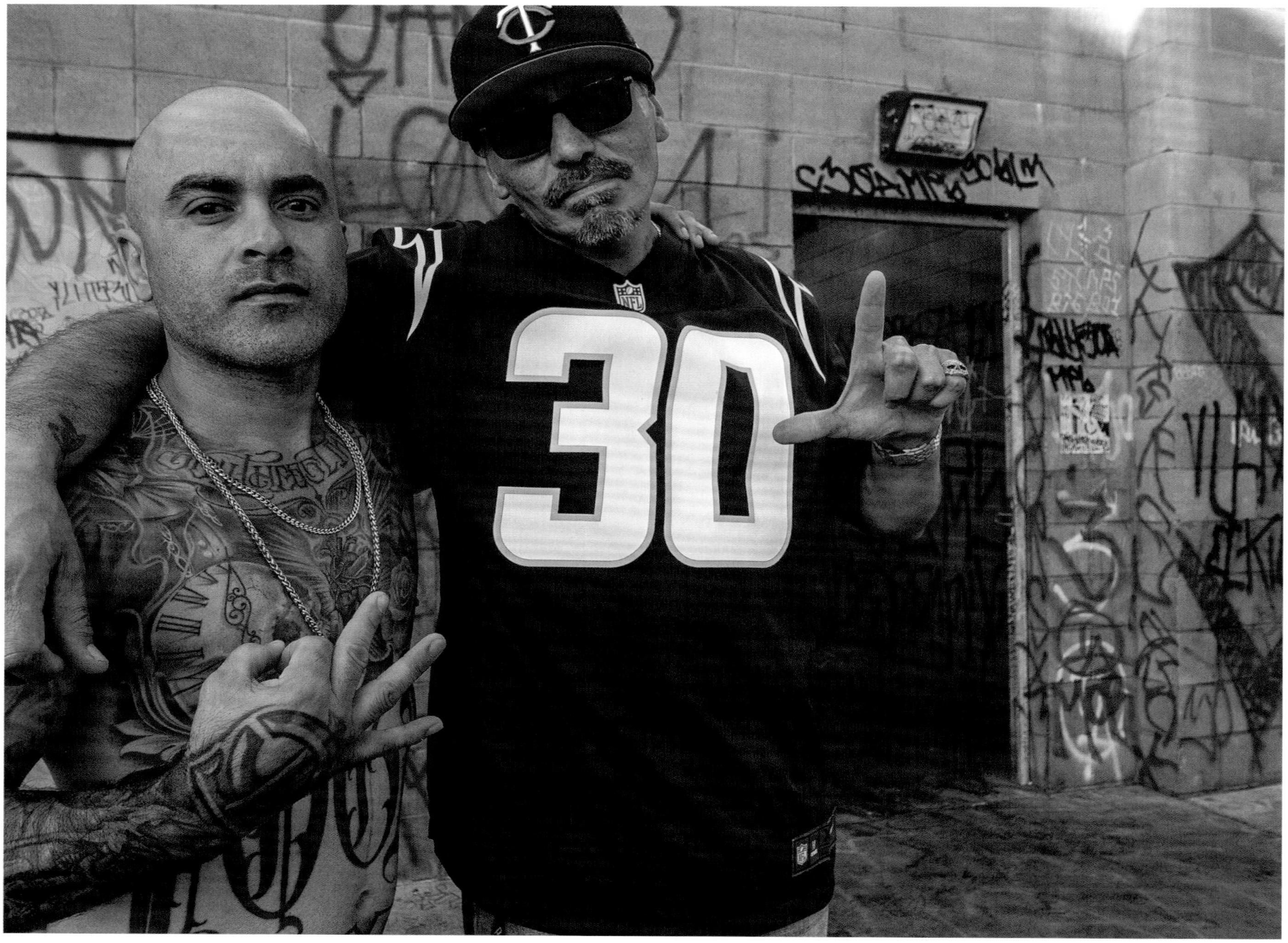

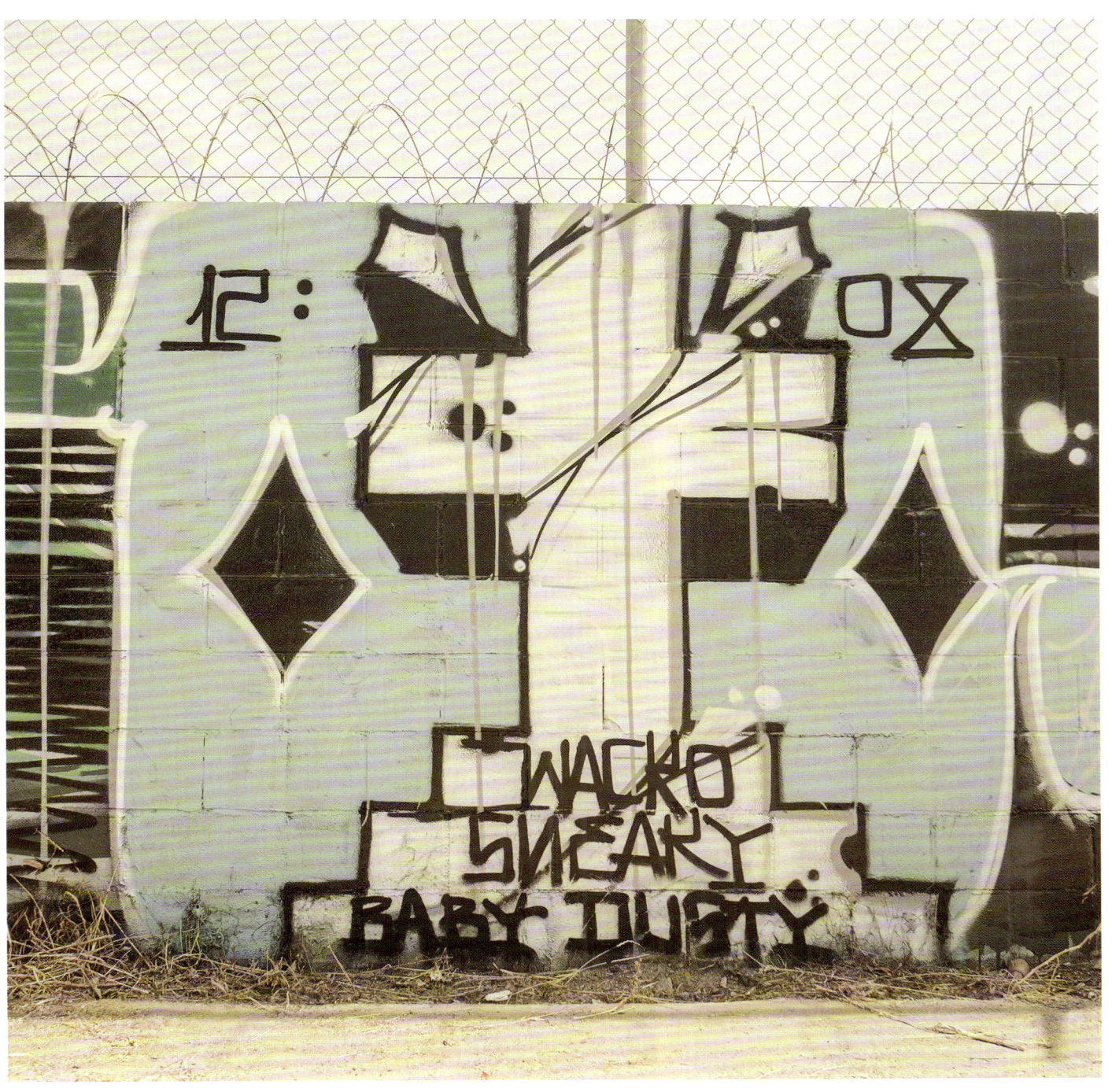

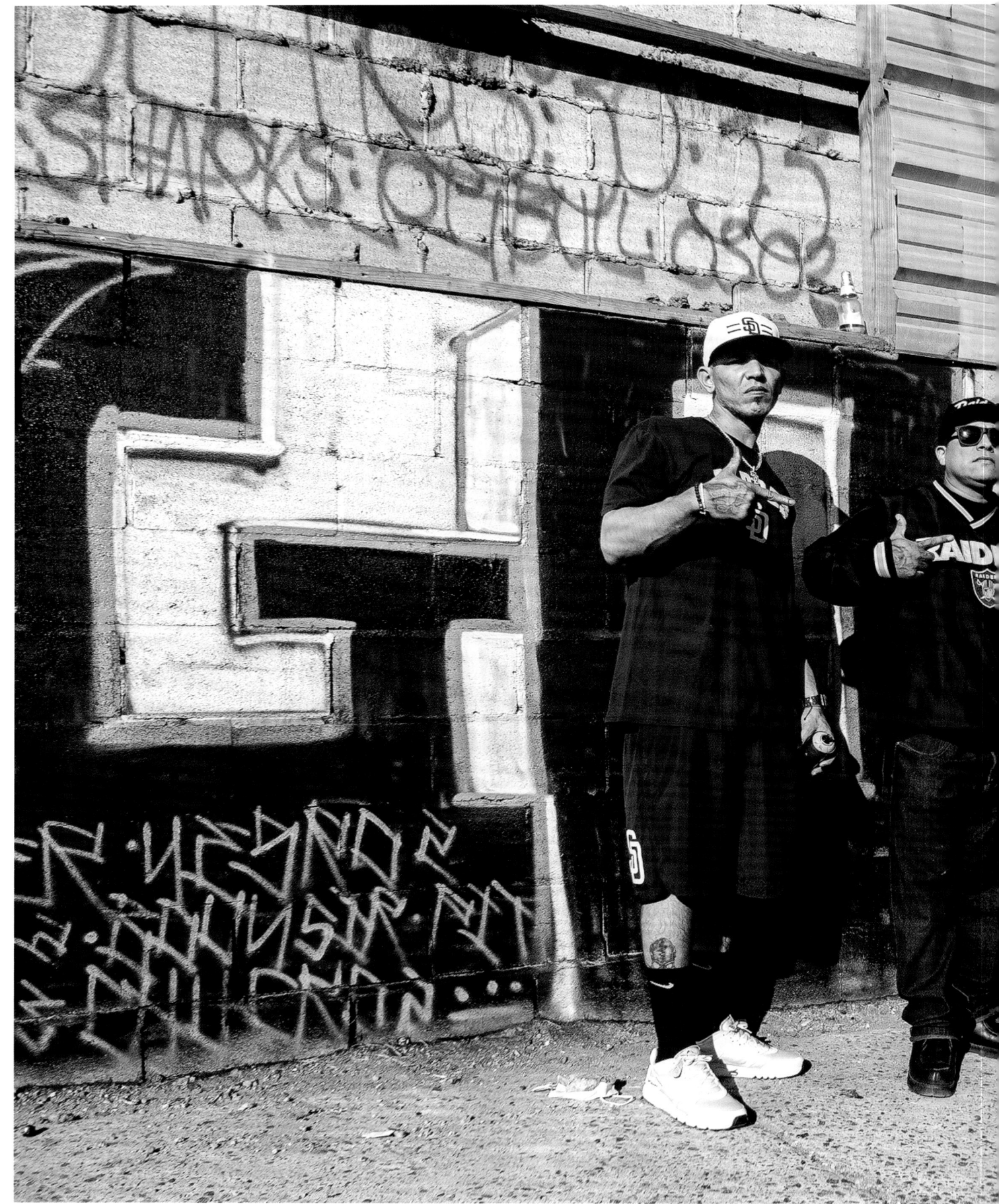

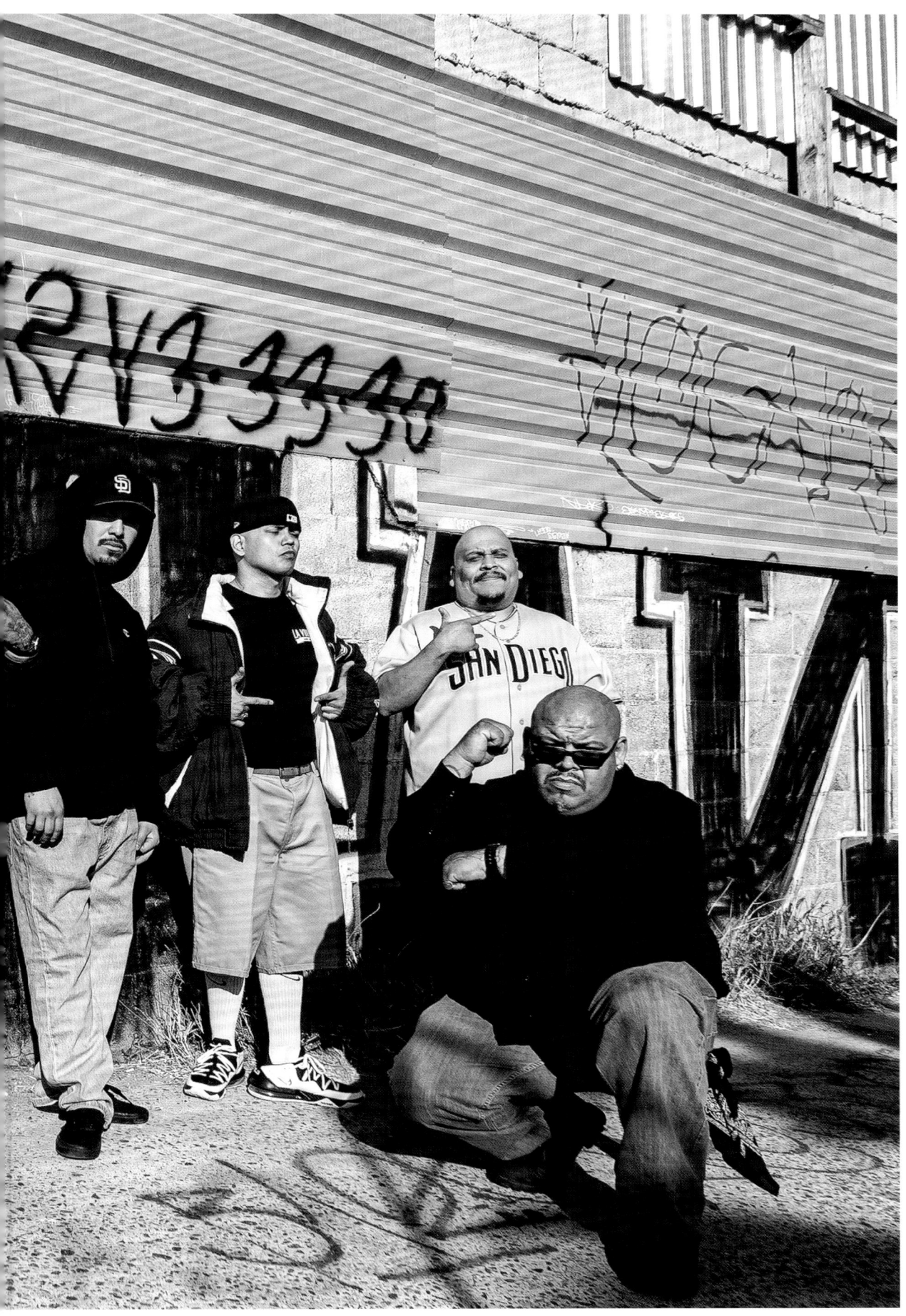

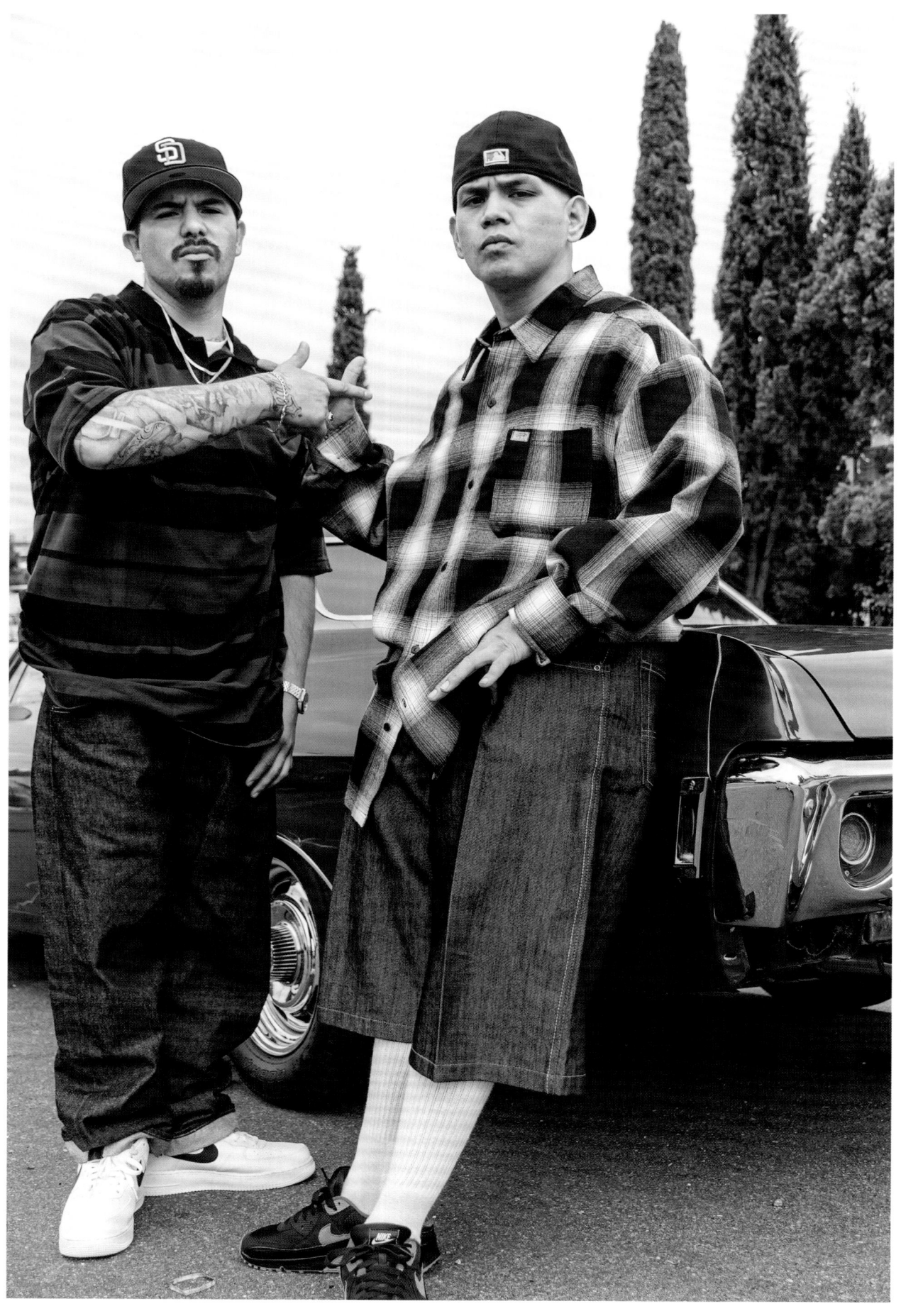

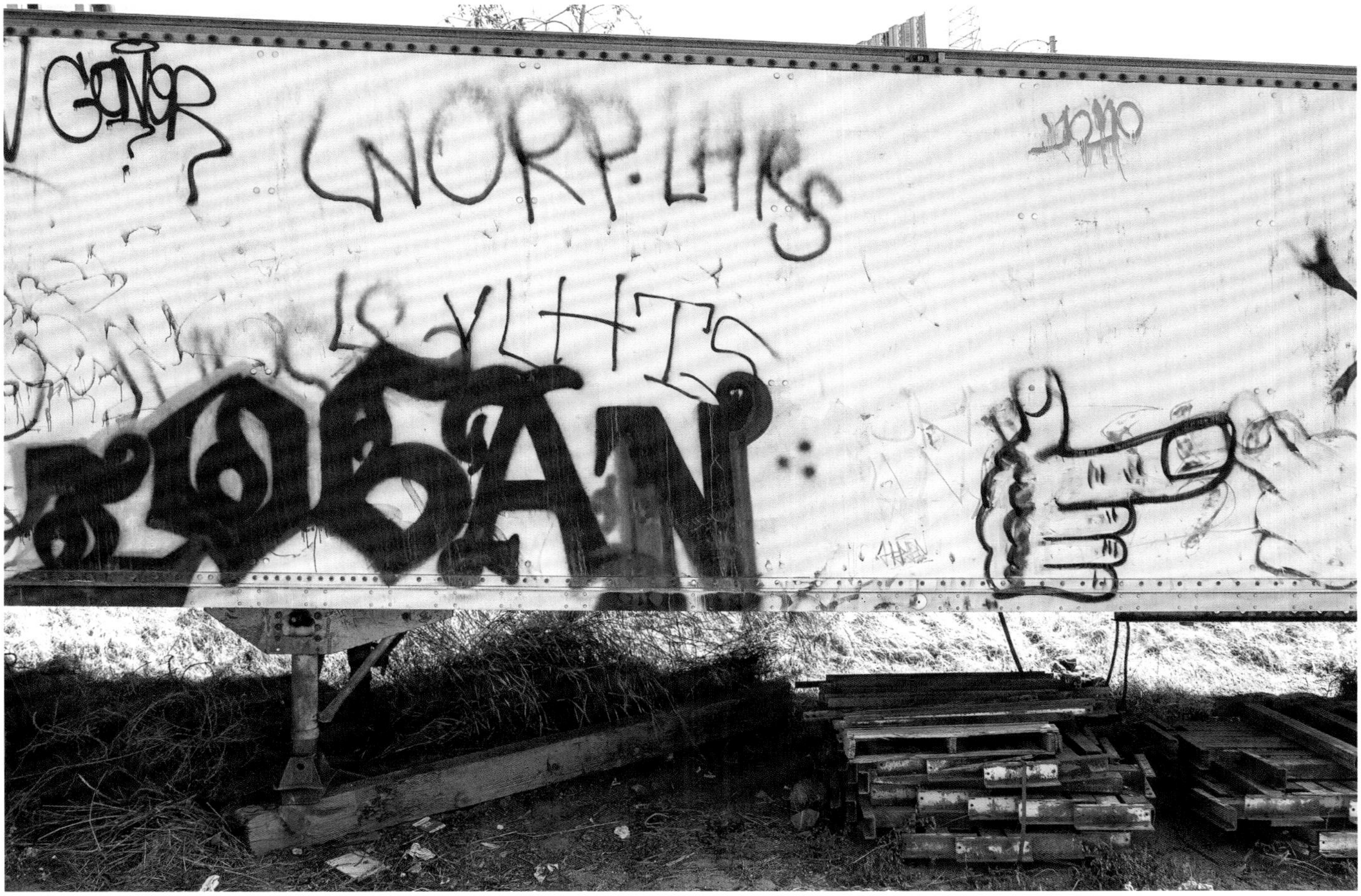

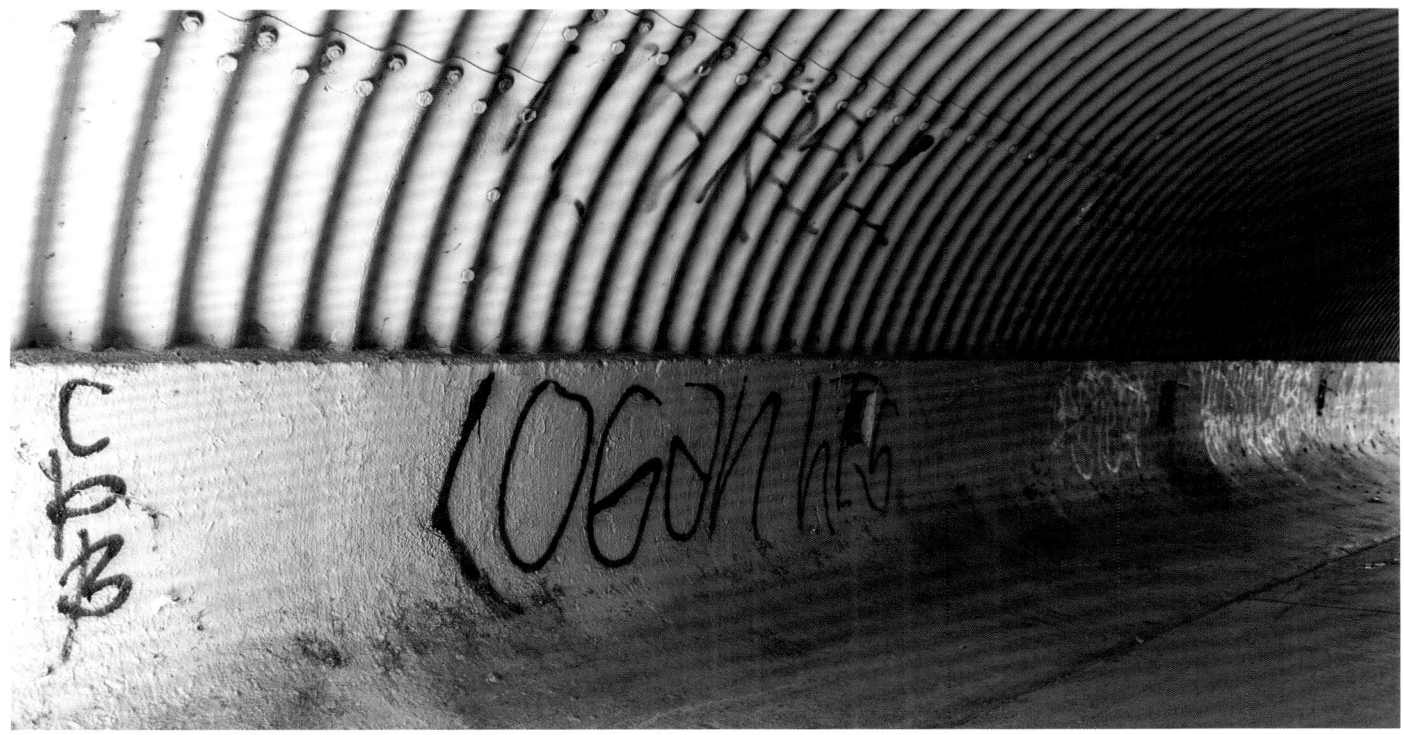

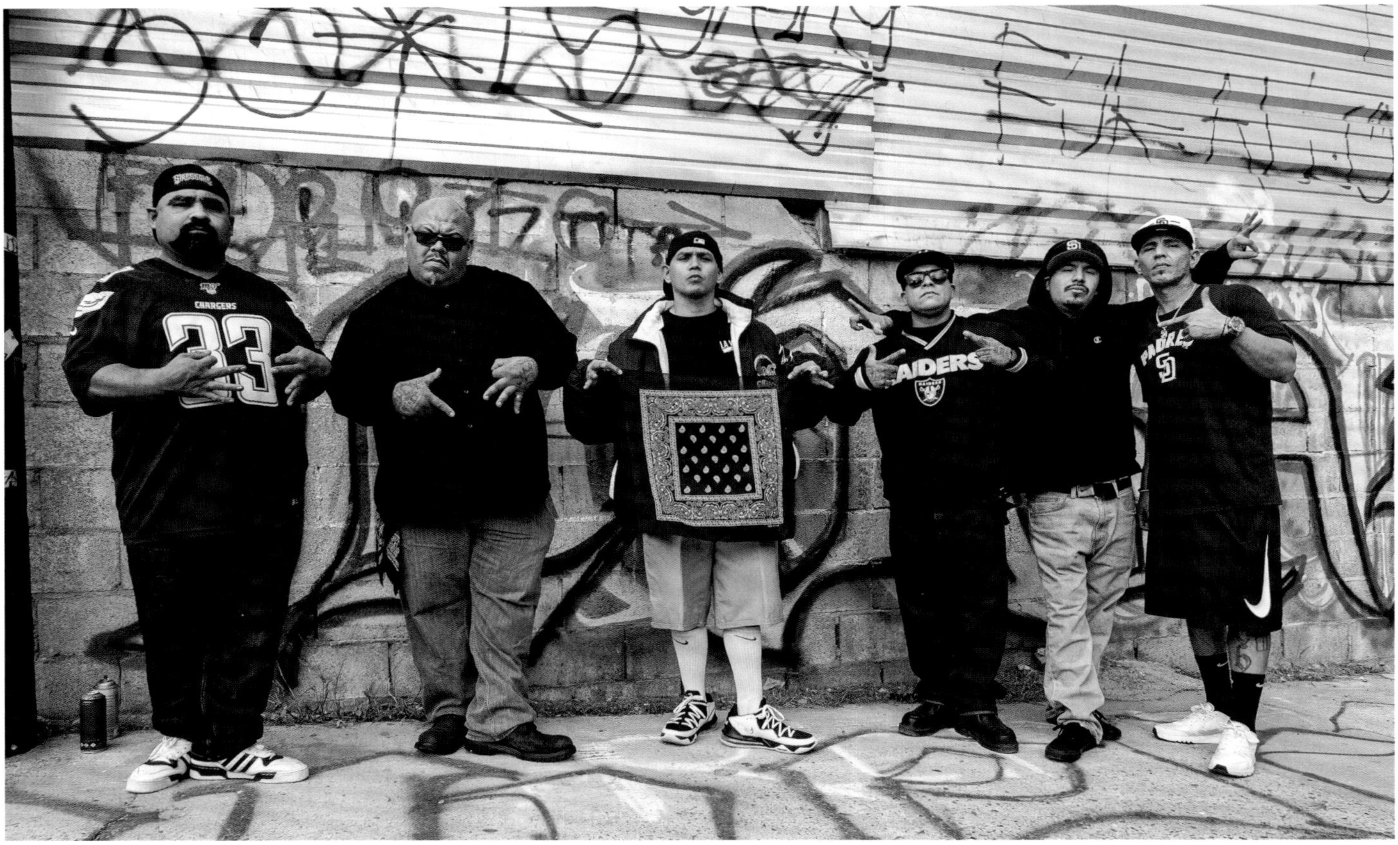

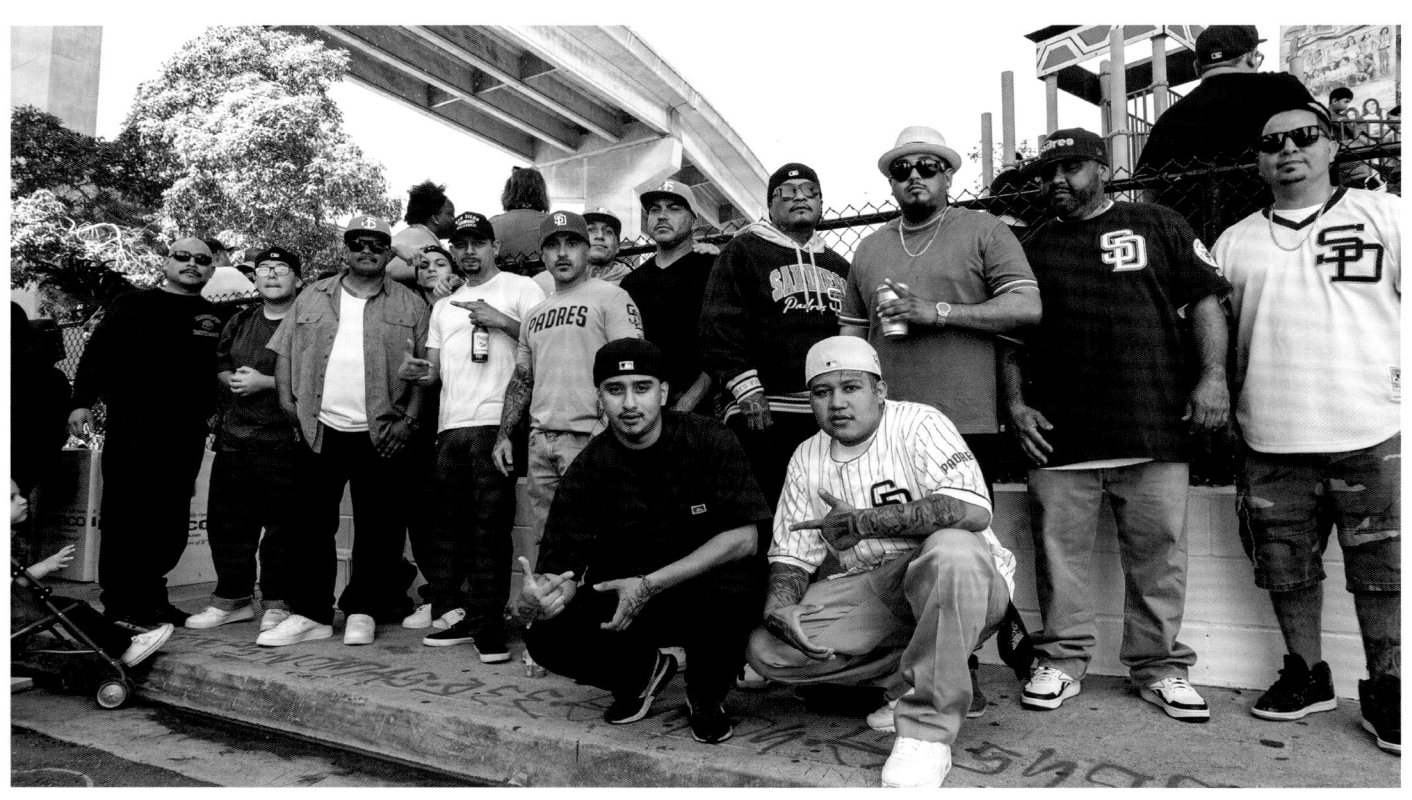

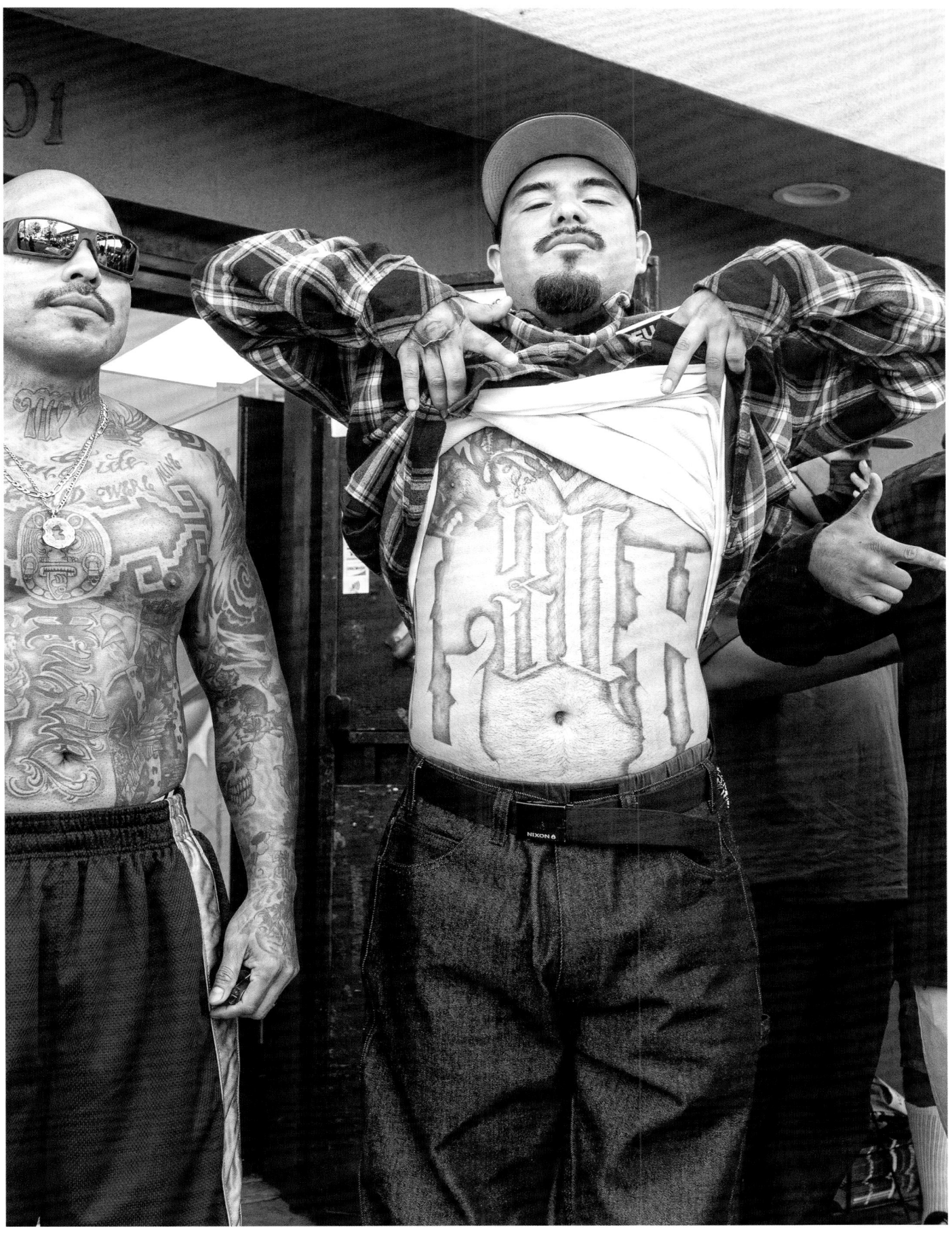

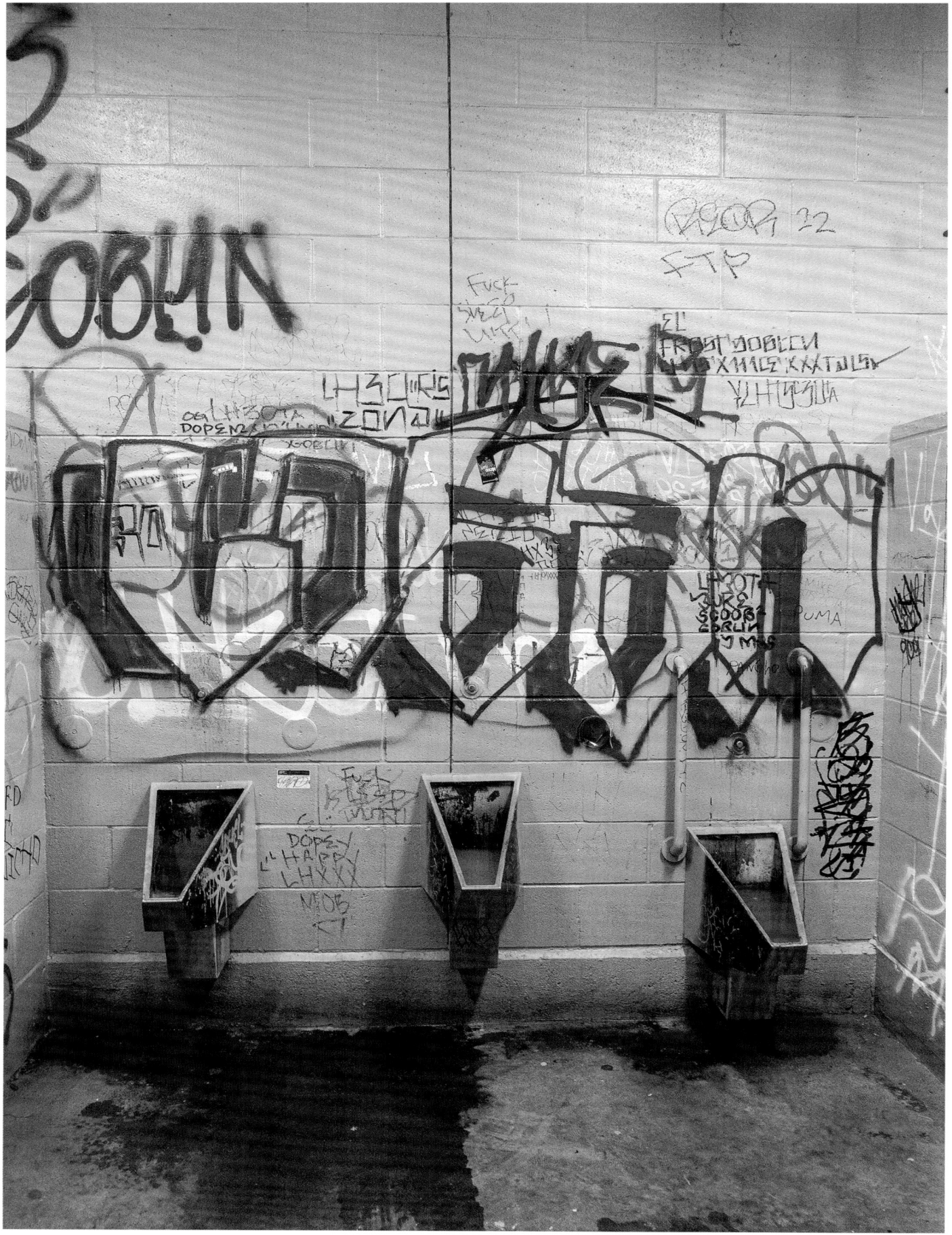

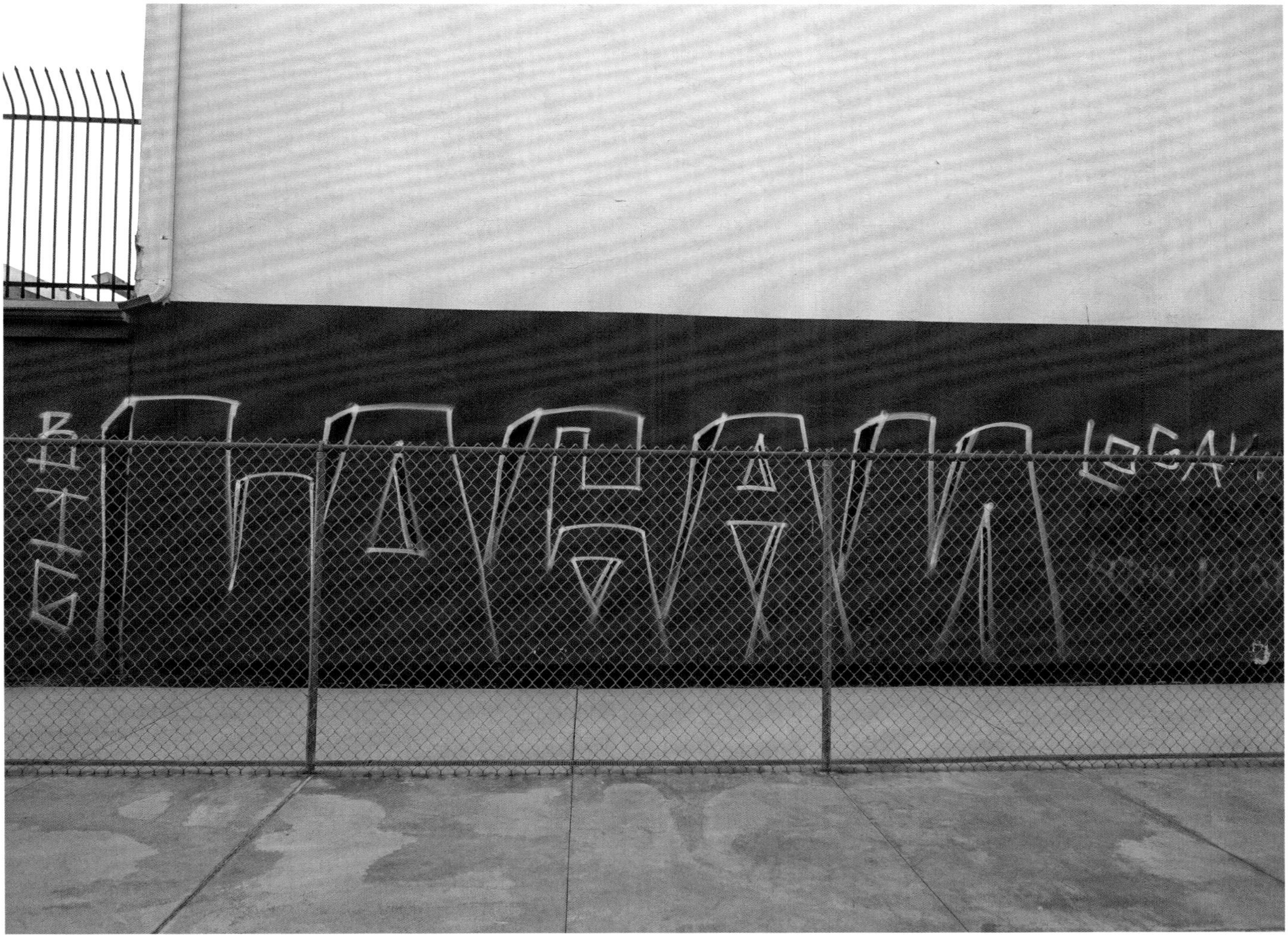

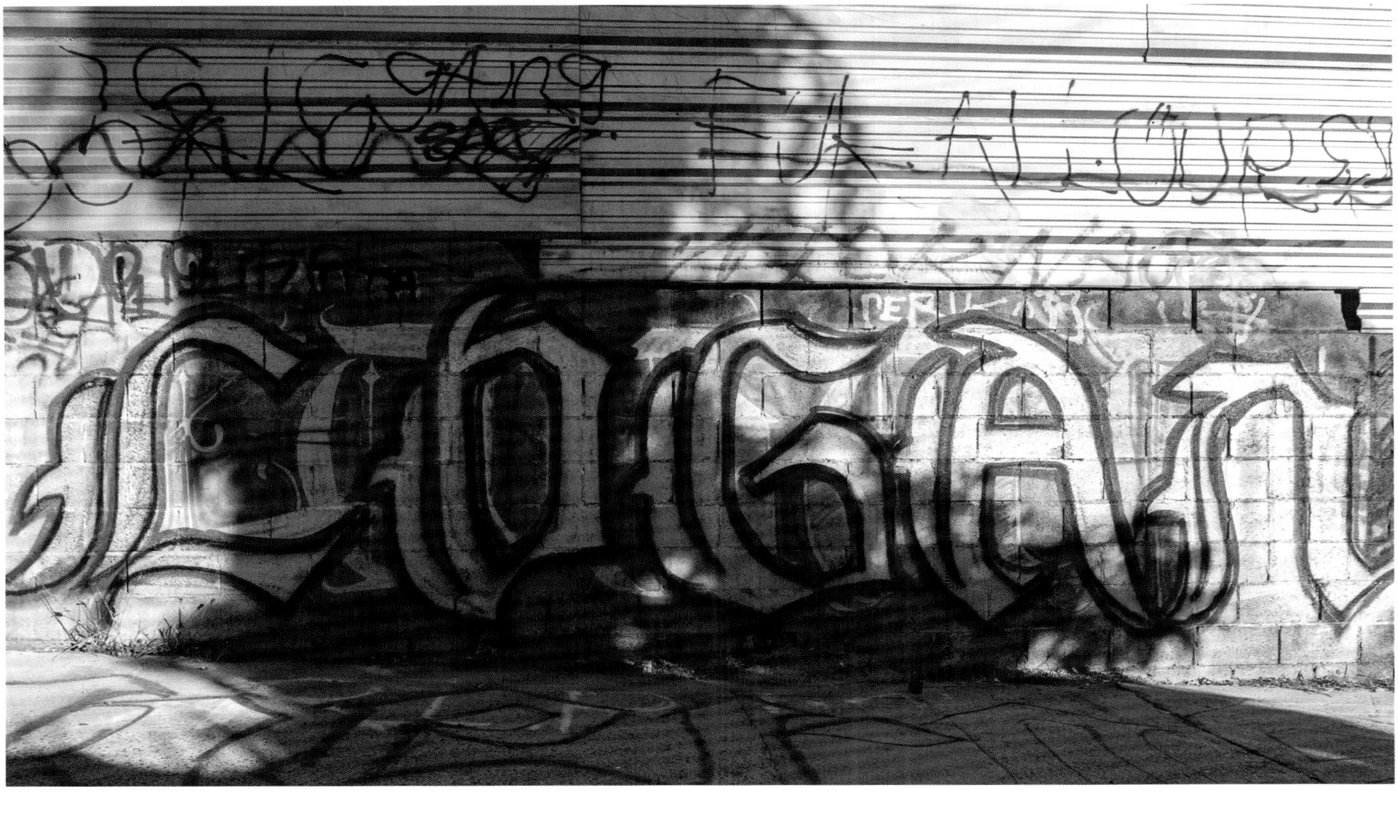

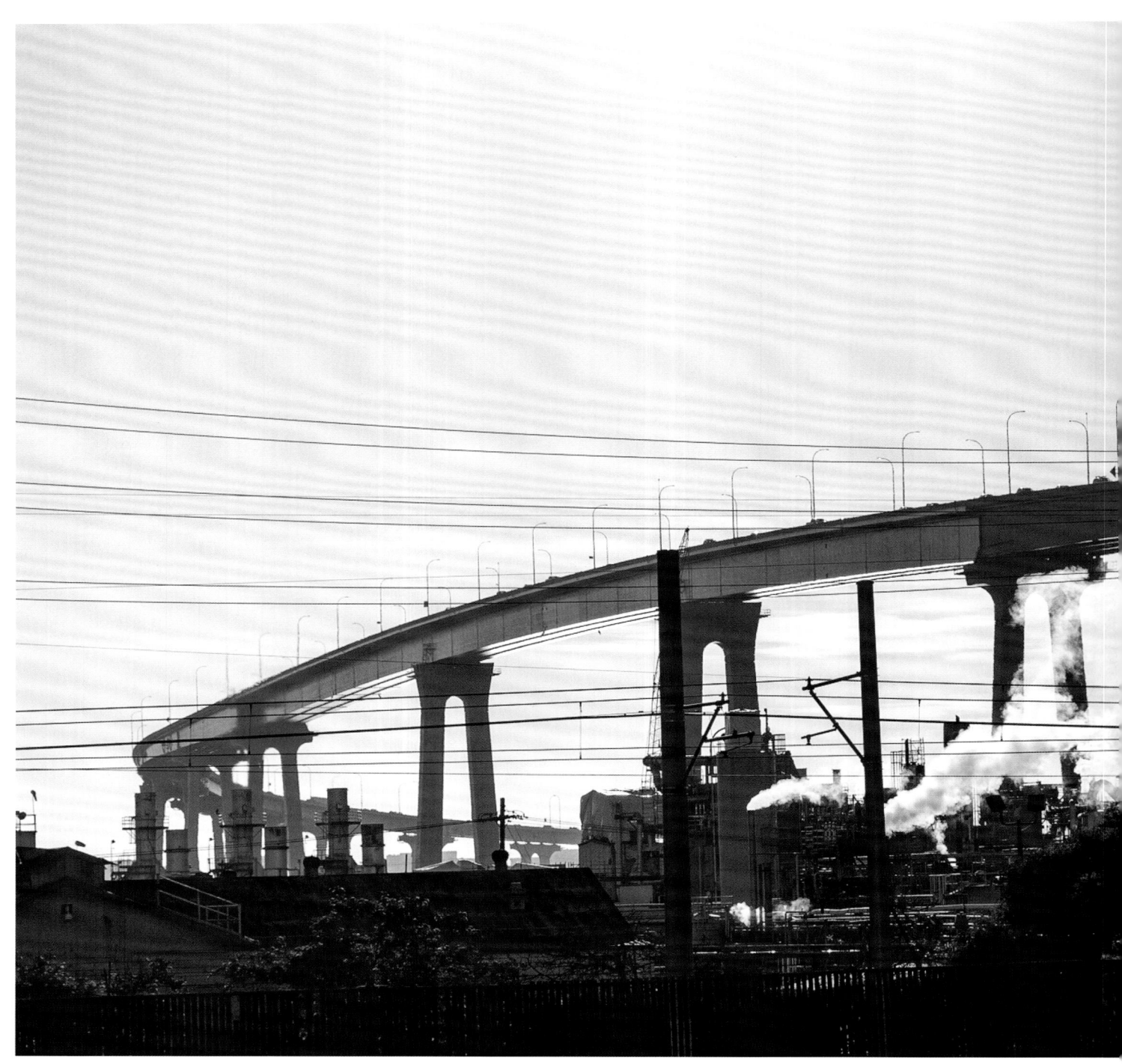

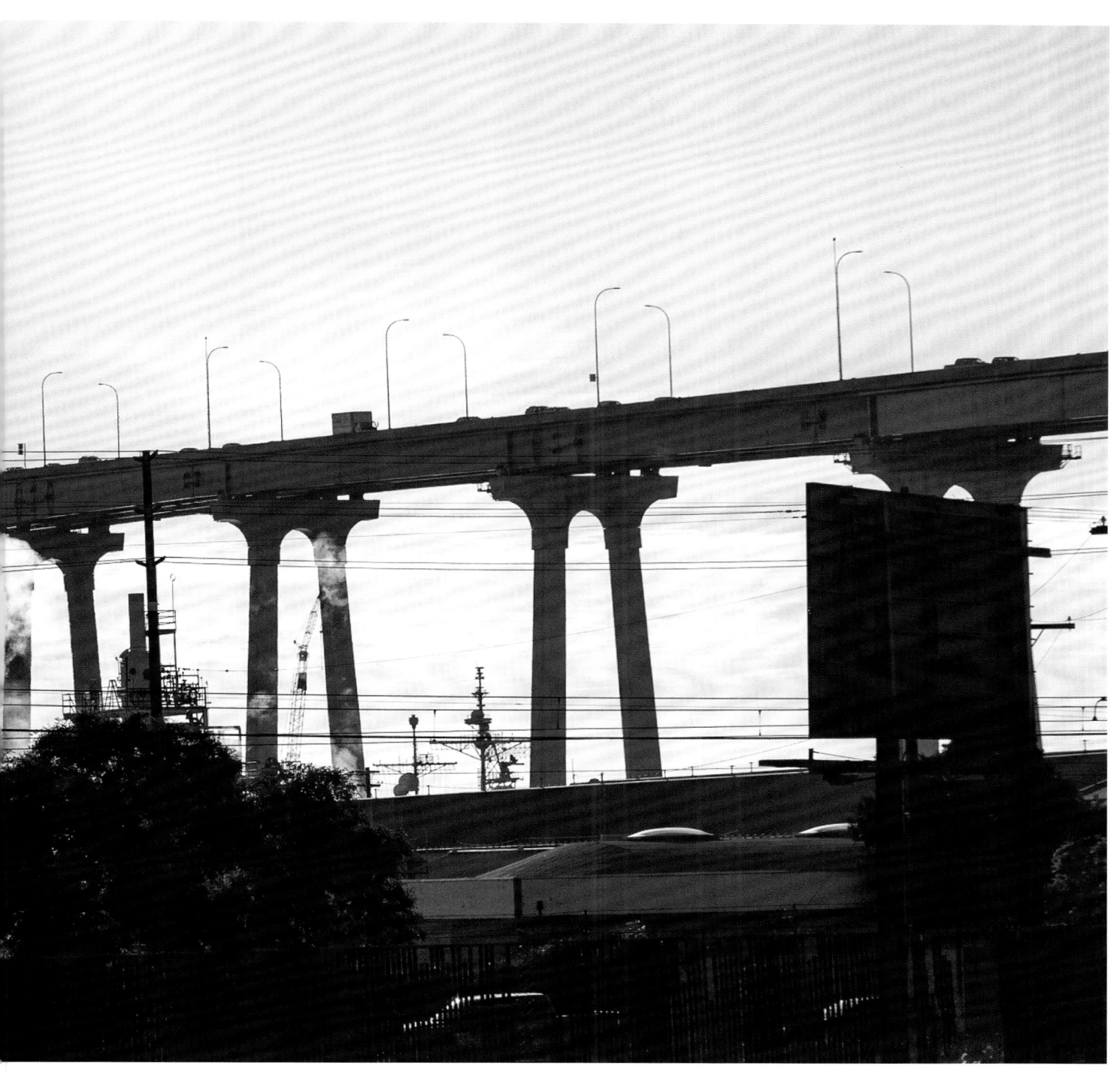

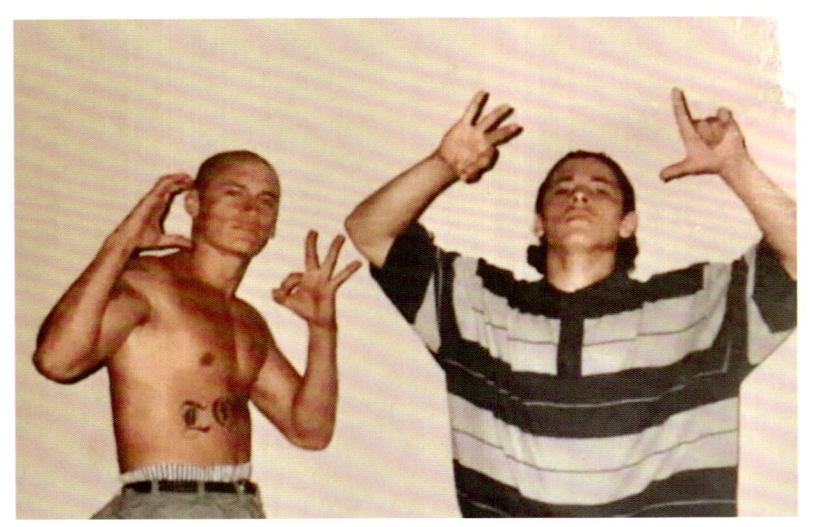

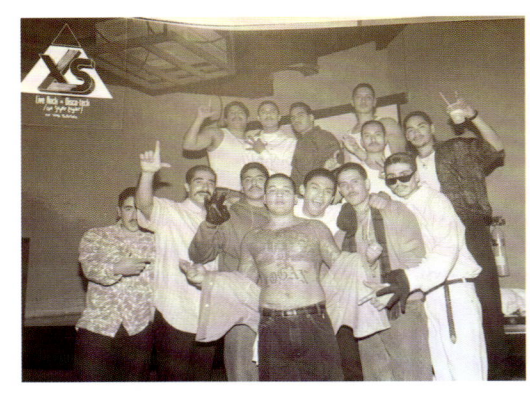

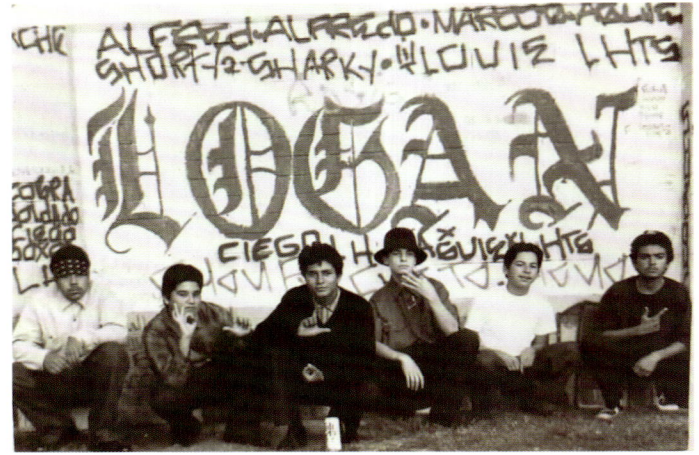

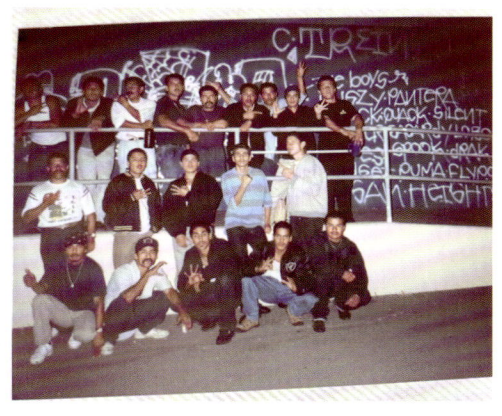

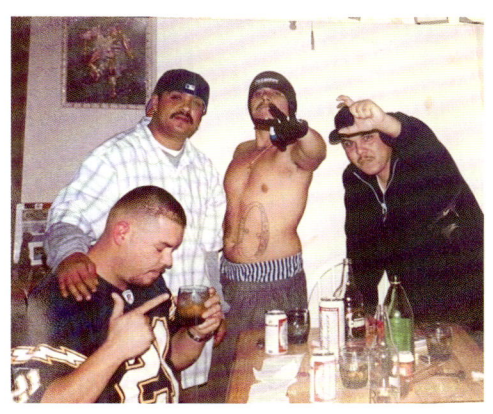

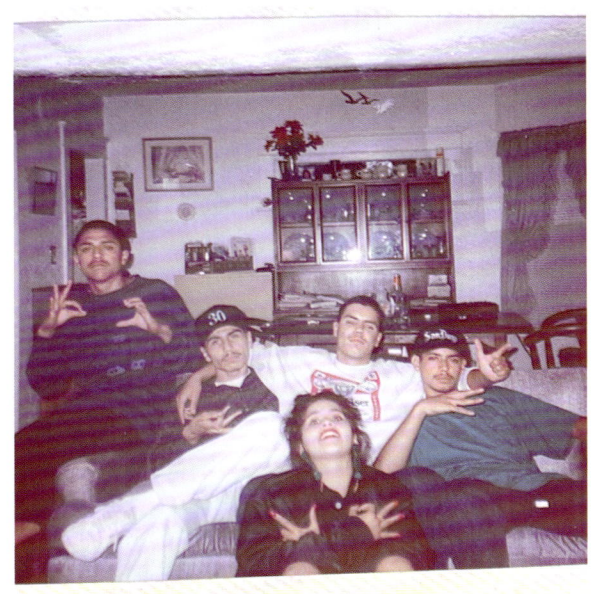

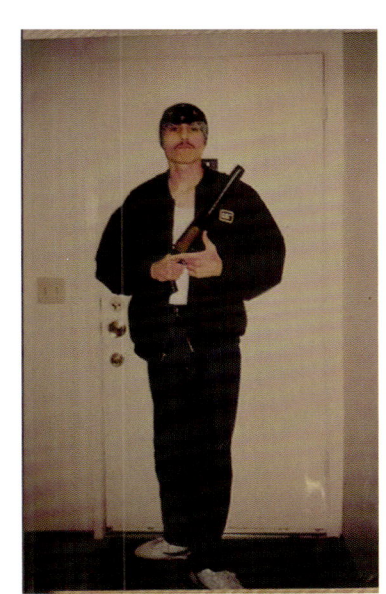

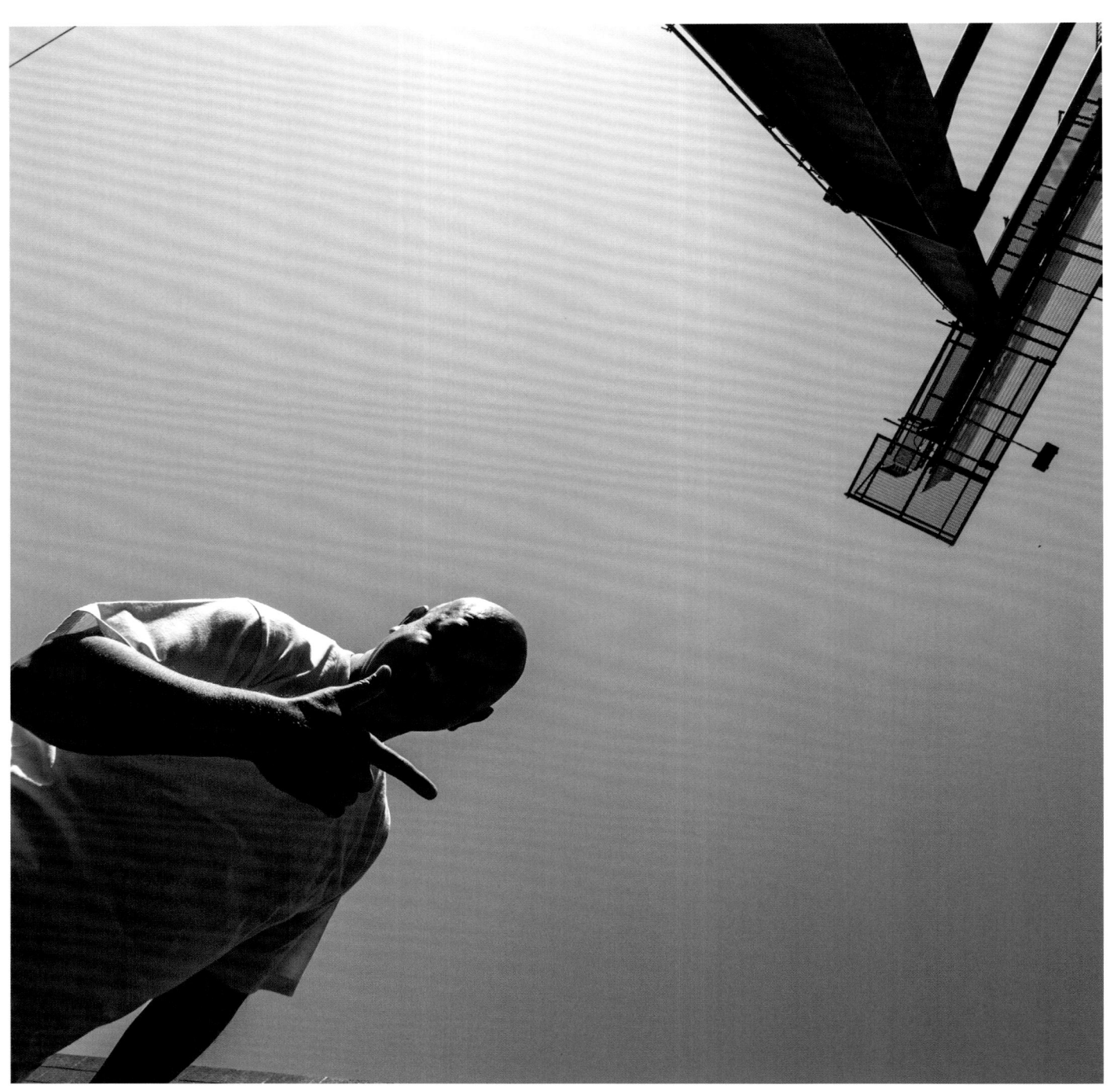

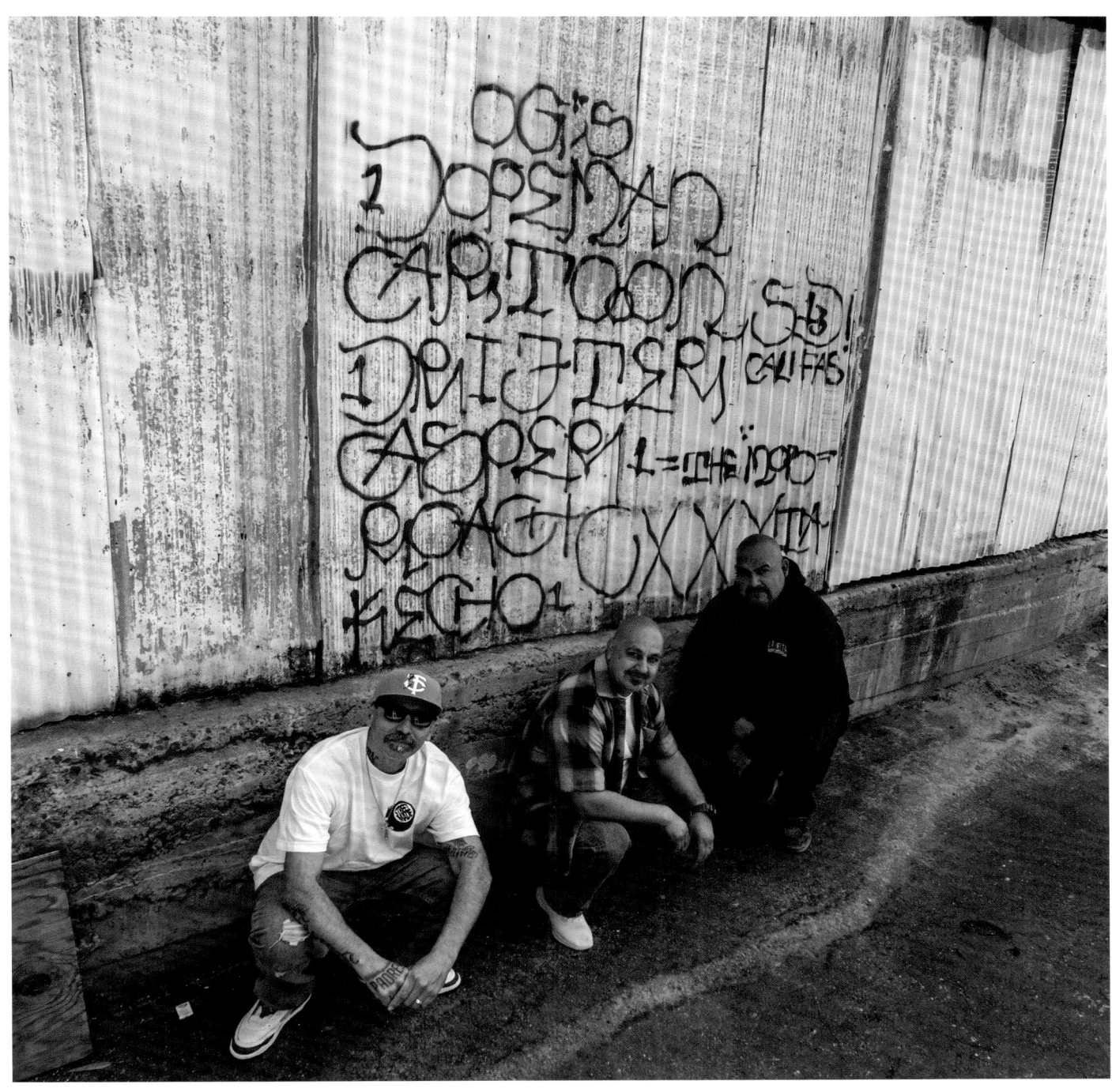

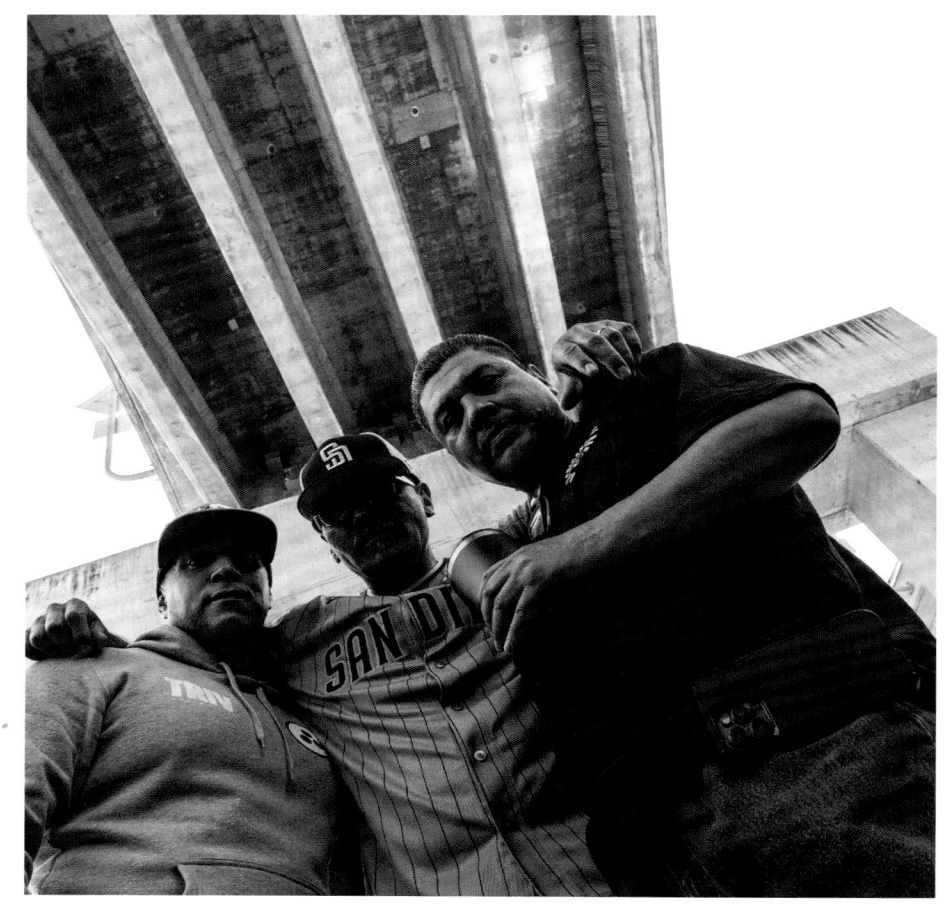

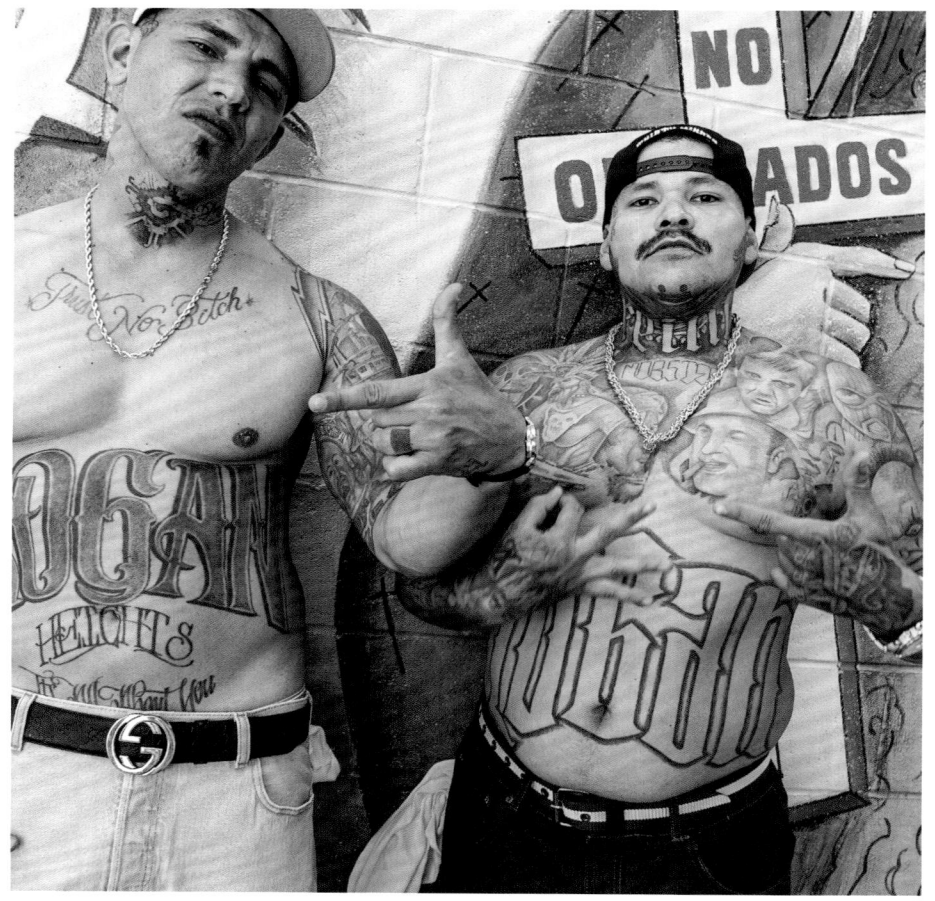

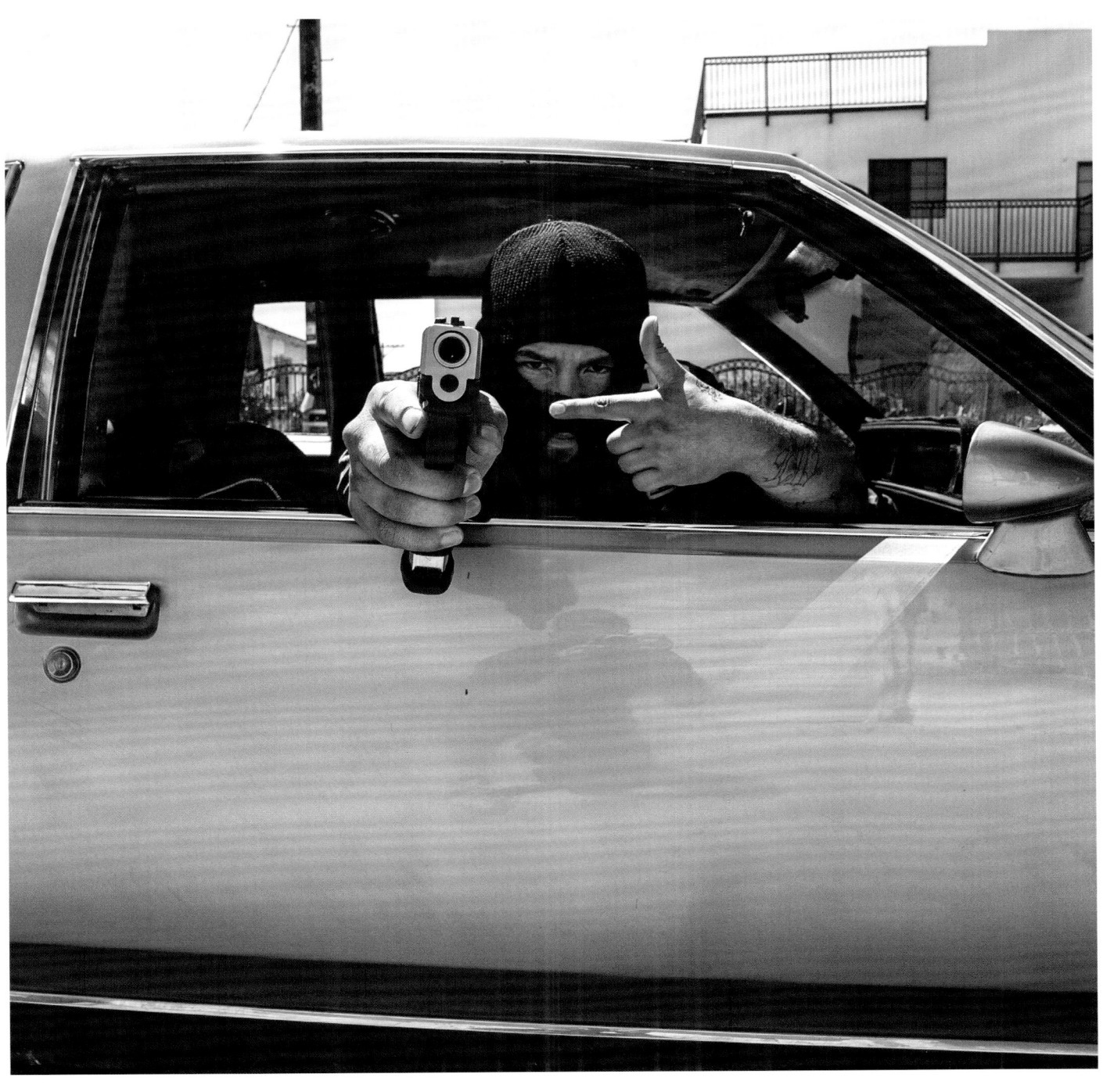

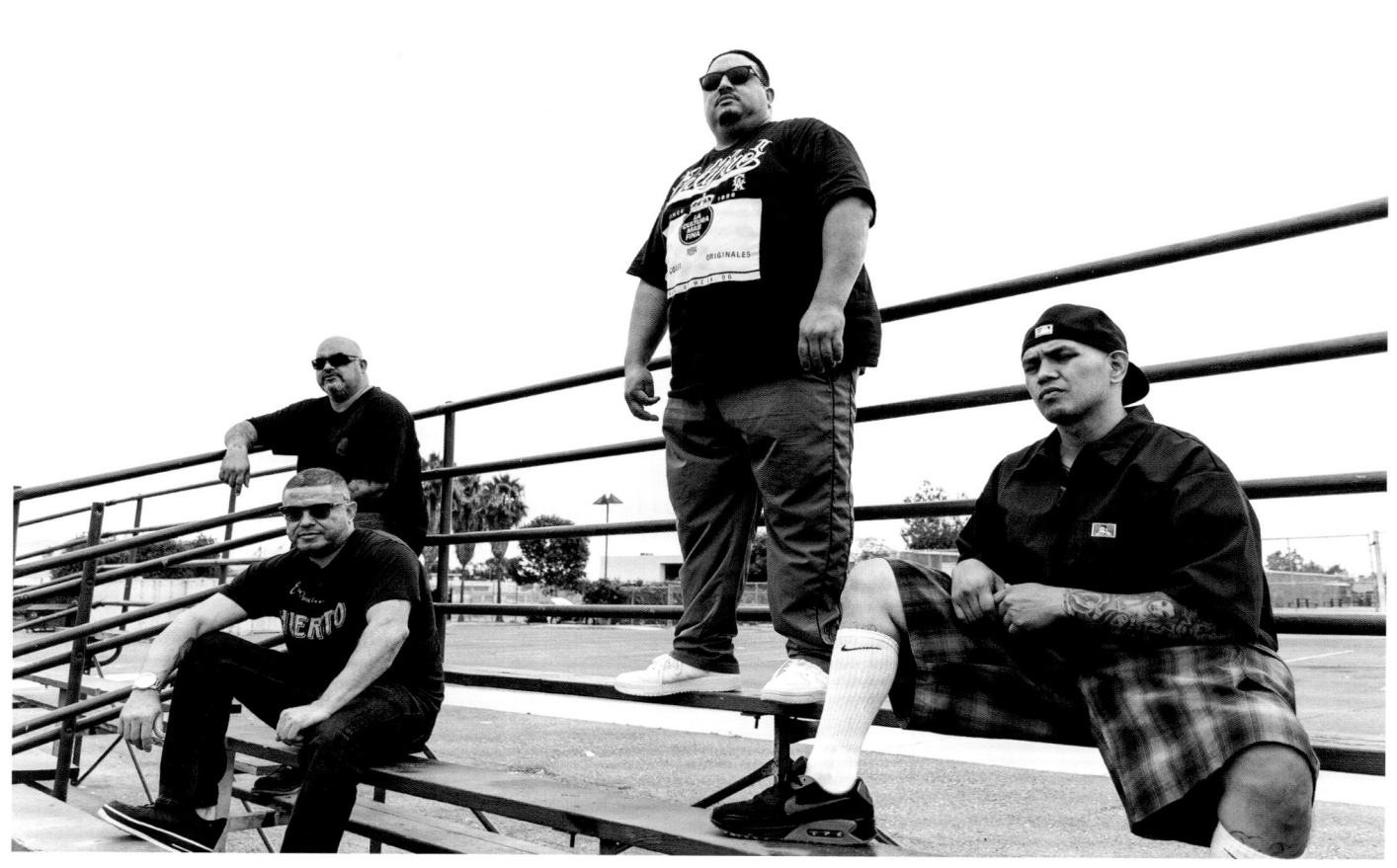

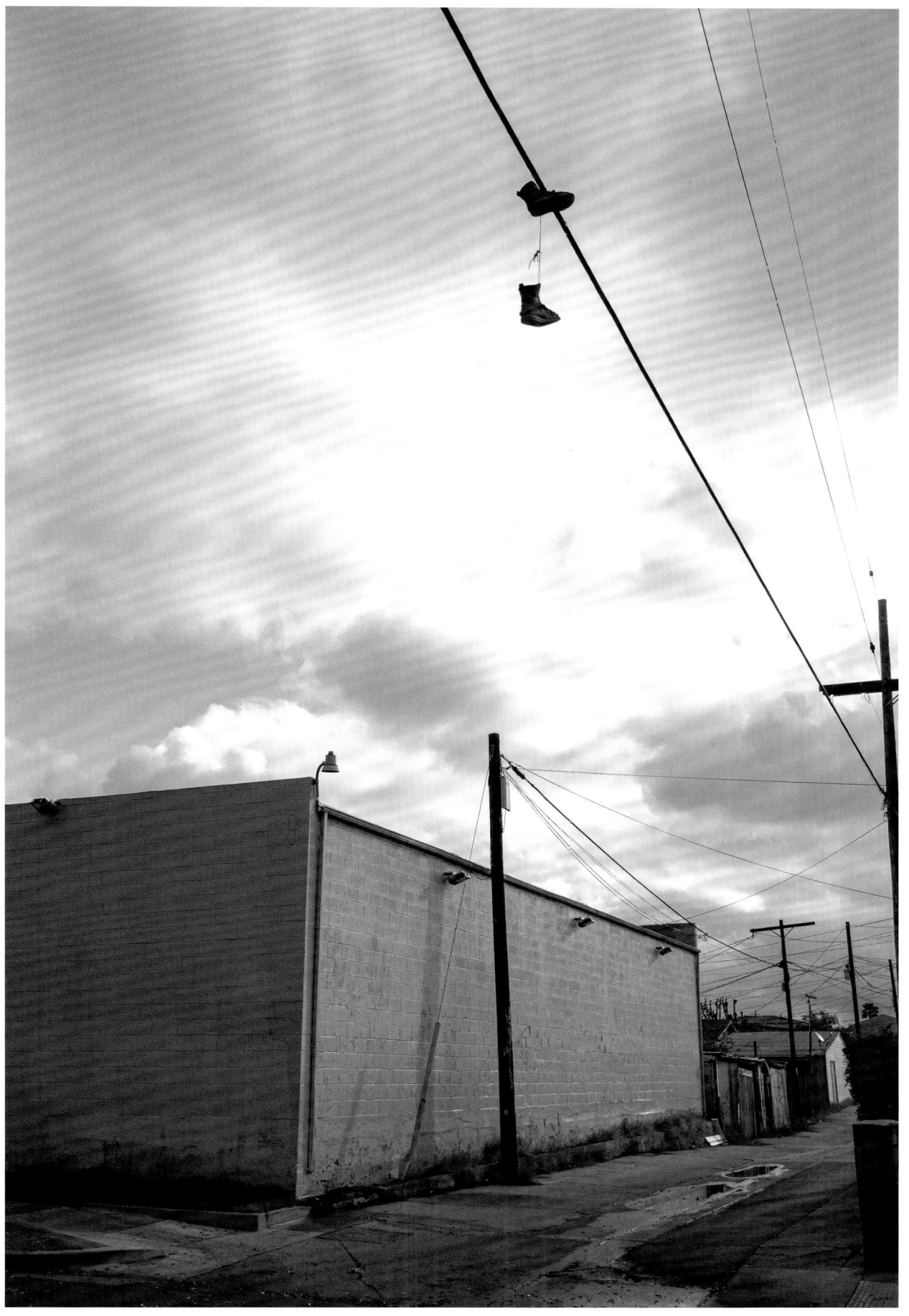

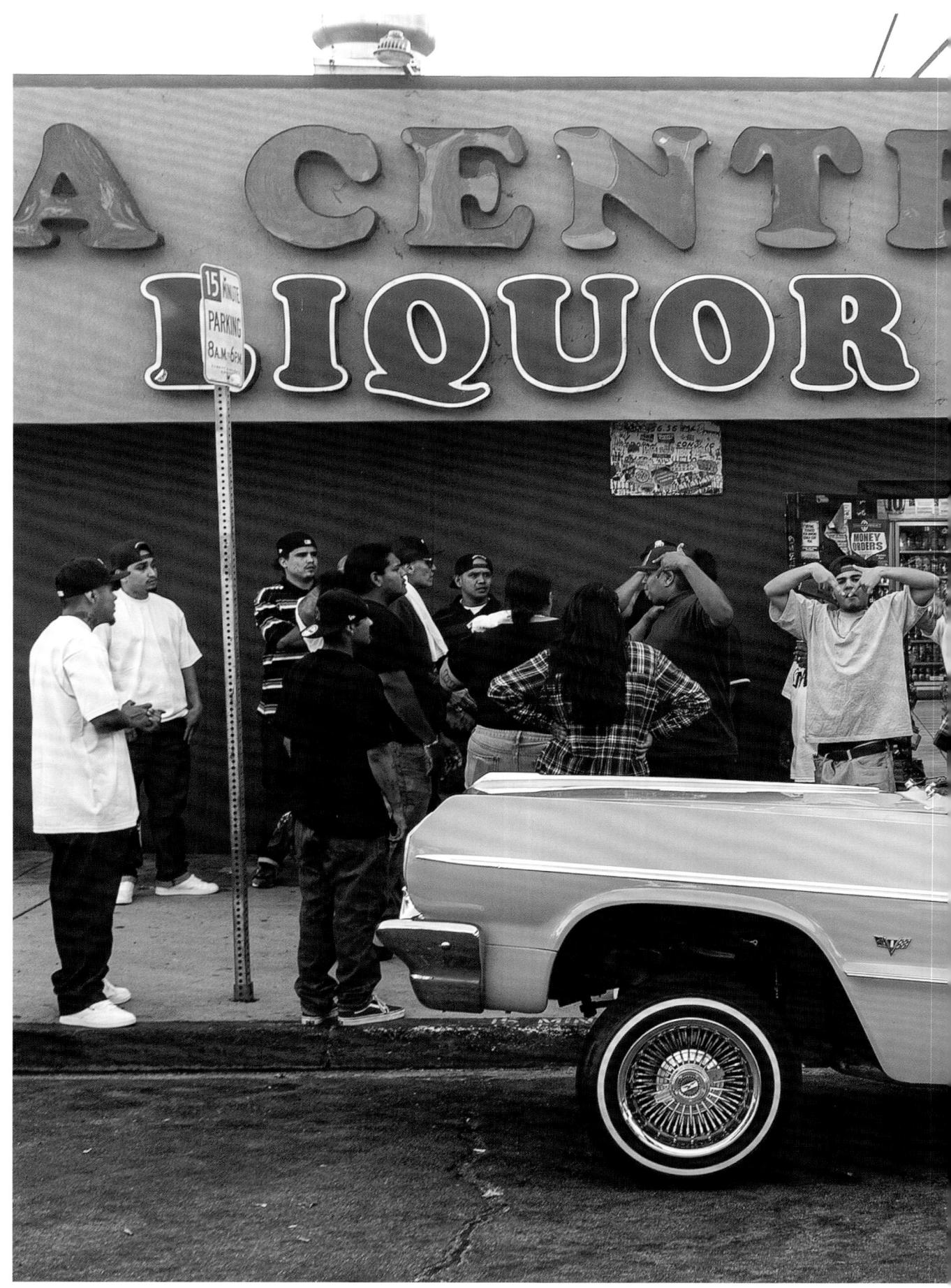

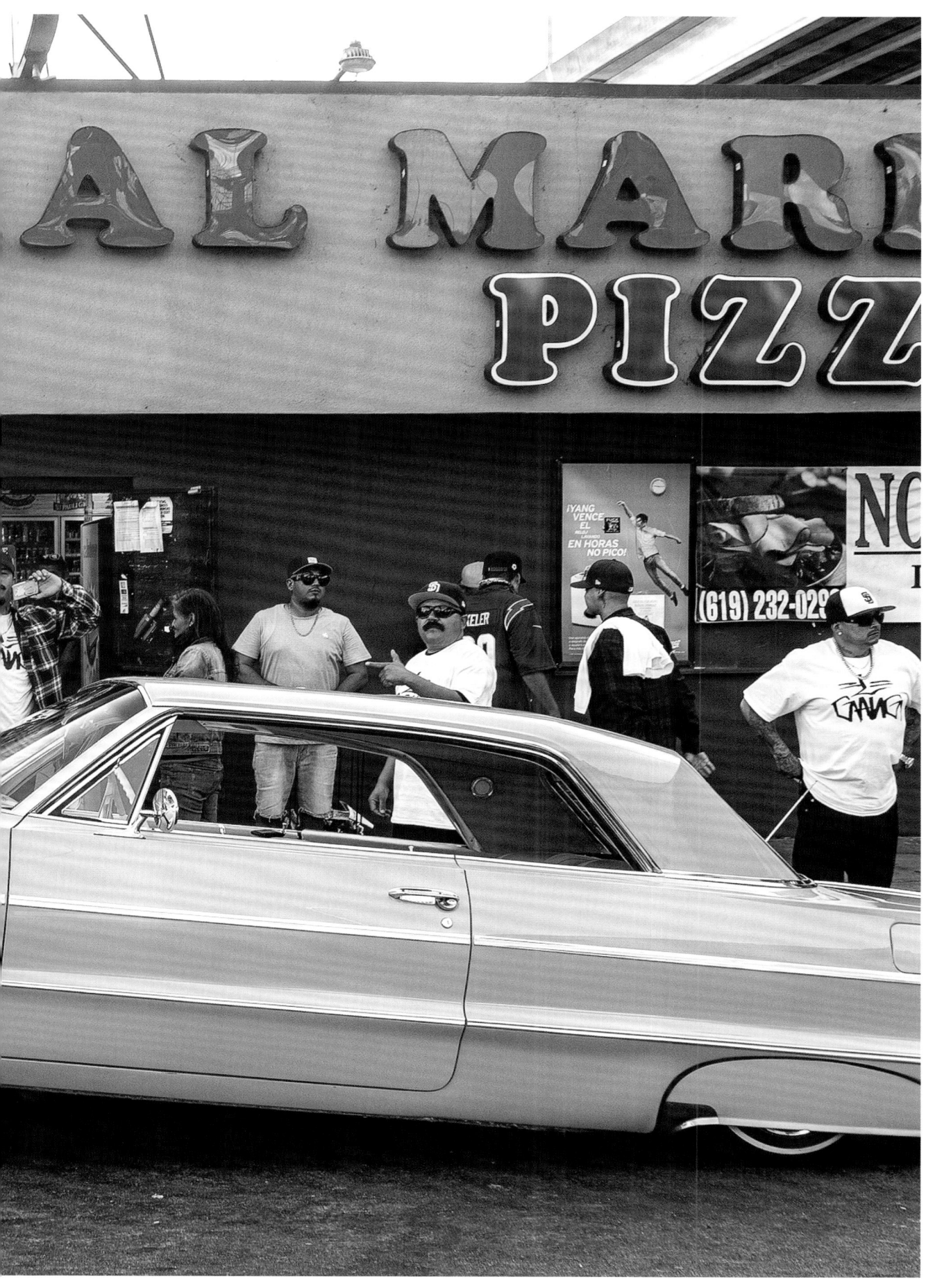

SHERMAN

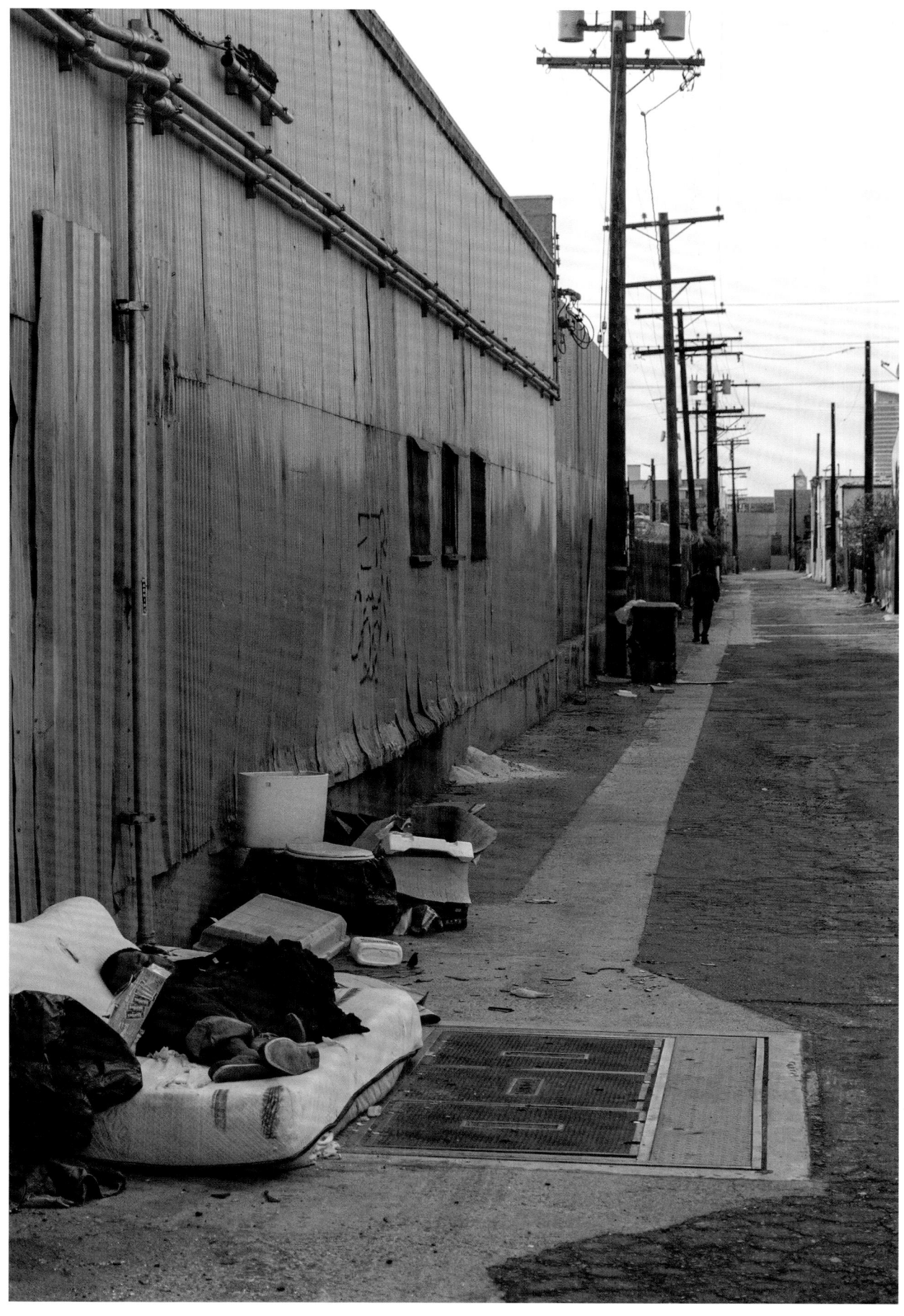

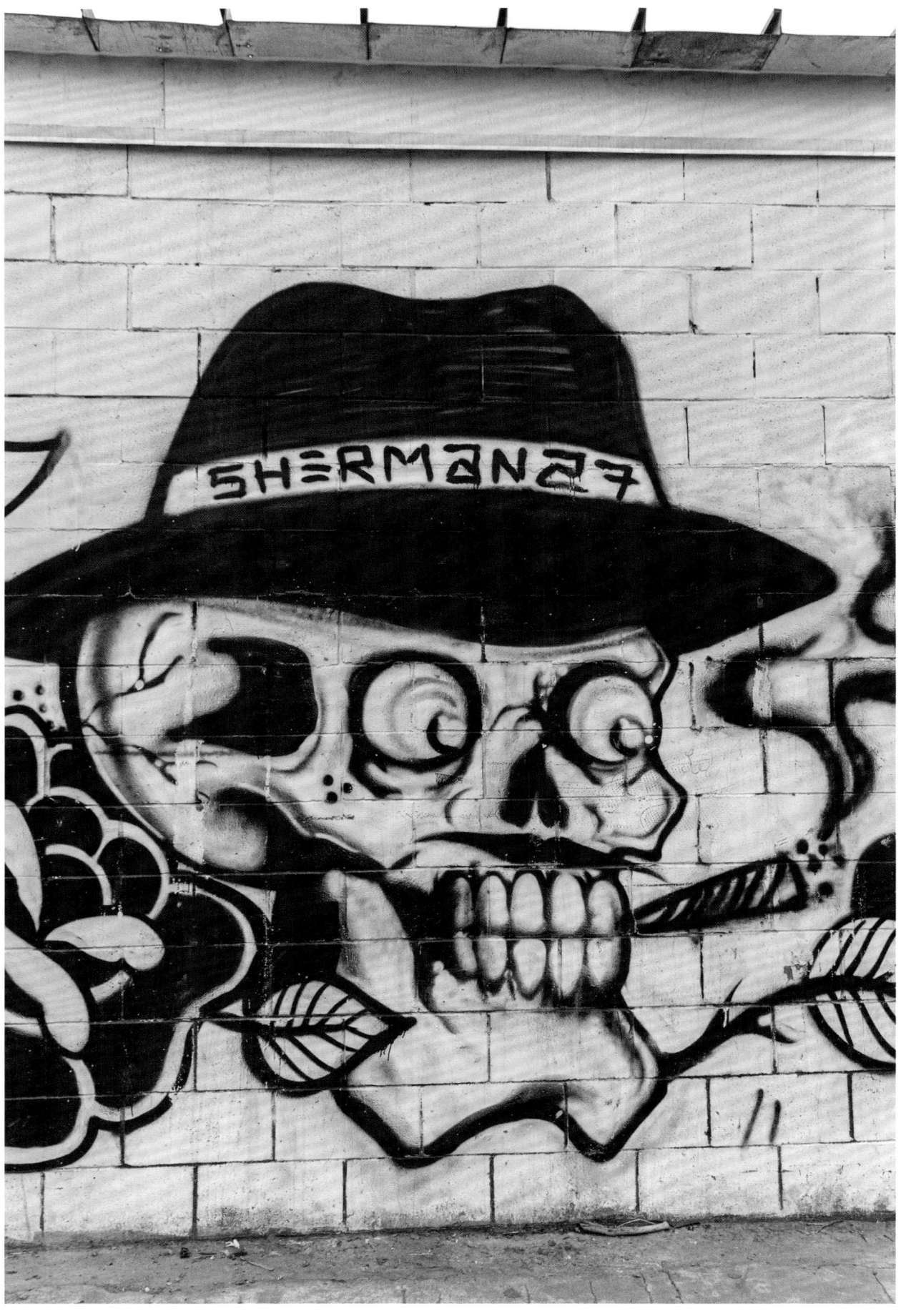

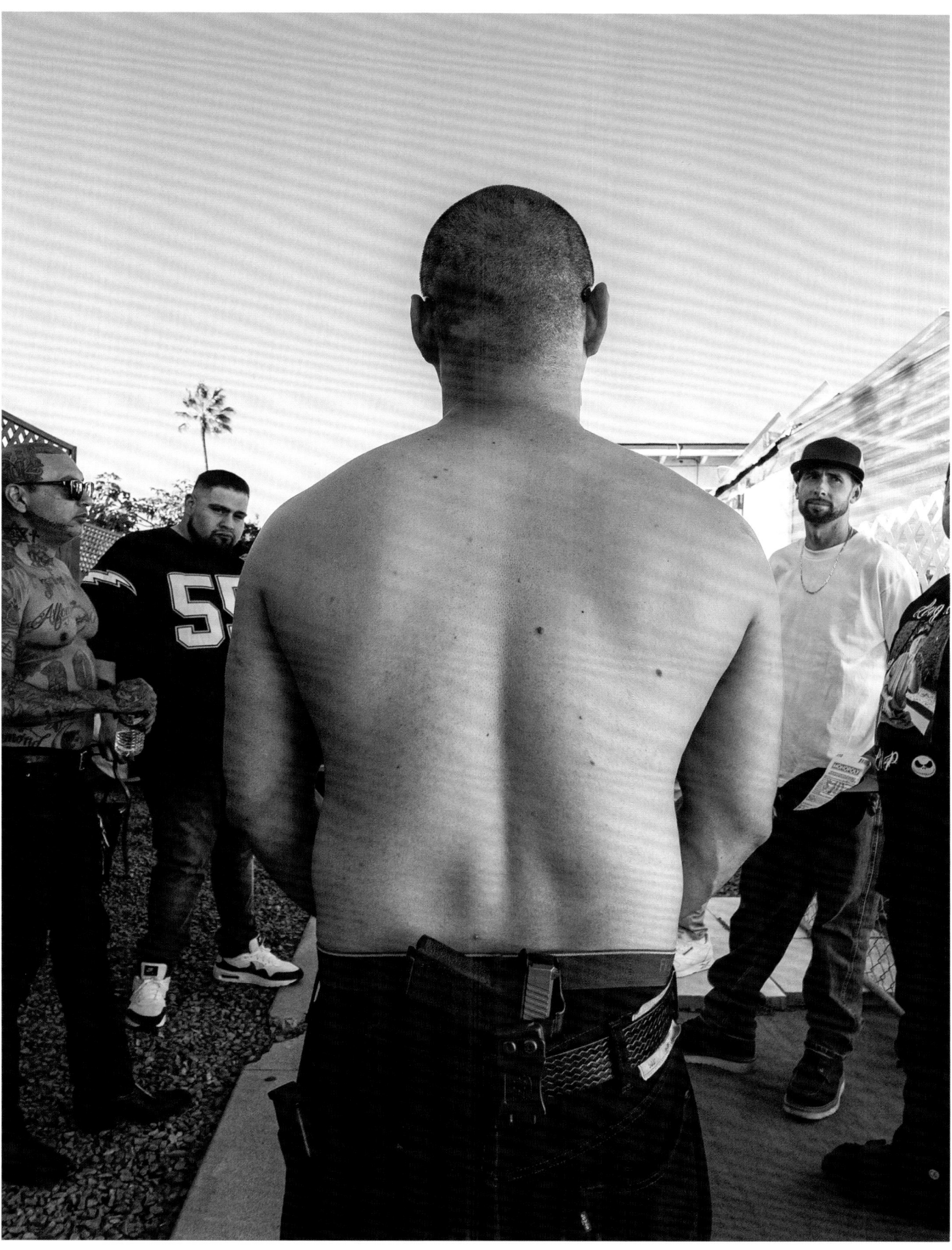

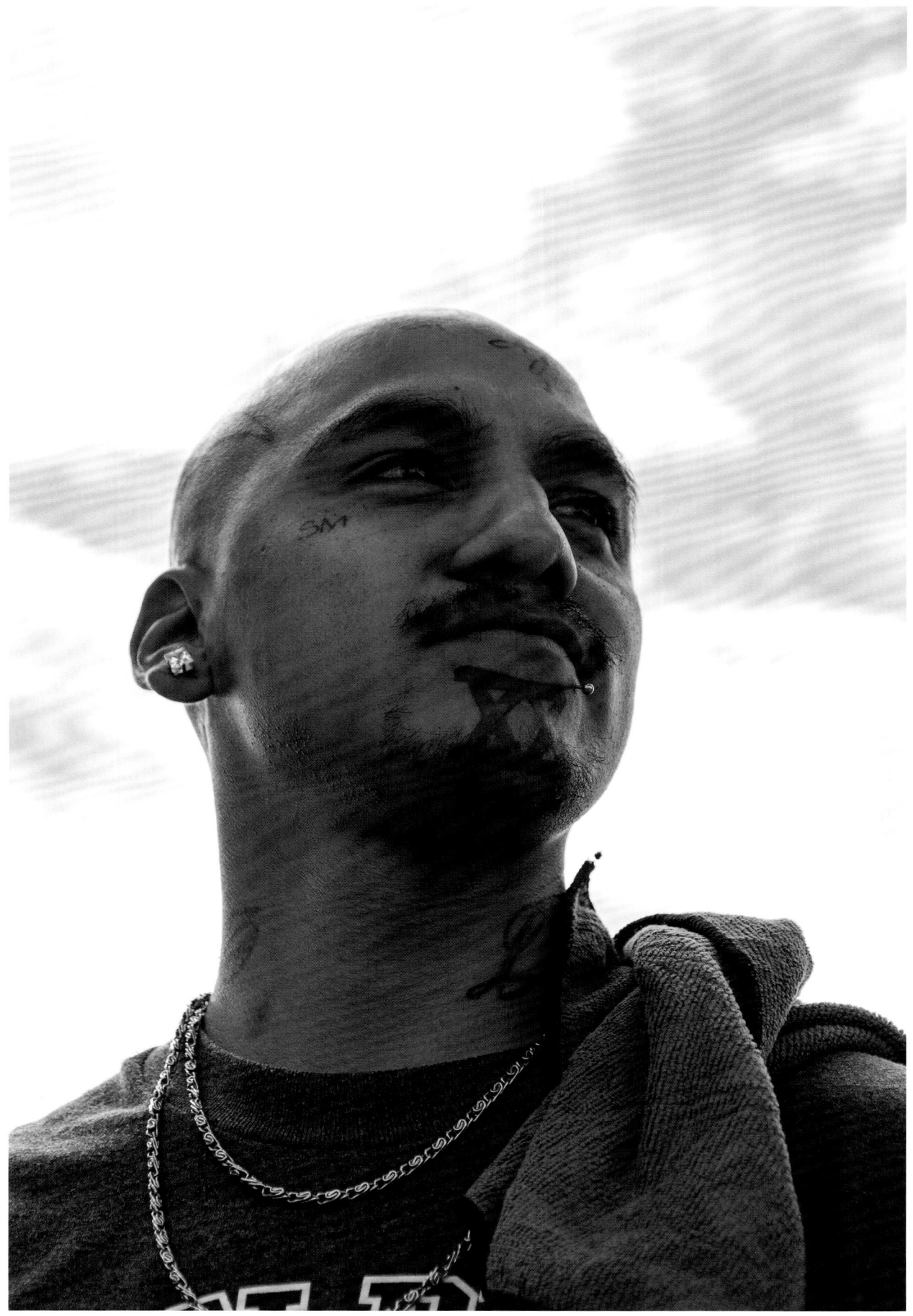

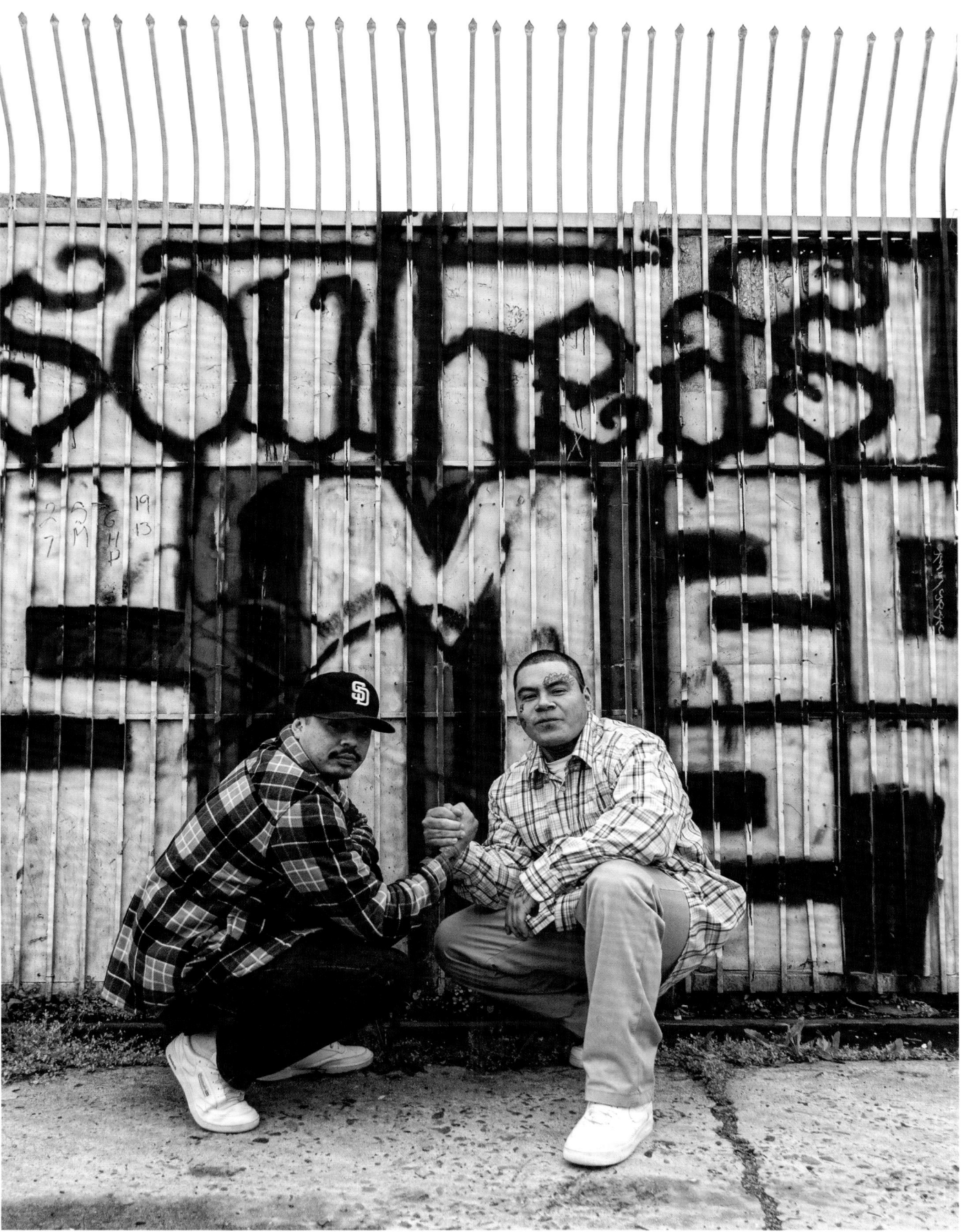

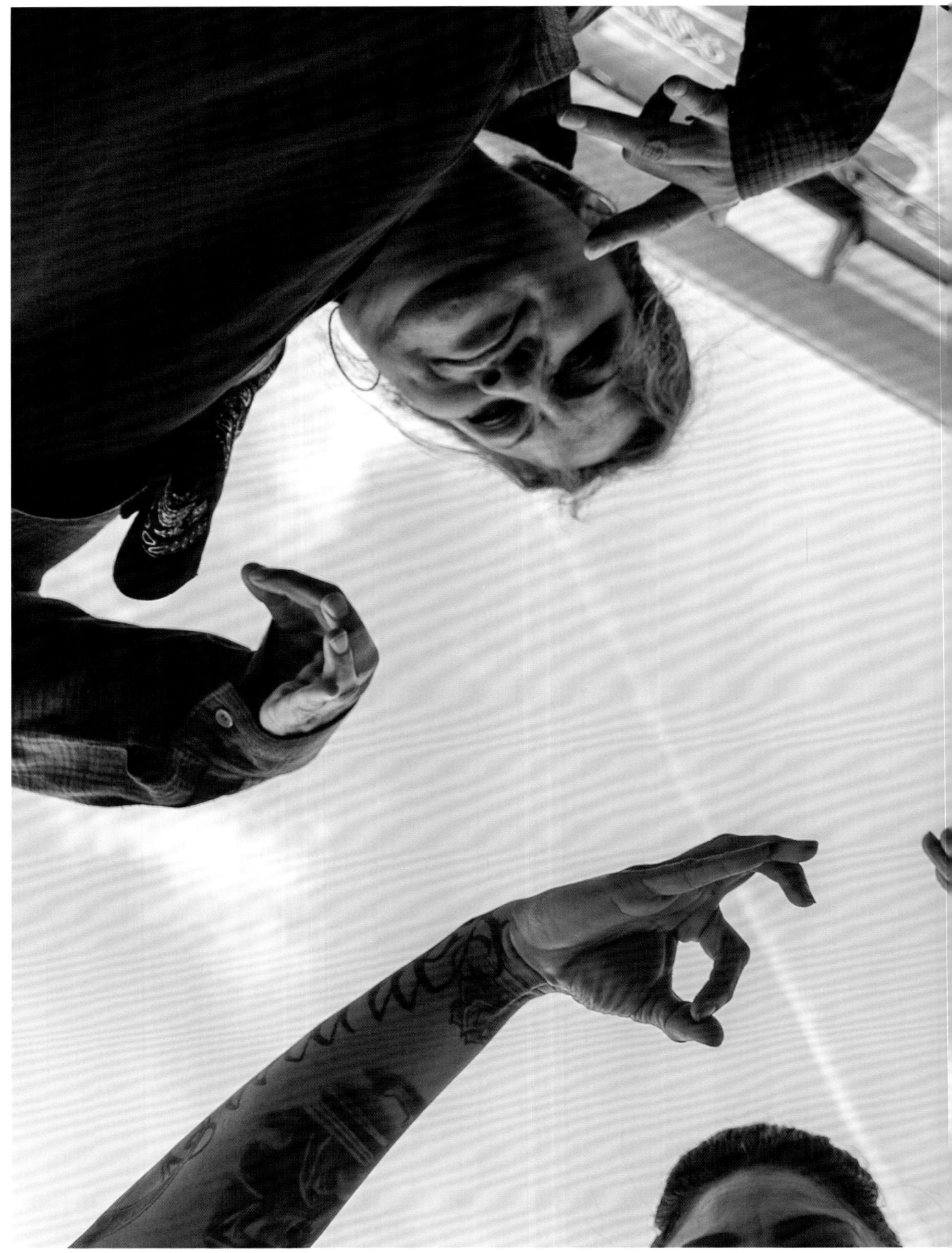

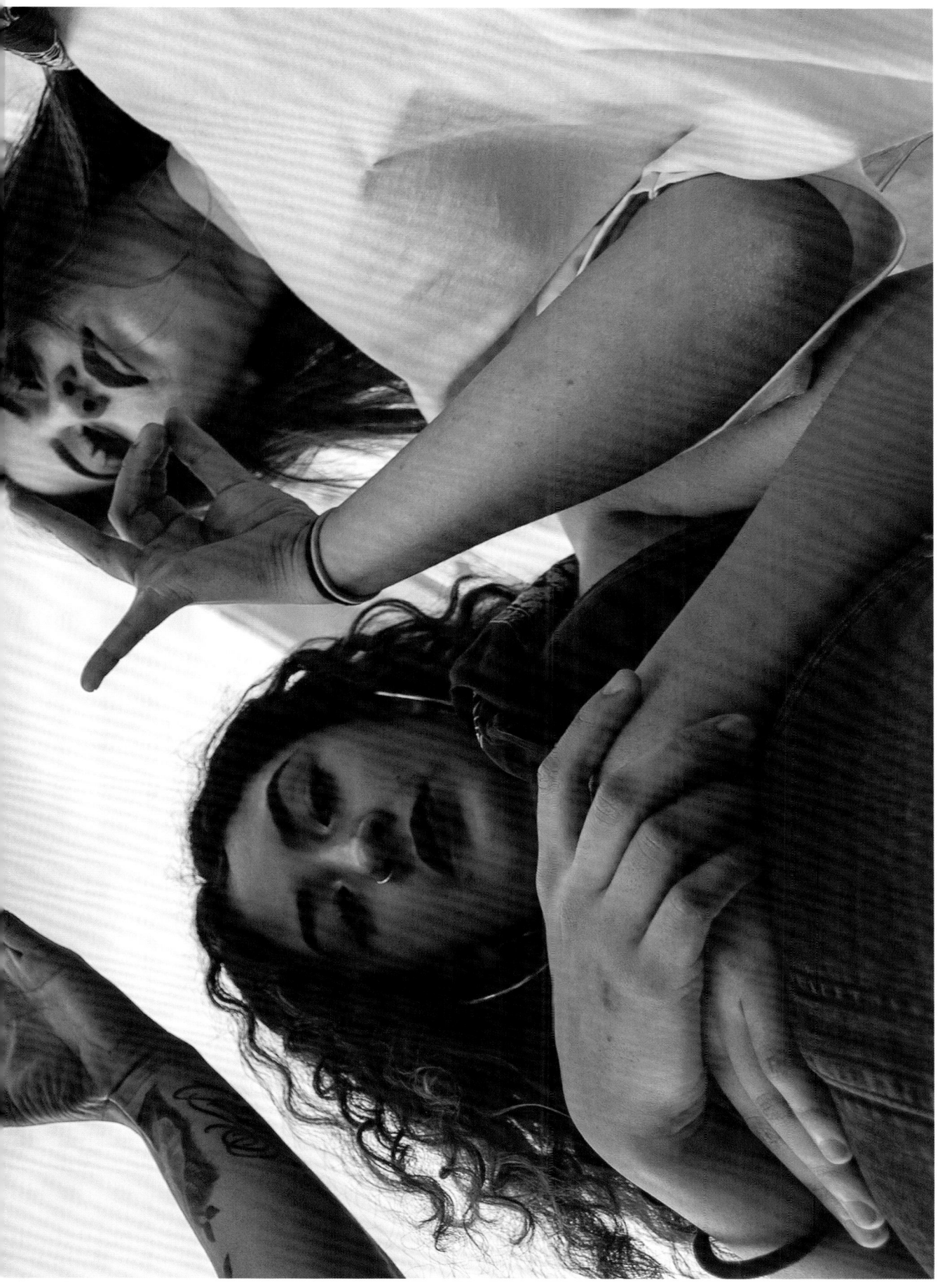

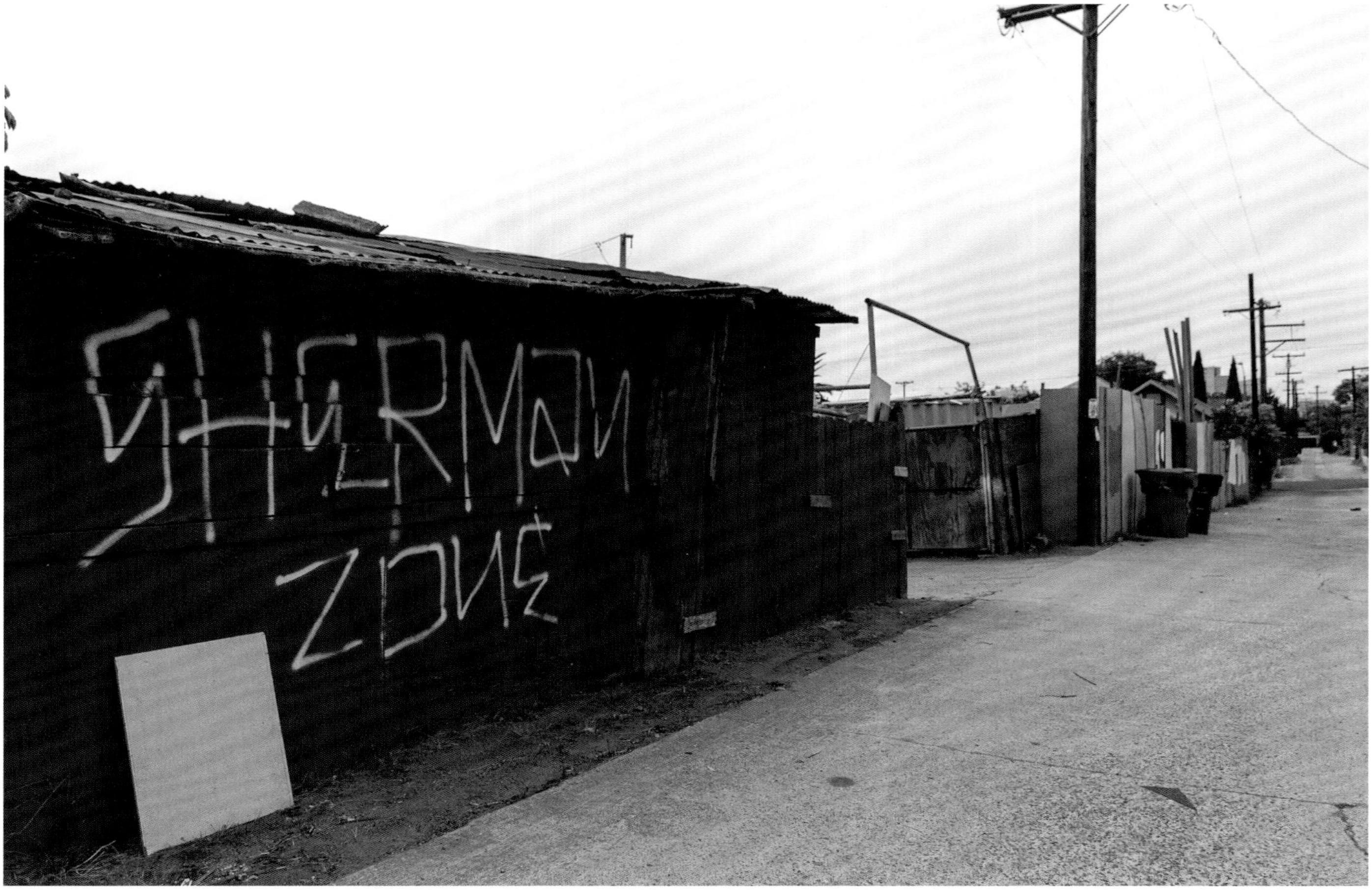
SHERMAN
ZONE

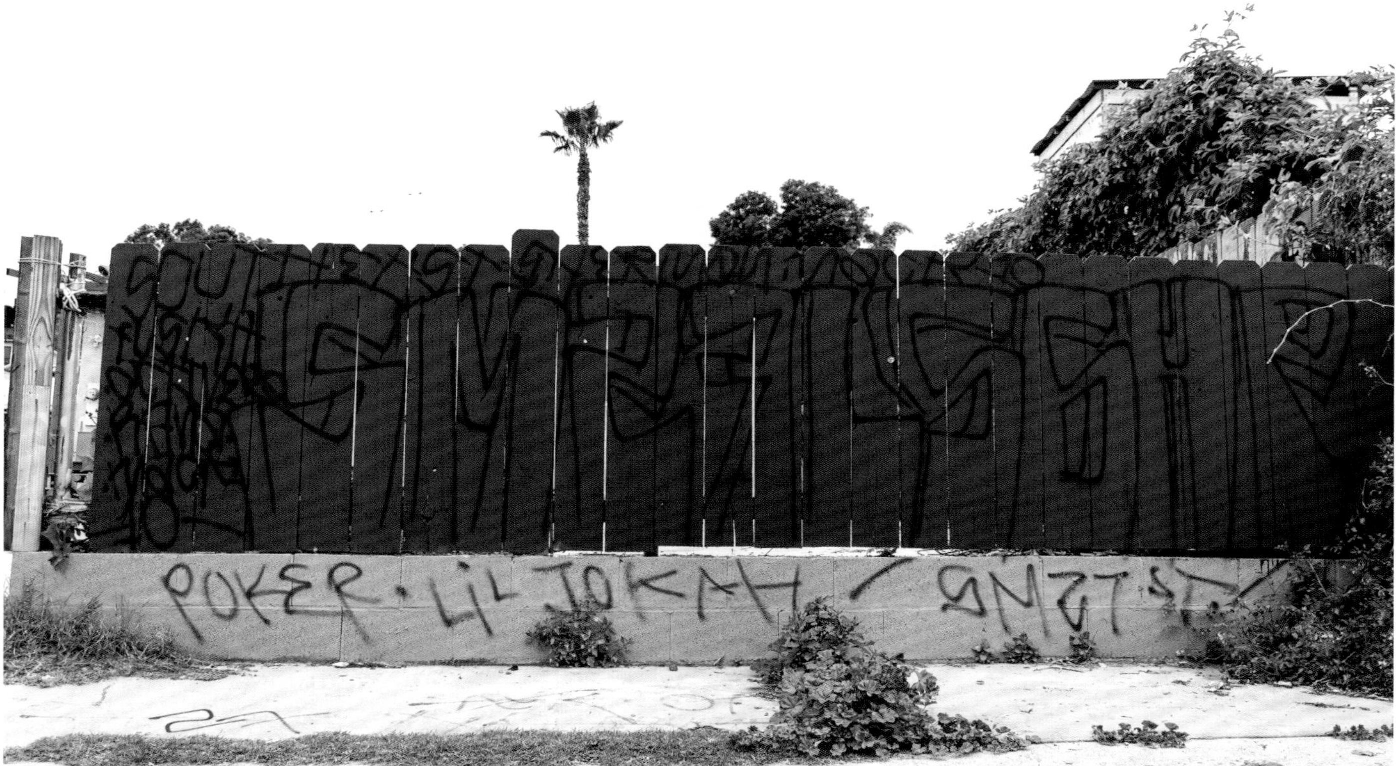
POKER · LIL JOKAH

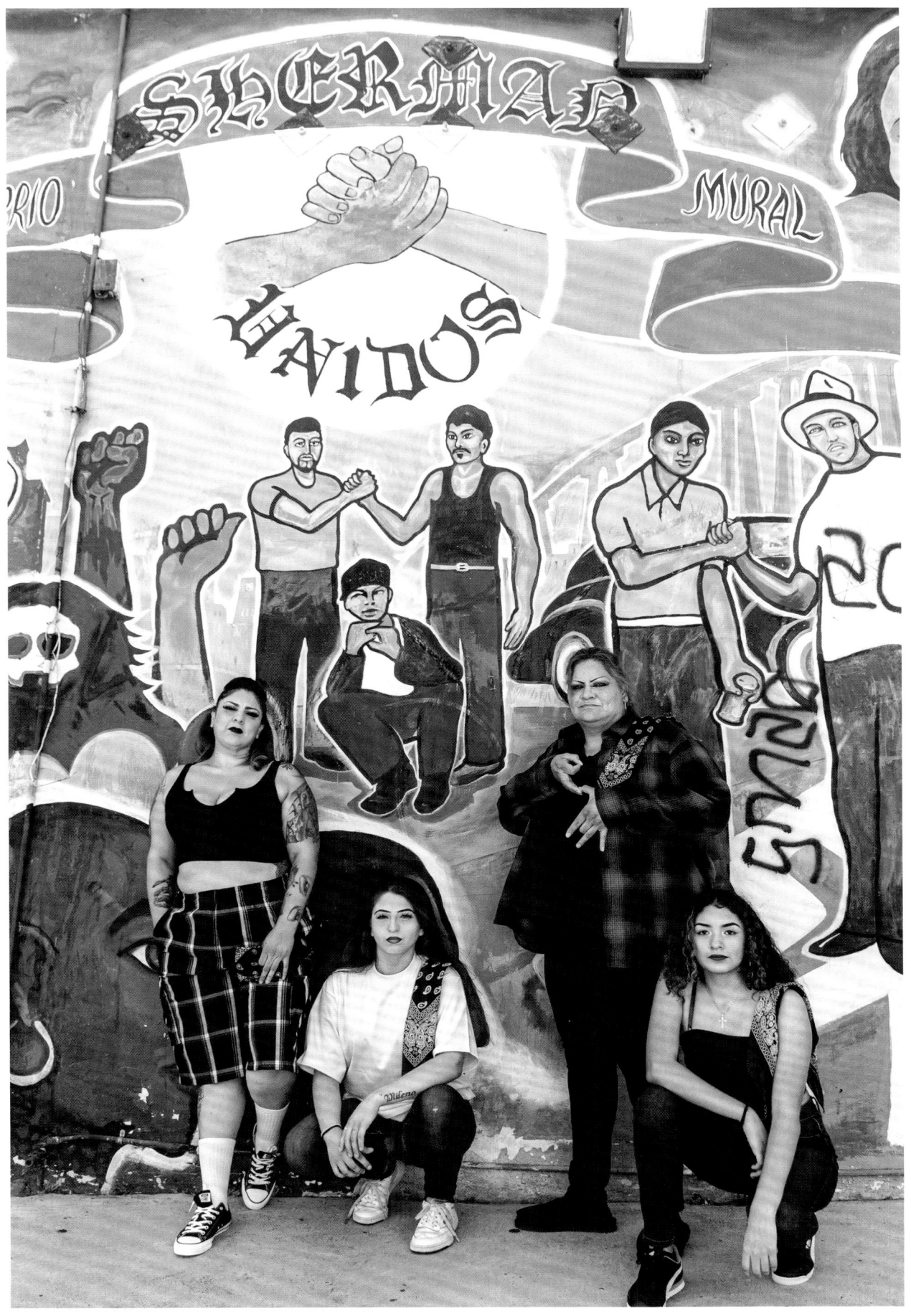

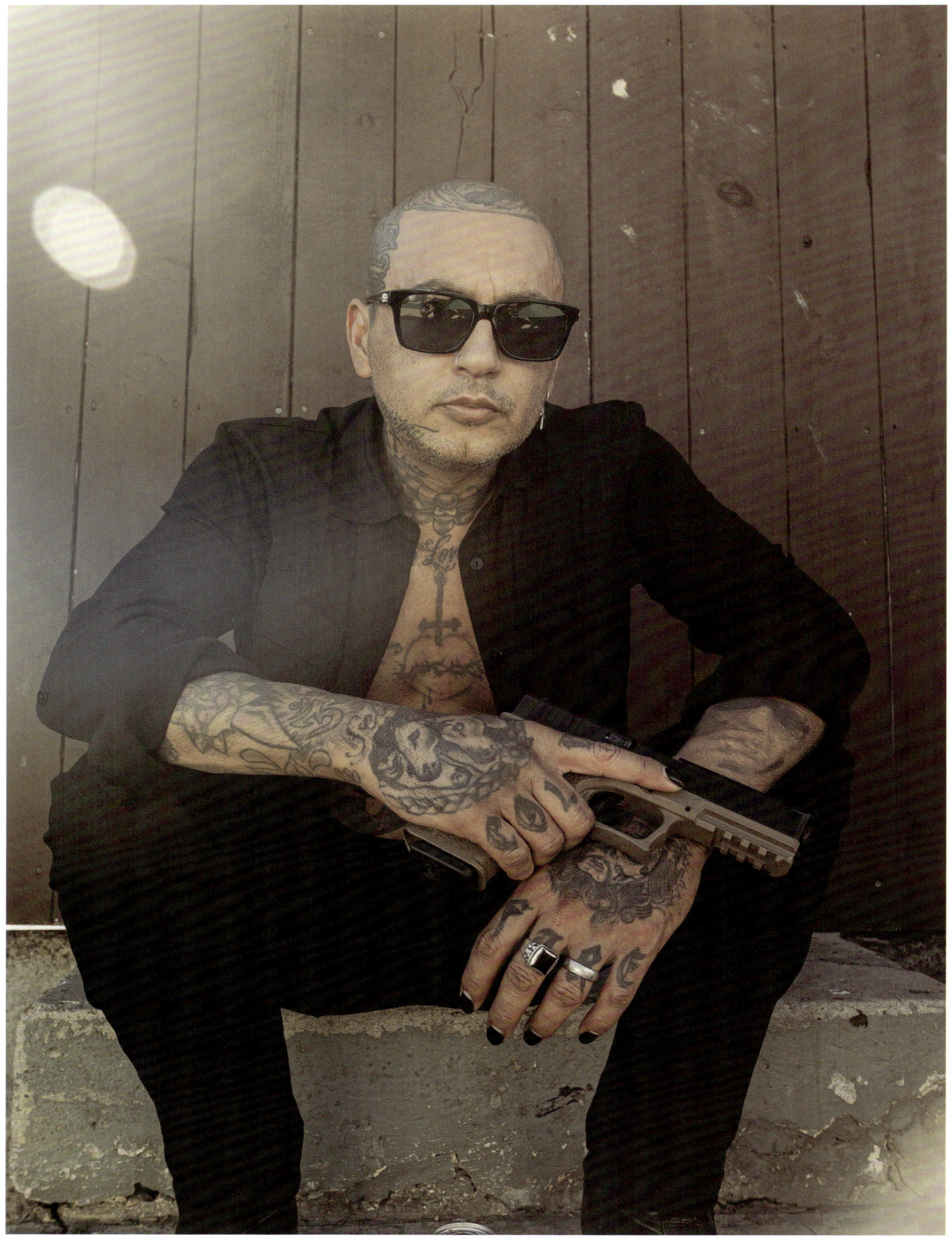

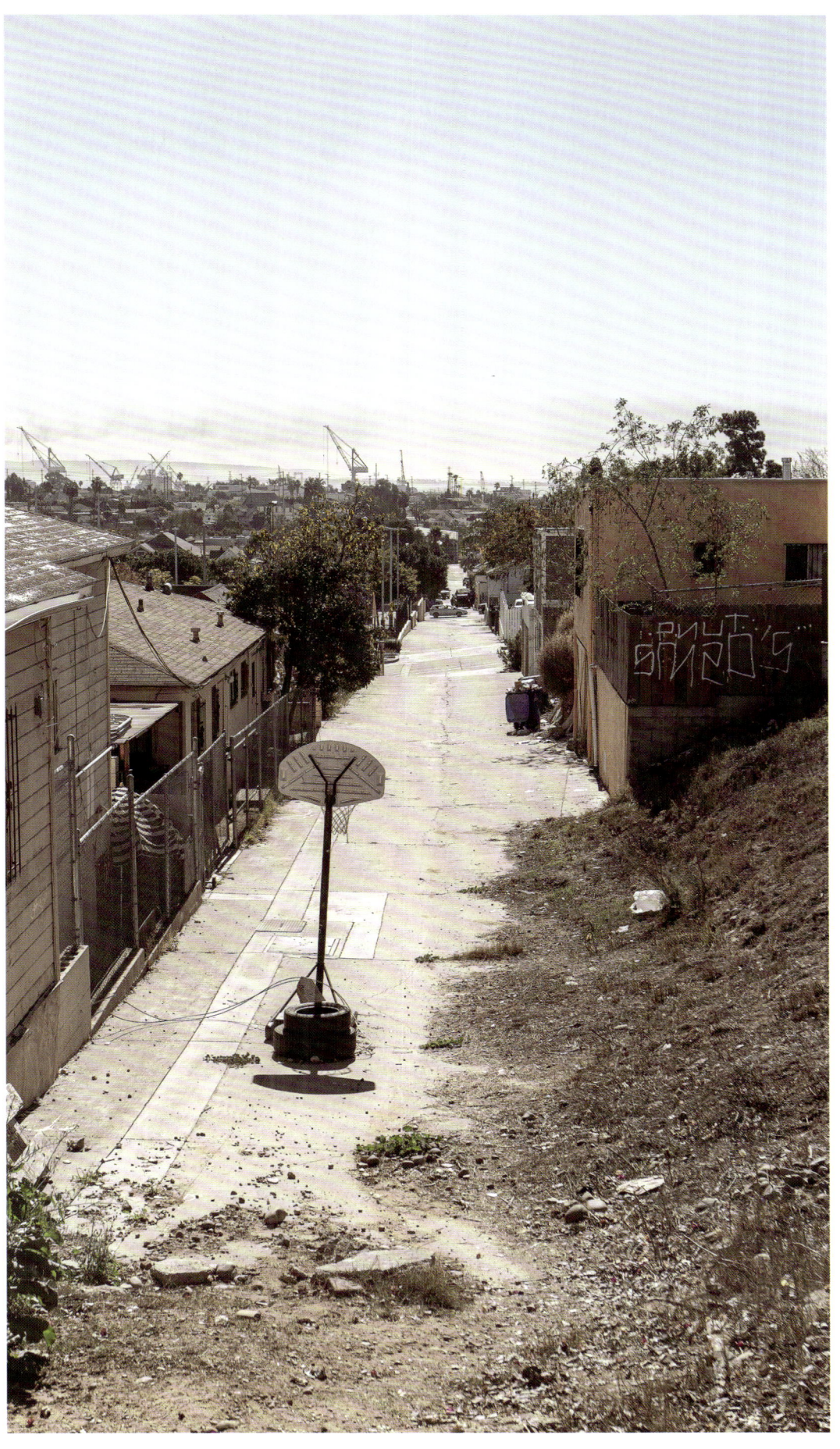

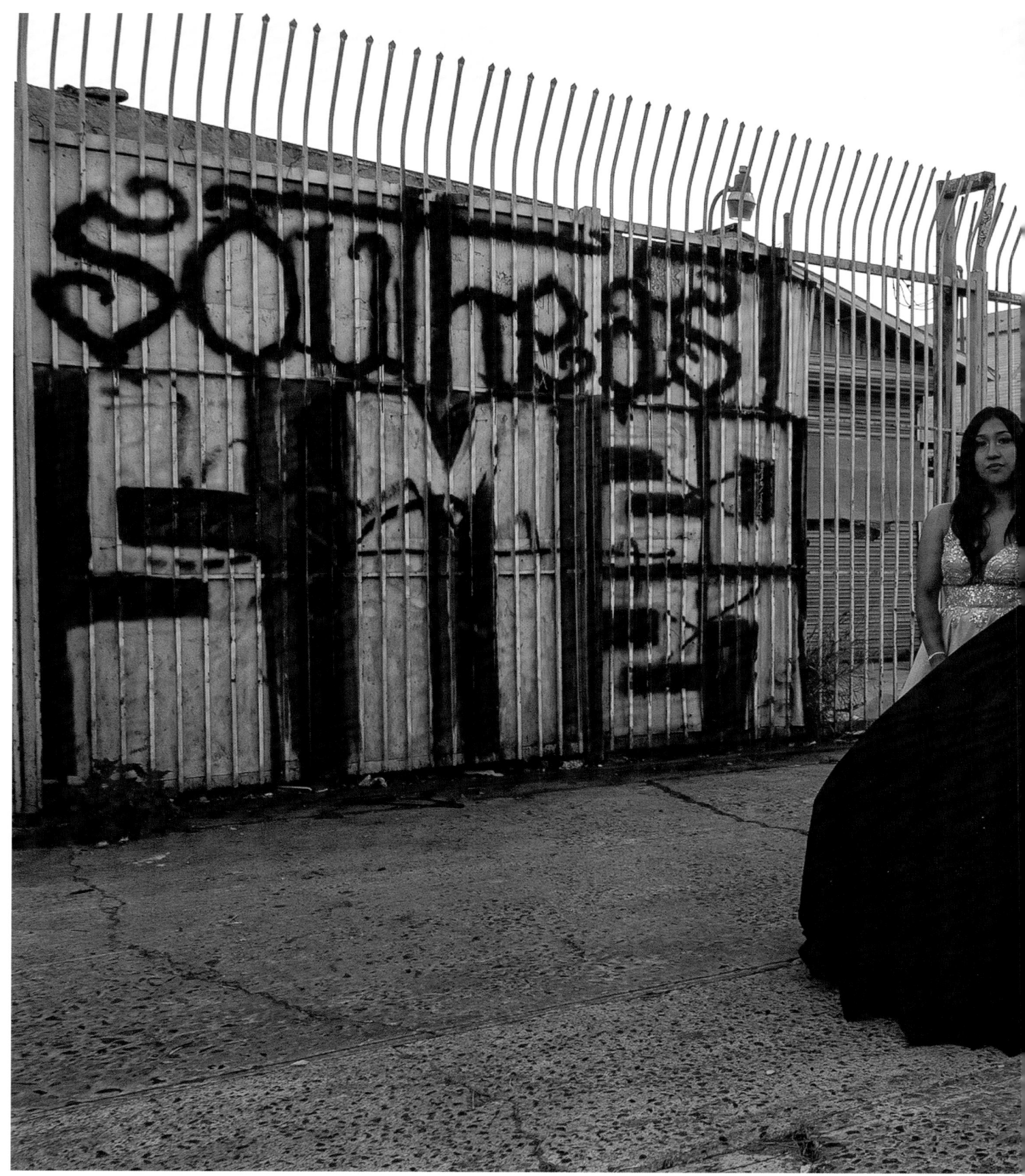

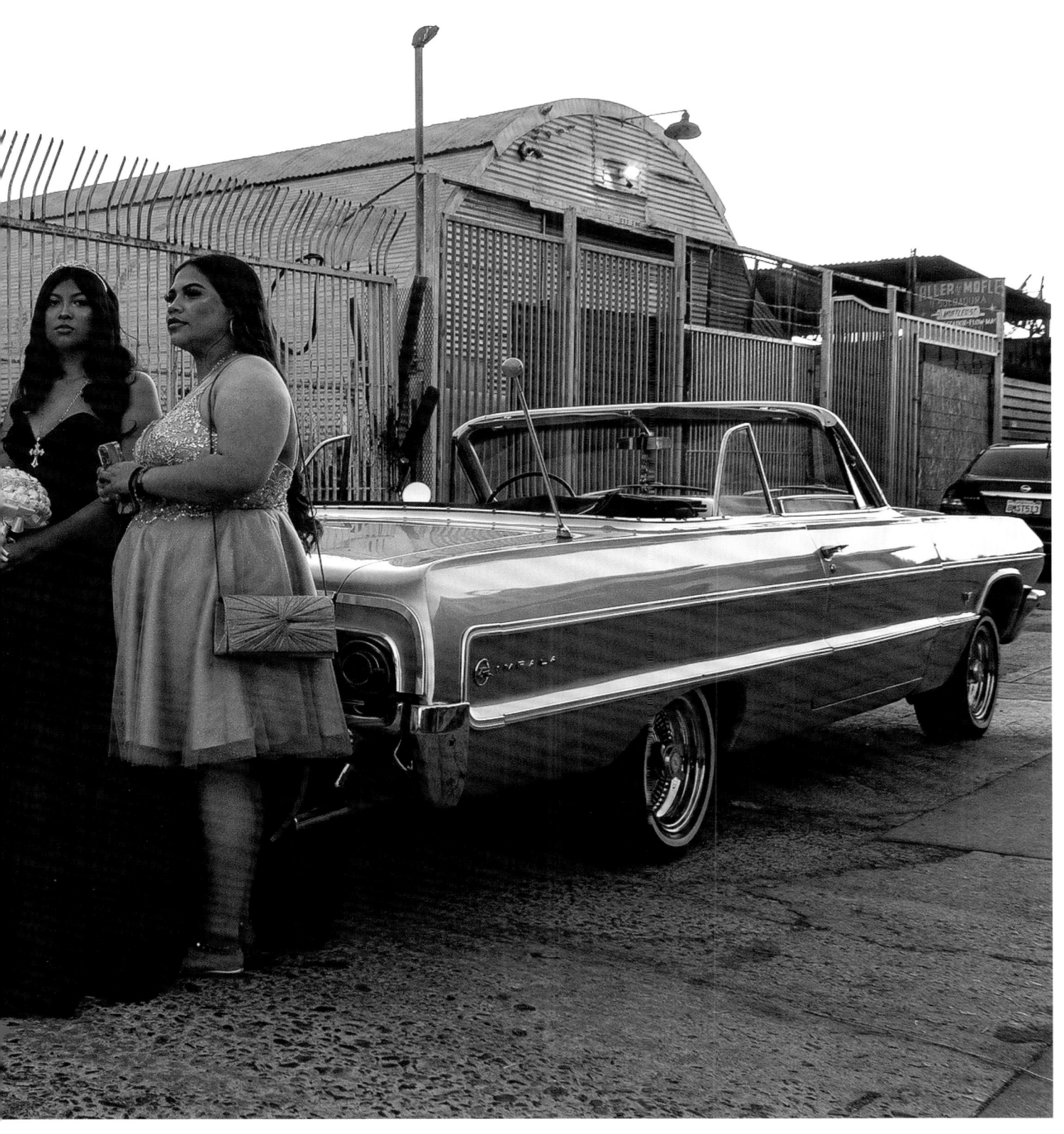

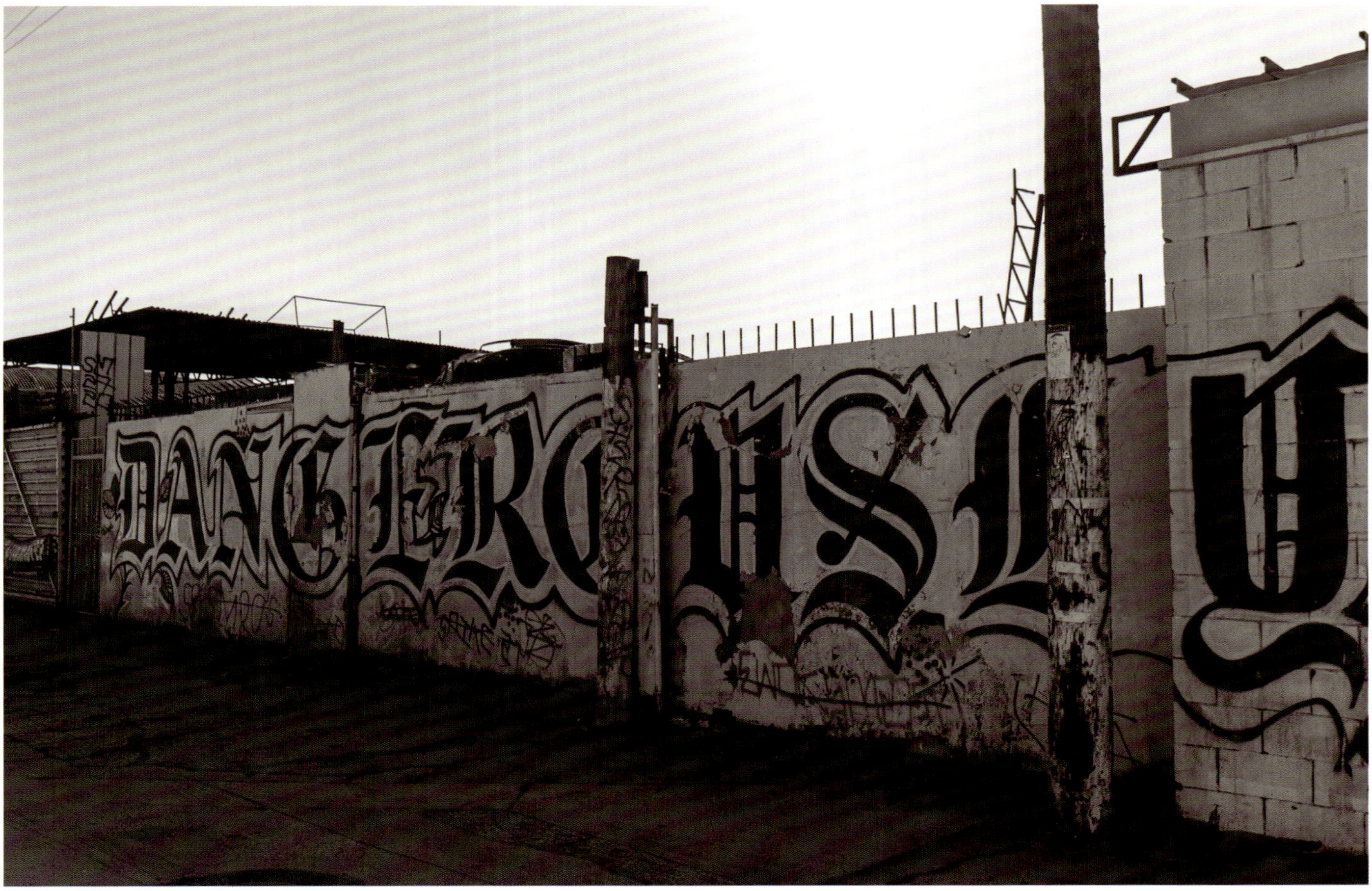

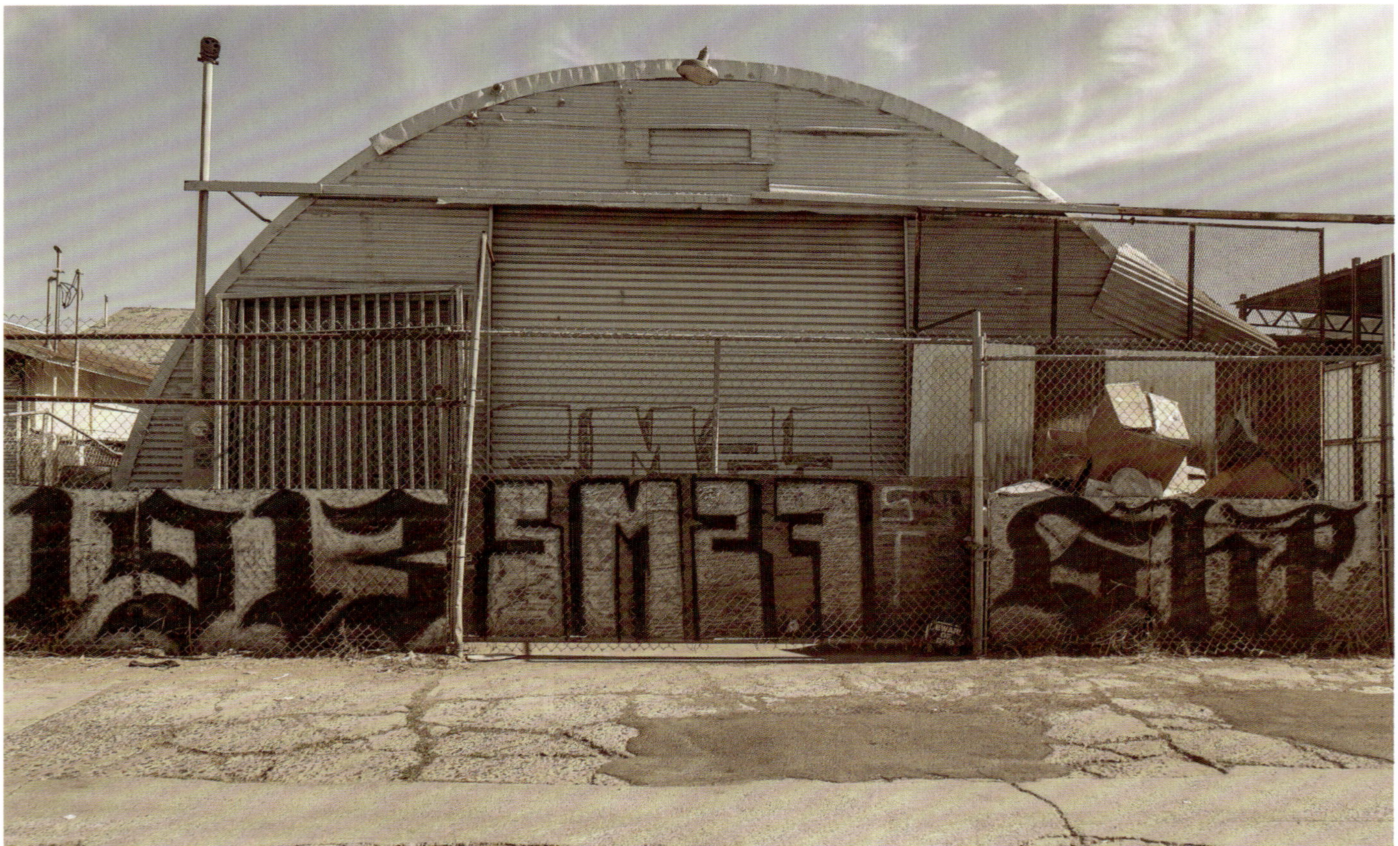

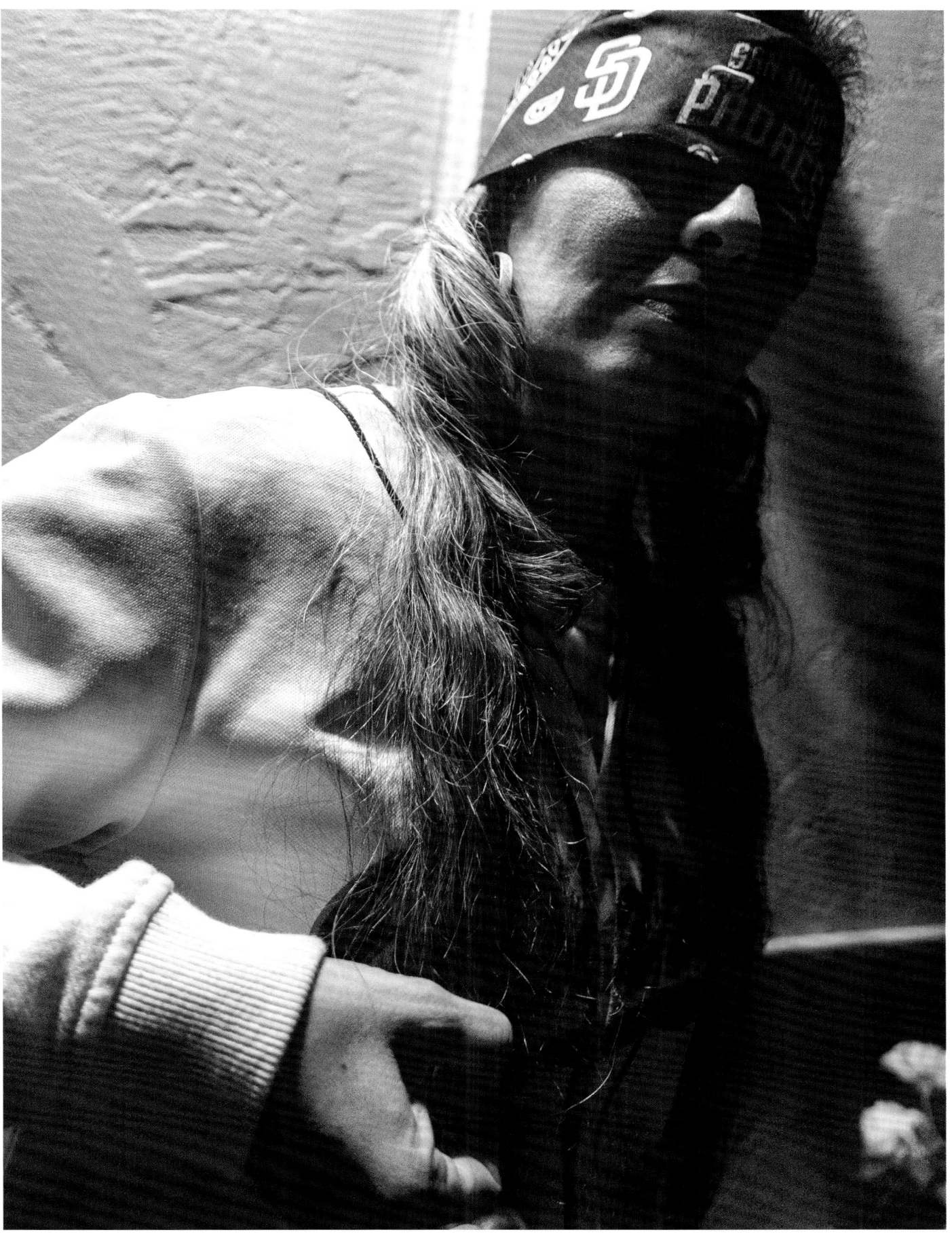

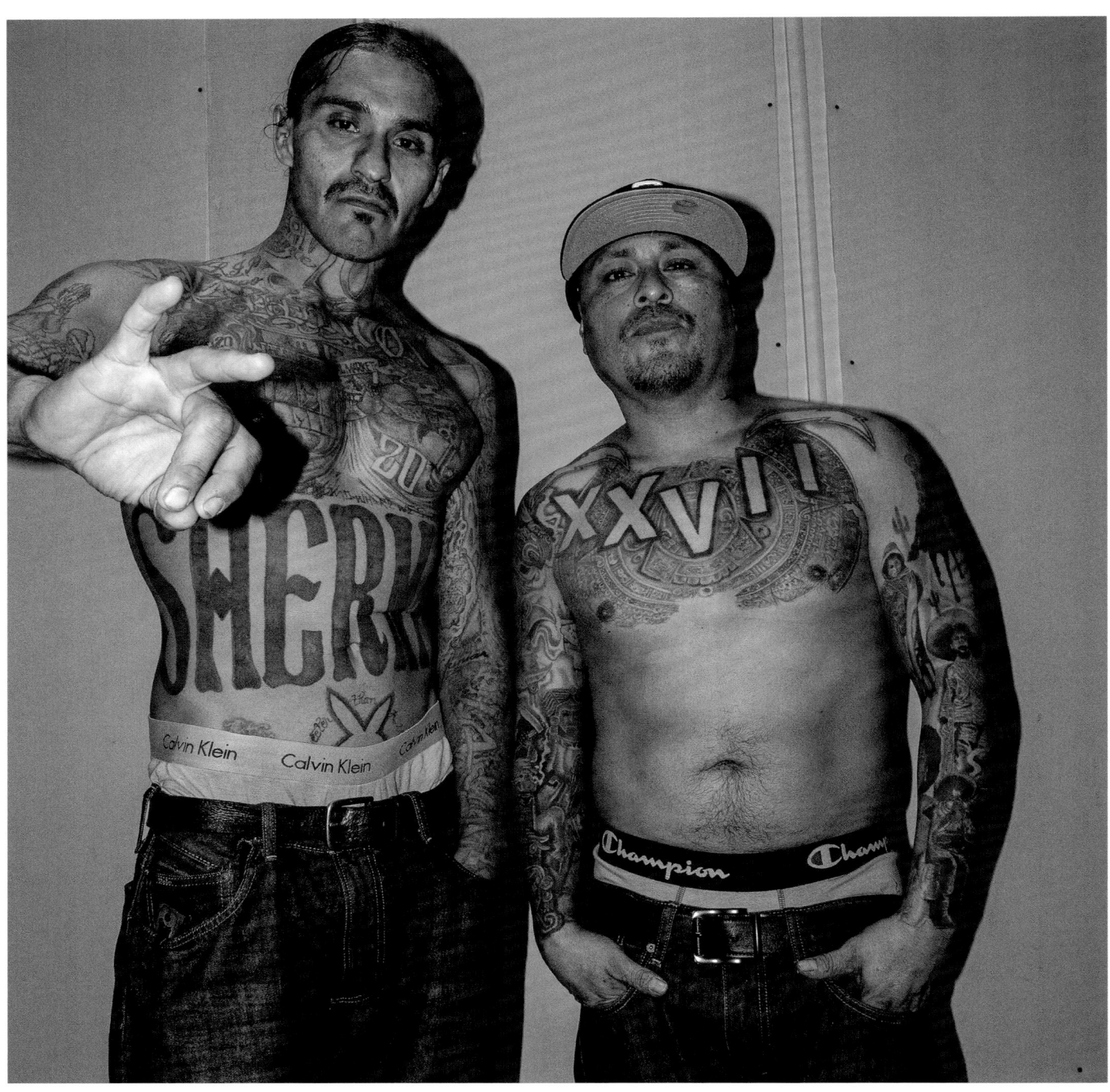

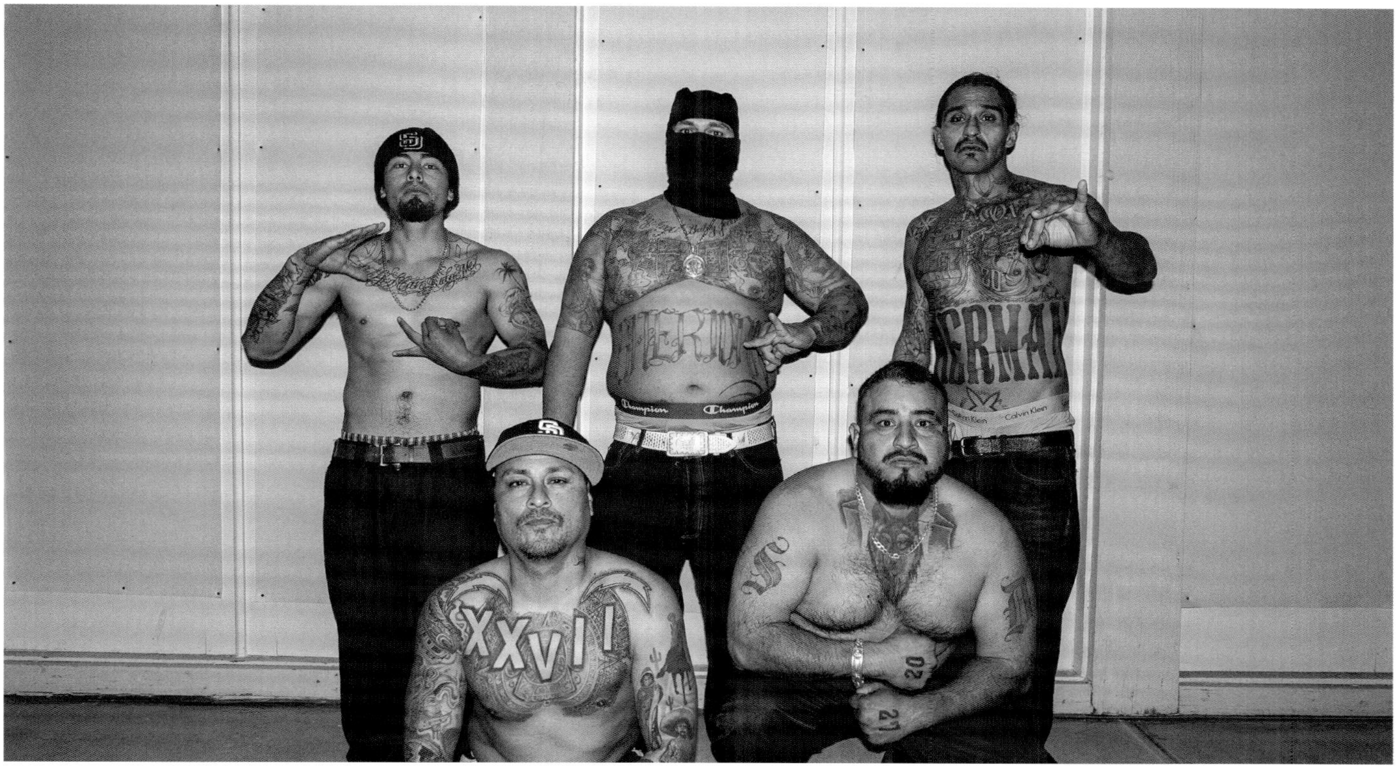

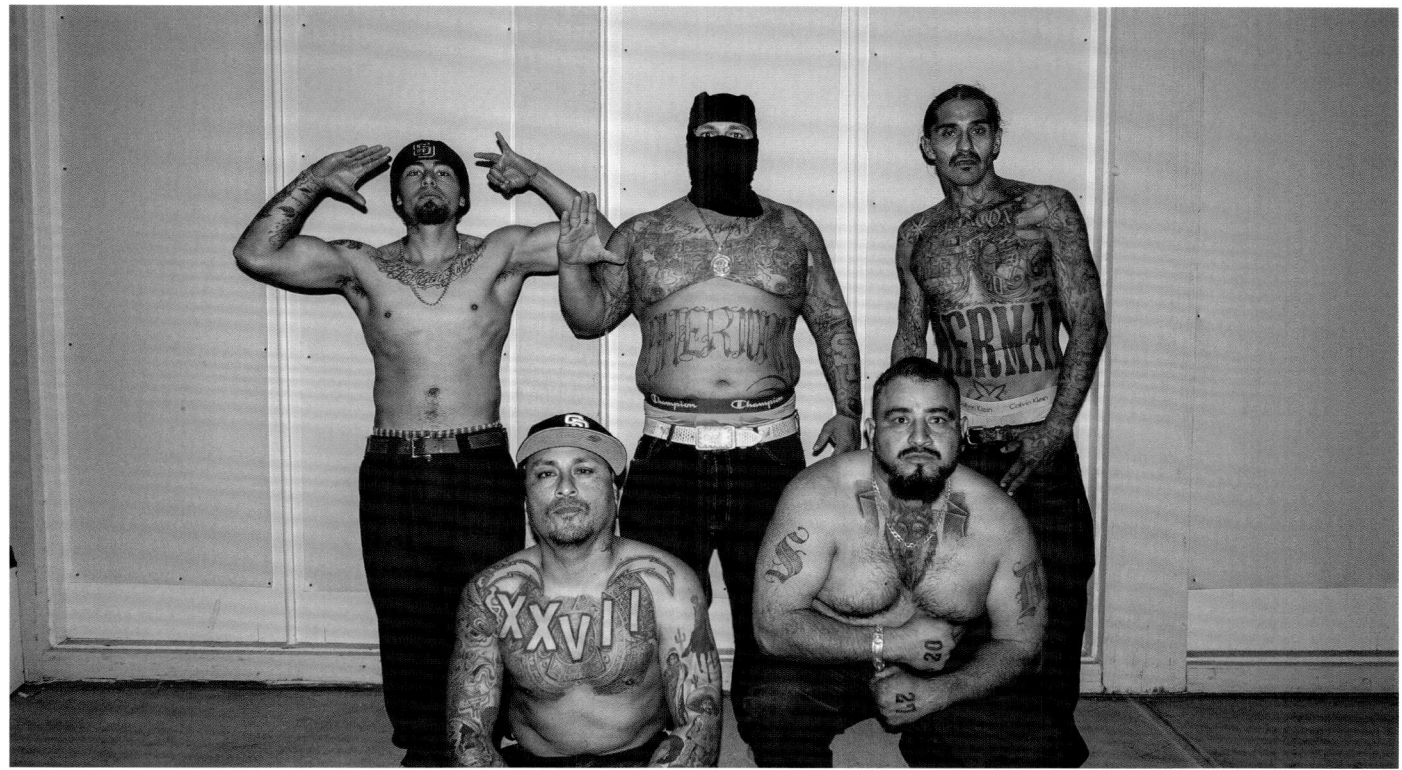

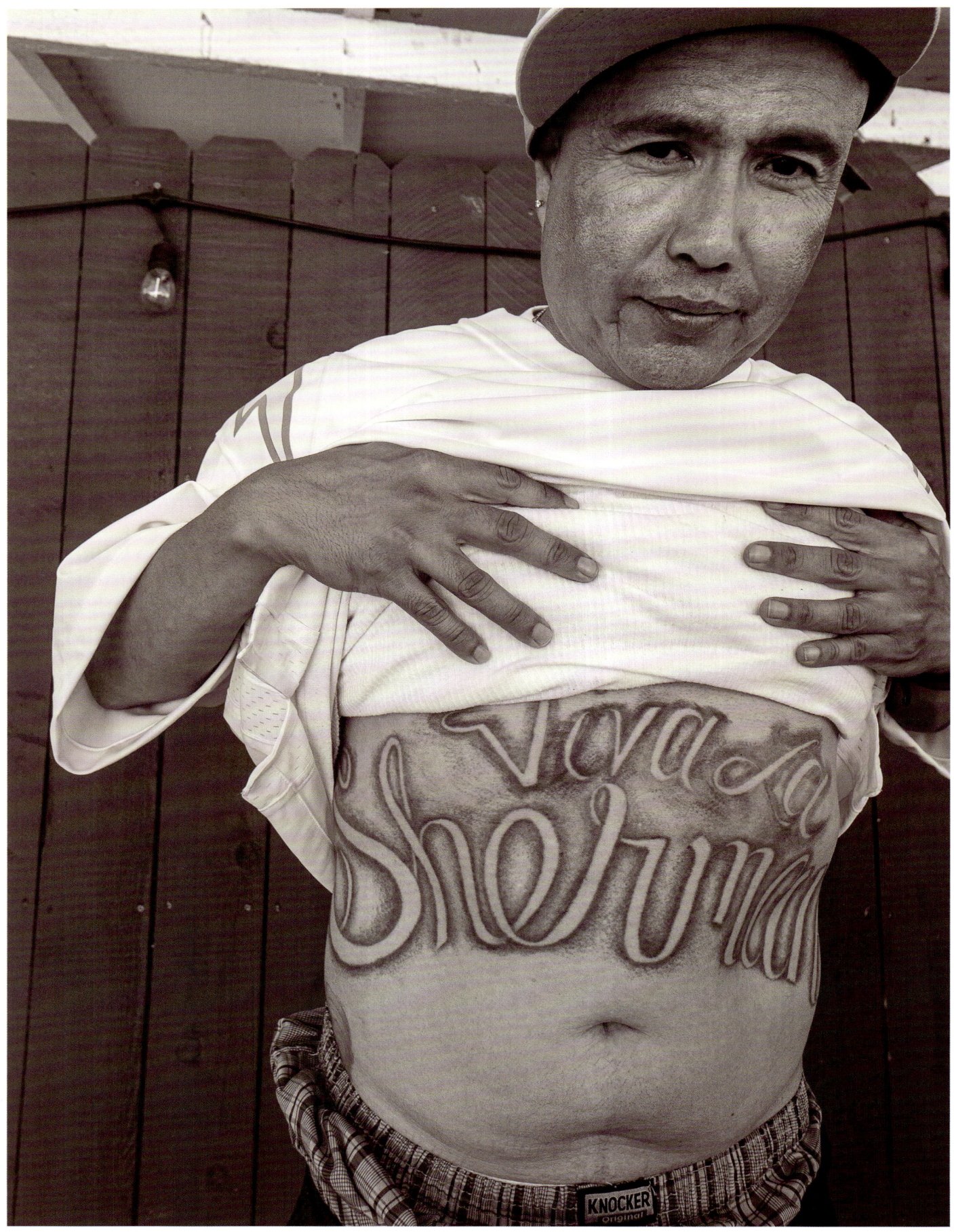

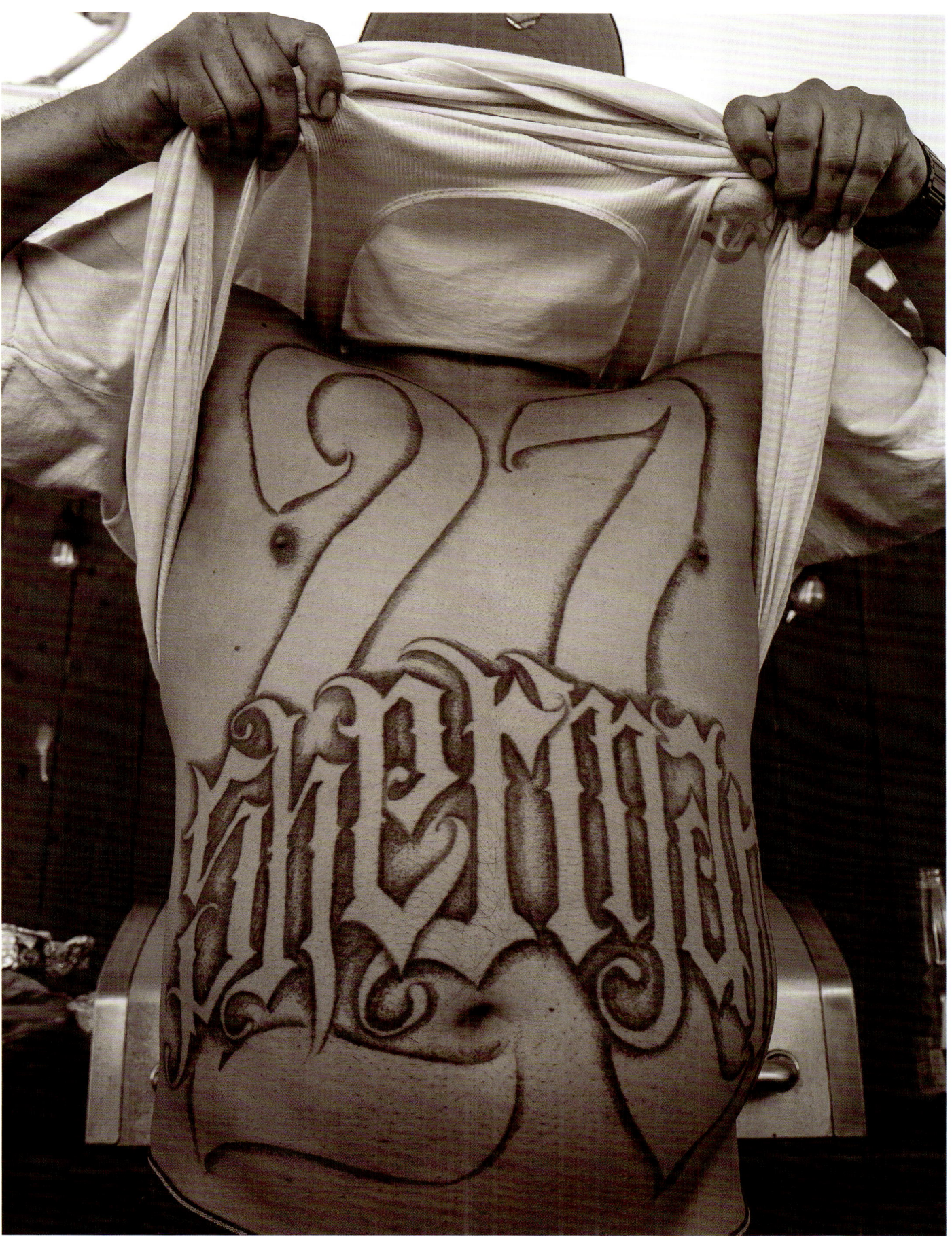

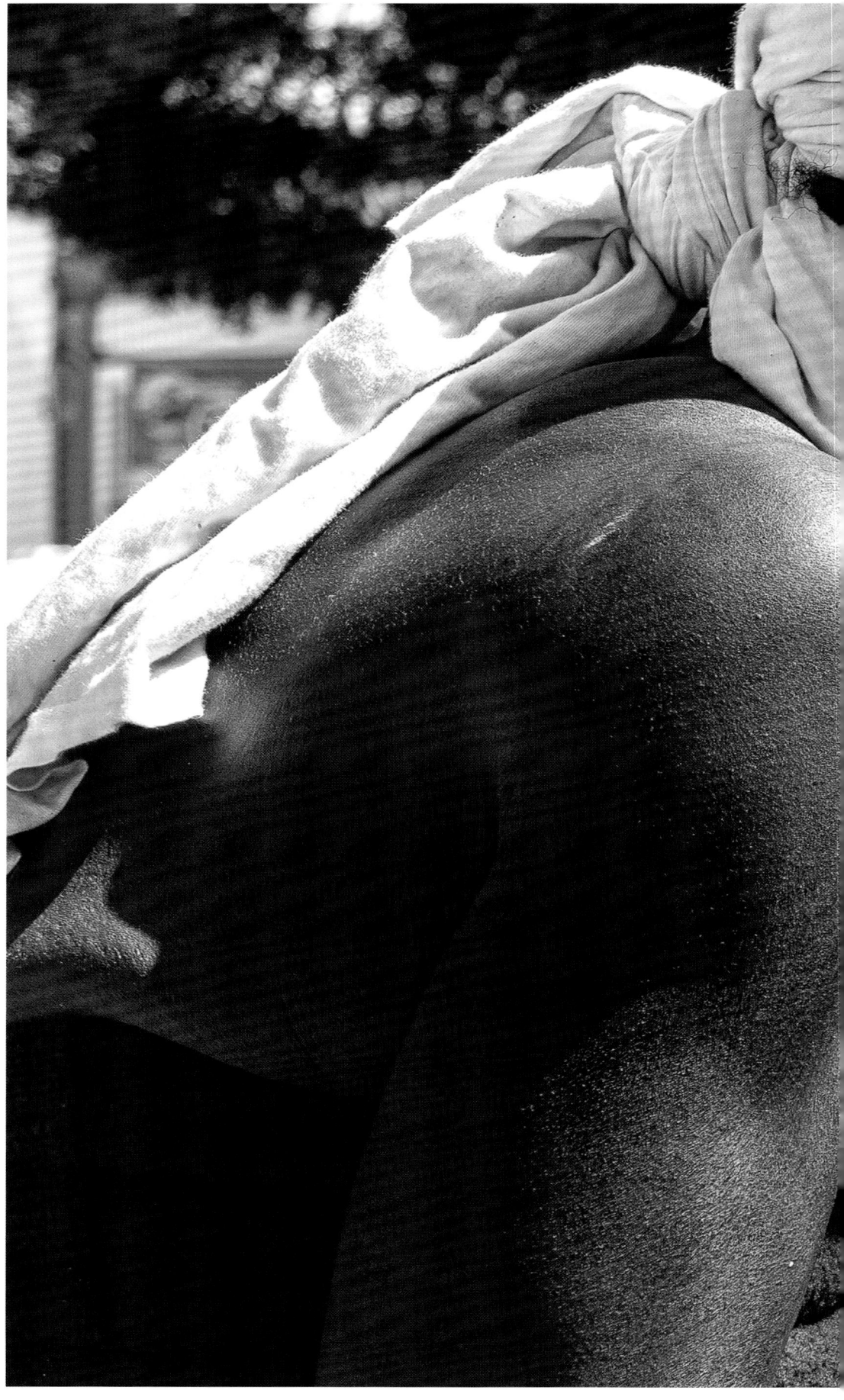

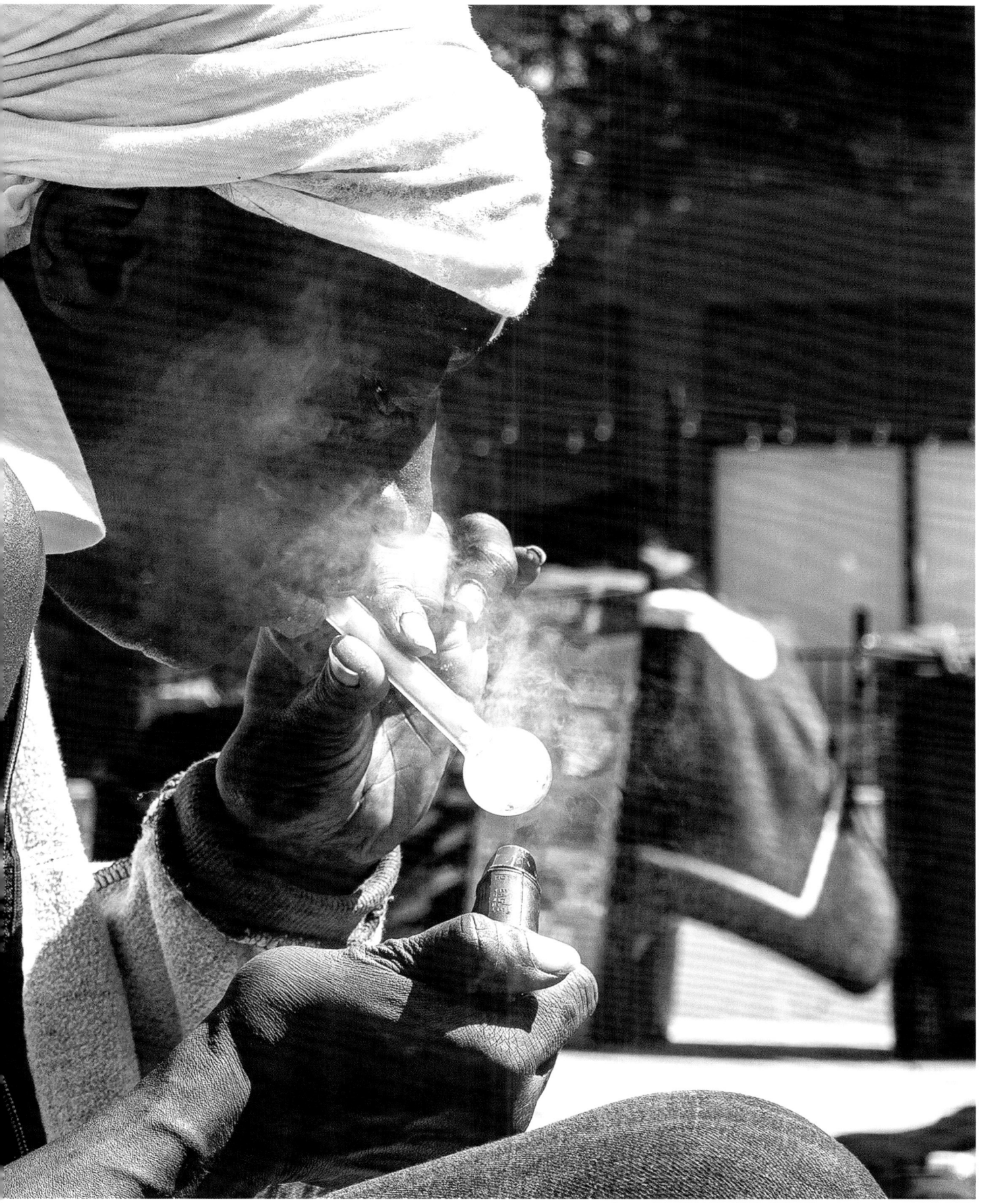

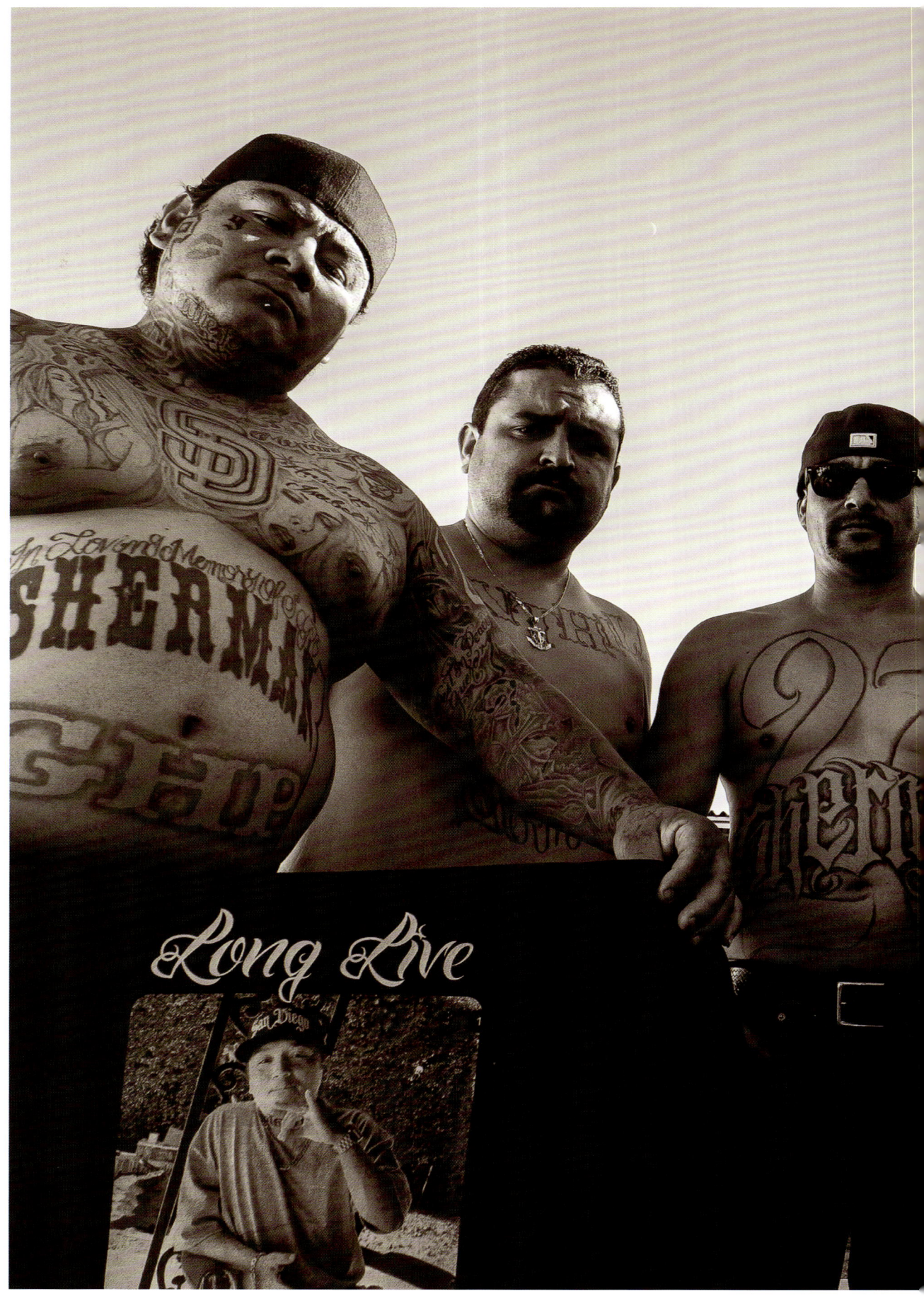

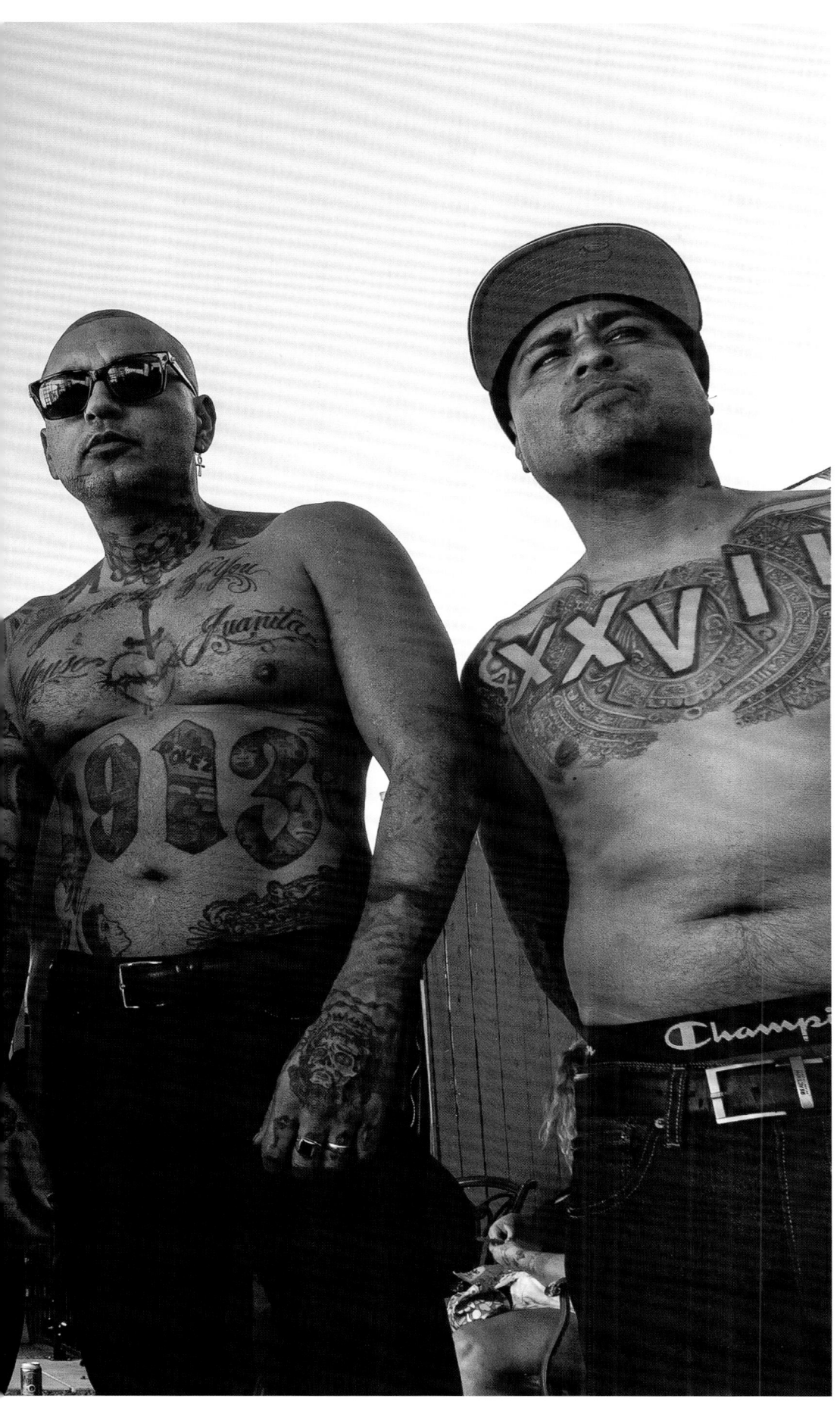

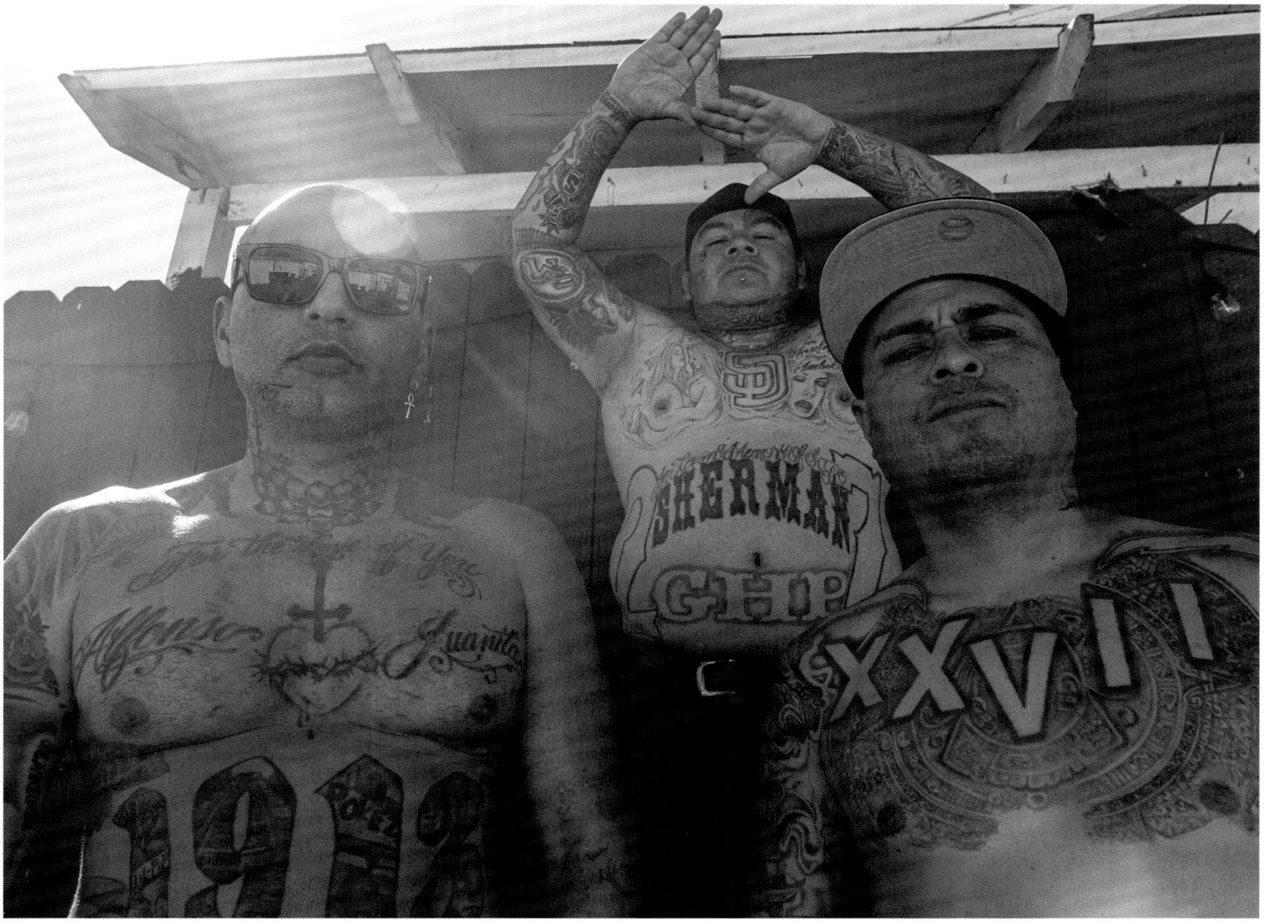

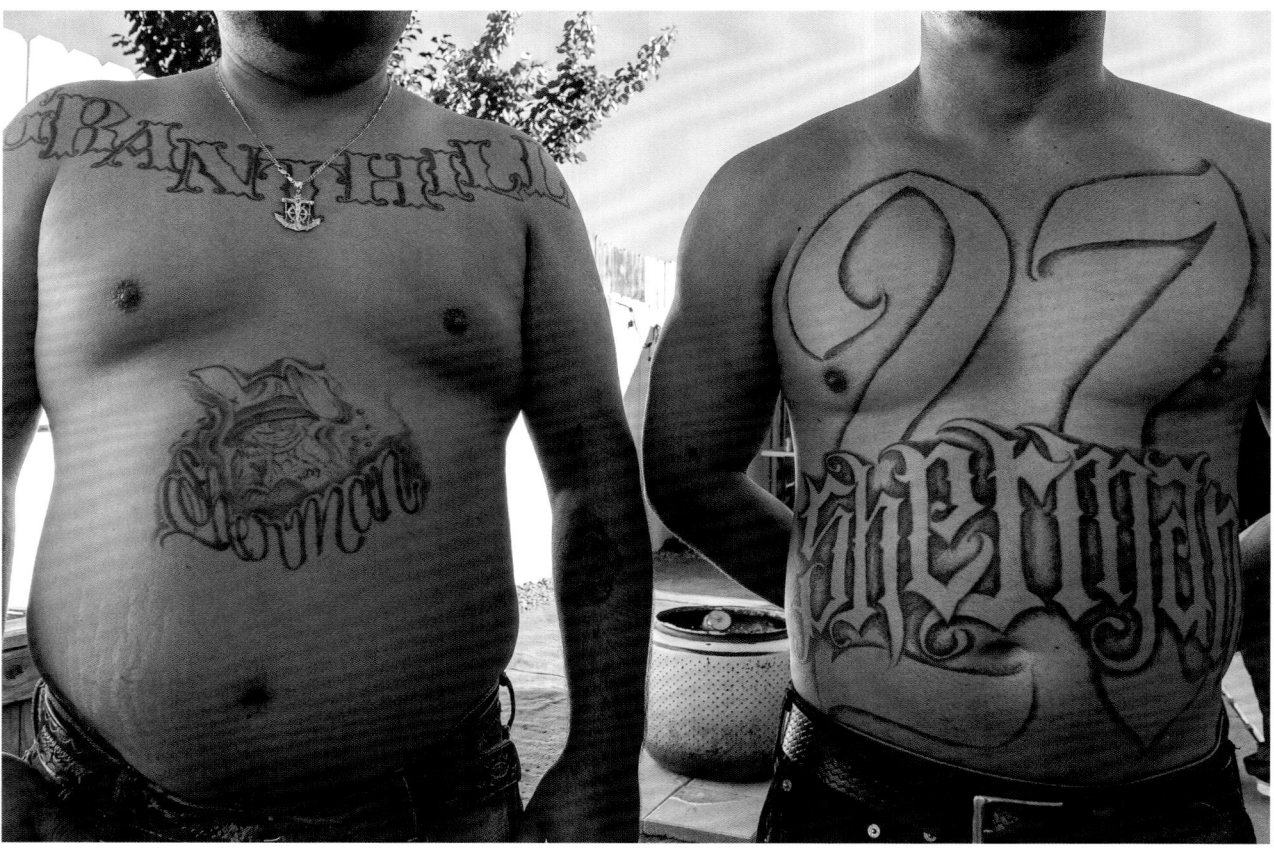

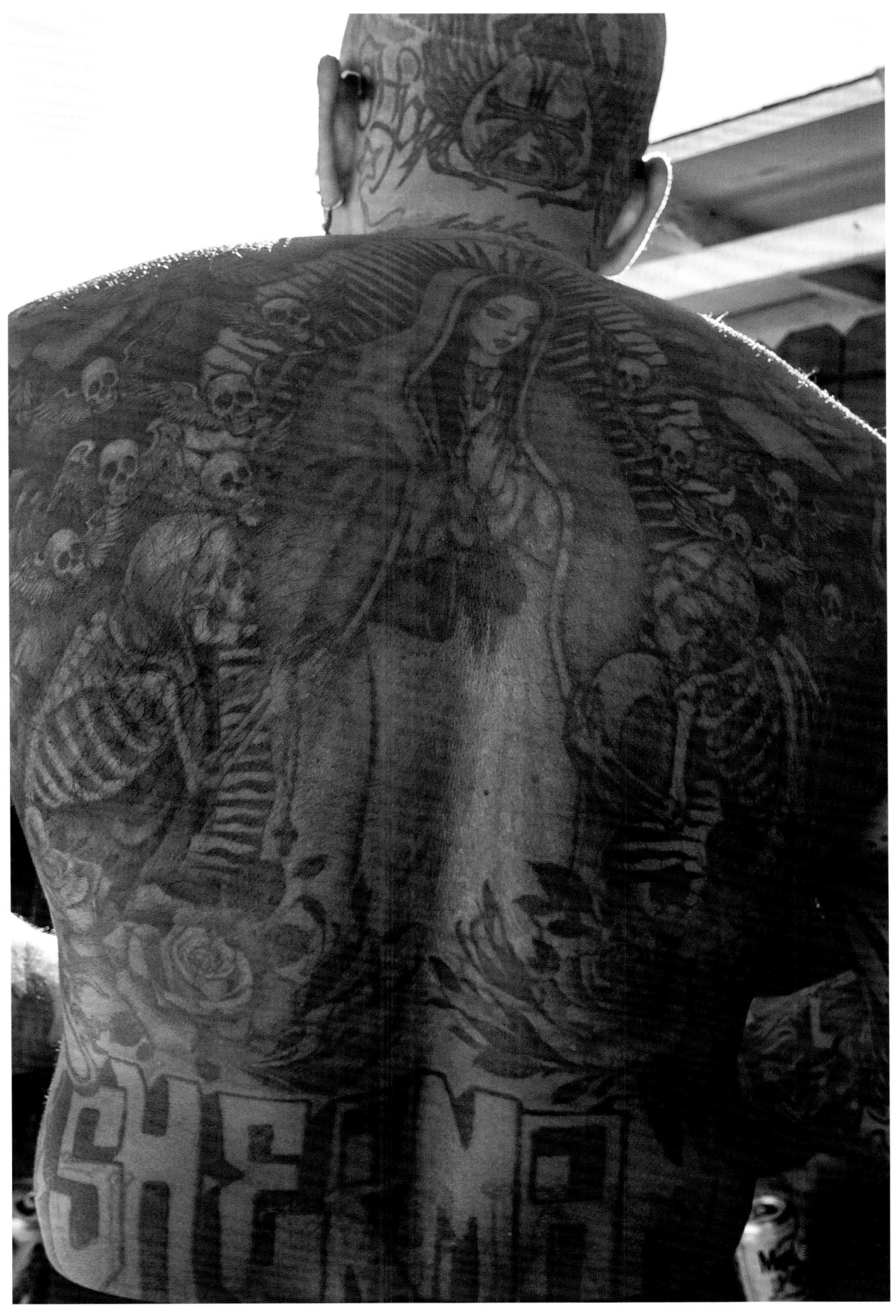

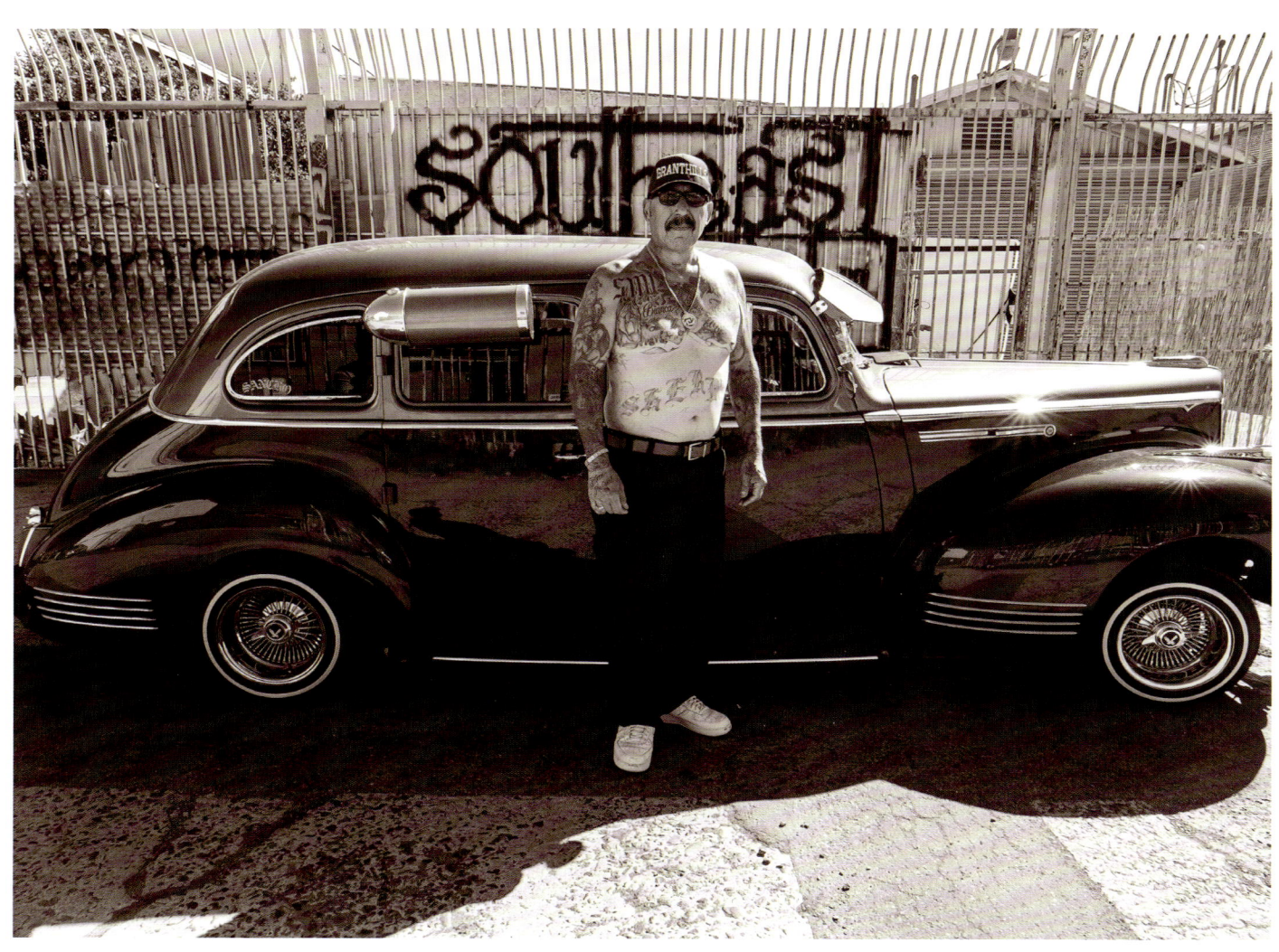

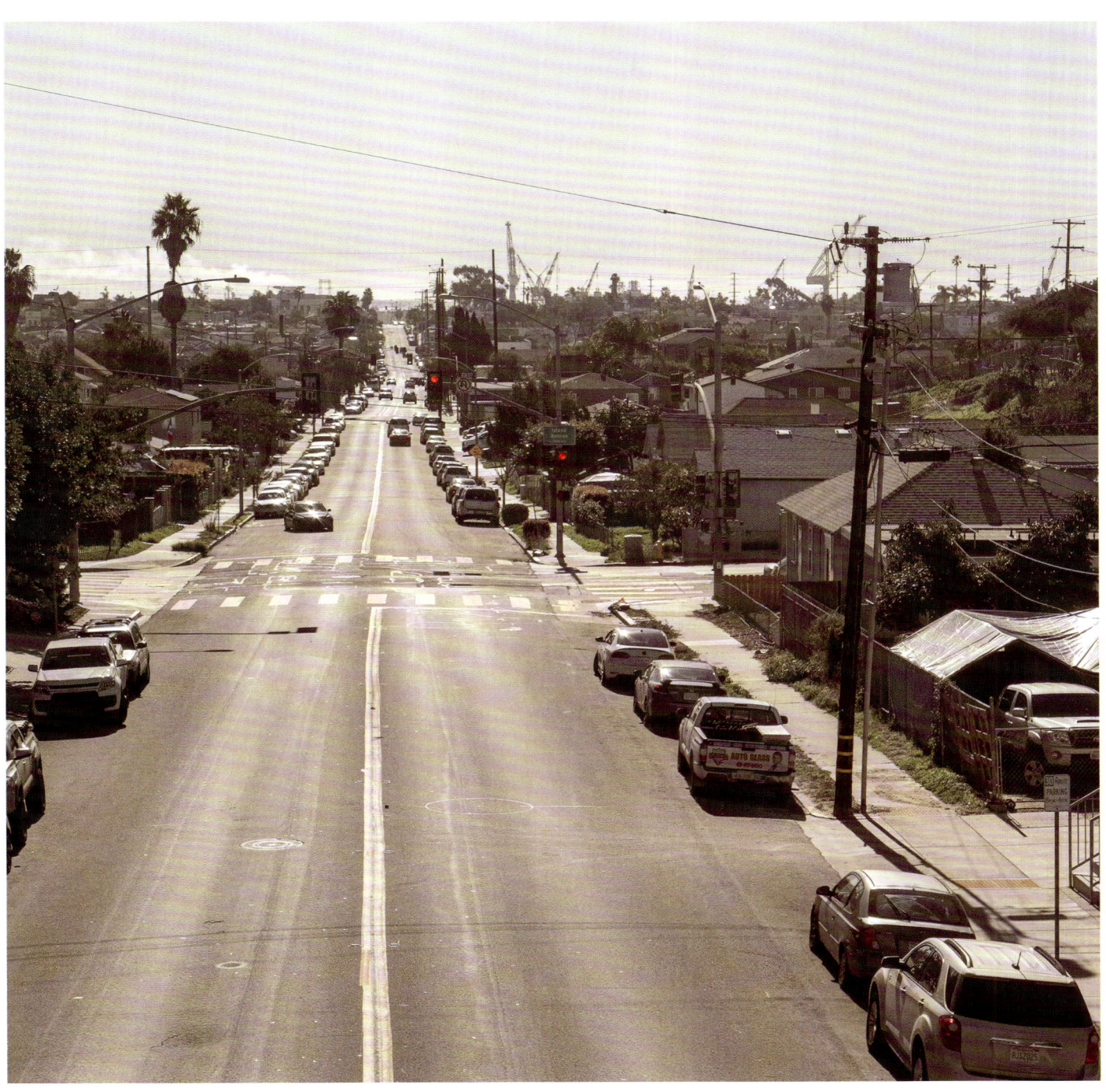

LOMAS

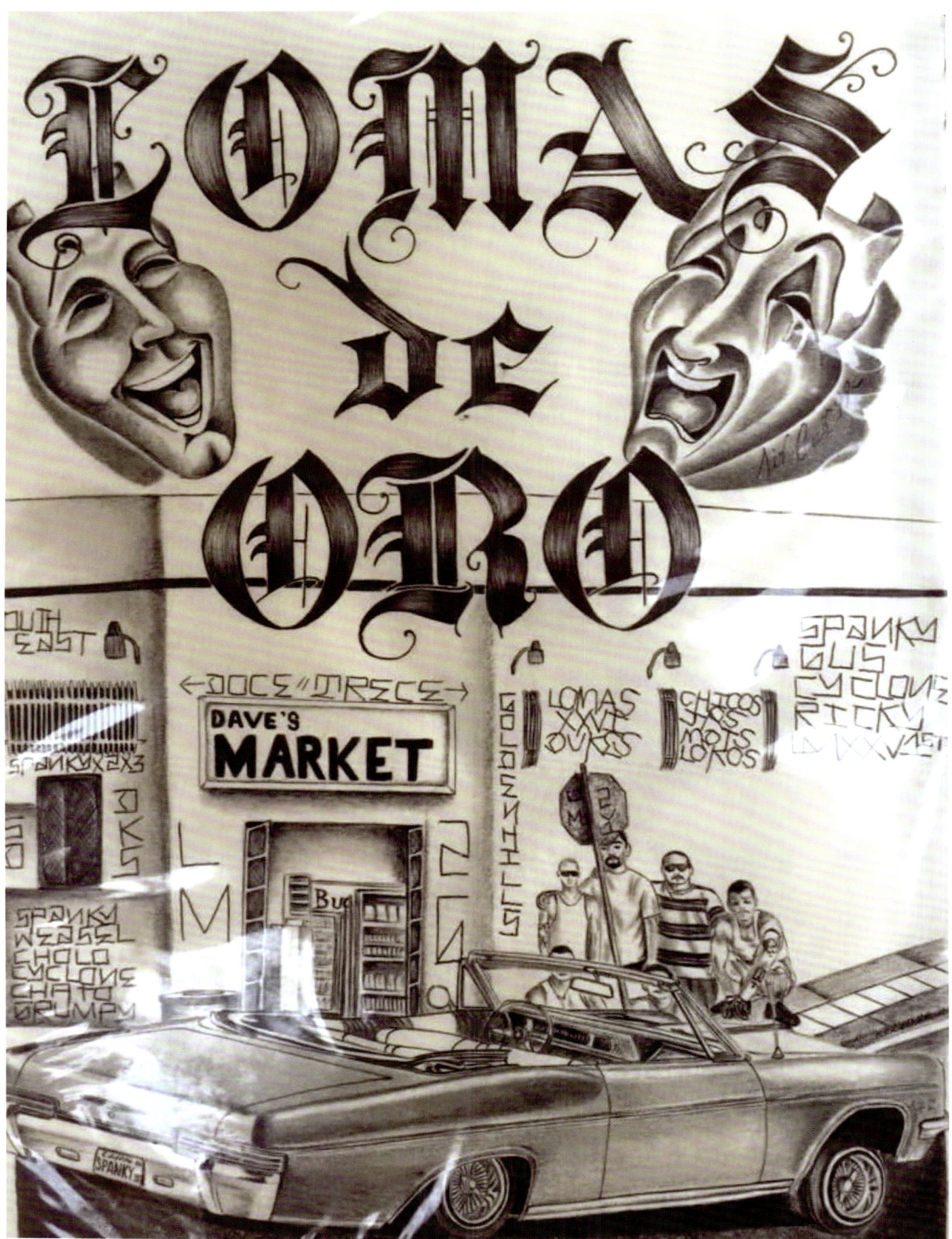

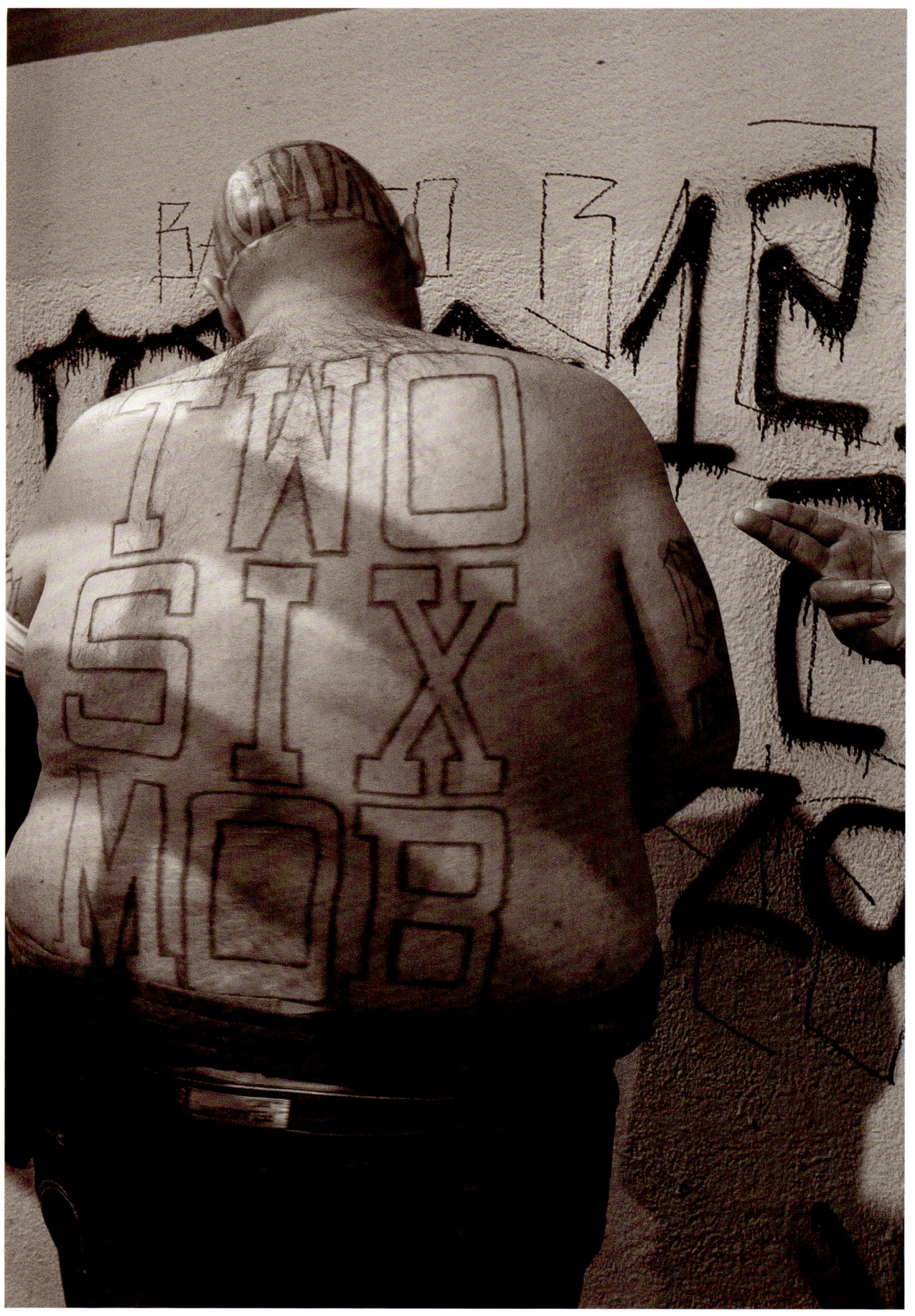

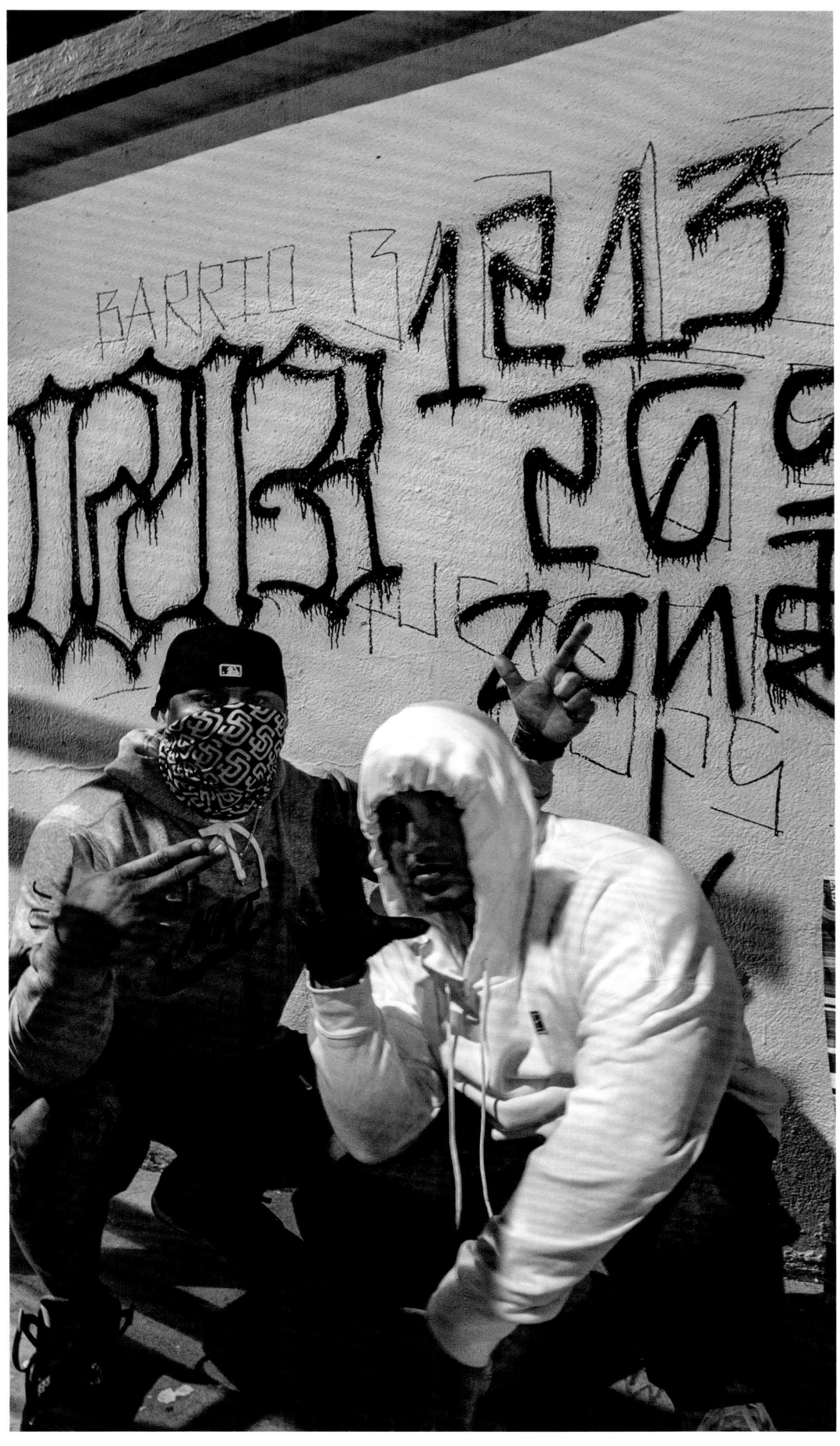

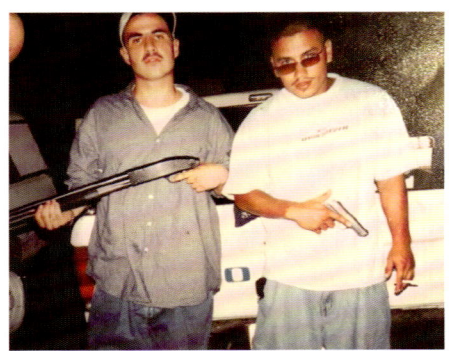

"Drugs have destroyed many of our generations so we made it a point not to let them break us down and yet eventually, they were our downfall. We are still here but not close like we once were back in the days because back then, we were like an army. We were disciplined in following our neighborhood guidelines and we always knew that we were different from other hoods. One day the juras had us hemmed up at the park and said,

'If you guys are not fighting your enemies, we get calls only to show up and realize you are fighting yourselves. We will put five of you to any ten and put our money on you guys.' True fuckin' story.

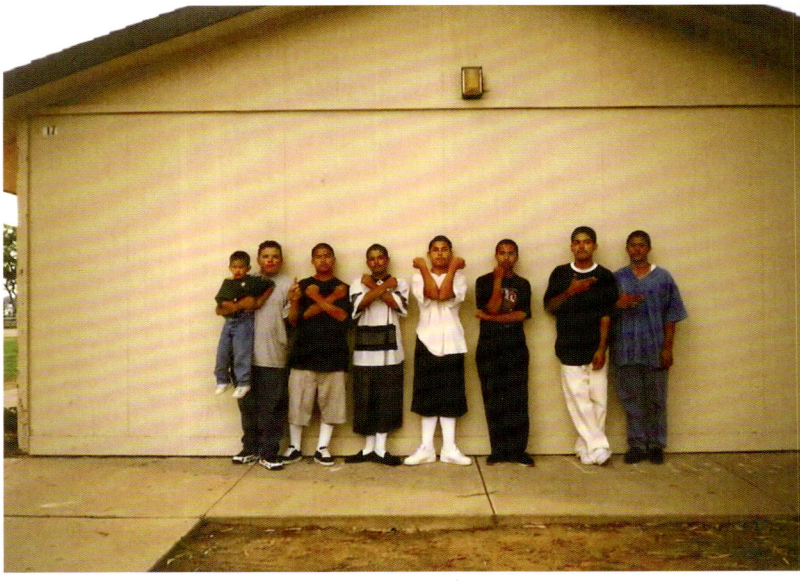

Our neighborhood in my days wasn't a walk in the park, Lomas boys didn't care about looking cool, it was a war zone back then. In the late '80s and the 1990s, it was on and cracking.

We had no idea what our future held. Our homeboy Mugzy, RIP, was our age but he was from the older clika: CLS Mob, Chicos Locos. He came to our junior high and told us the homeboys wanted to meet us so there was a mandatory meeting Friday night.

As soon as we showed up to Twenty-Sixth and Broadway, Dave's Market, it kicked off. The homeboys rushed us and told us to leave and to quit claiming their hood. We here about twenty deep, only ten of us stayed. That's when the clecha began, from that point on all they wanted were riders. The Nasty Too Sick Duke's clique was formed in 1989. It was a war zone back then and the Lomas boys were strapped, ready and anxious to put in work.

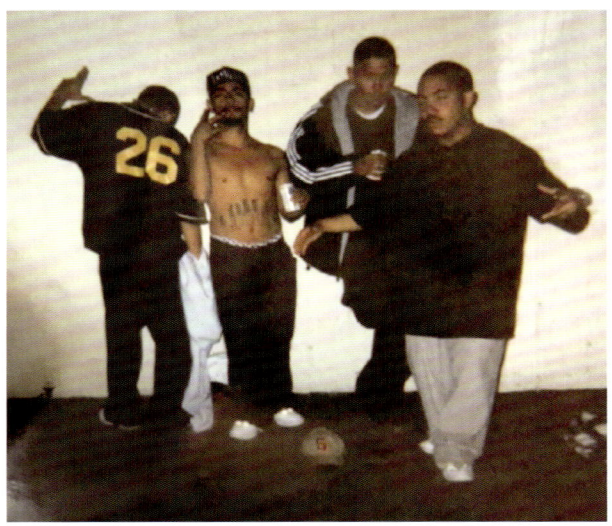

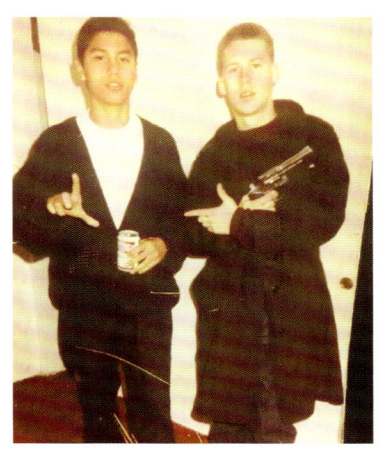

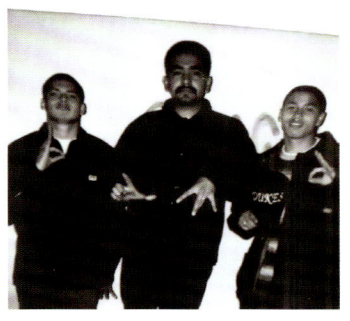

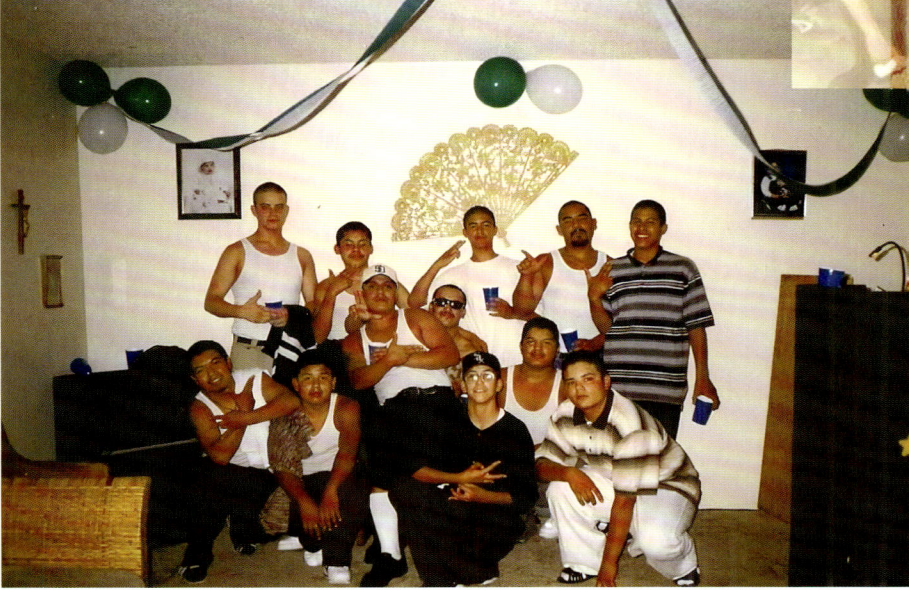

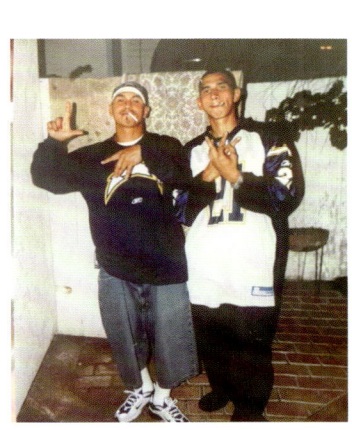

It was always gauchos, homie, fuckin' gauchos. When they saw me they knew what it was gonna be. A lot of homies knew that I was about it and that I was down to get it if they wanted it, that fade, because I was all about it. For that, many talk about me or avoid it because they knew the outcome, either it went down or they backed down."

—GRUMPY, LOMAS 26

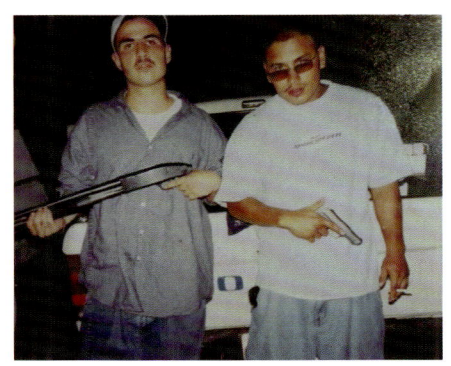

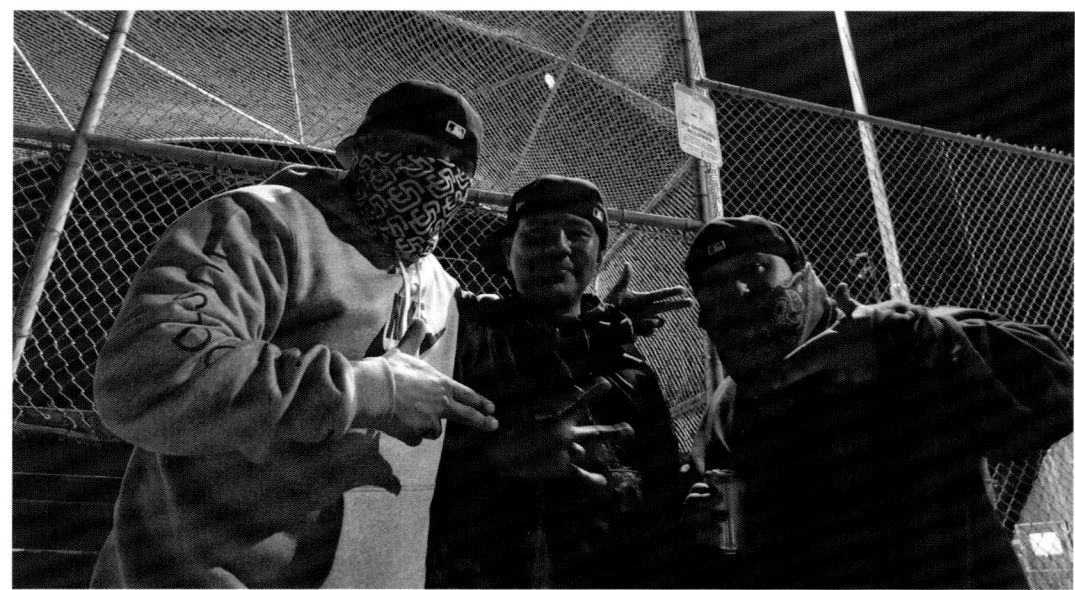

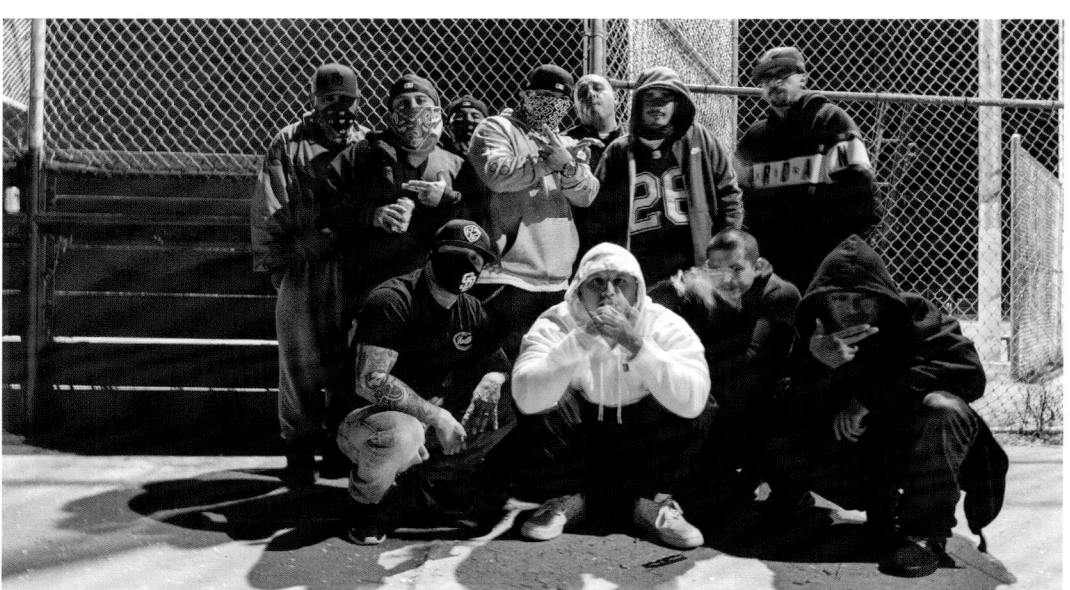

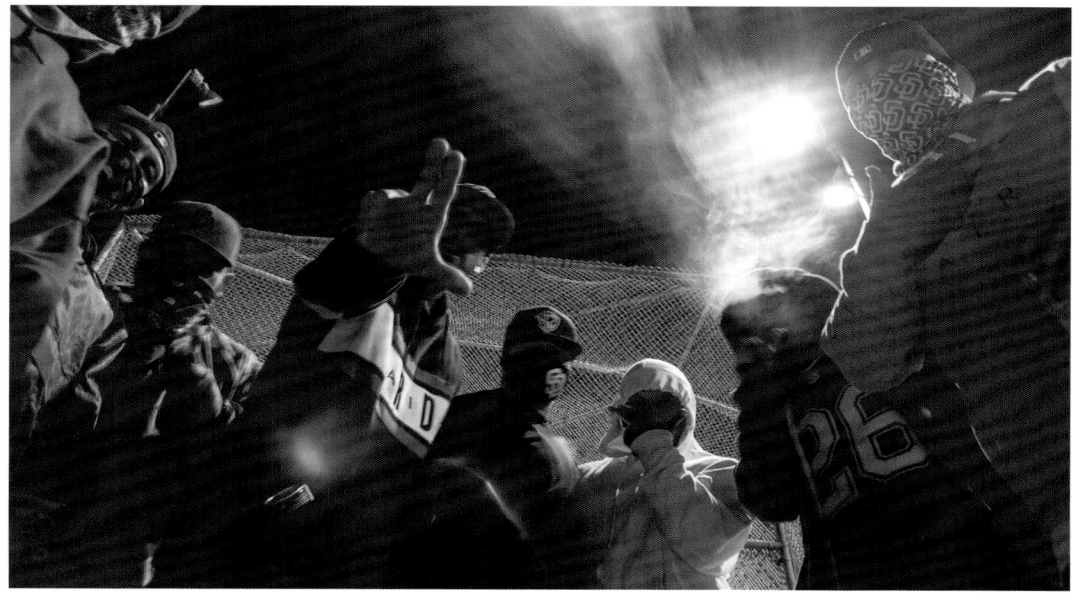

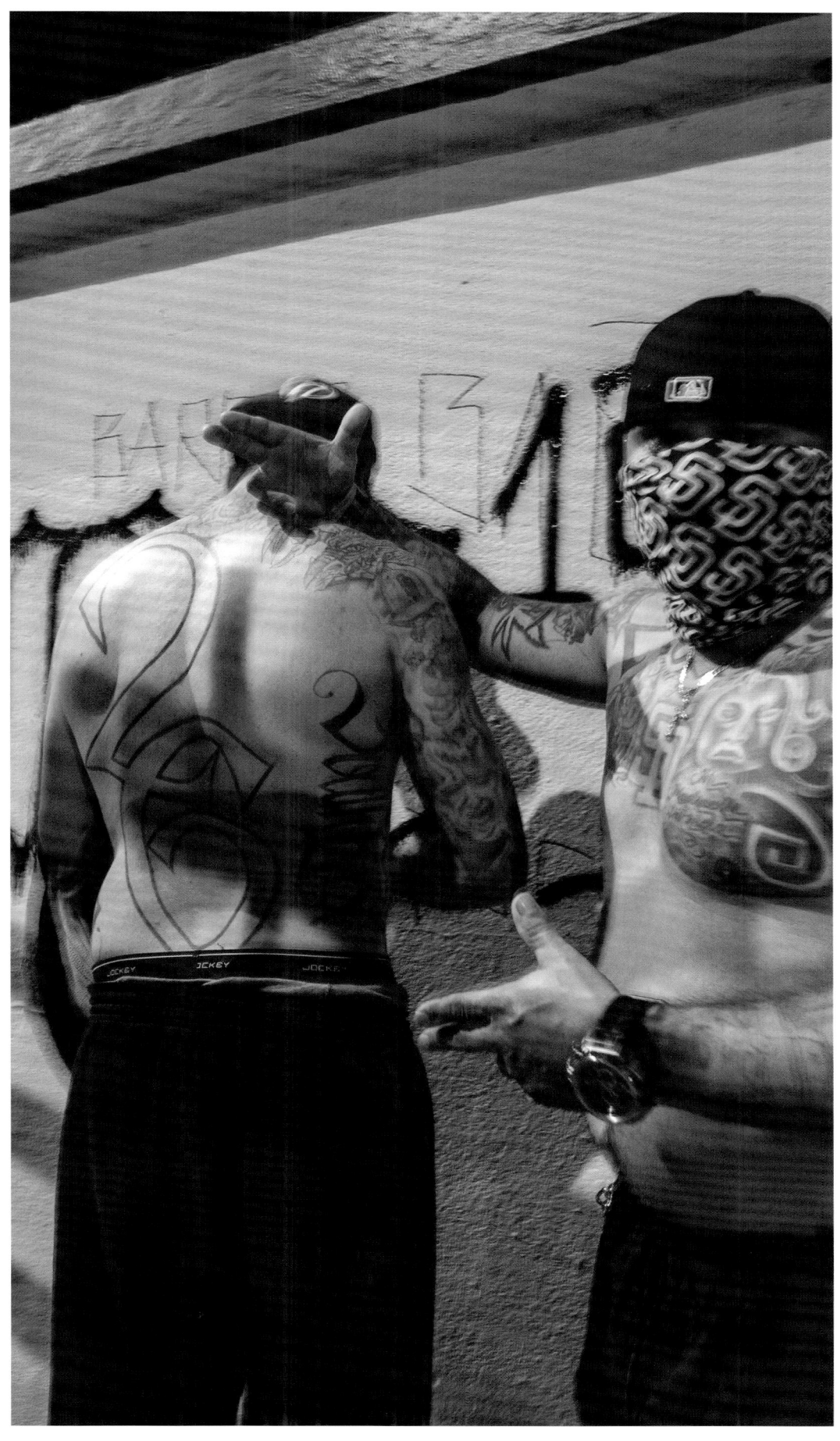

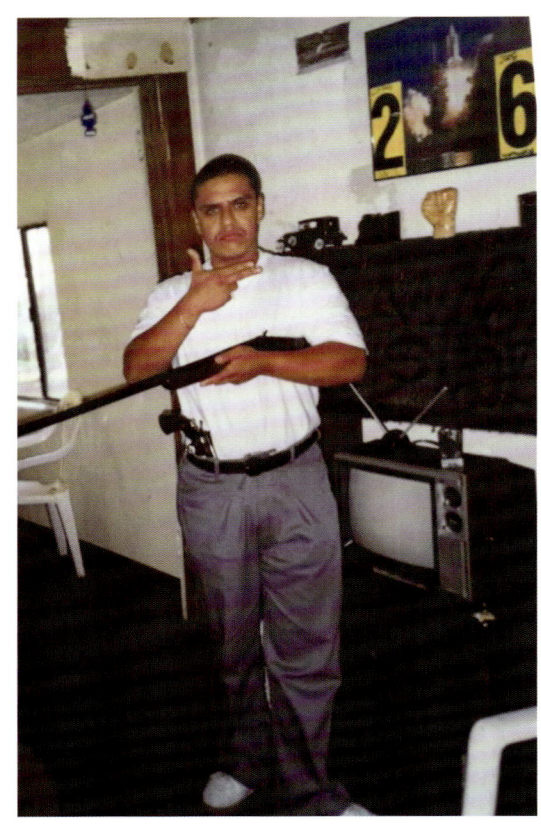

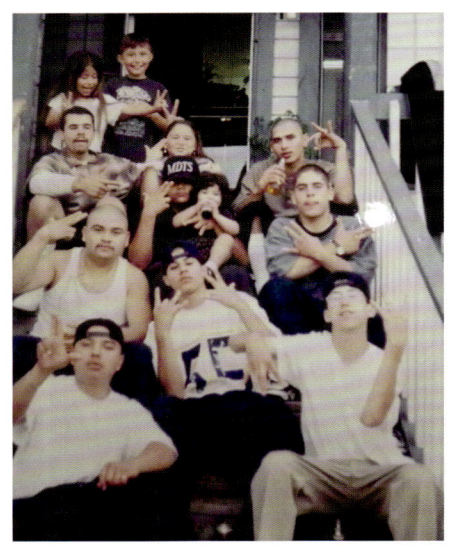

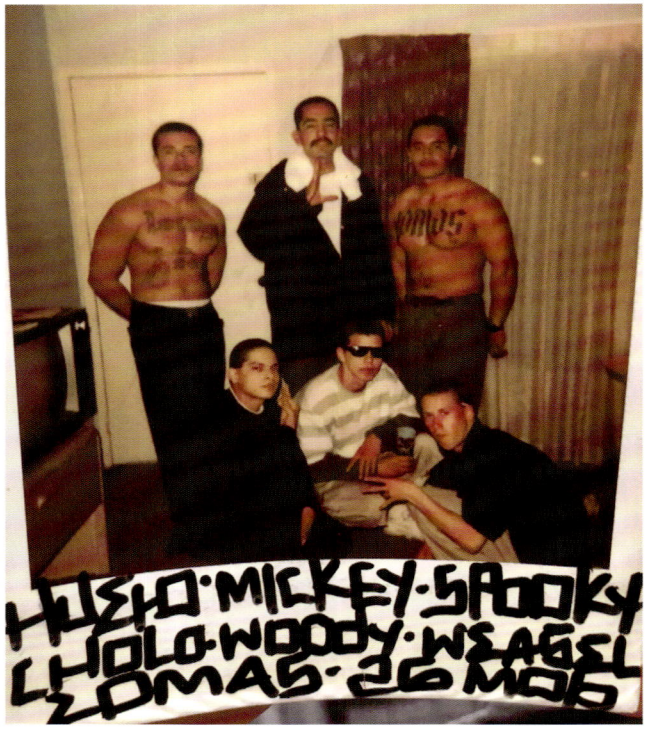

HOELO·MICKEY·SPOOKY
CHOLO·WOODY·WEASEL
TOMAS·26 MOB

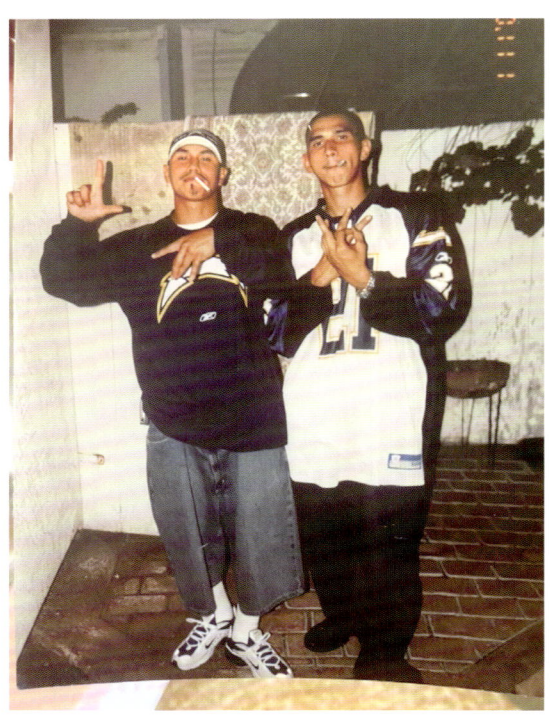

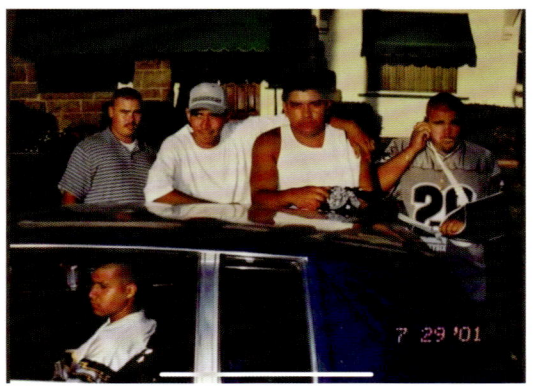

7 29 '01

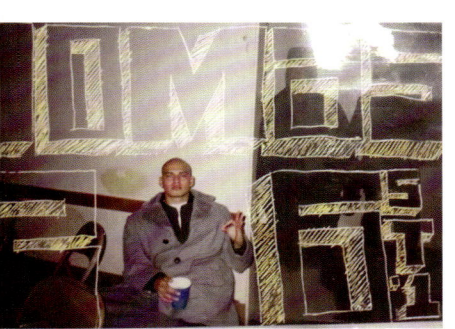

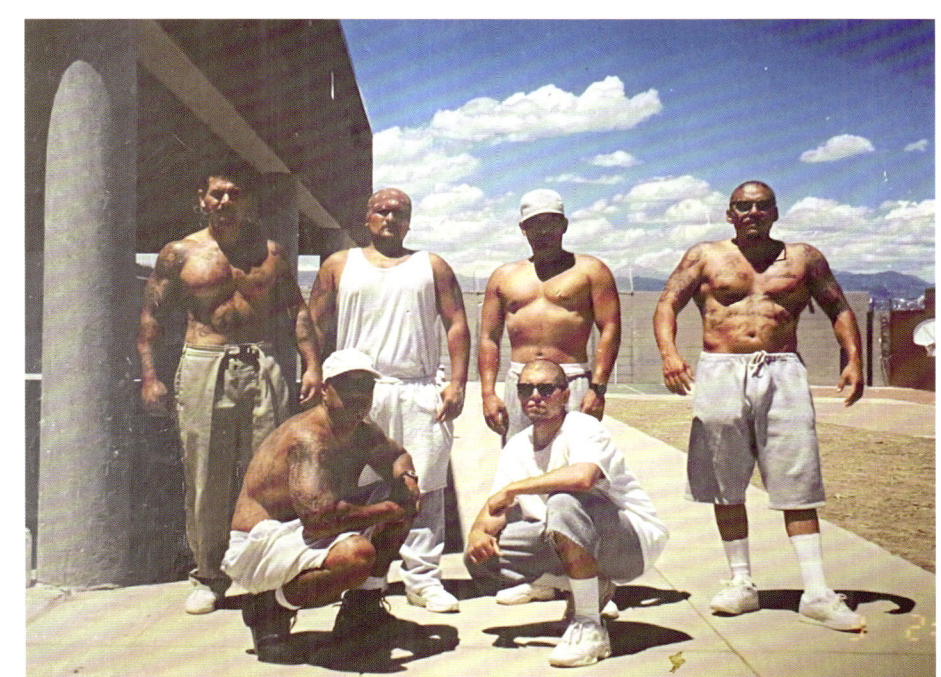

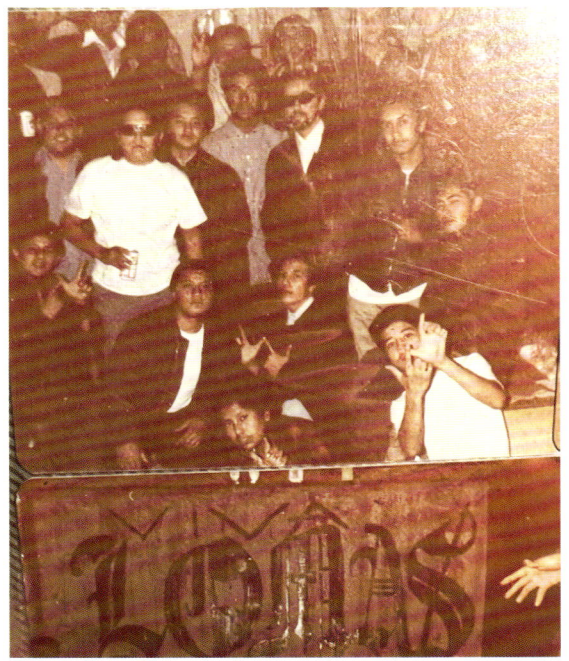

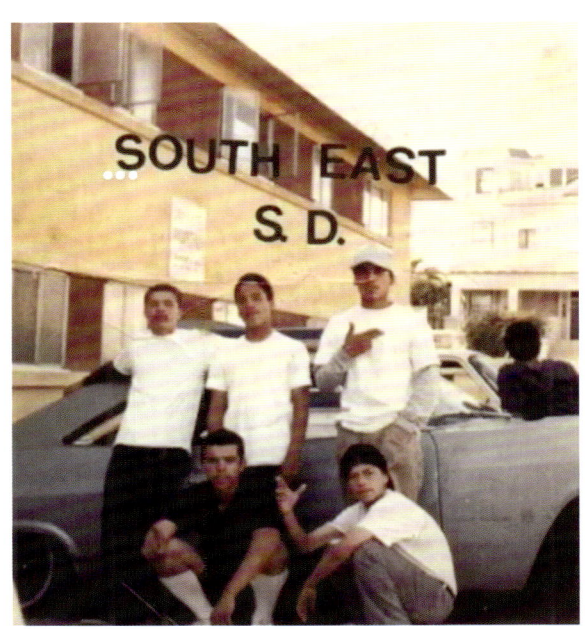

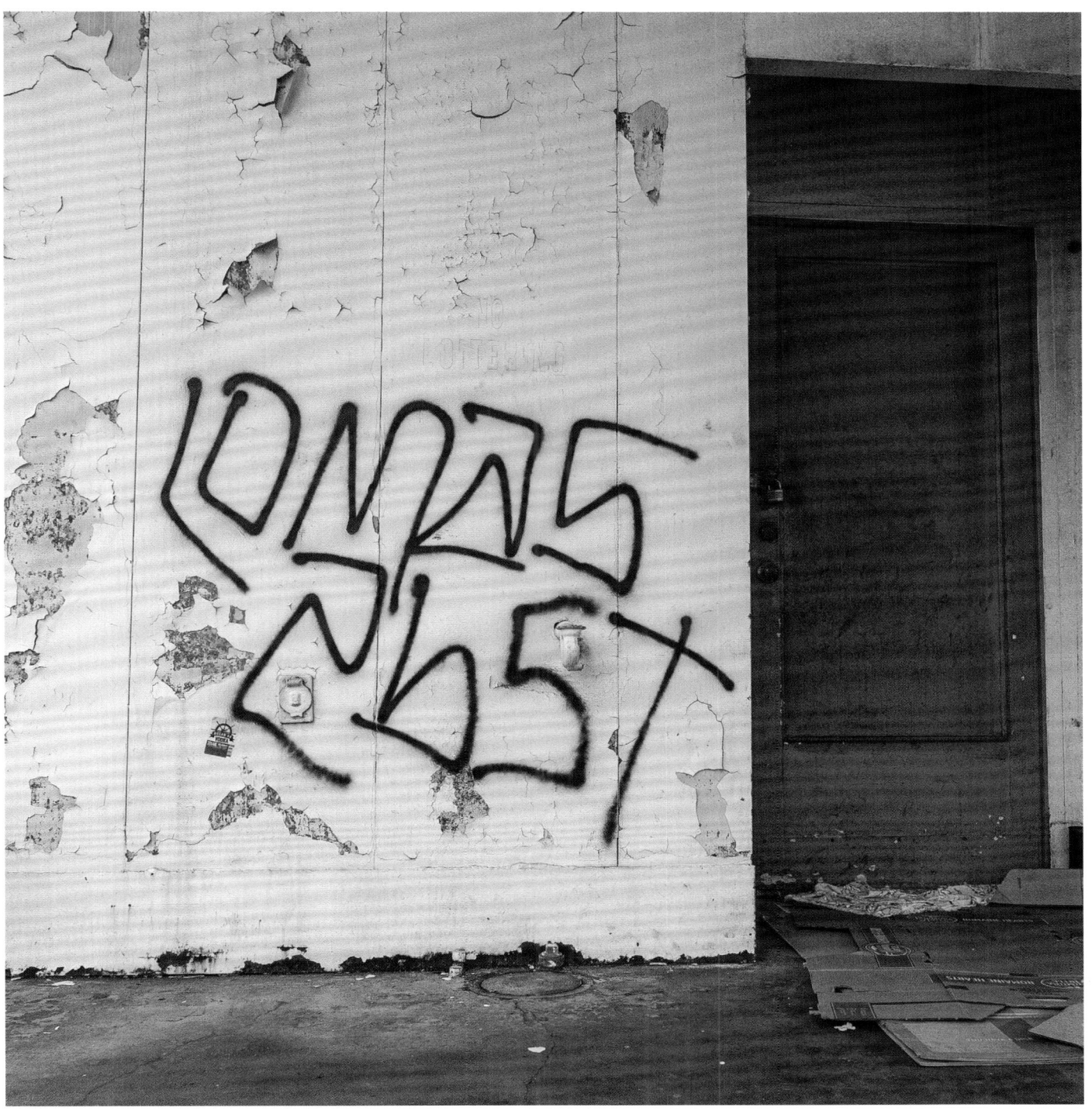

DEL

SOL

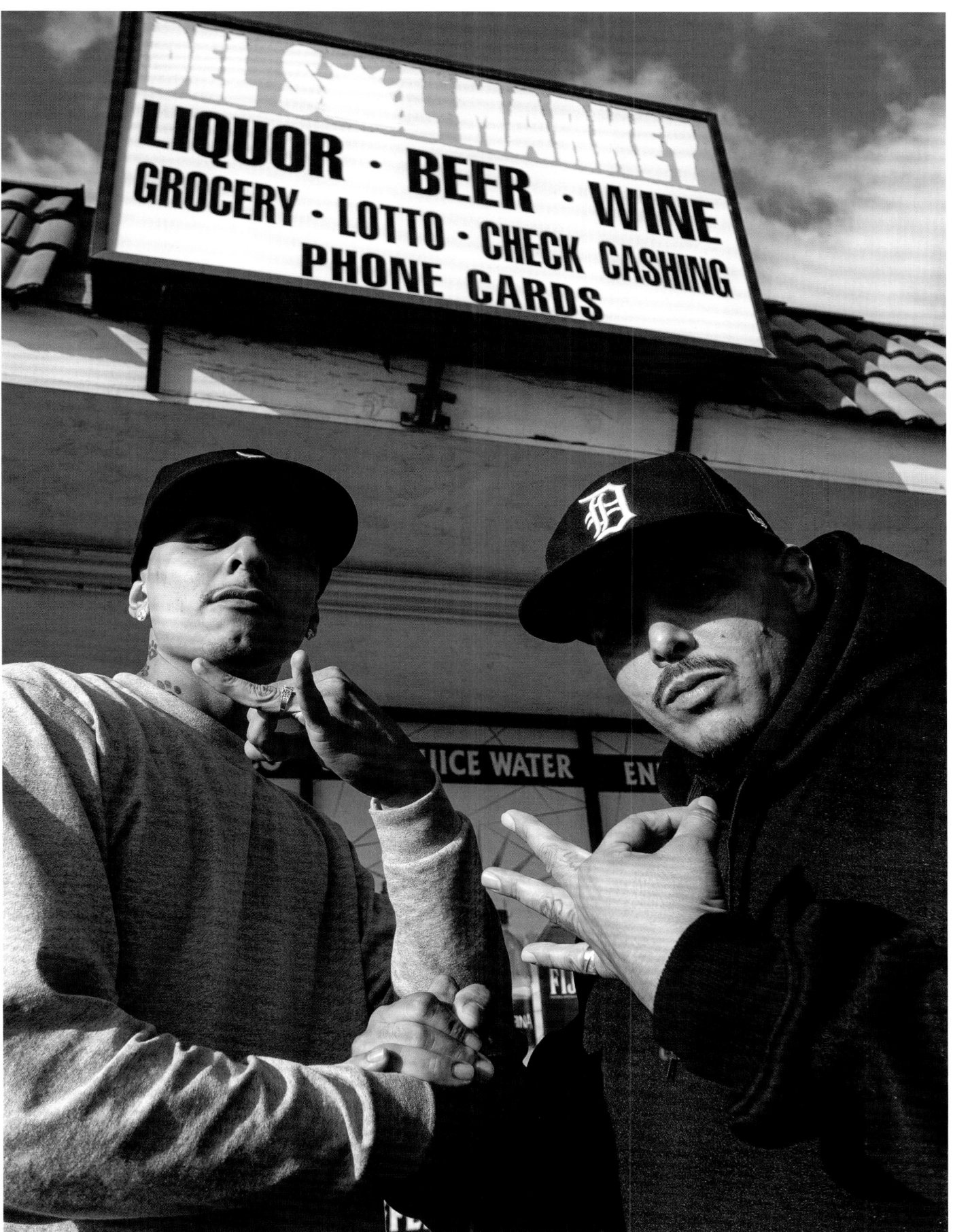

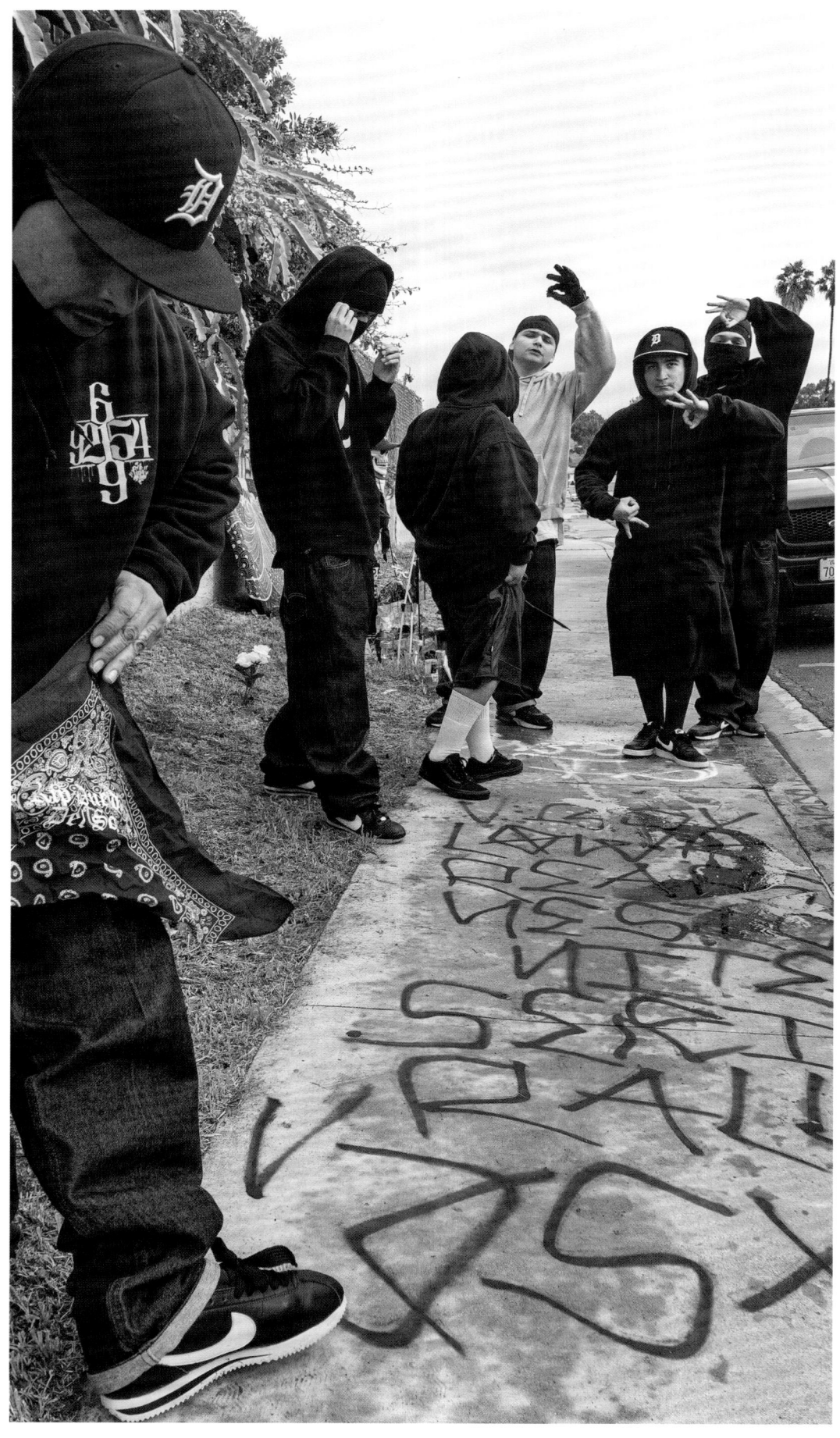

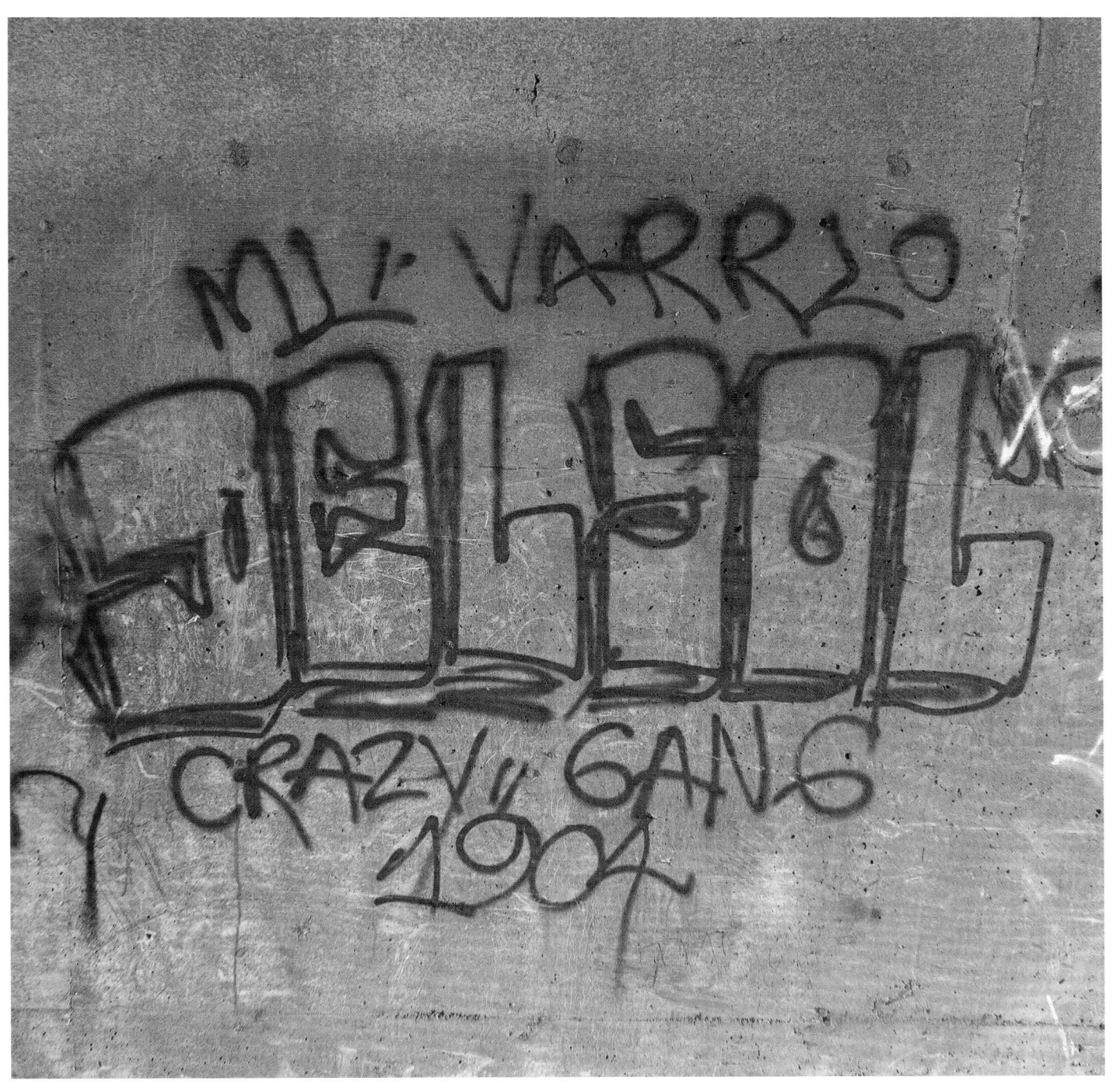

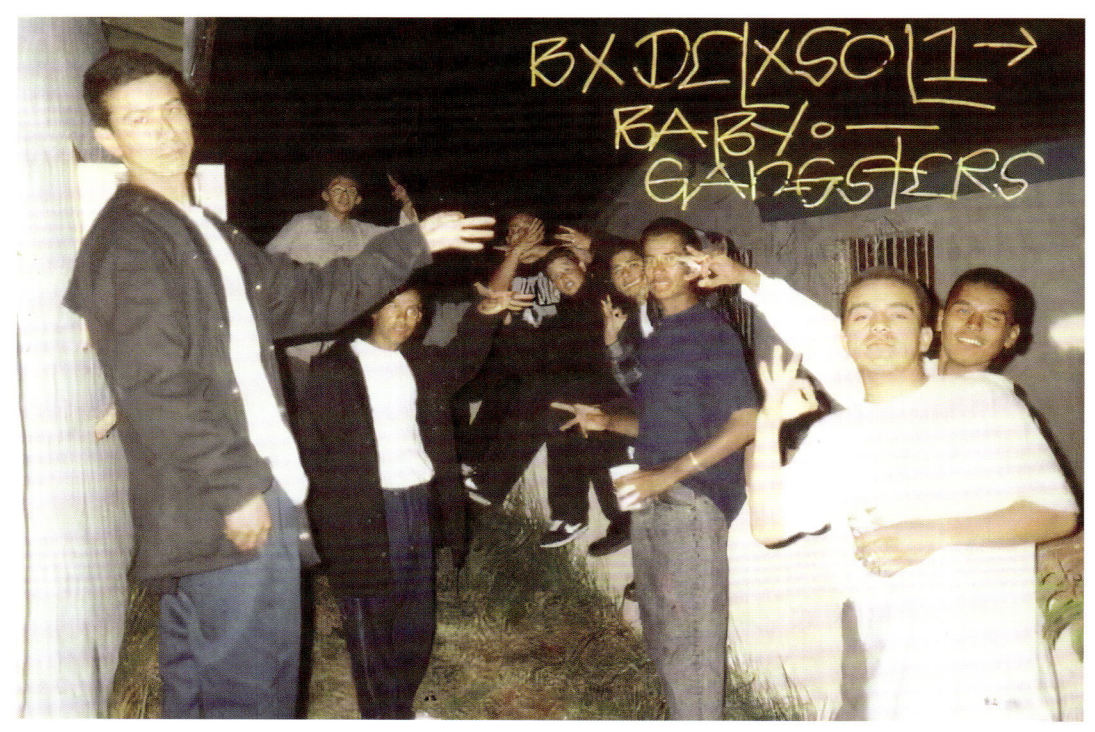

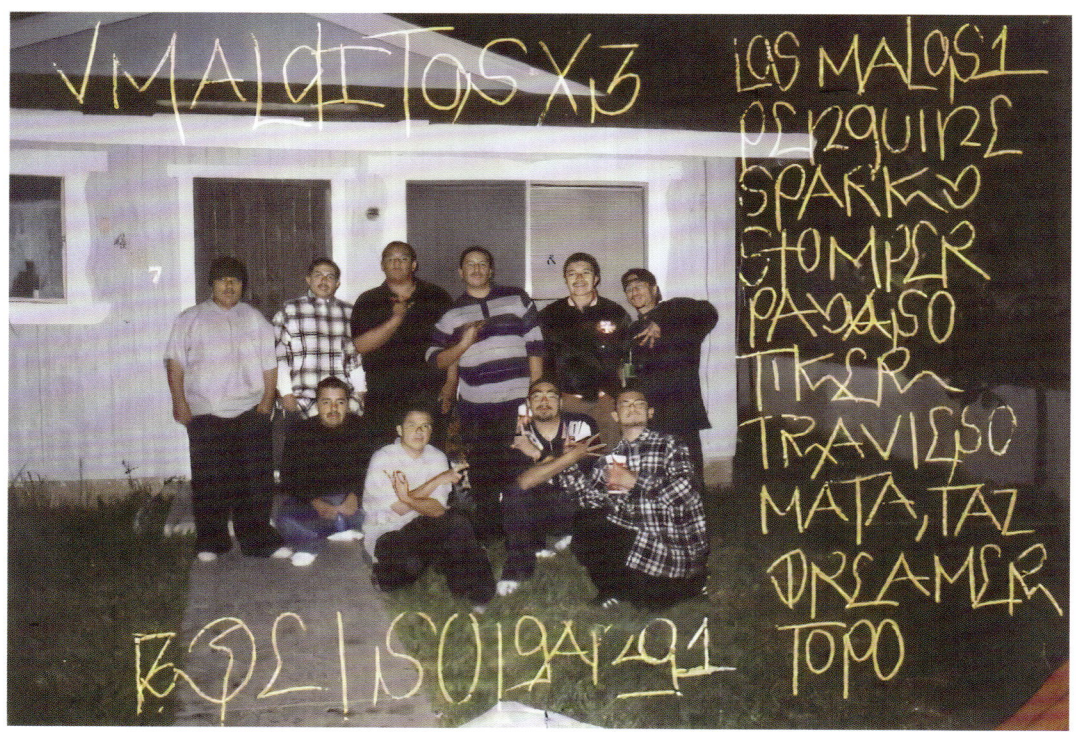

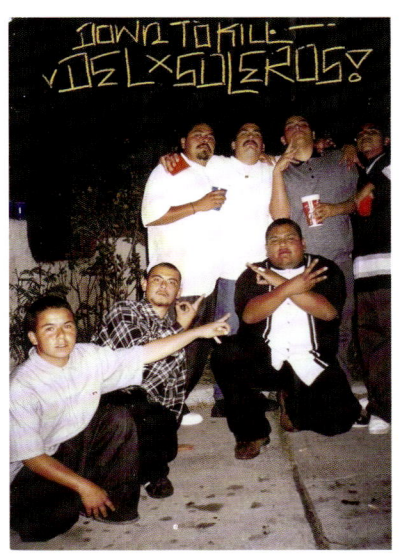

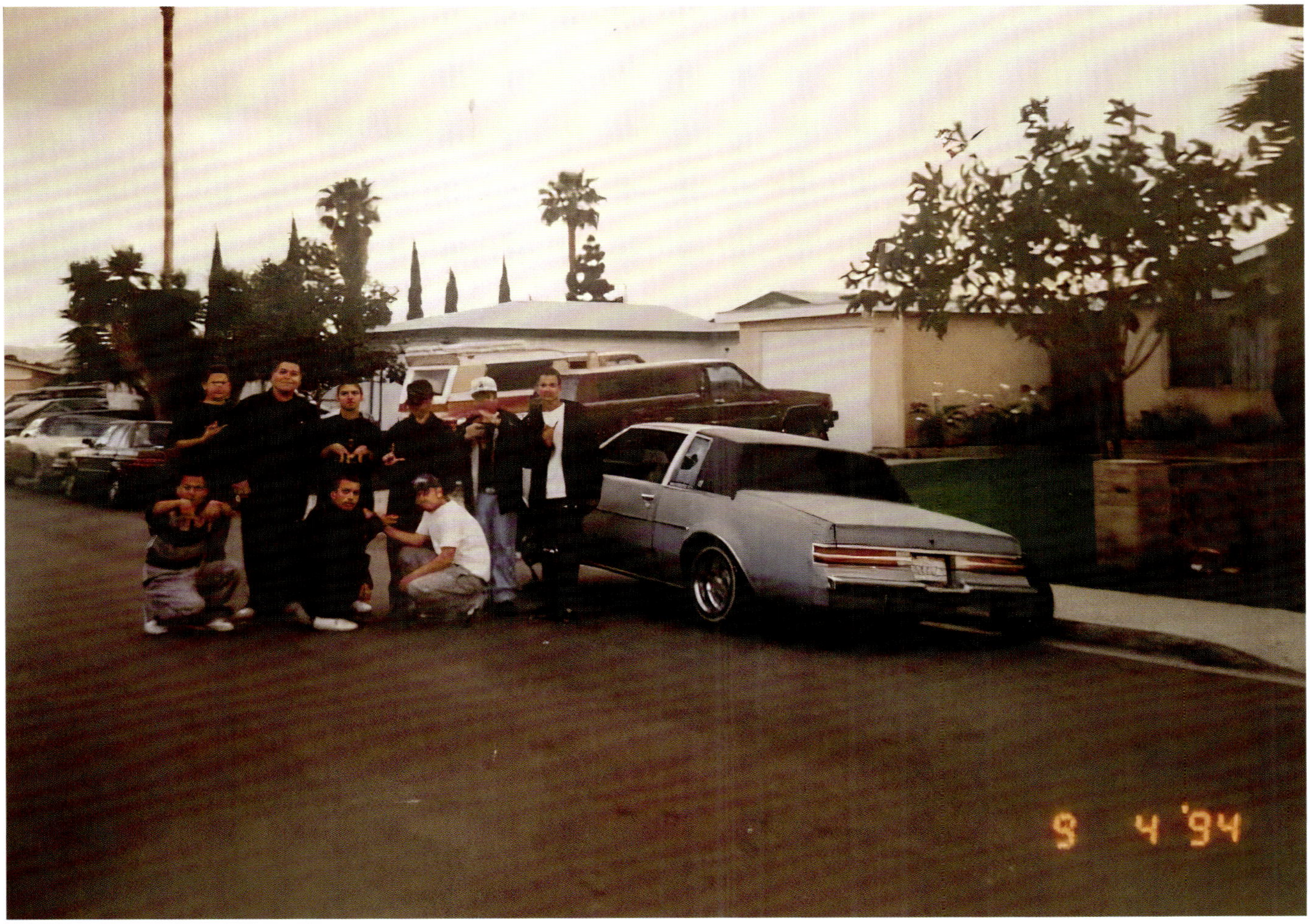

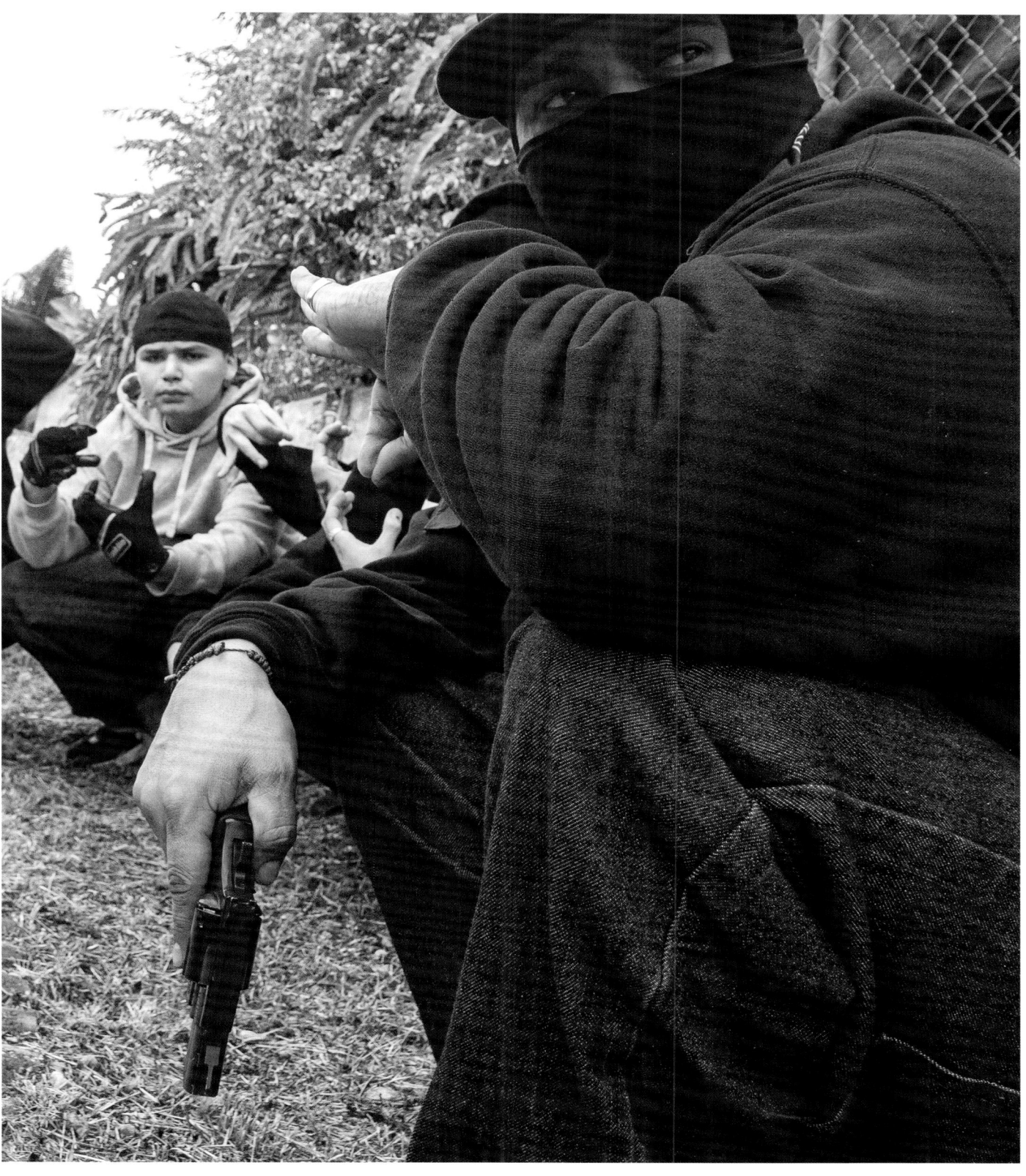

EAST

SIDE

POSOLE

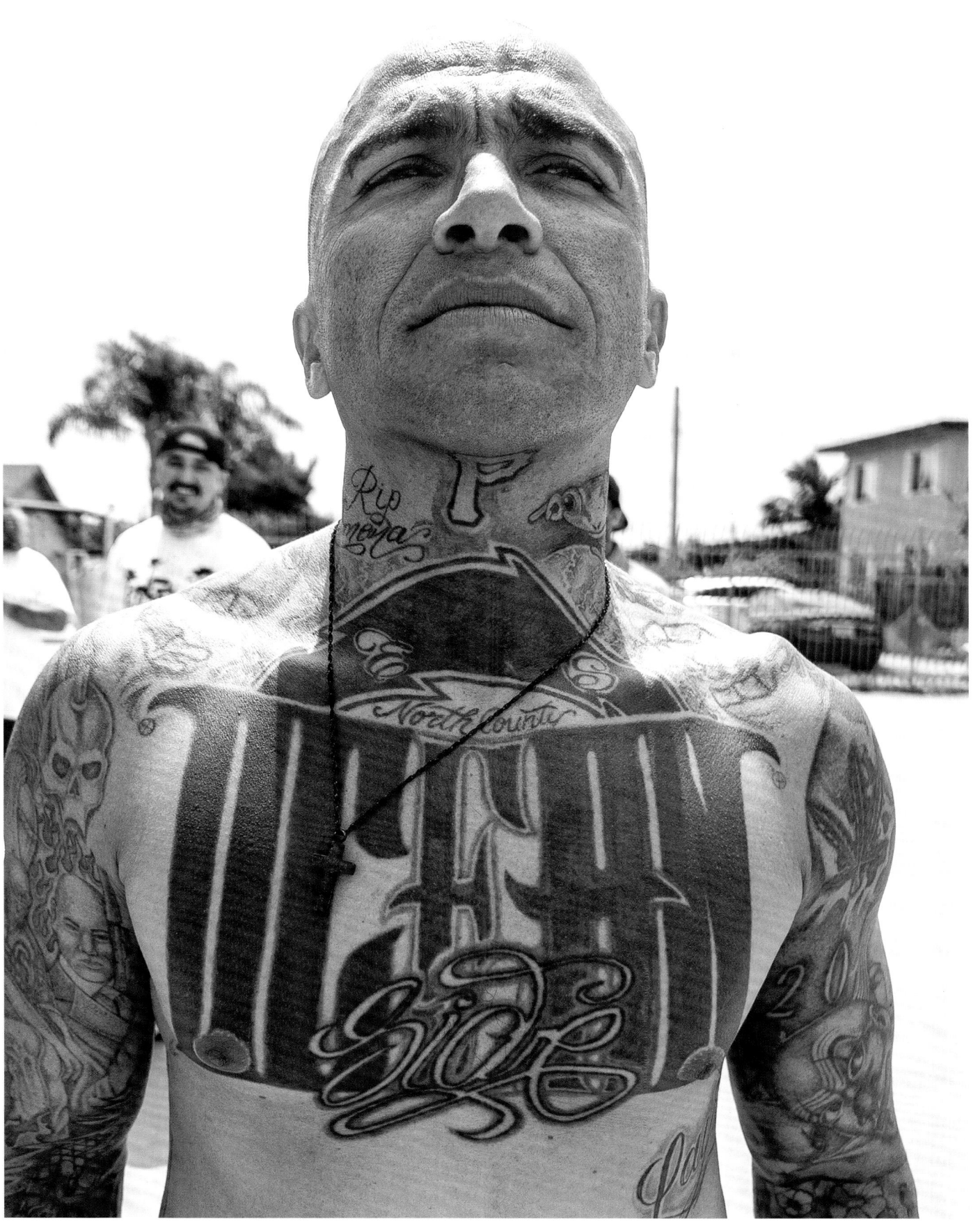

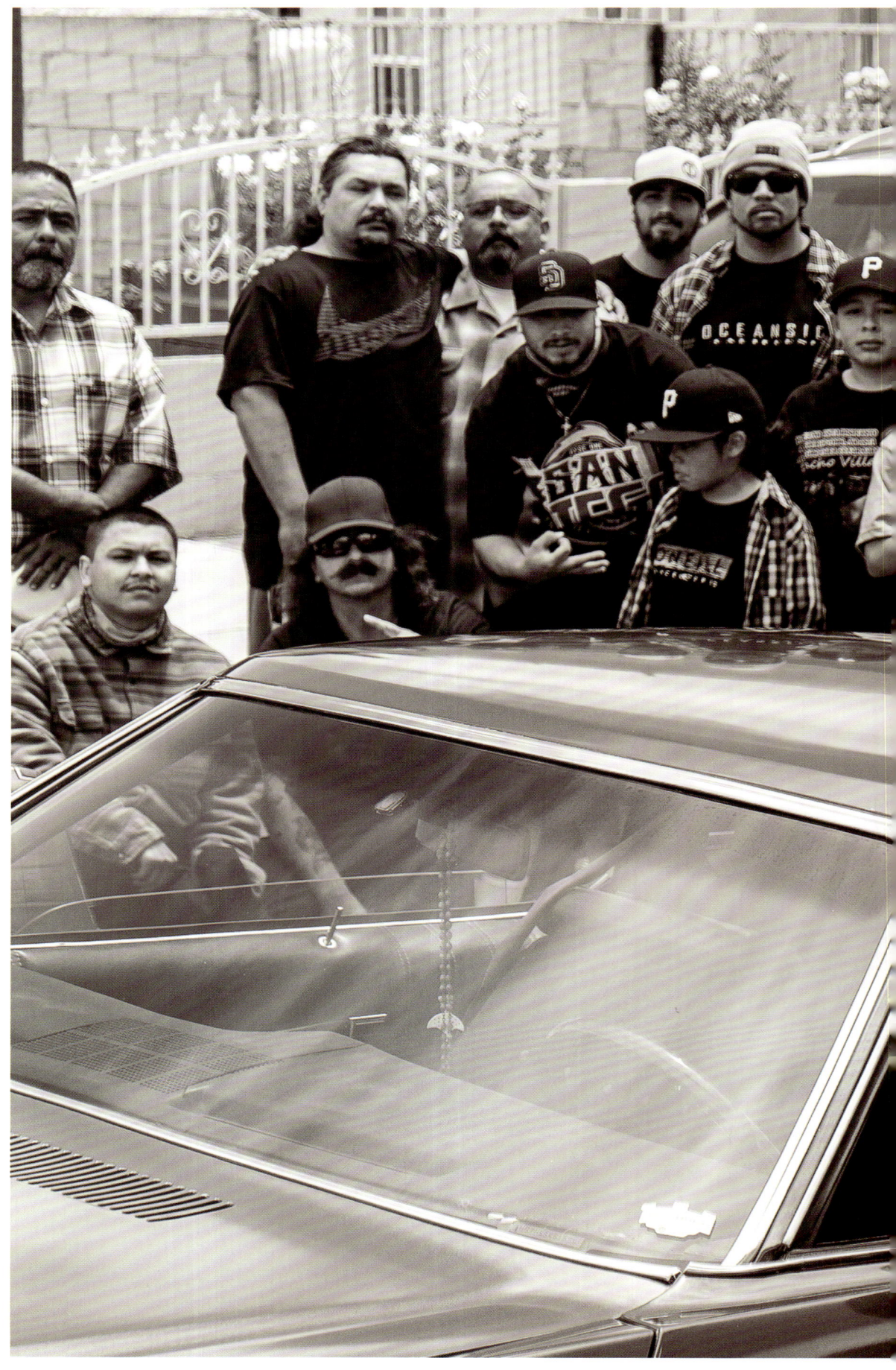

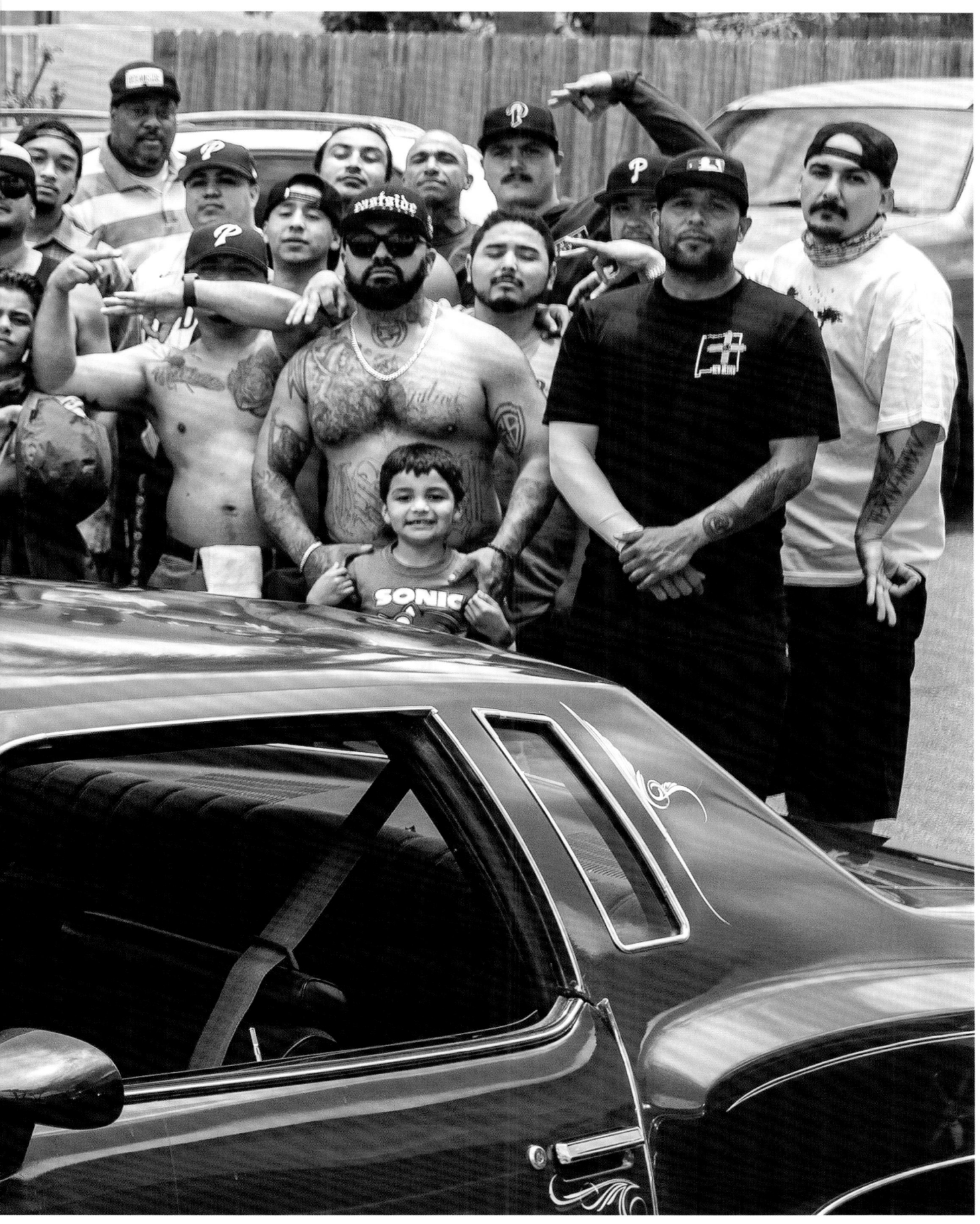

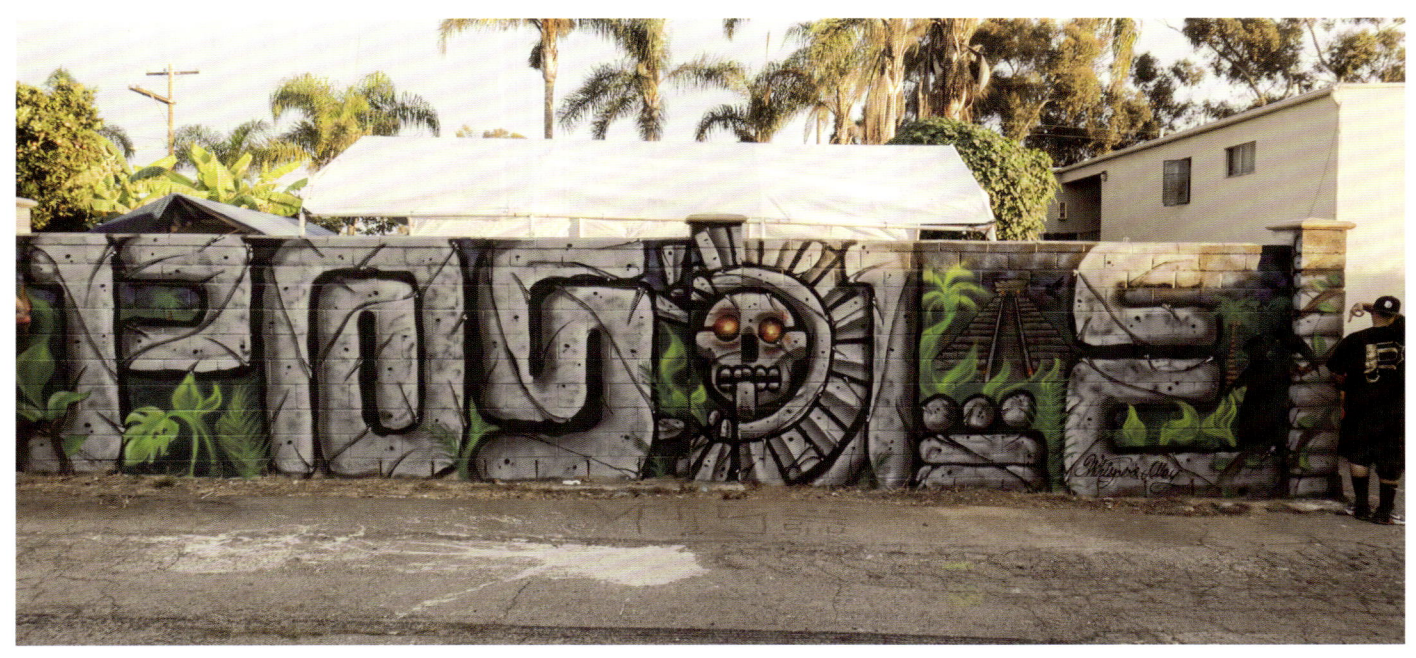

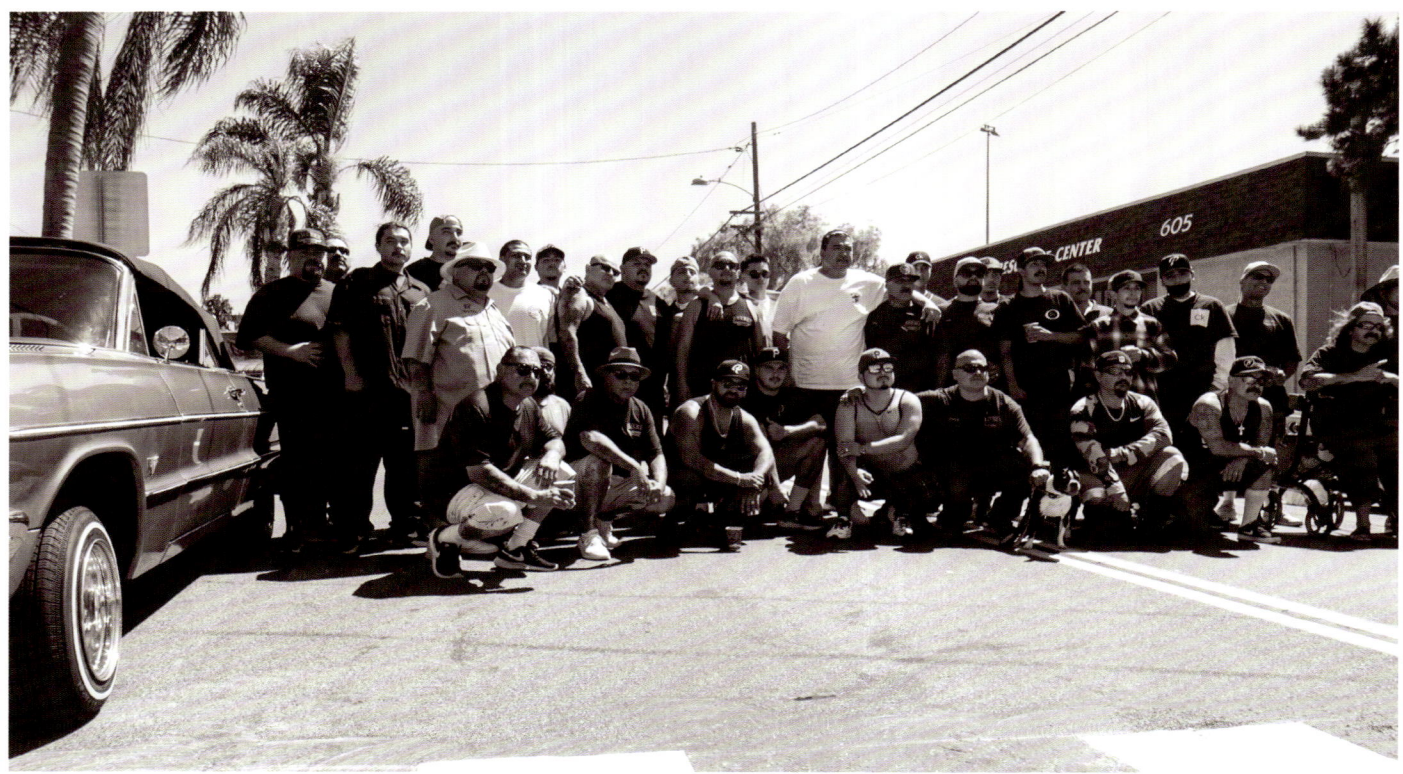

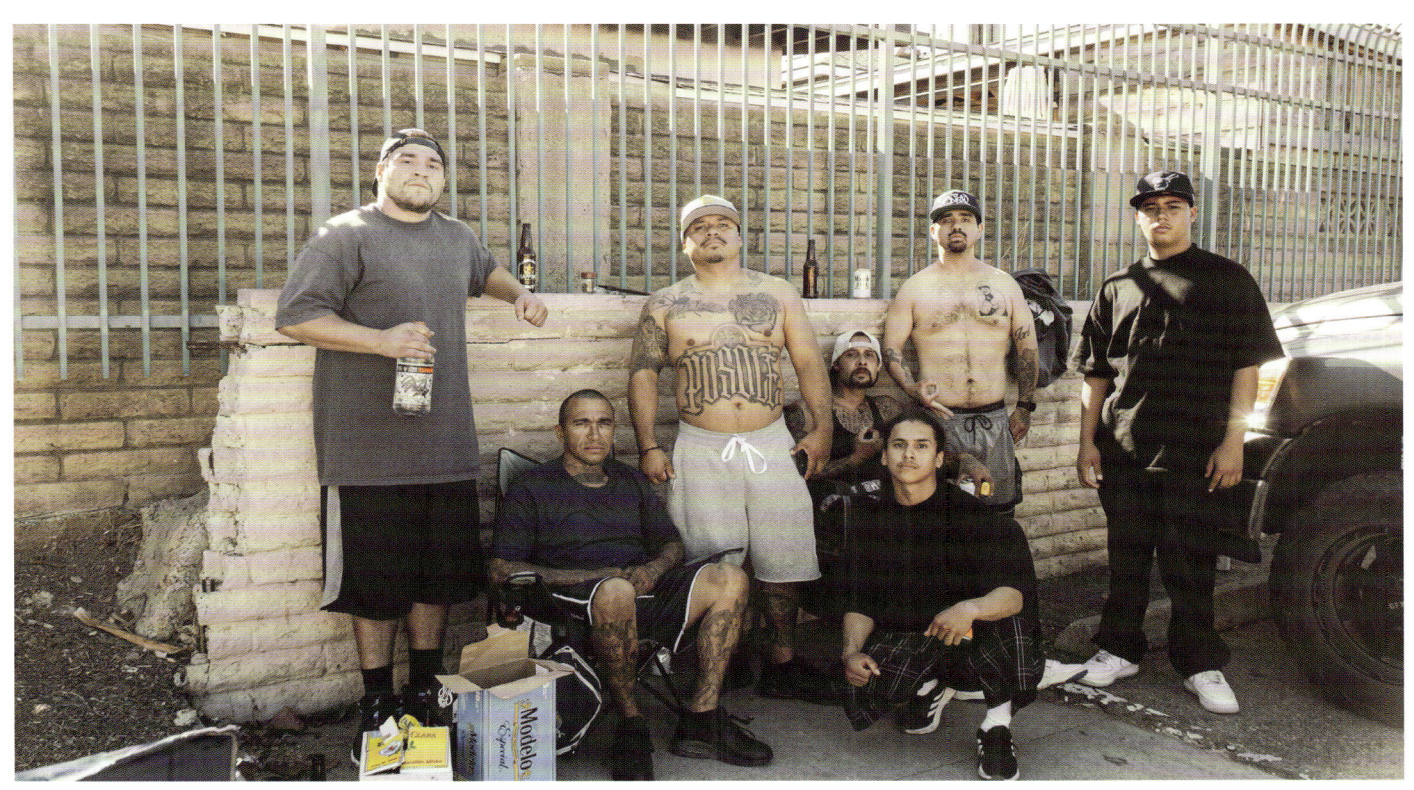

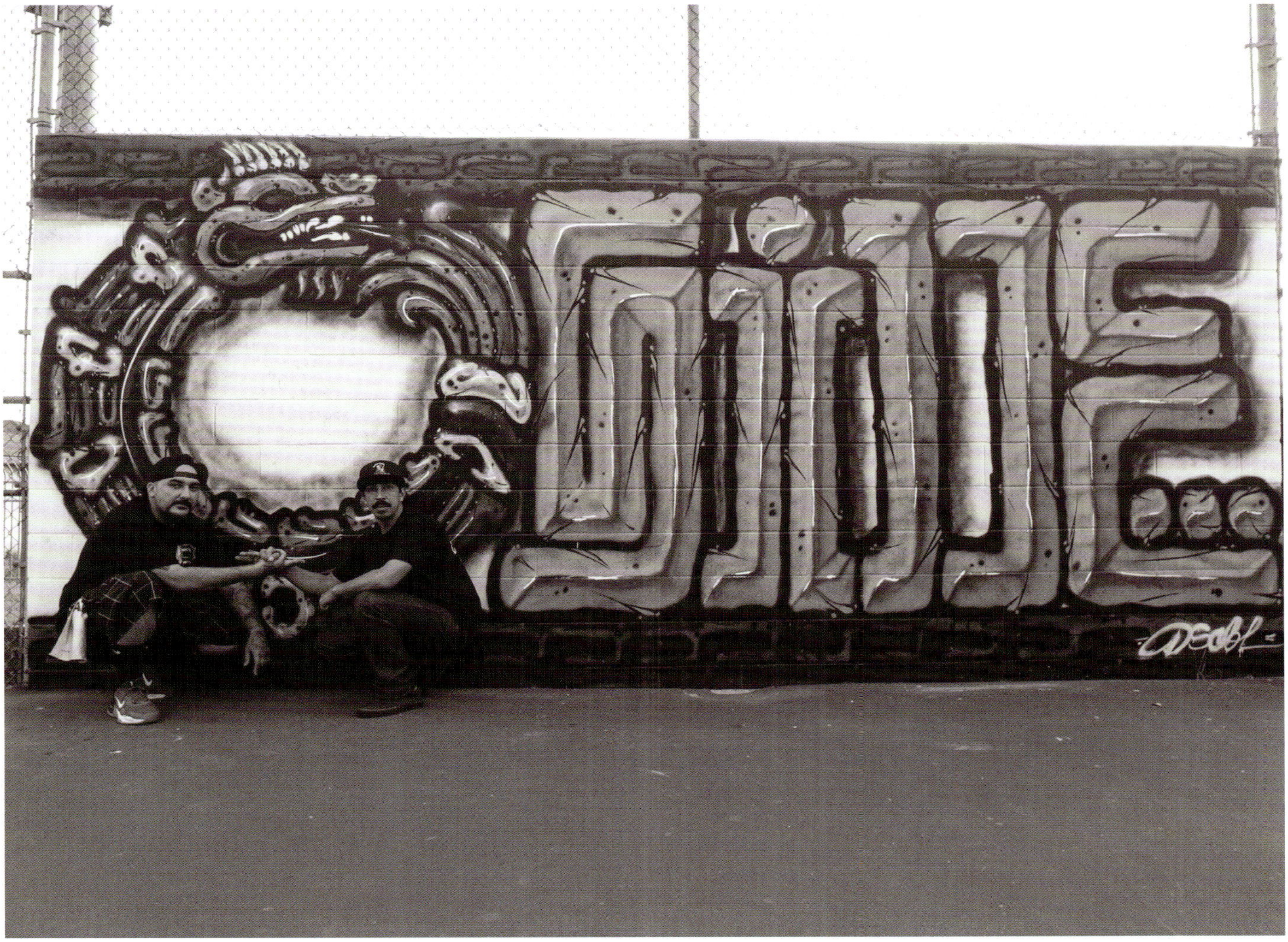

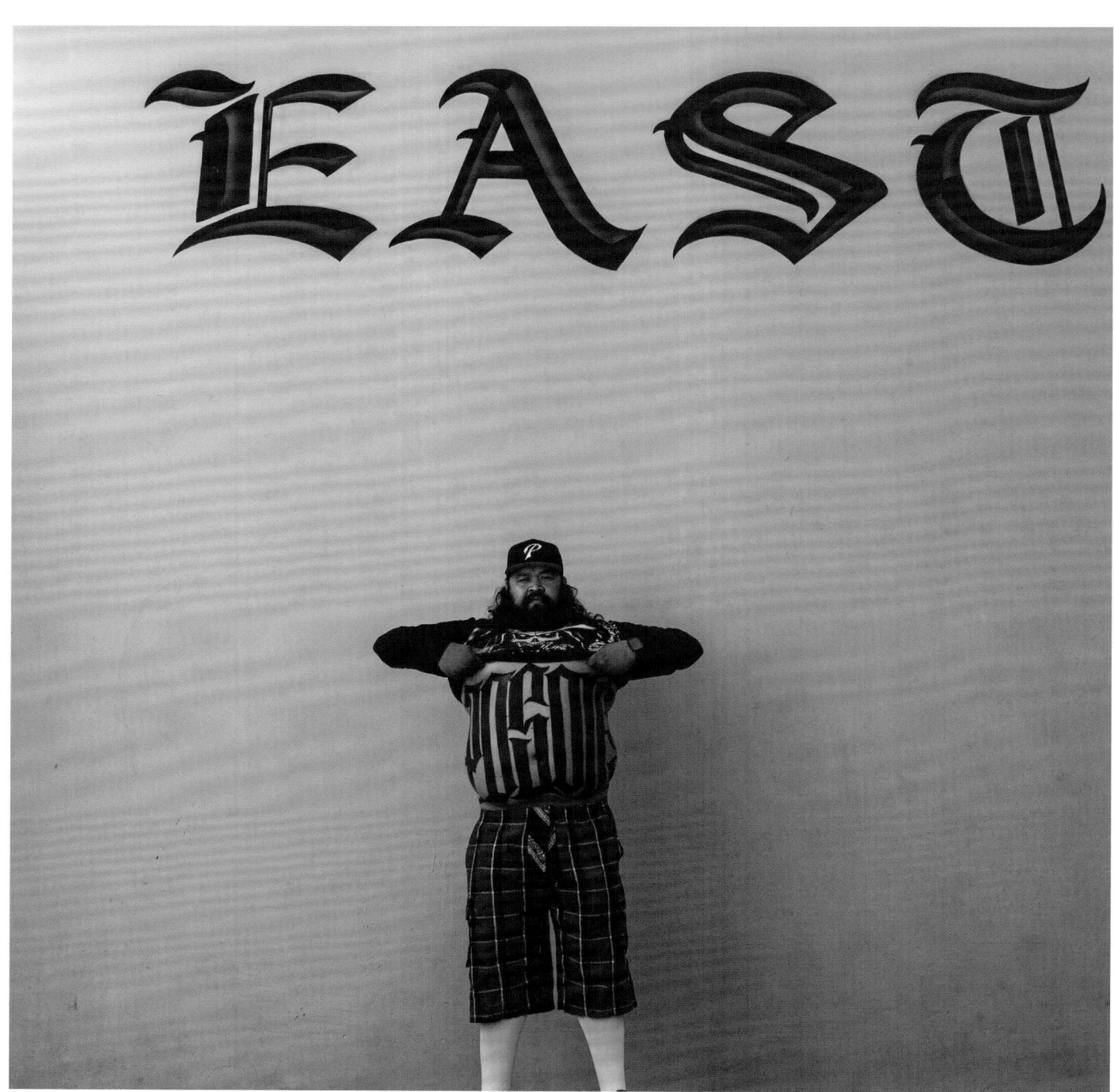

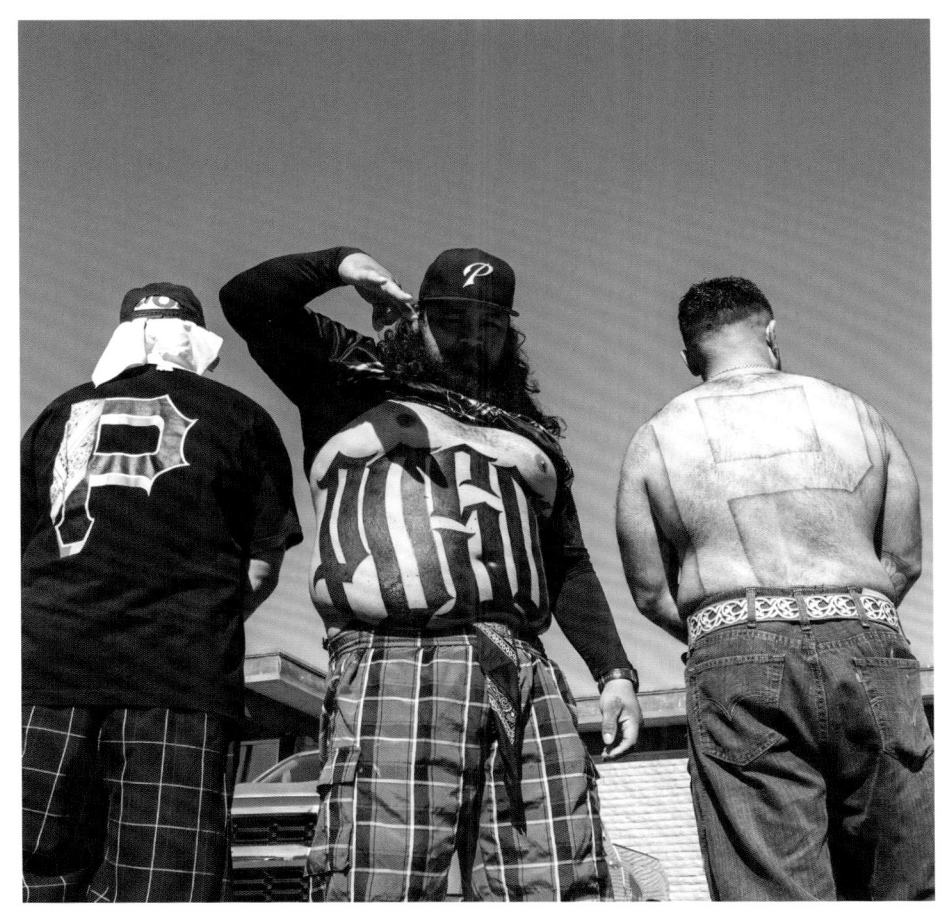

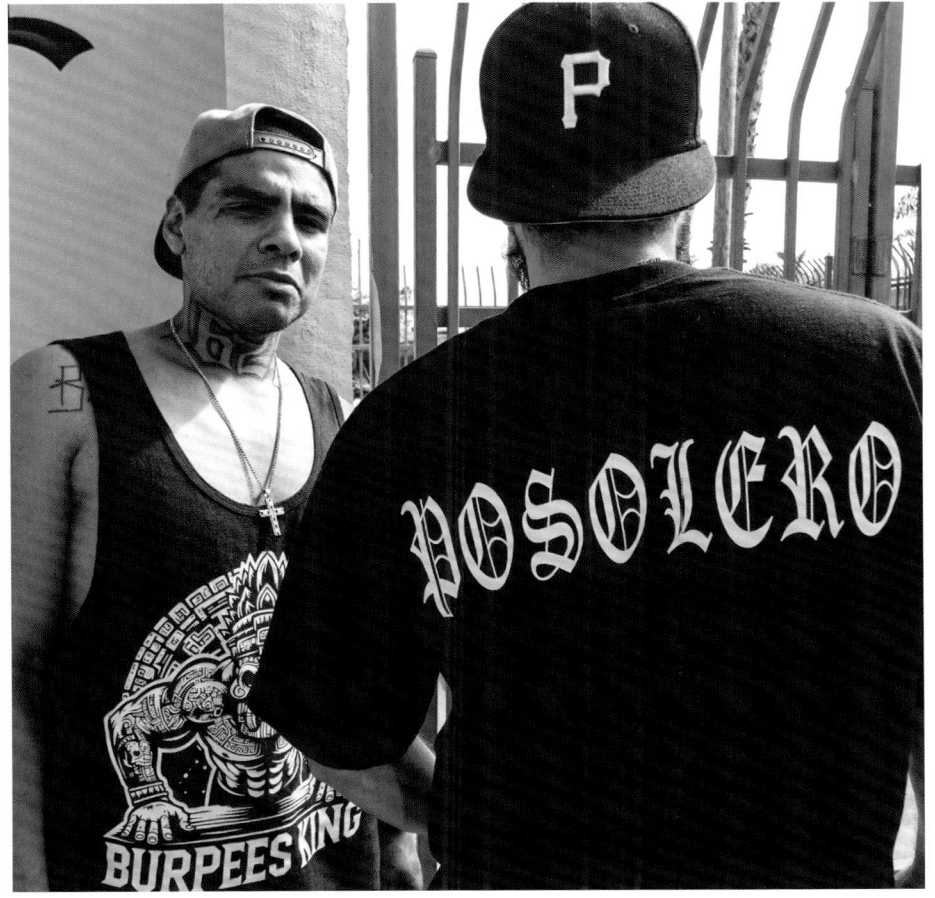

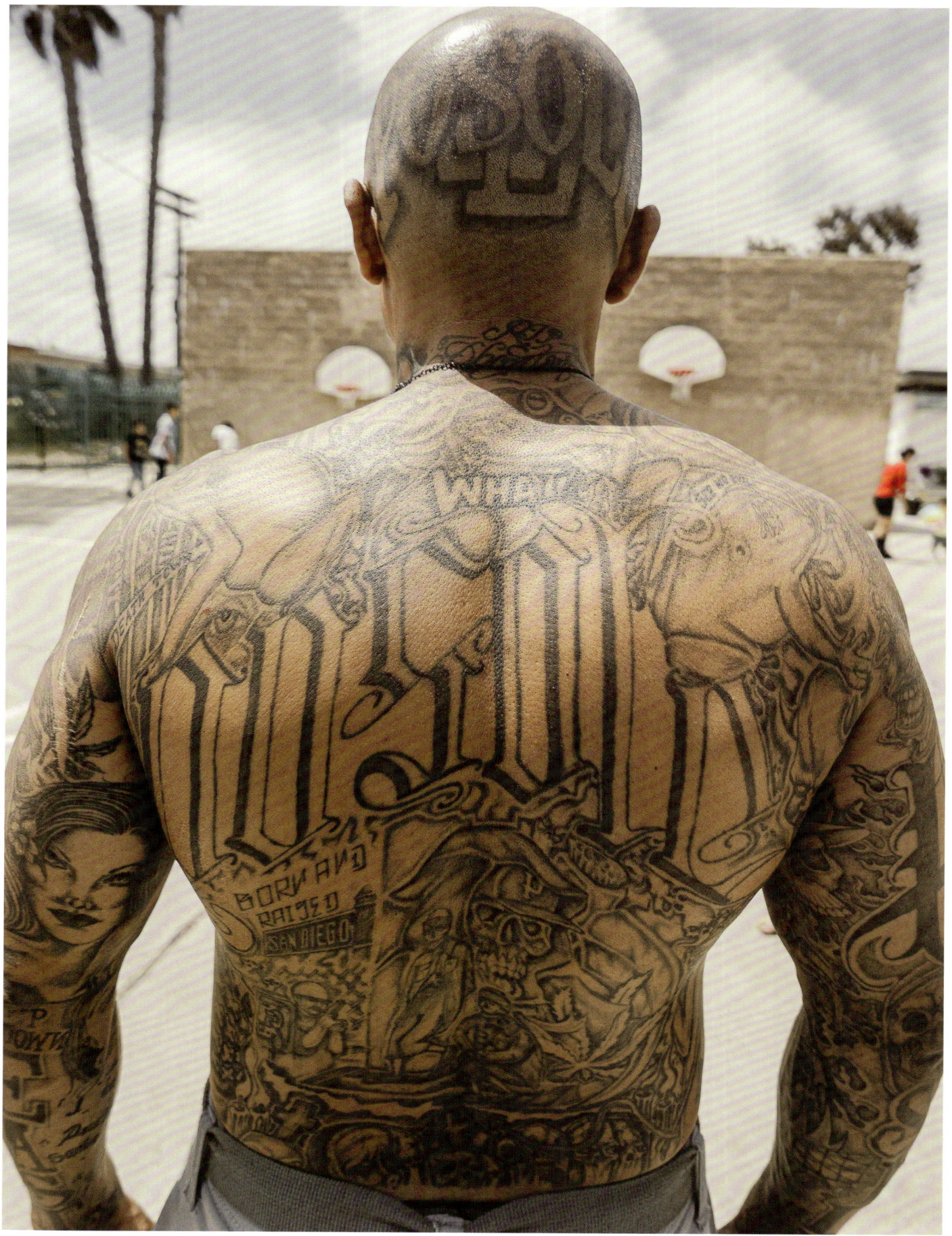

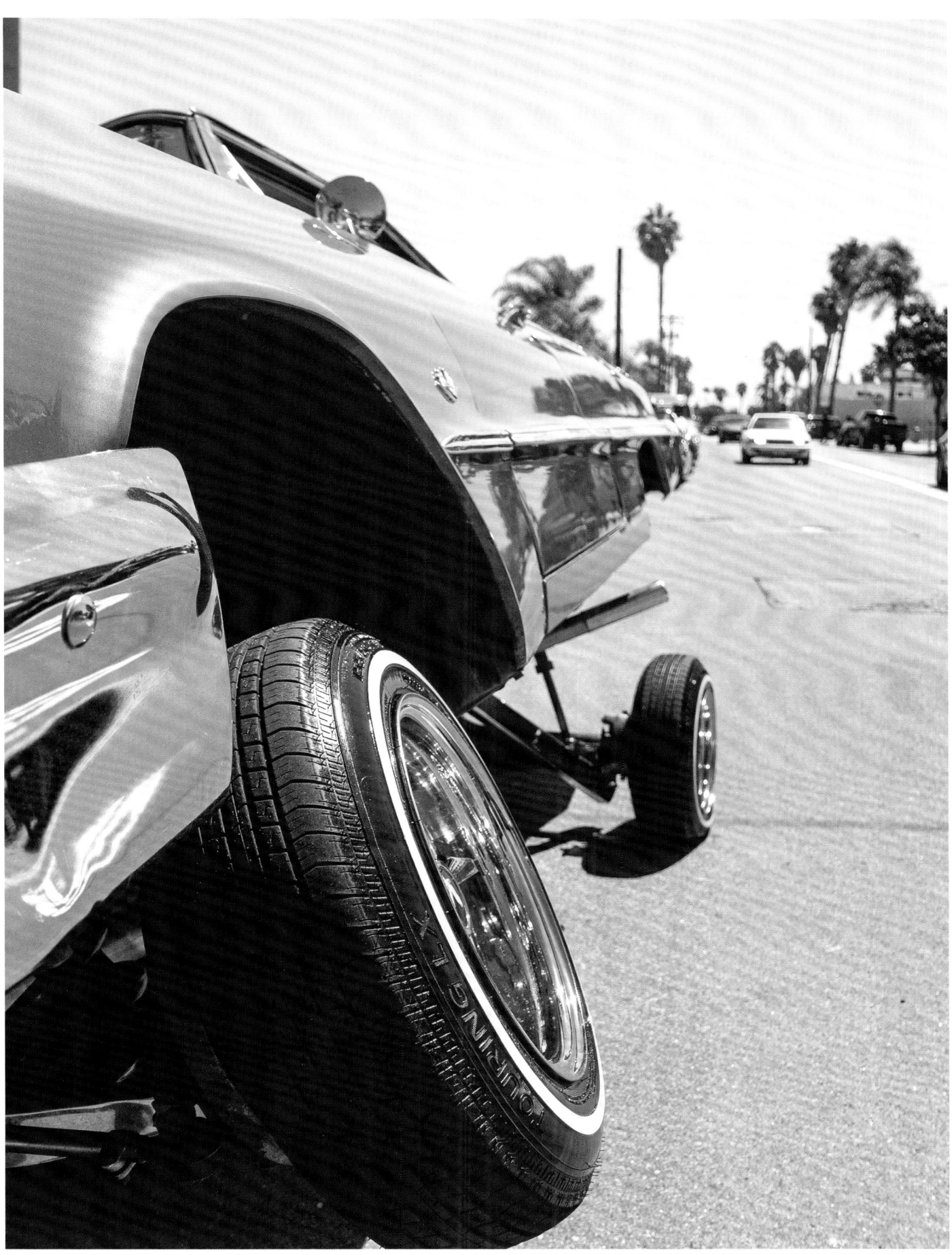

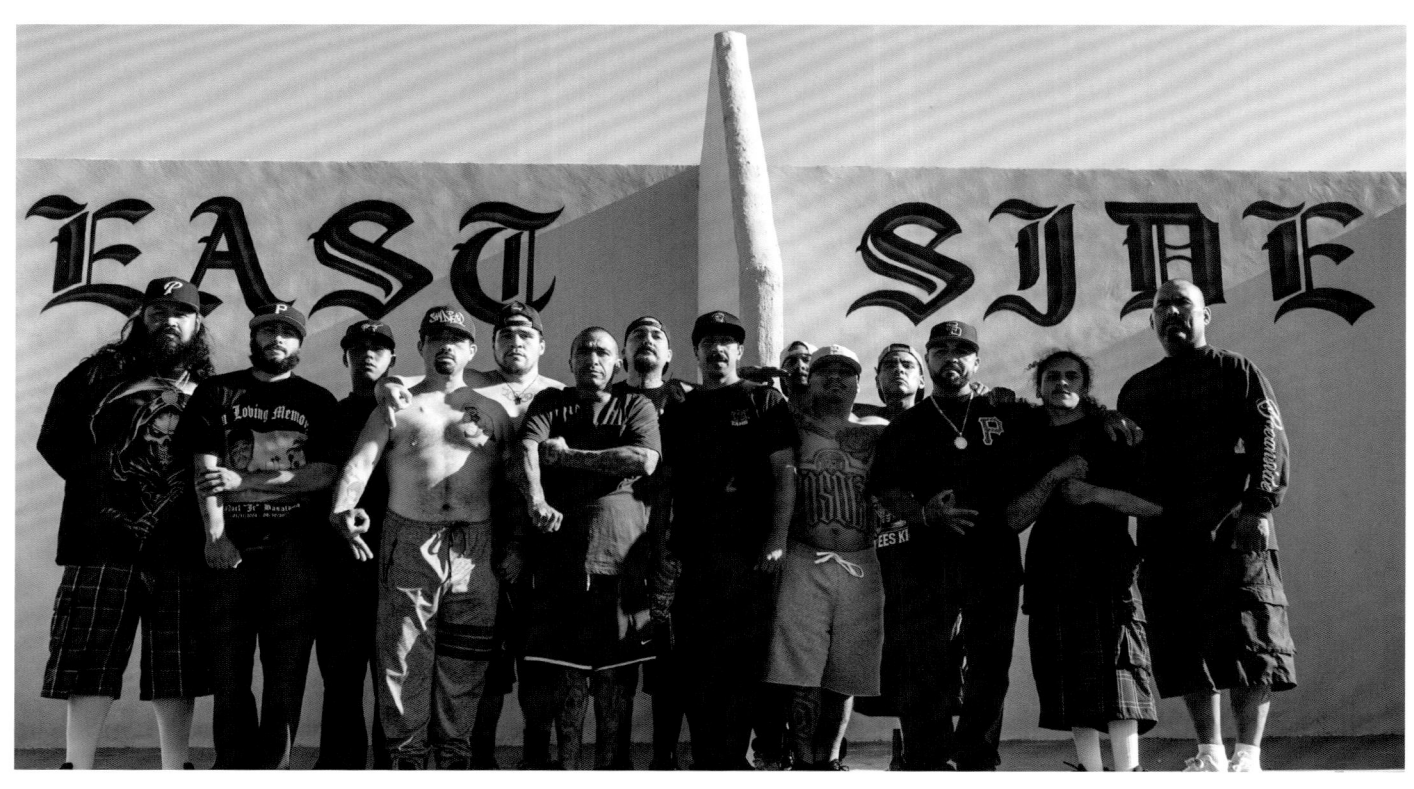

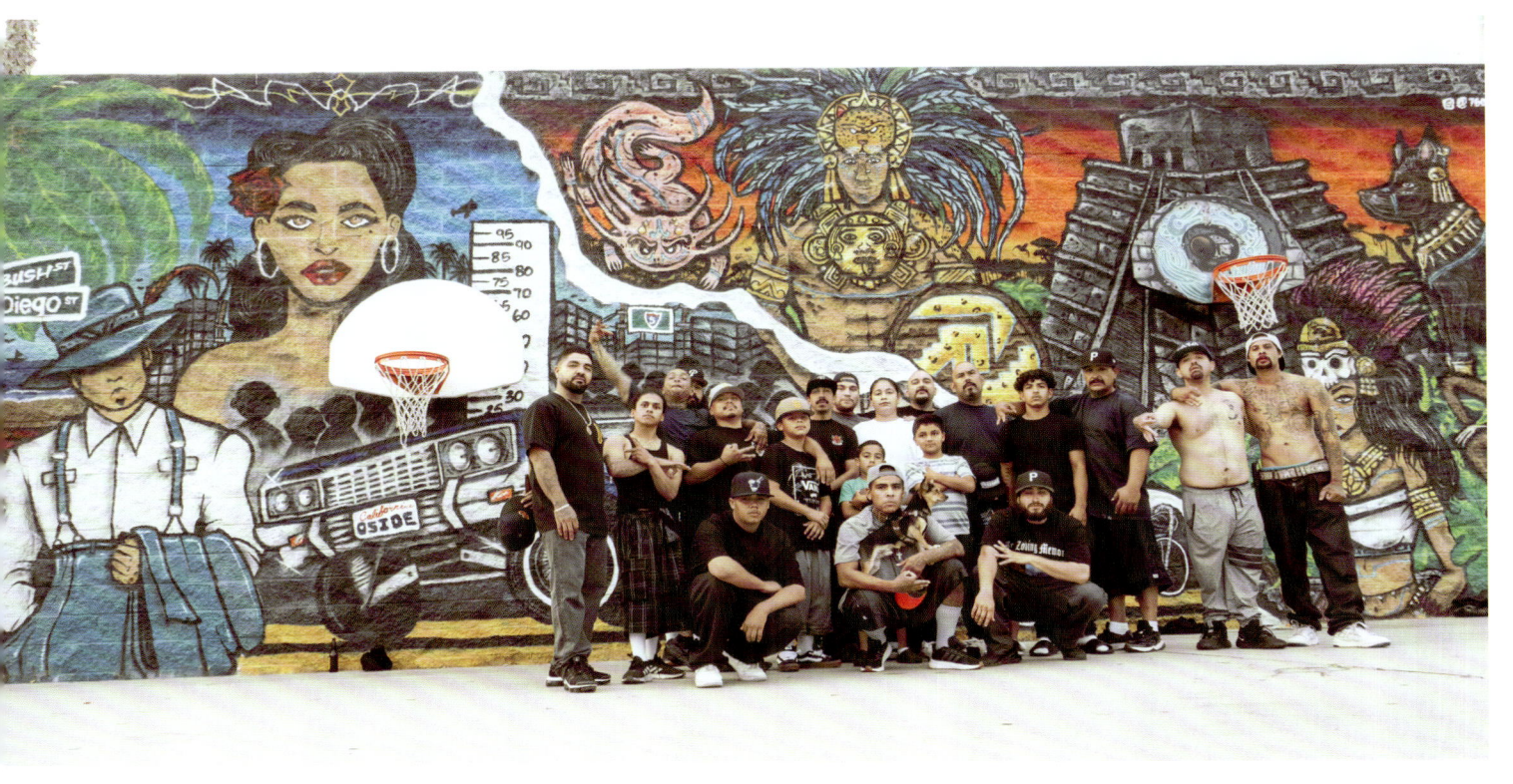

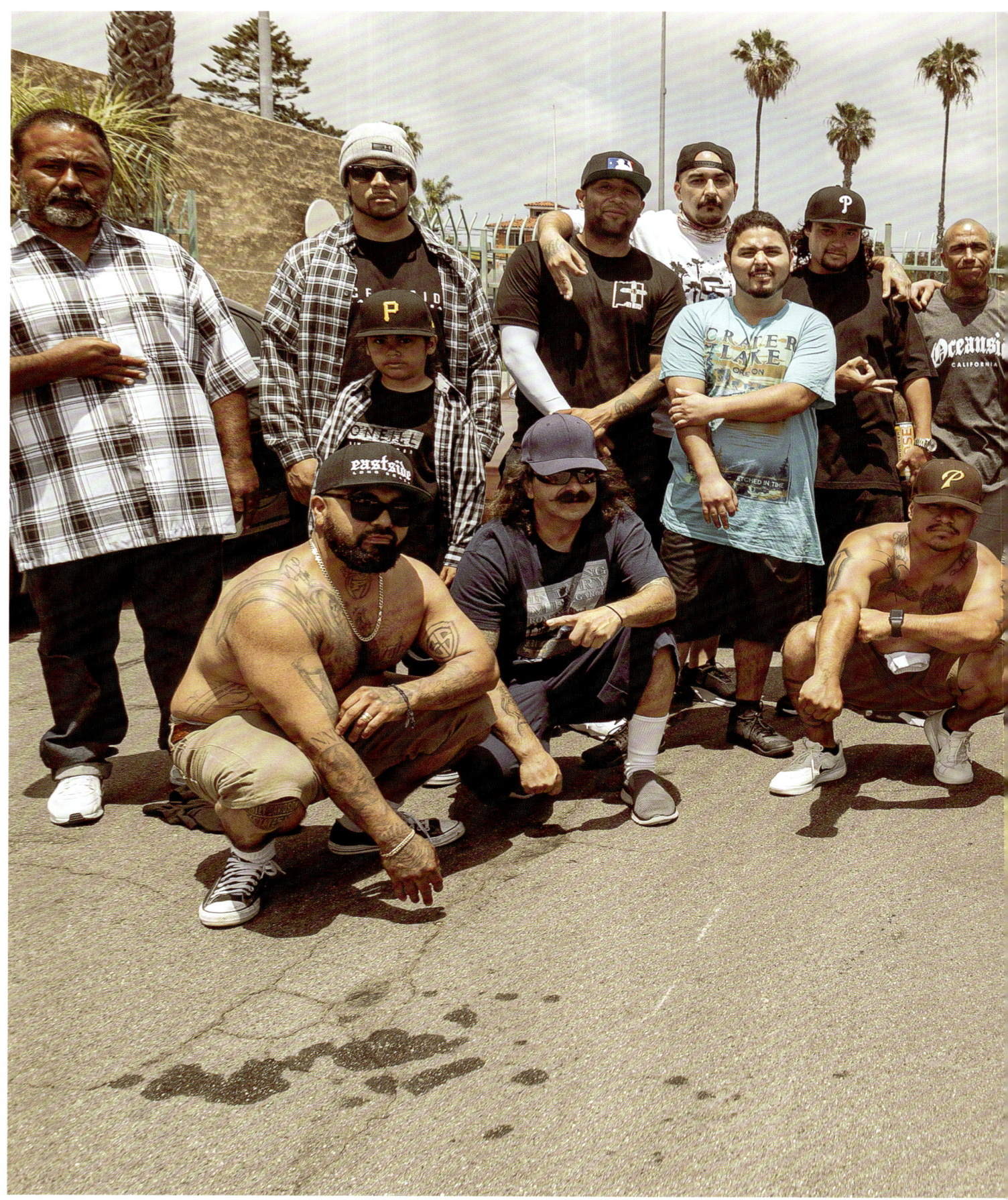

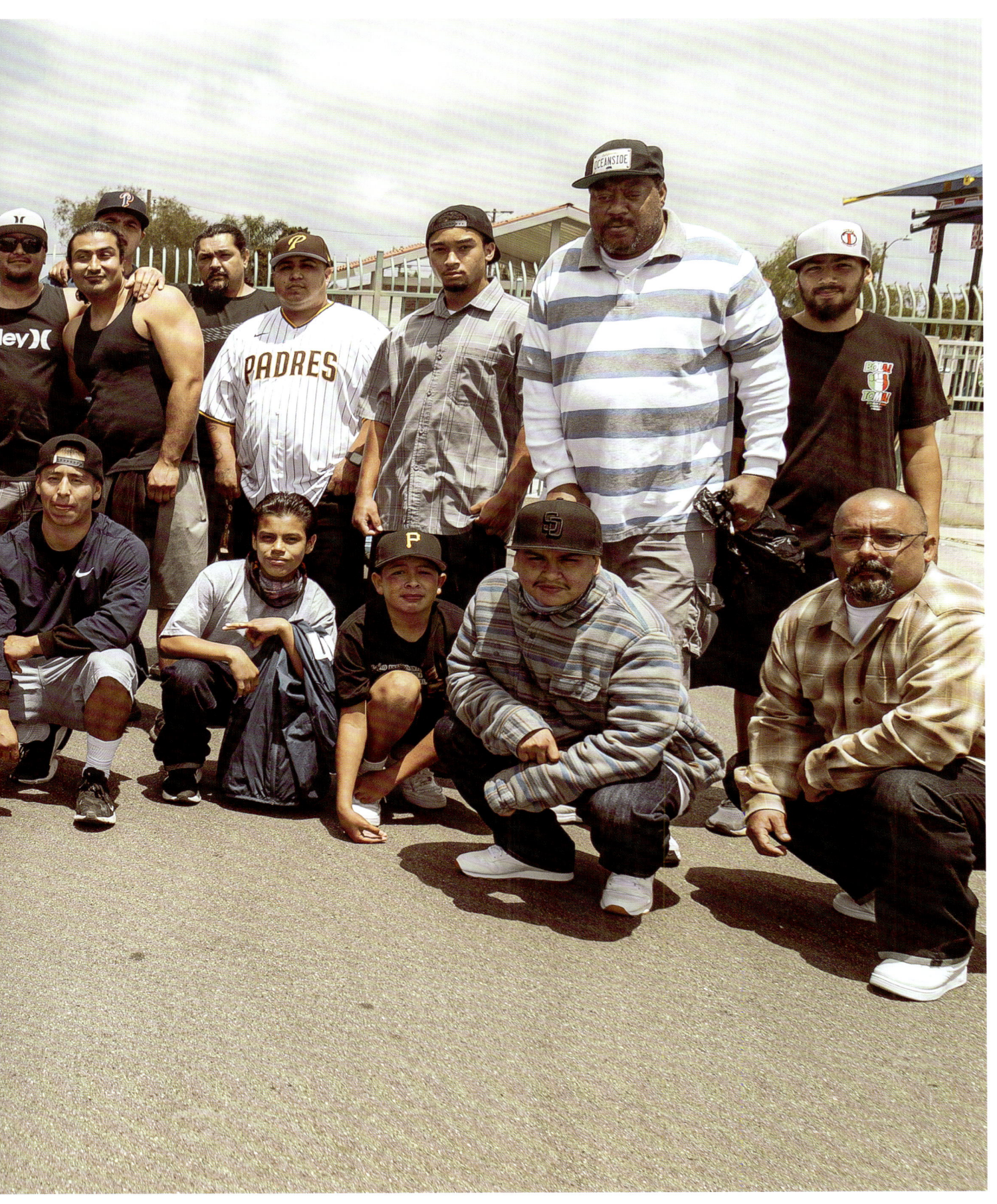

141

BEACH

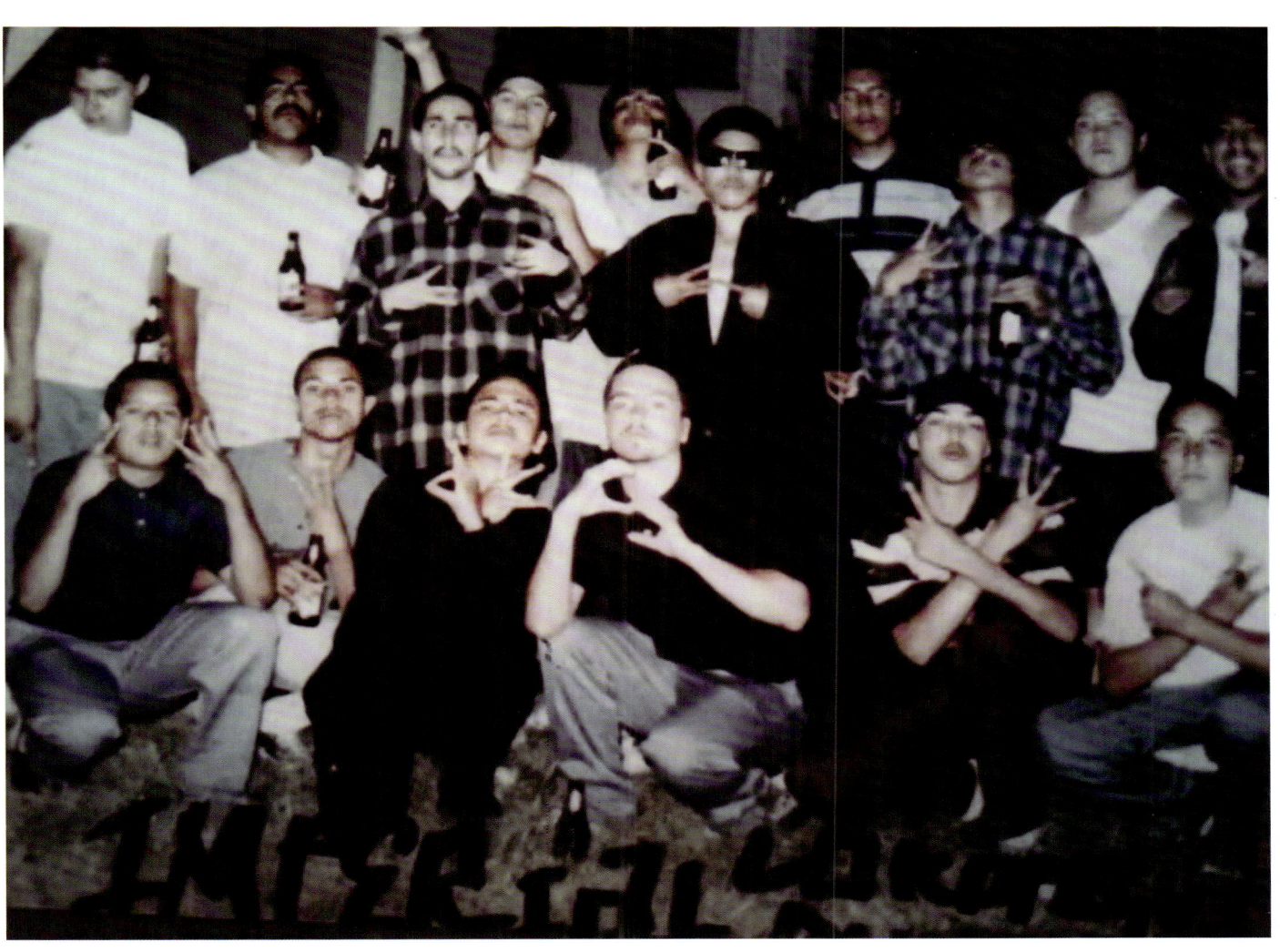

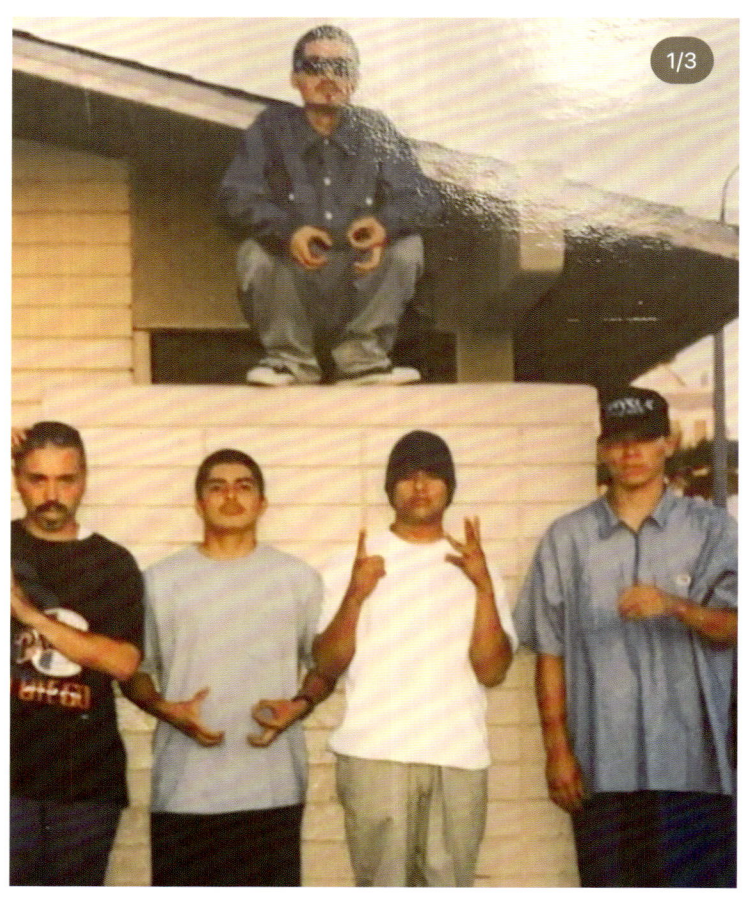

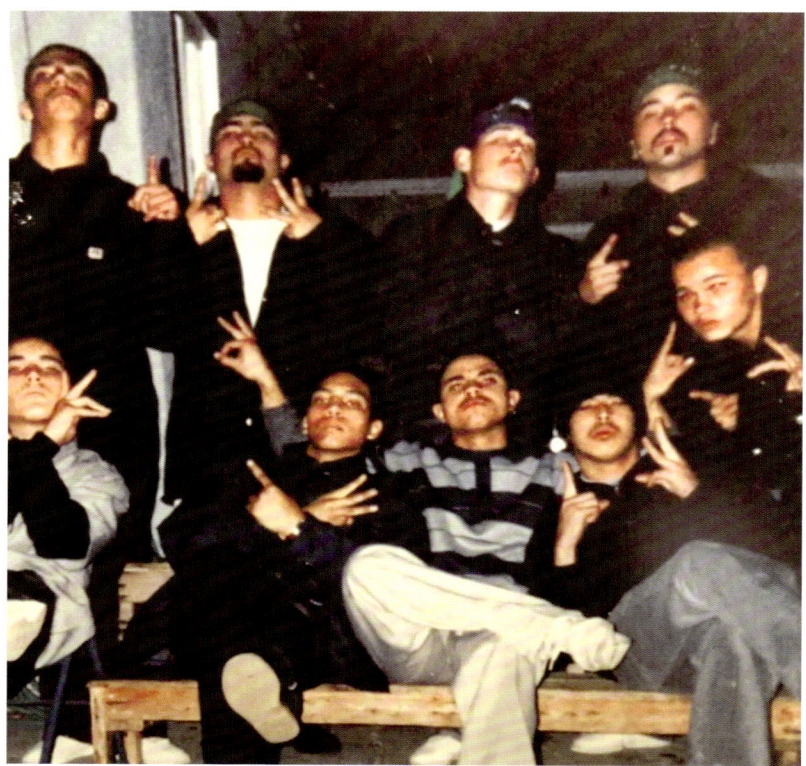

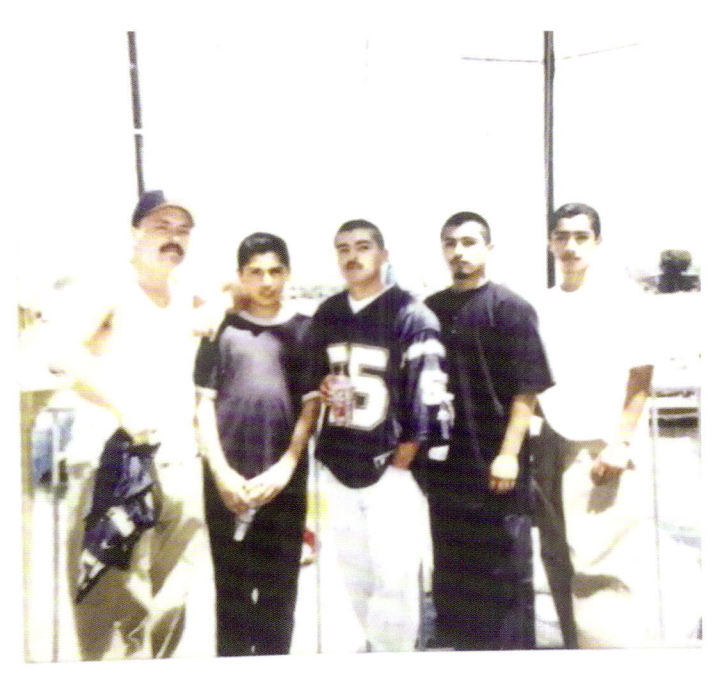

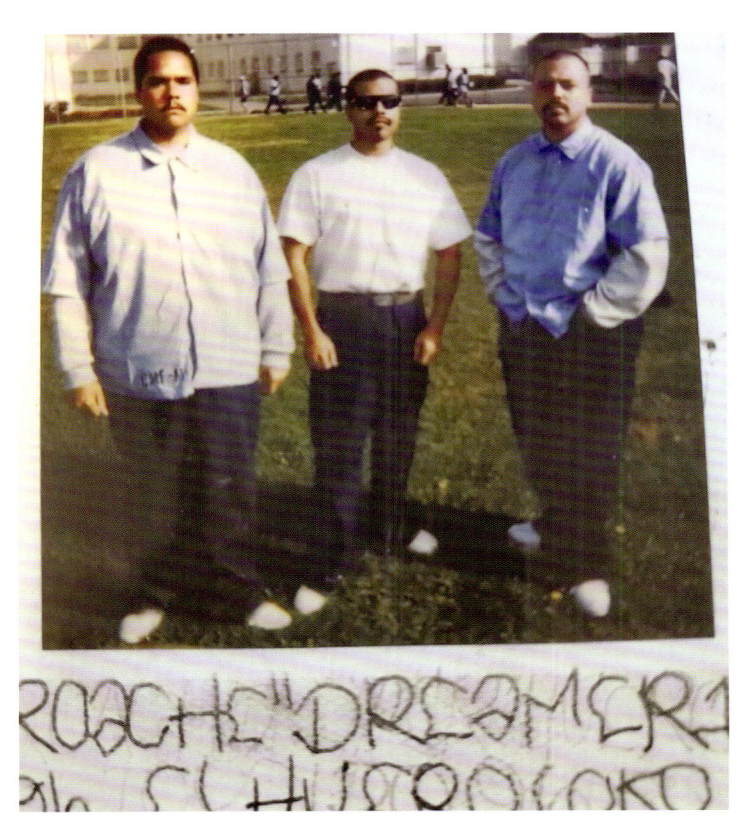

MARKET

STREET

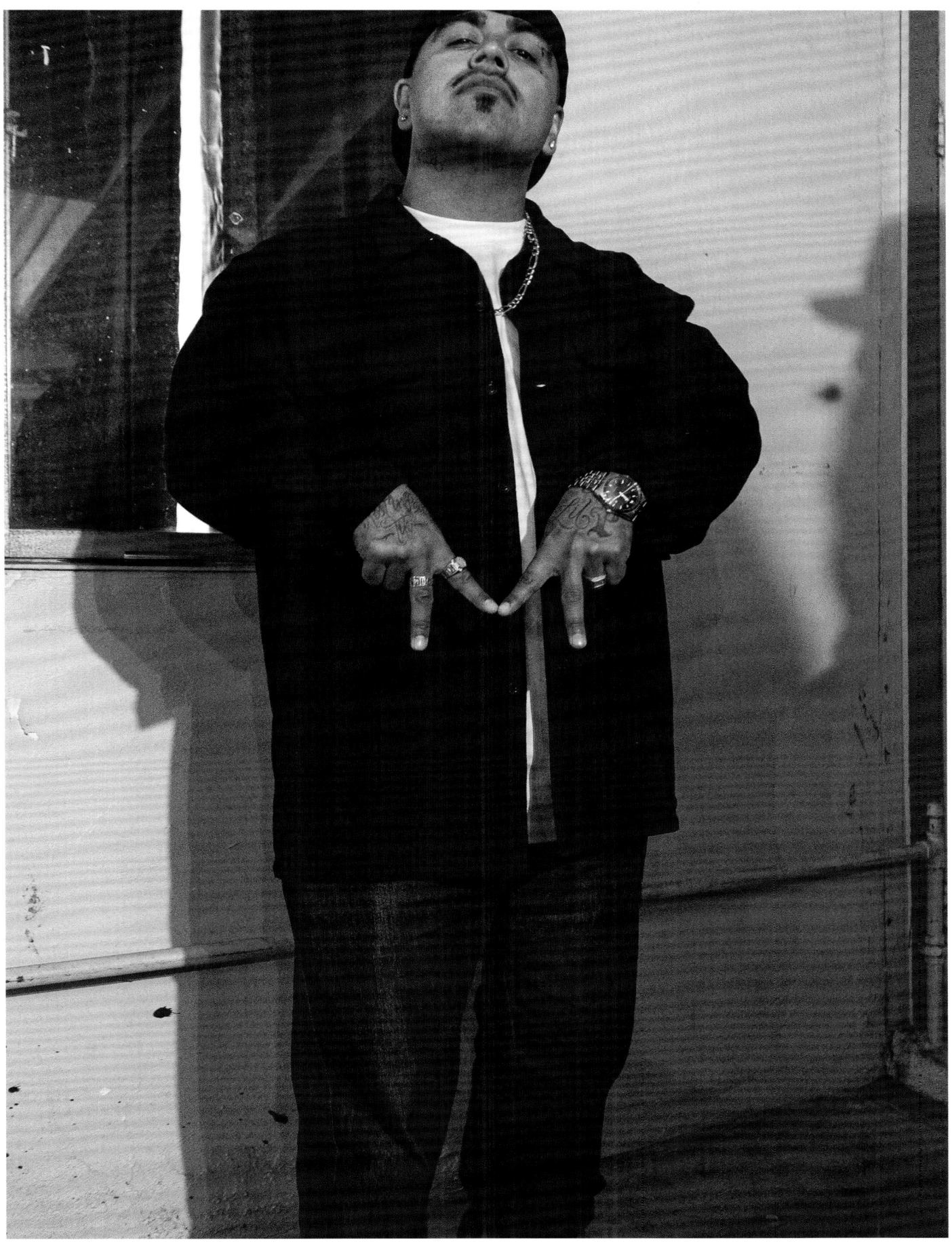

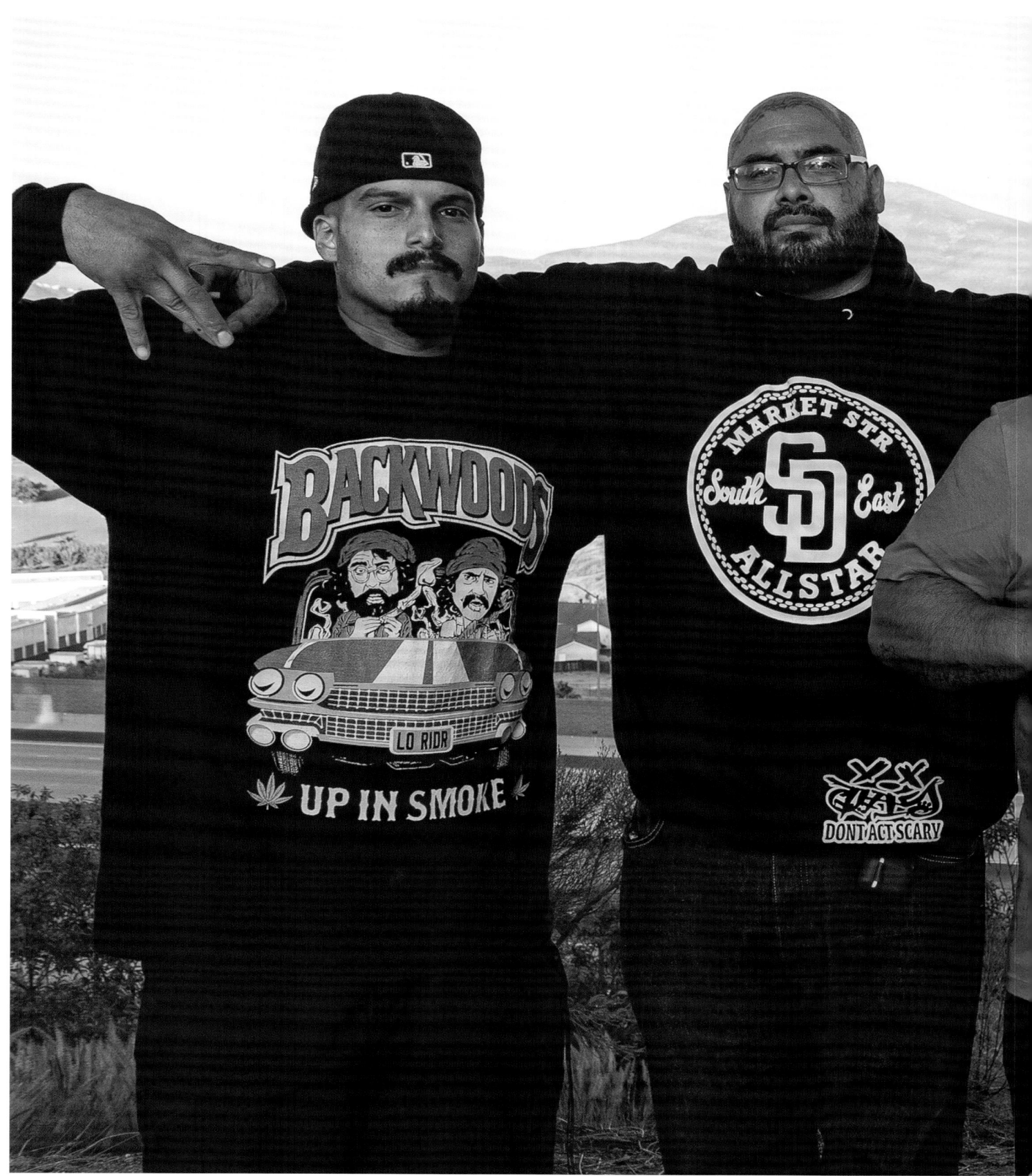

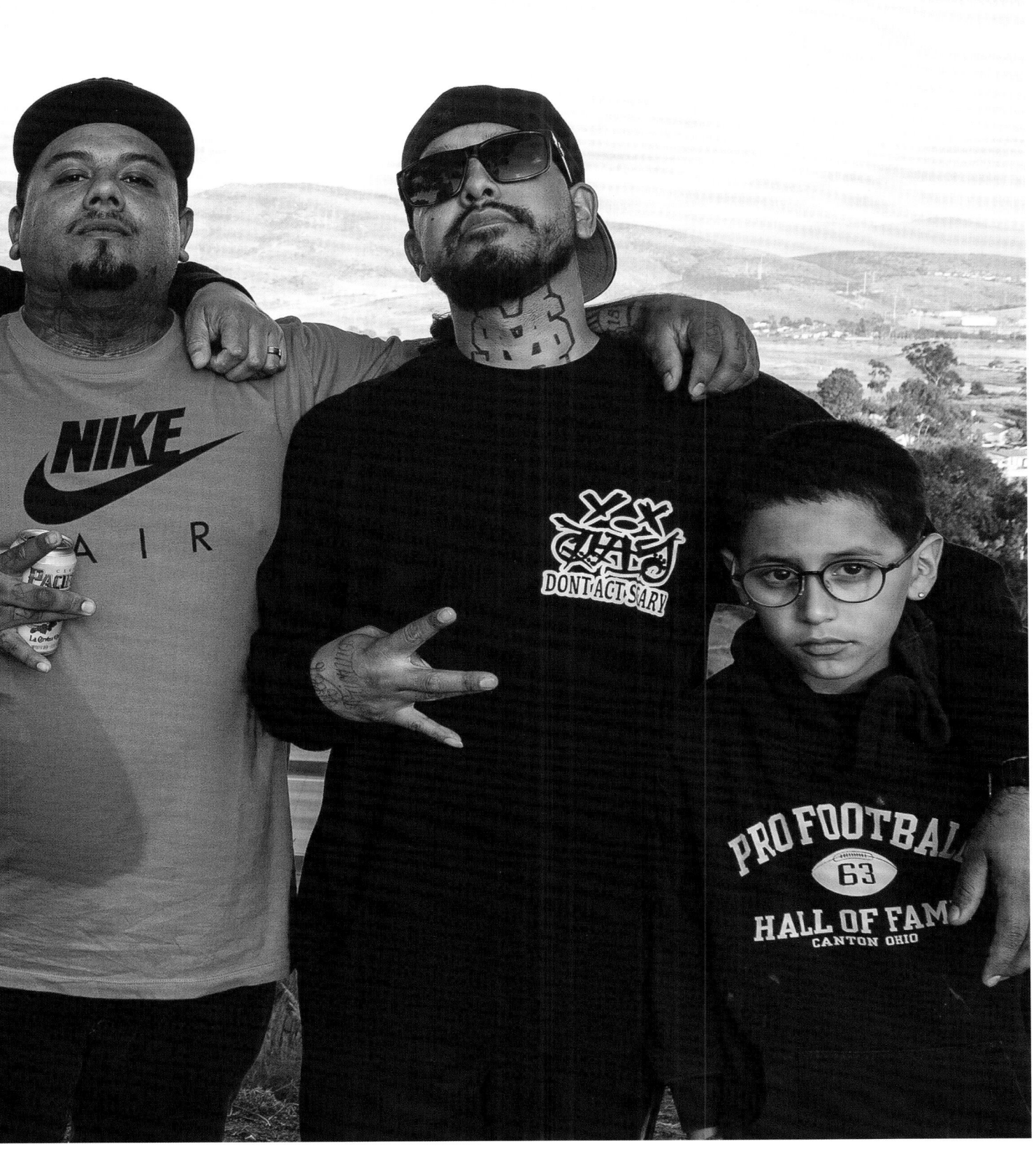

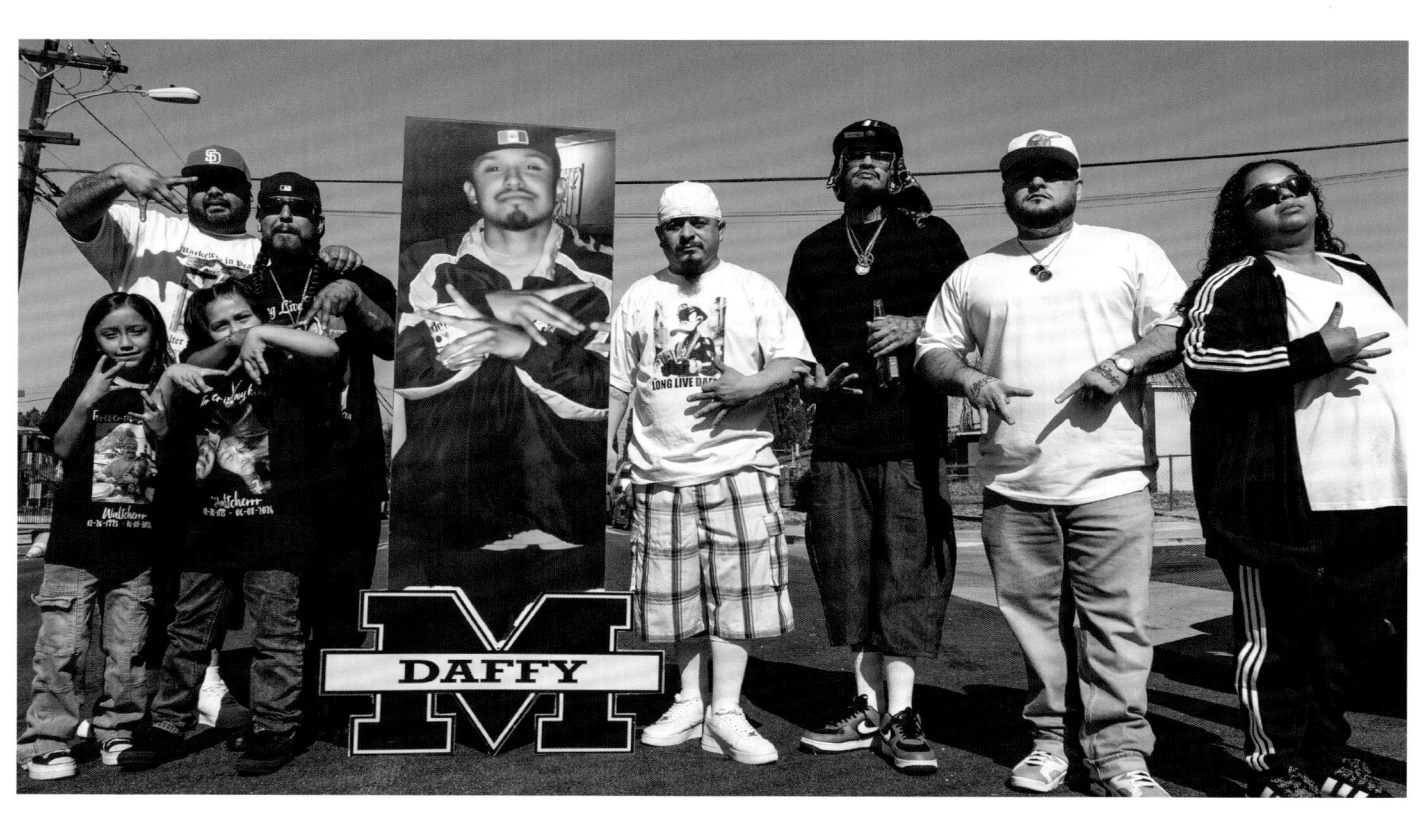

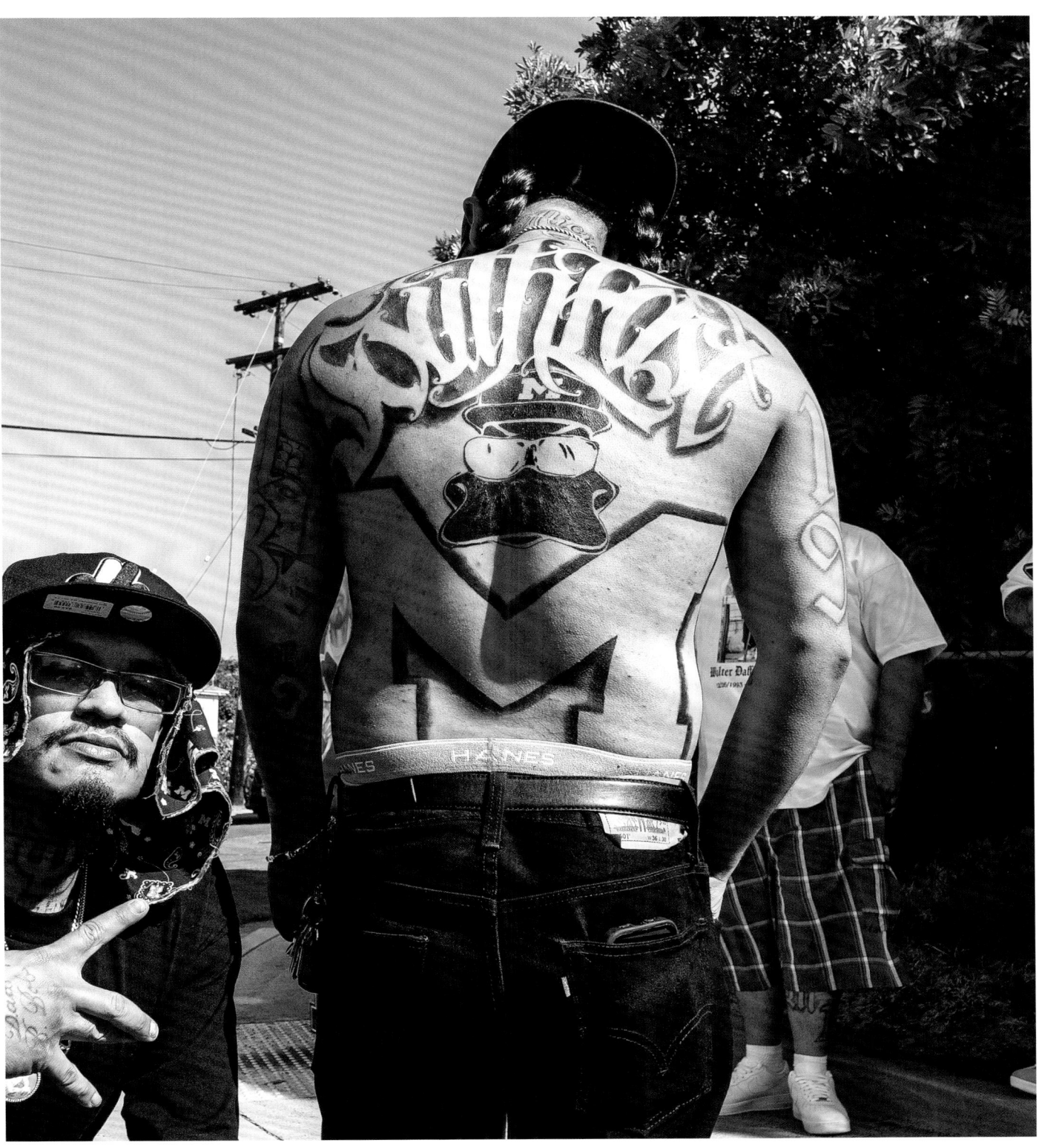

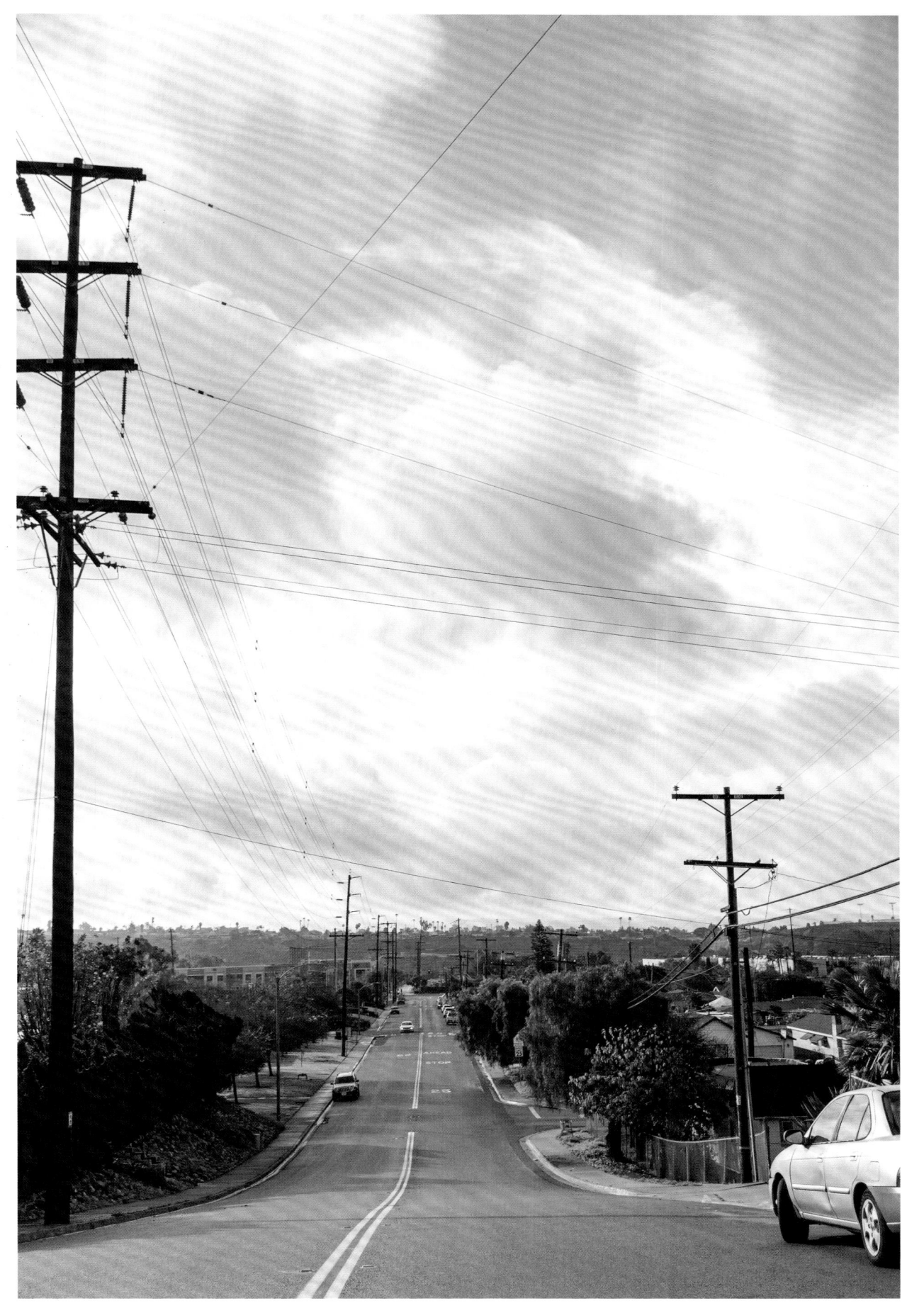

Like I tell everybody, I'm always gonna be from Otay, I grew up here all my life, I never forget where I come from. I'm here every day! You never forget that, cause that's what makes you the person you are today. All my uncles are from Otay, I used to look up to my uncles when I'd go to my grandma's house. I used to keep watch while they were slamming heroin, I was like fuckin' nine, eight years old.

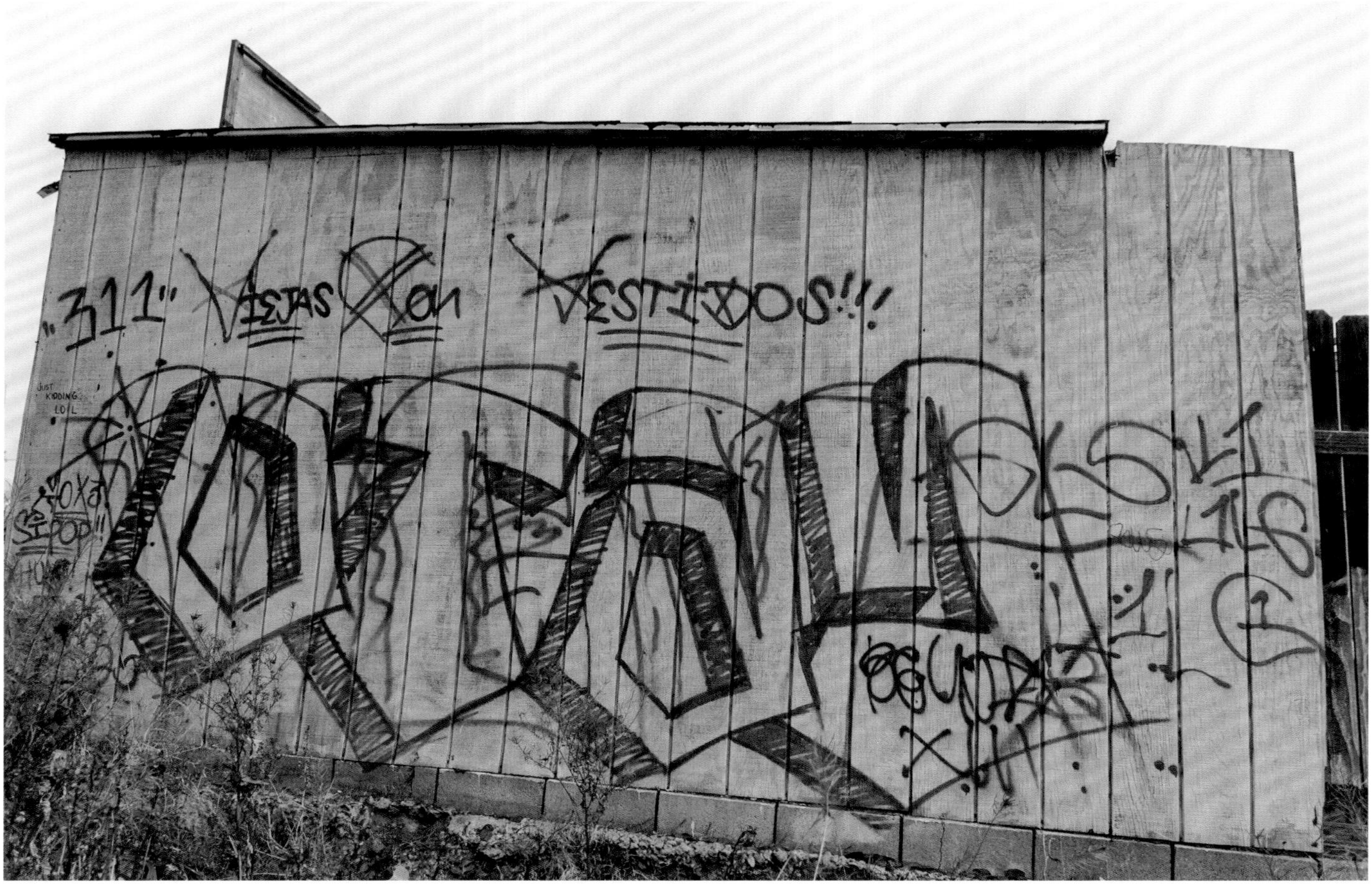

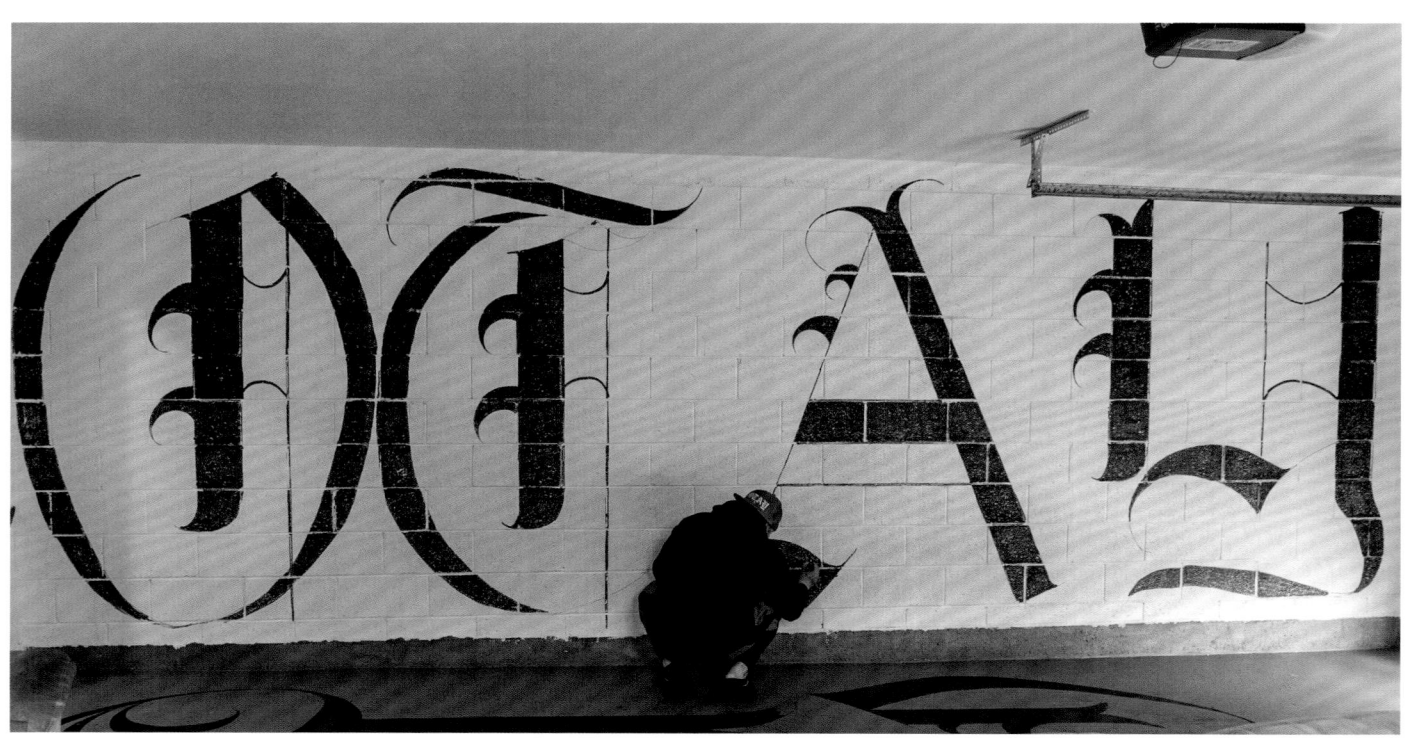

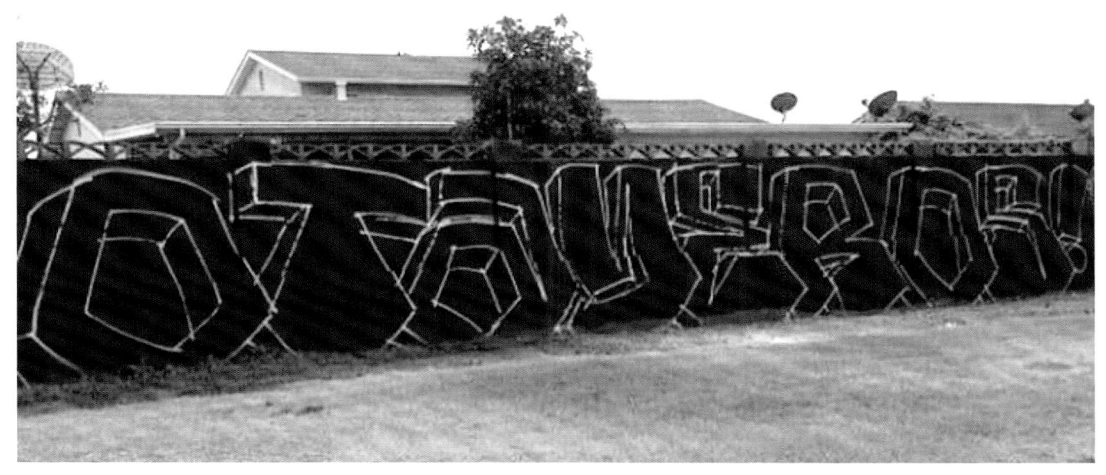

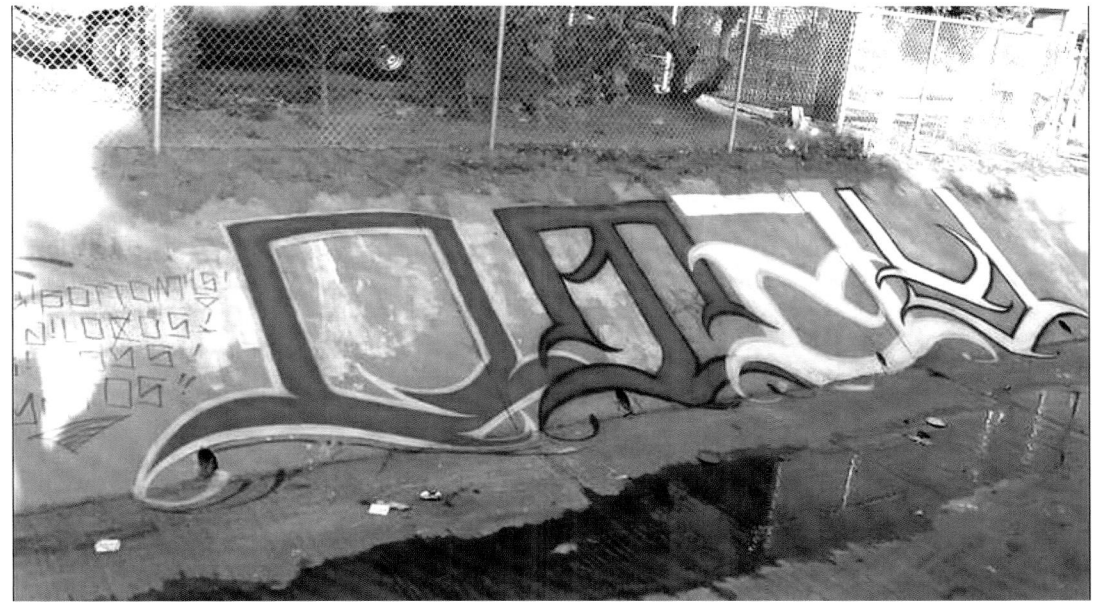

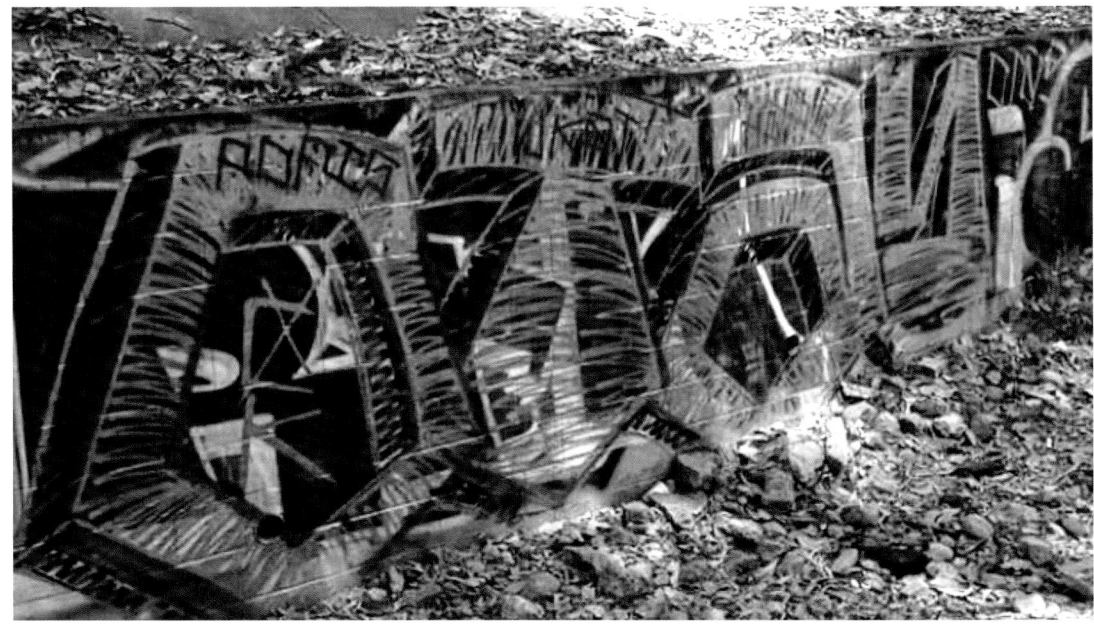

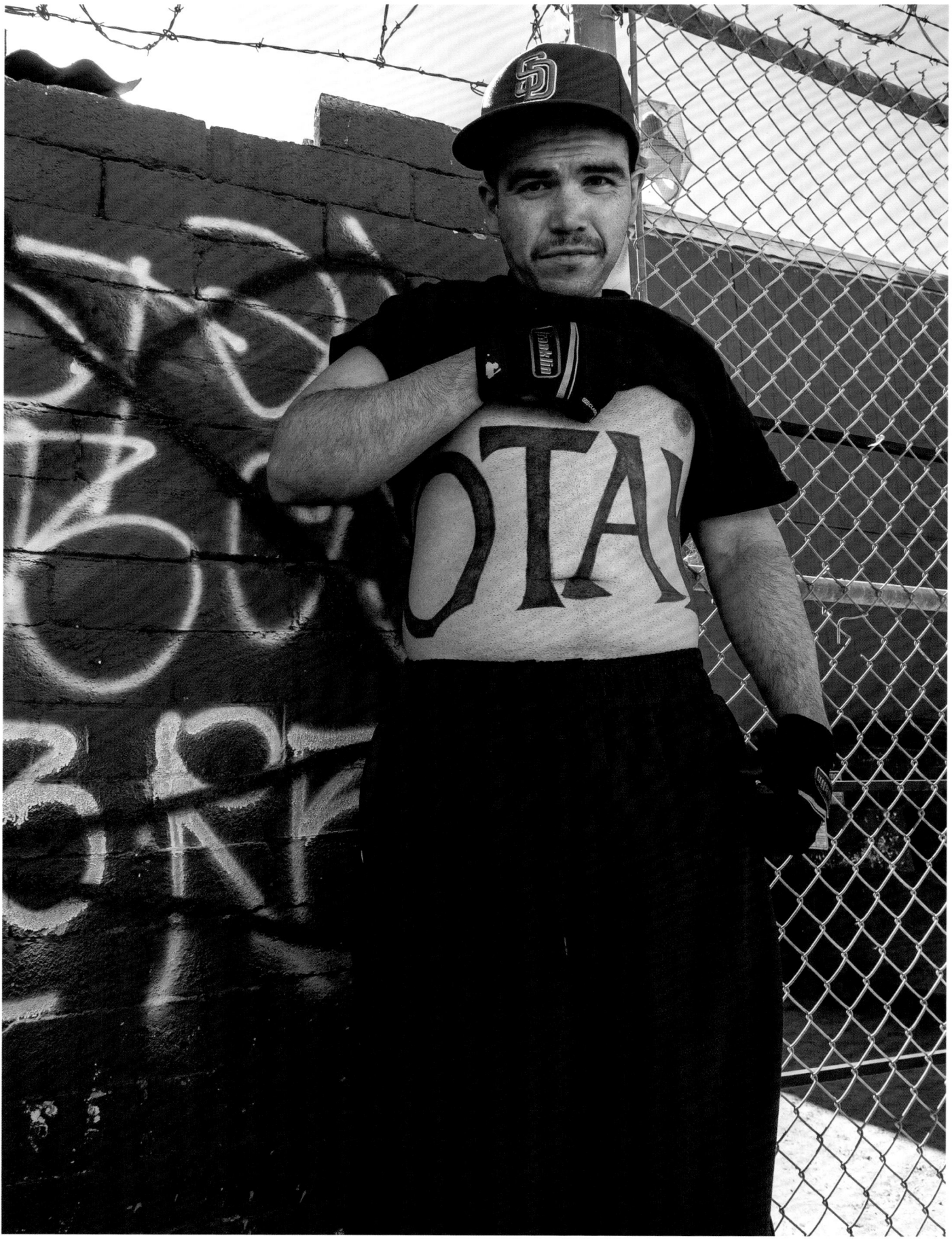

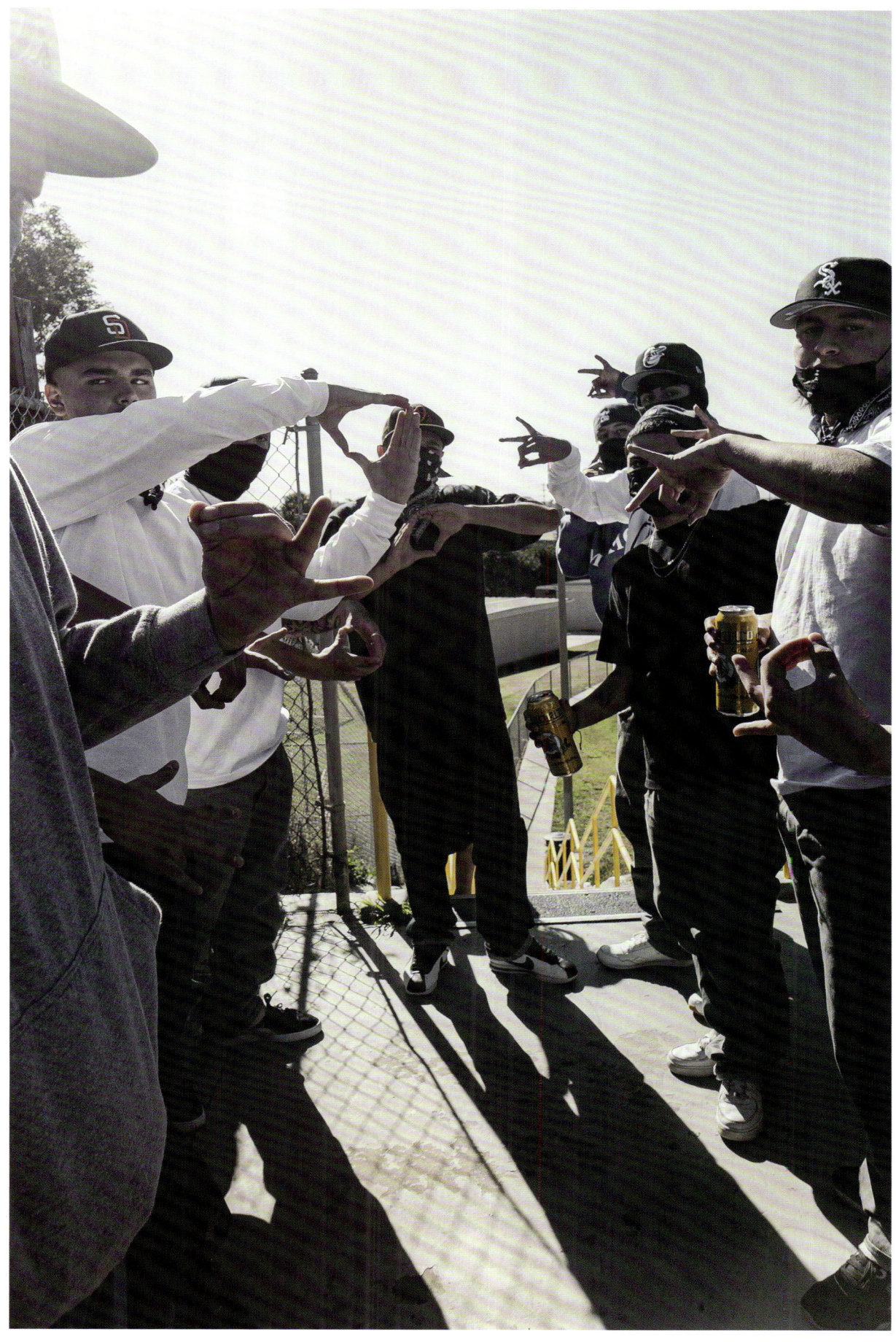

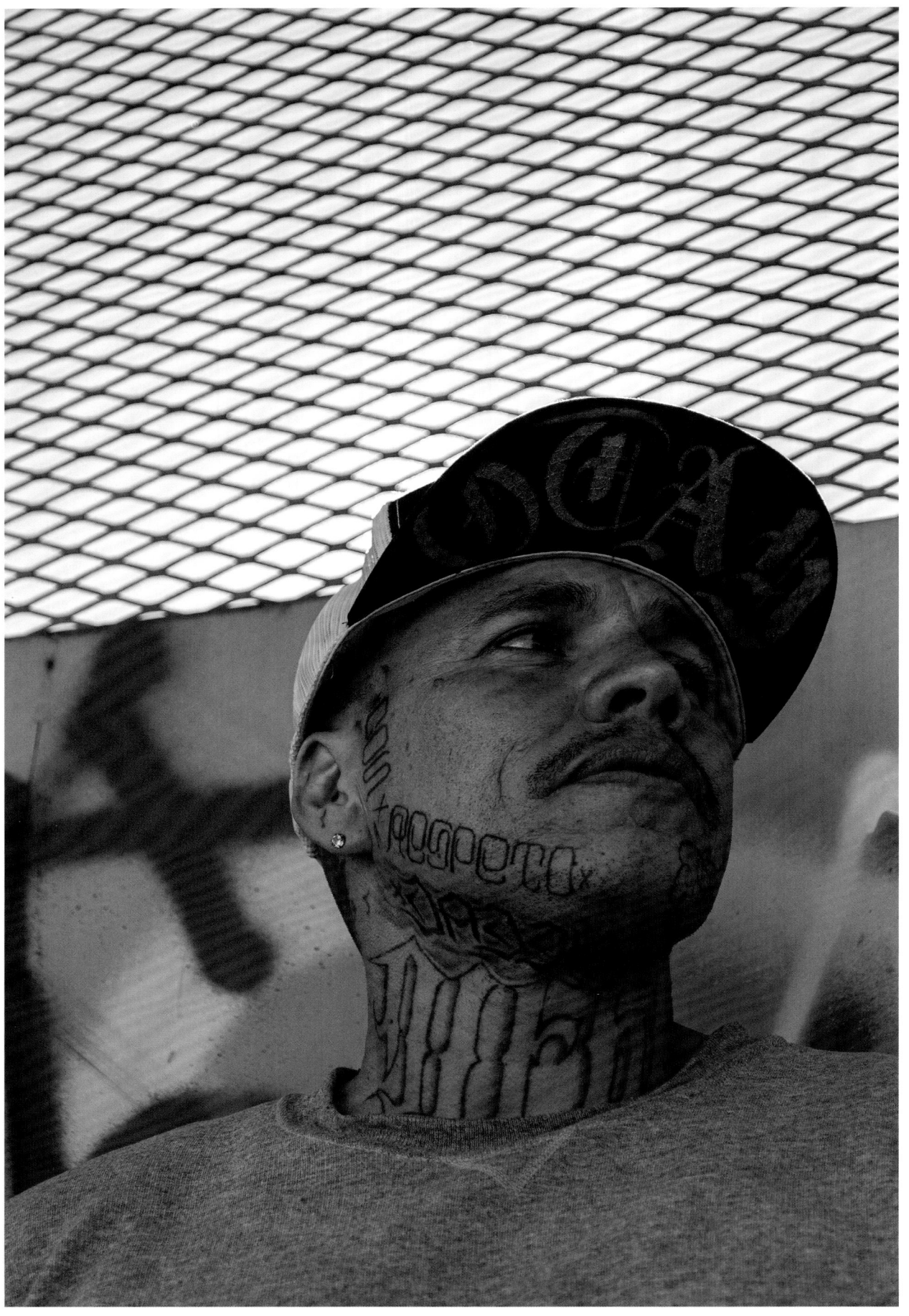

"My first gun, one of my older homeboys didn't give me it, but handed it to me. I still remember those muthafuckers, it was like a .357, all chrome big ol' fuckin' gun and I was like fuckin' ten years old and that's how I grew up. I grew up around tecatos, I grew up around gangsters, straight gangsters, know what I mean.

It kinda molded me into the person I am now, as a 'de es moroso'—'the fuck up'—more as a respectful person, because they always taught me respect! Even though they kind of influenced me in a sense, but they always taught me or they showed me like '. . . Don't do drugs! Don't be doing this shit. Never fuckin' snitch! Never tell on nobody! Mind your own business and respect everybody.' That's how I grew up and that's how I carried myself till this day, that's why I have this—[points to the side of his face]—the "Con Respecto," 'cause that's the way I carry myself, with respect! I respect everybody, whether you're Black, white, Mexican, I don't give a fuck who you are! I respect you, period! You respect me! The day you disrespect, it's on! We're gonna have issues, and so that's how I grew up, around that. Like I said, I have cousins all from my neighborhood, uncles, aunts, and even my mom, so I grew up with the oldies, with family Otay parties, stuff like that, I mean, you see it as normal.

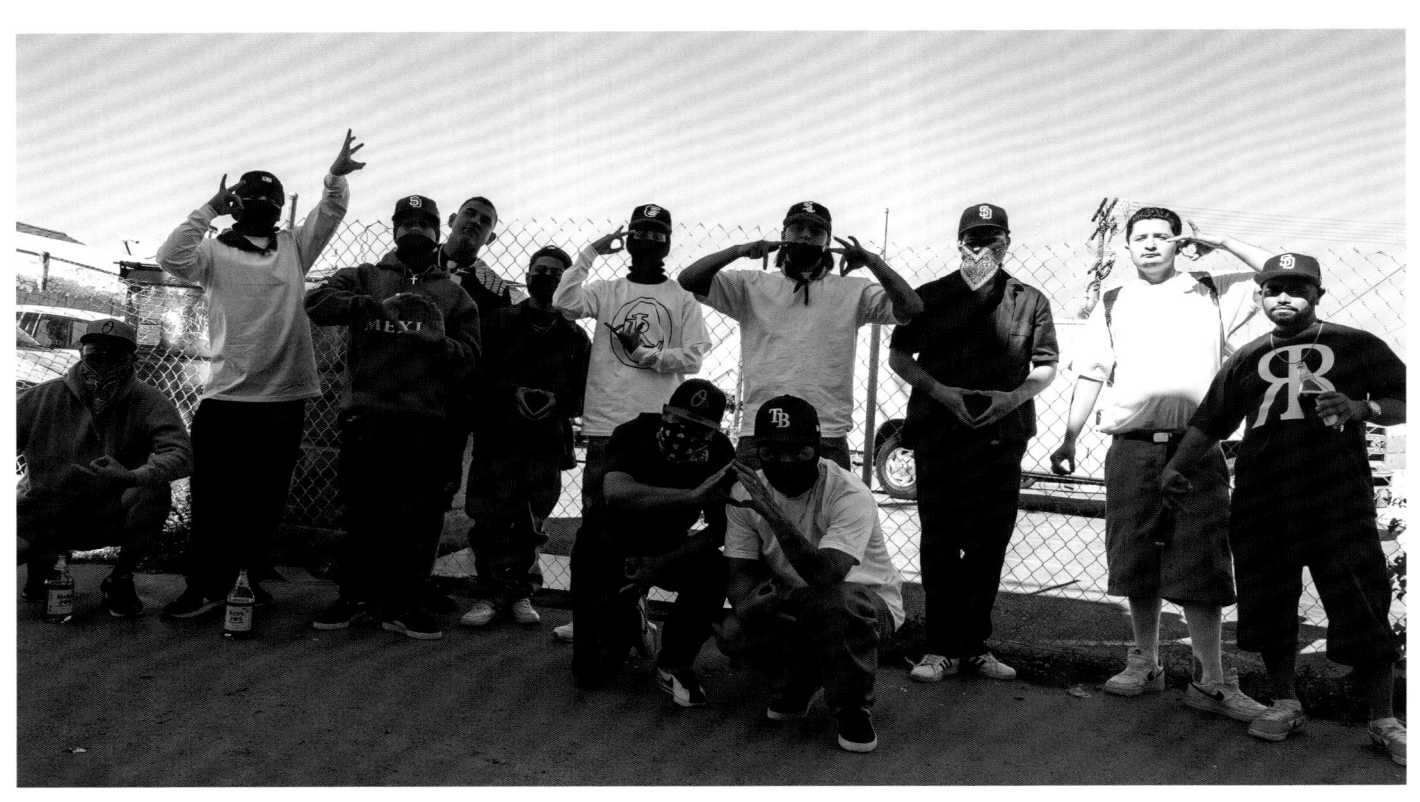

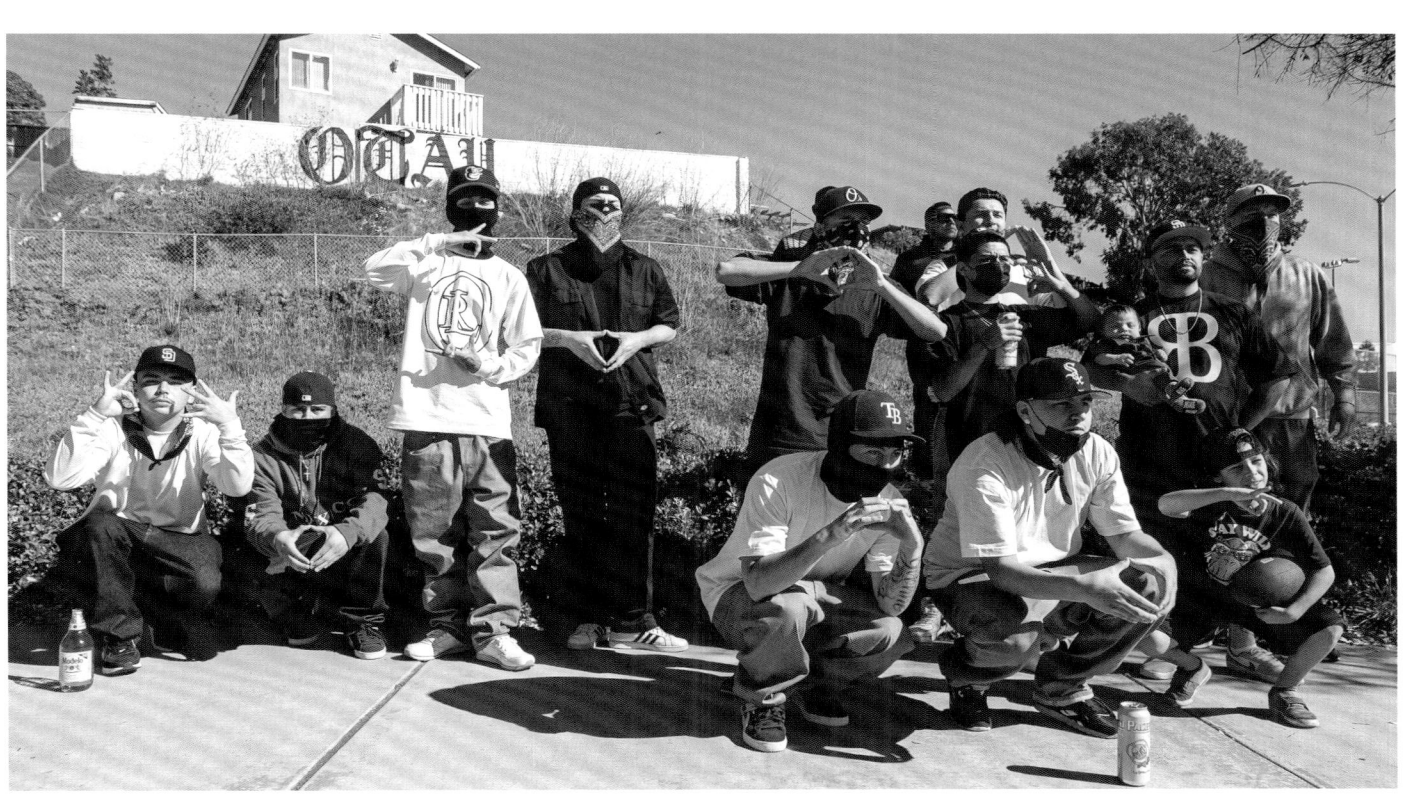

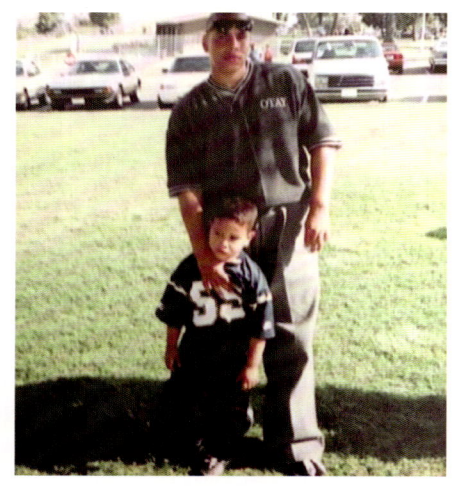

What honestly changed my life was just seeing everybody going to prison and never having a chance to get out anymore. A lot of my friends, a lot of homies of mine, a lot of people that I felt were 'untouchable' at the time, you know? Because, like I said, a lot of people act like they are with the business—but! They don't know what the business is!

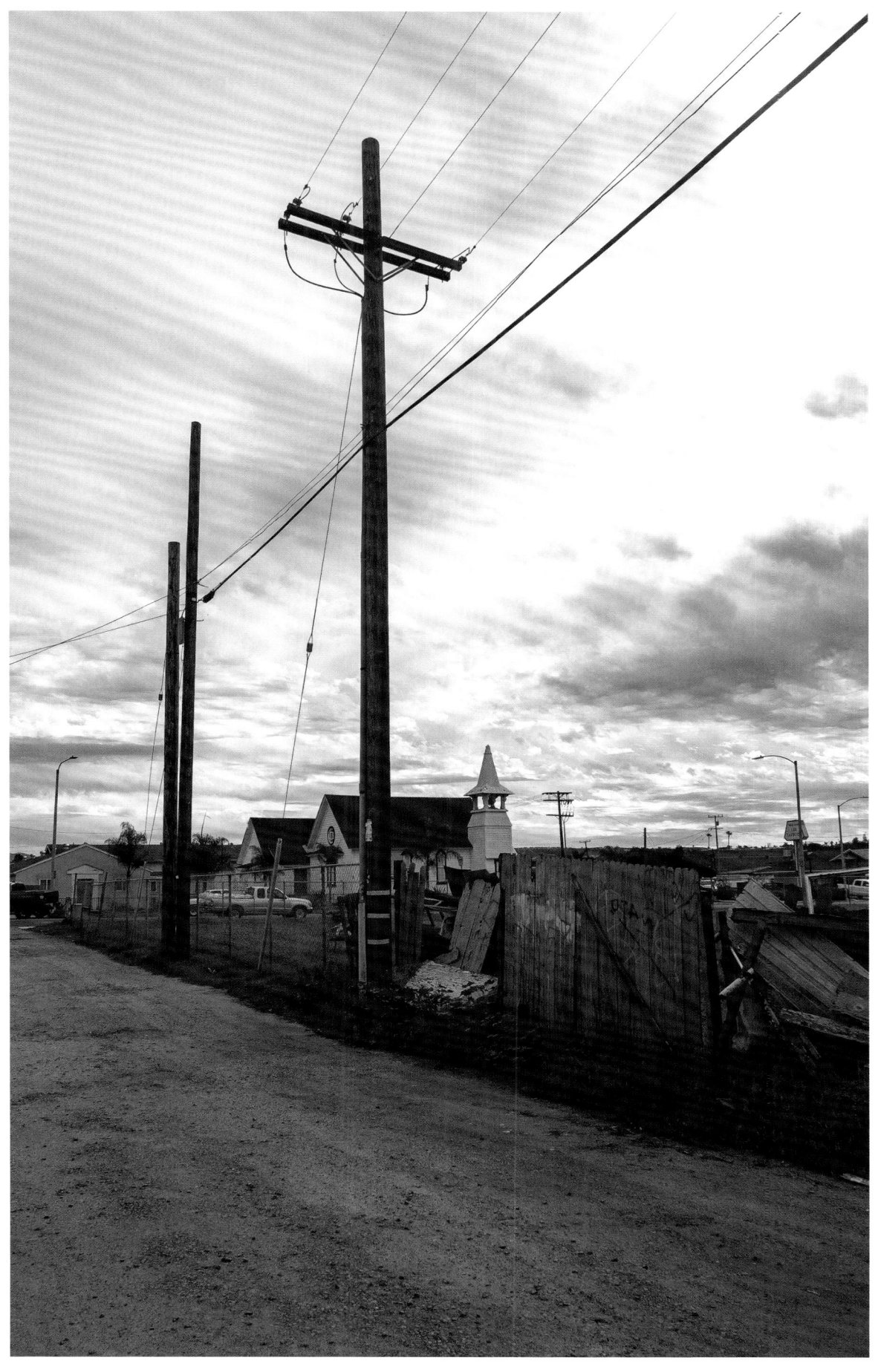

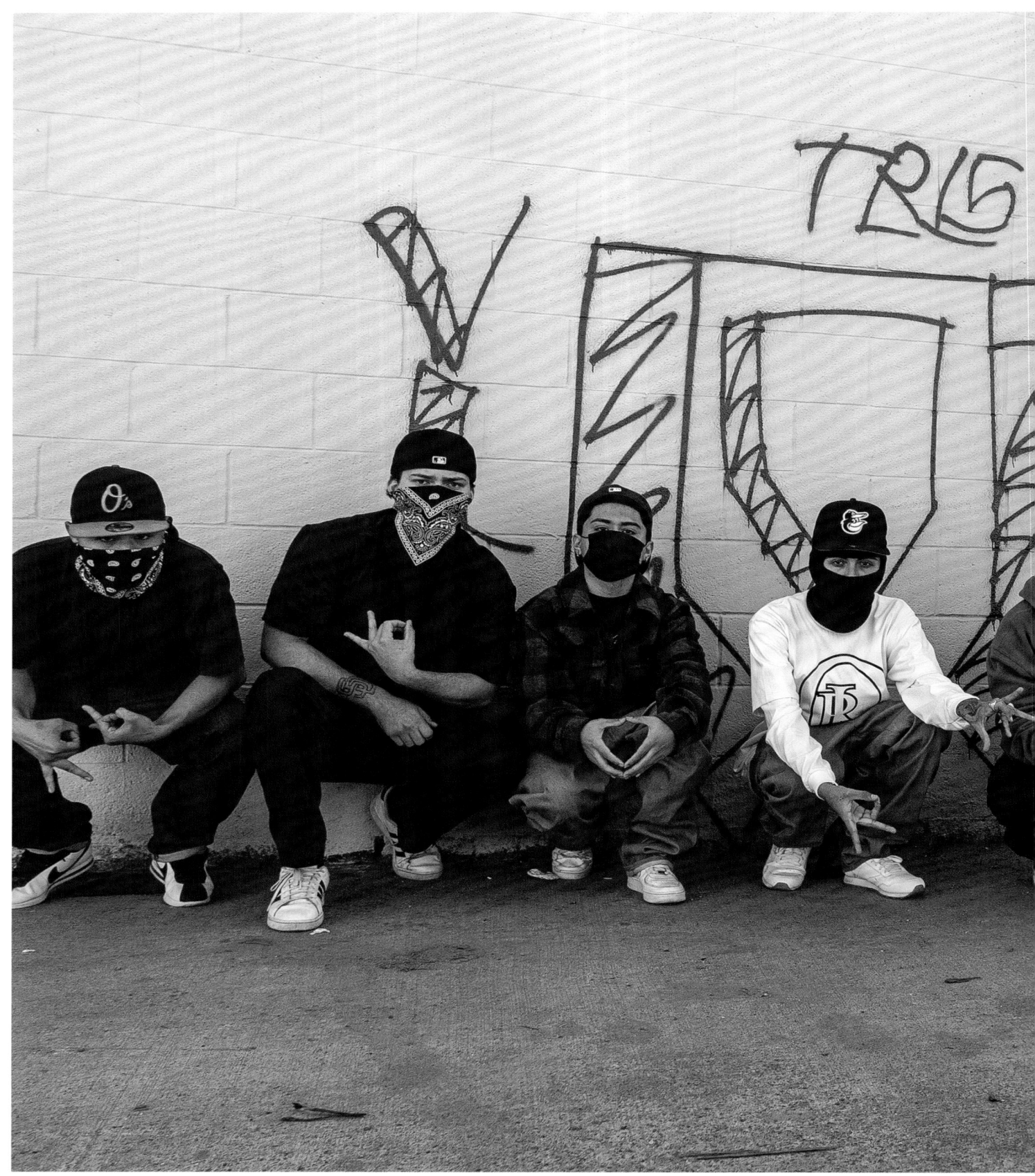

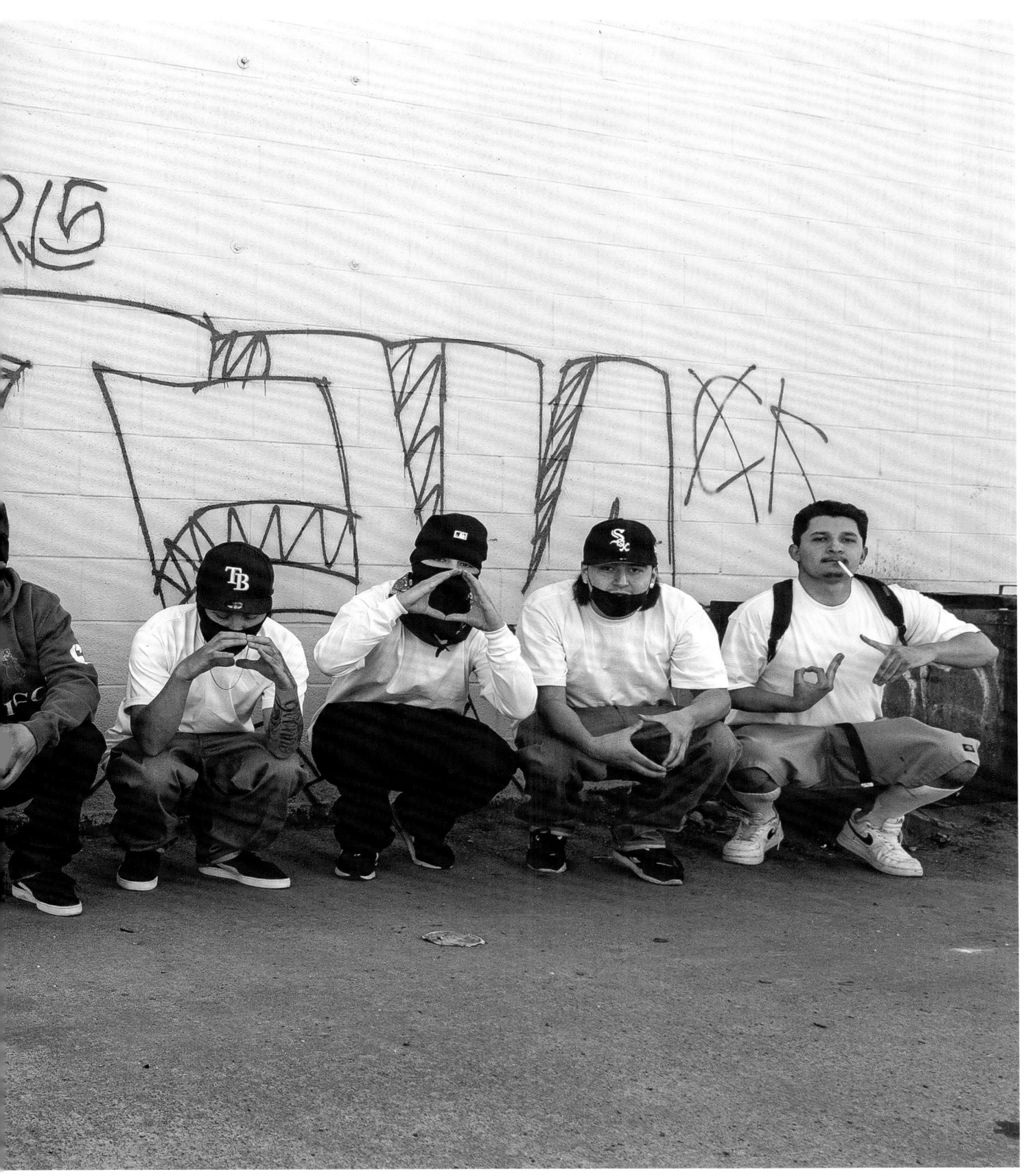

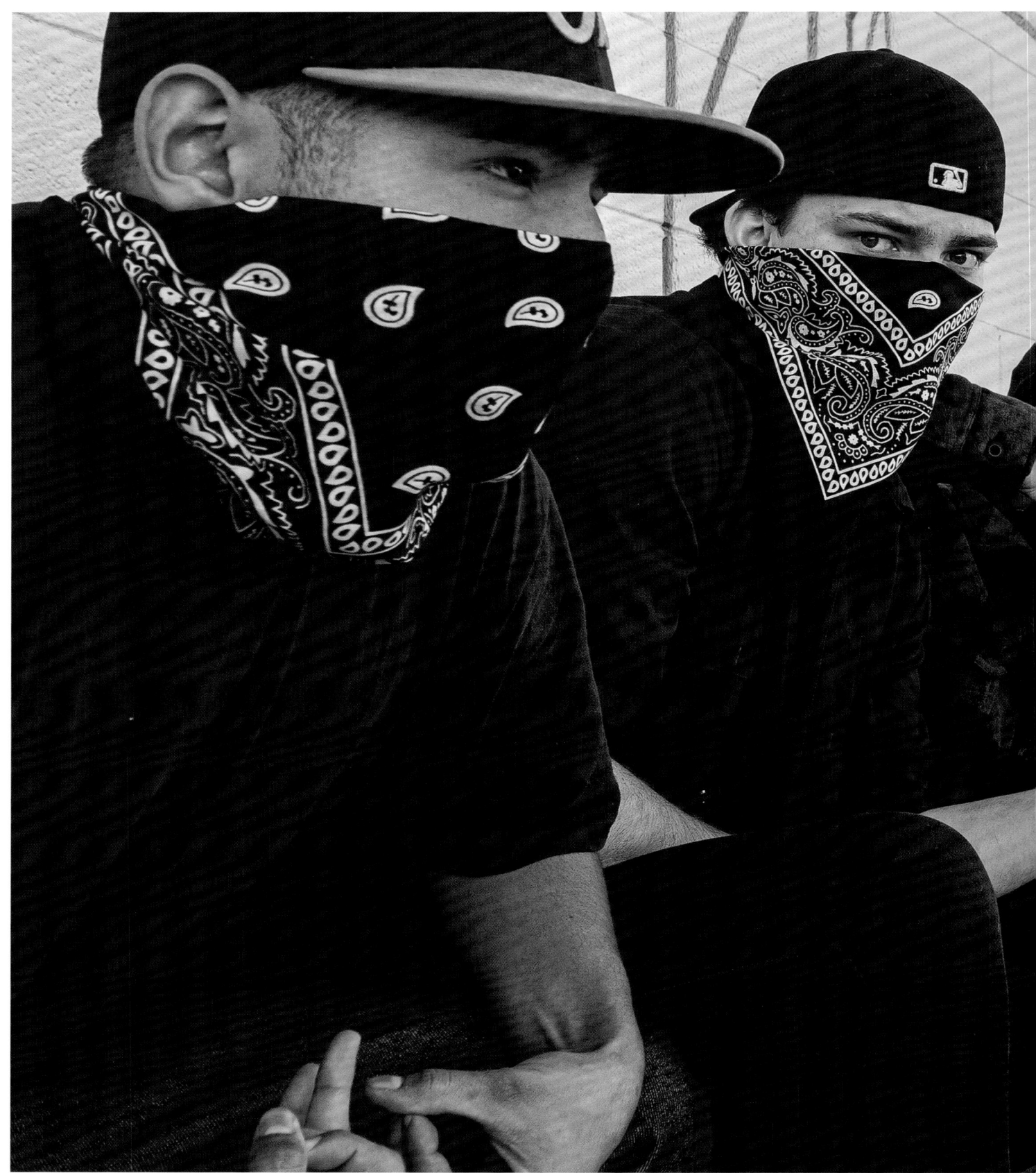

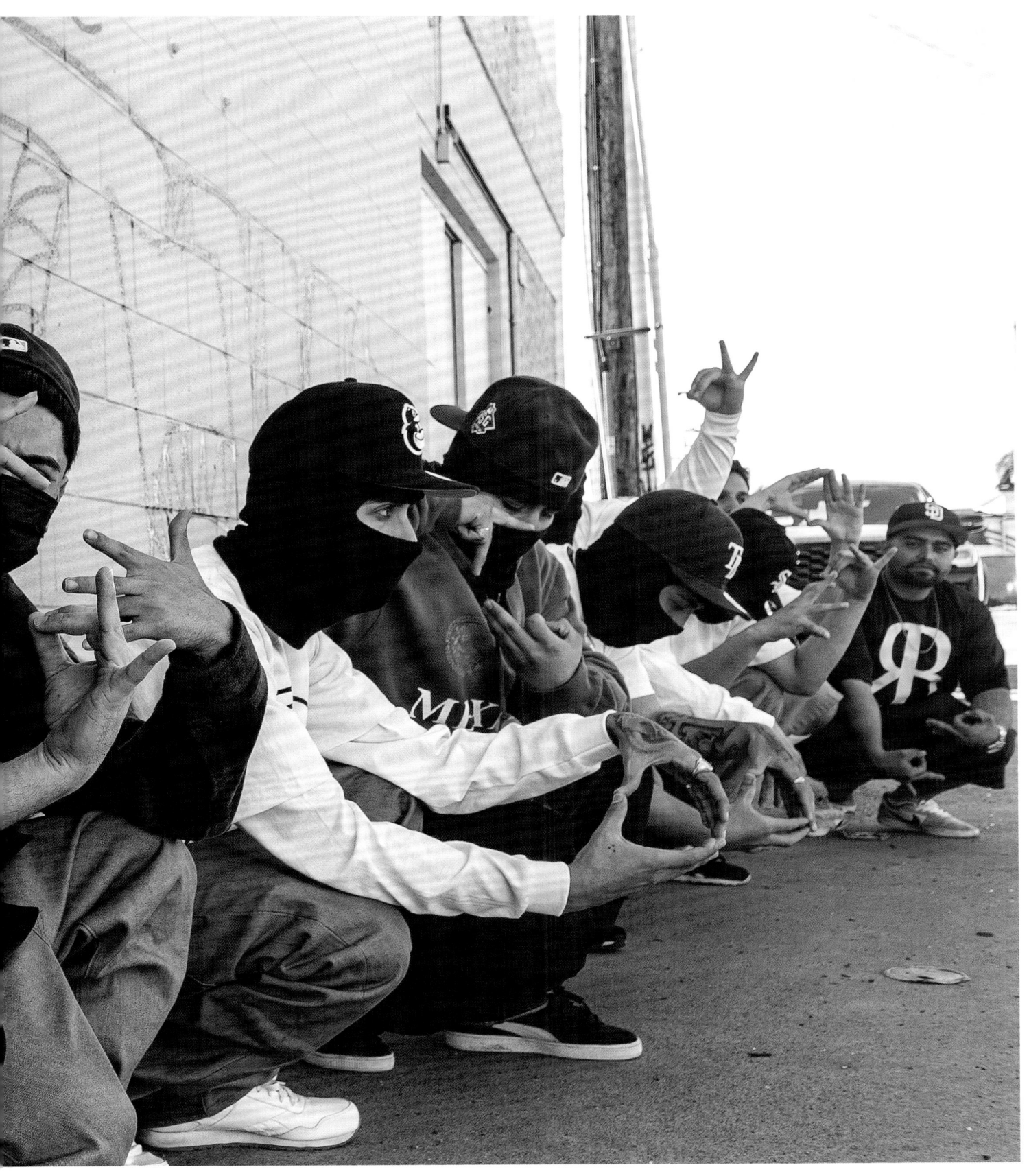

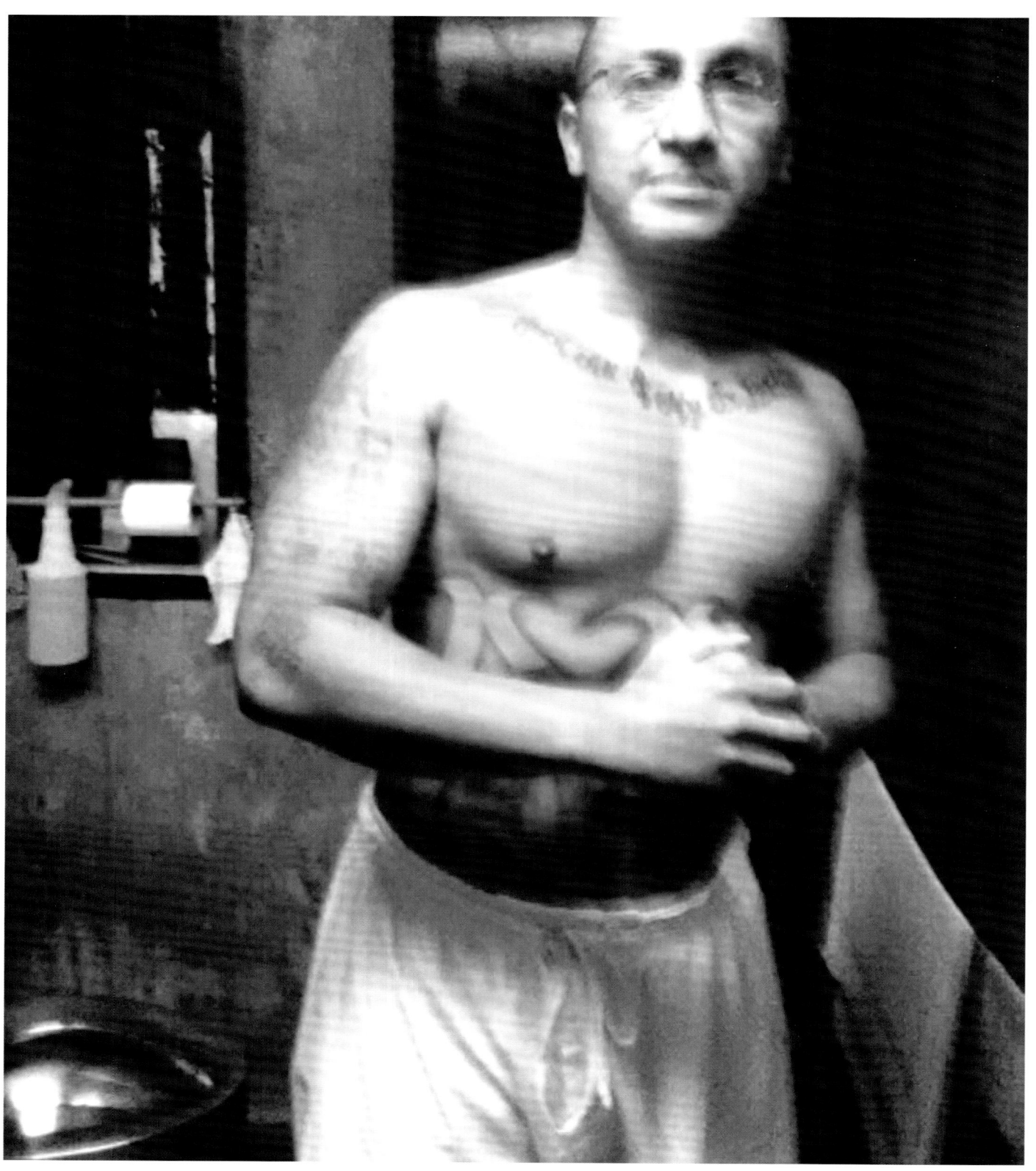

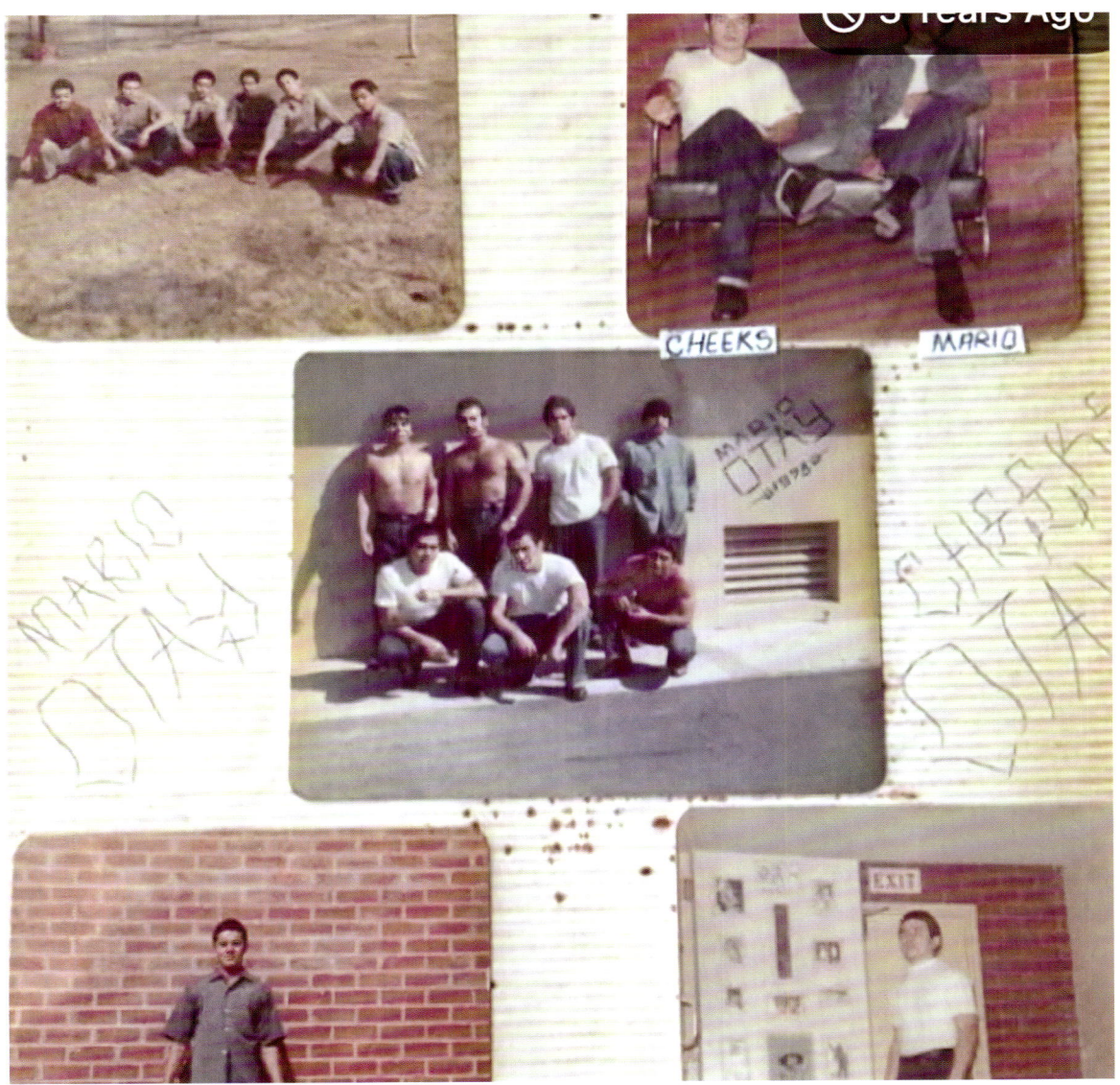

I really fucked around! I was really with the business! And when I say with the business, I mean like I was with the shit, know what I mean? I fucked with everybody and I knew everybody, I knew them! I affiliated with them in whatever way it was, and I respected everybody, but little by little, I would start seeing those guys going to jail, snitching on each other and, uh, even getting killed. That opened my eyes and it's like, fuck all that, I'm my own man so it's like I just started doing me.

Live for the day because tomorrow's never promised, you know, I've lost a lot of homies to these streets, drugs, a lot of shit, and just muthafuckers opening their mouth. I was that 1 percent that liked it, I enjoyed stabbing muthafuckers, I enjoyed getting into fights, I enjoyed doing big-ass block walls in my enemigos' neighborhood.

I enjoyed all that, I did that, all the time I was by myself. I'd hop on the trolley and get off right in the enigmas' neighborhood and start spray-painting everywhere. I enjoyed it, a lot of these people are peer pressured to do it nowadays, and I never blamed any of my family for the shit that I've done or for my upbringing. I've done a lot of negative shit in my life but I feel all the positive shit has paid off. Now I'm not saying I'm perfect, but I feel that I'm doing good considering the shit that I've been through and the shit I've done. I feel like I'm doing good, I just gotta maintain it and stay sucka free and keep pushing forward and stay on the positive shit."

—BIGG SOLO, OTAY

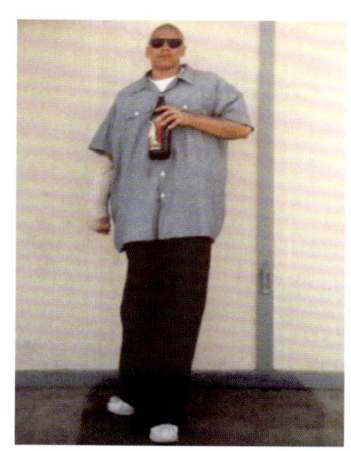

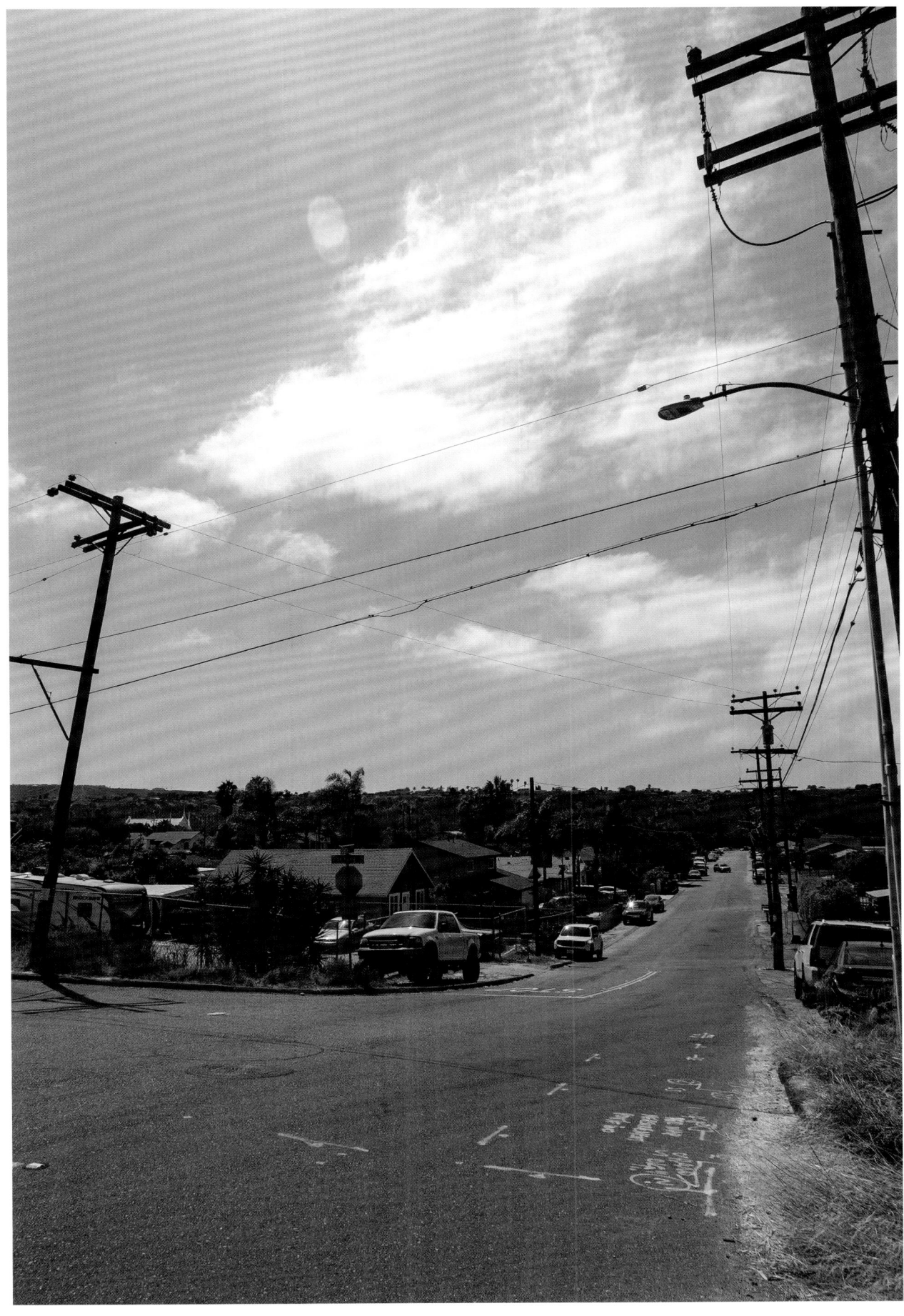

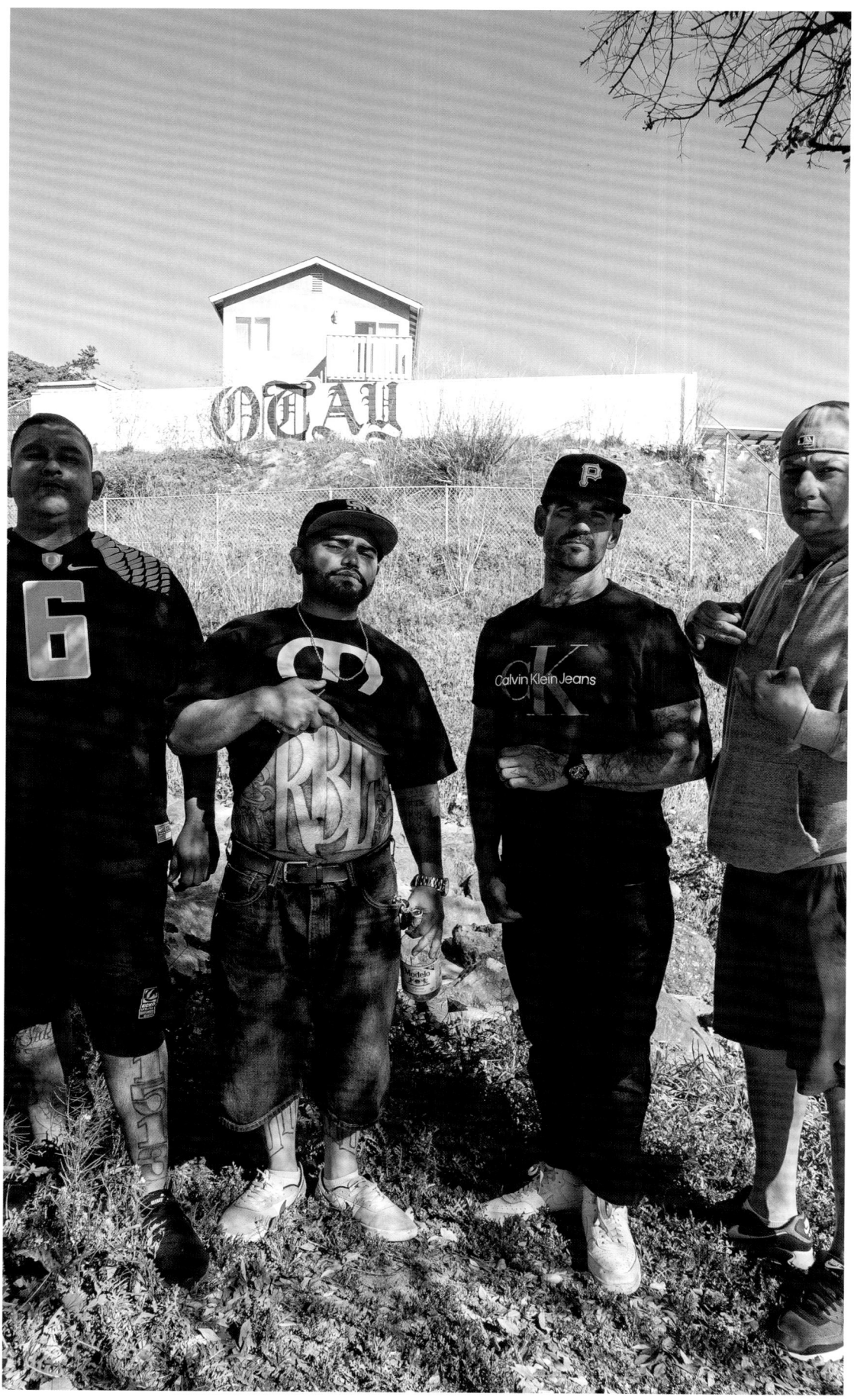

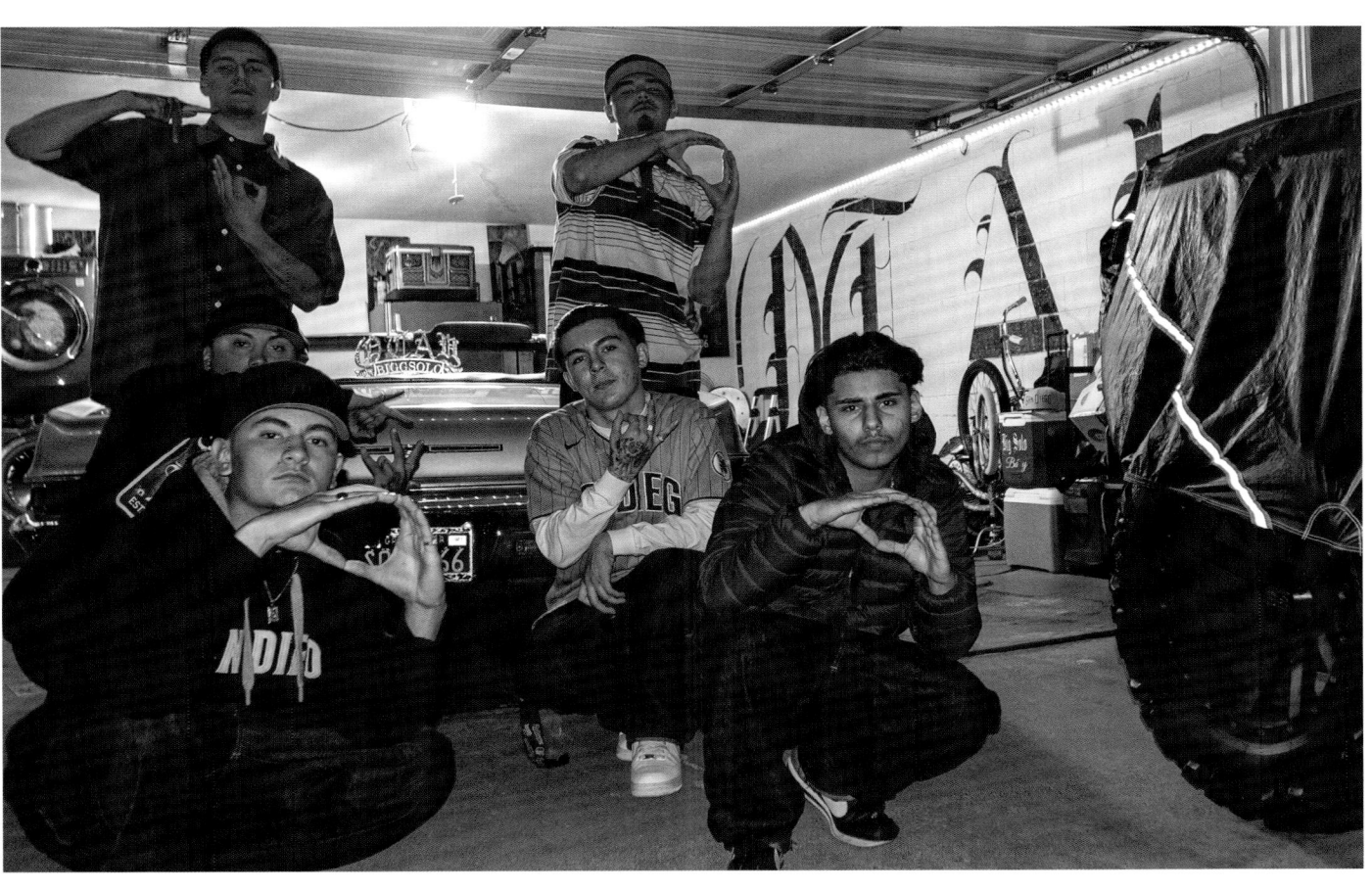

PARADISE

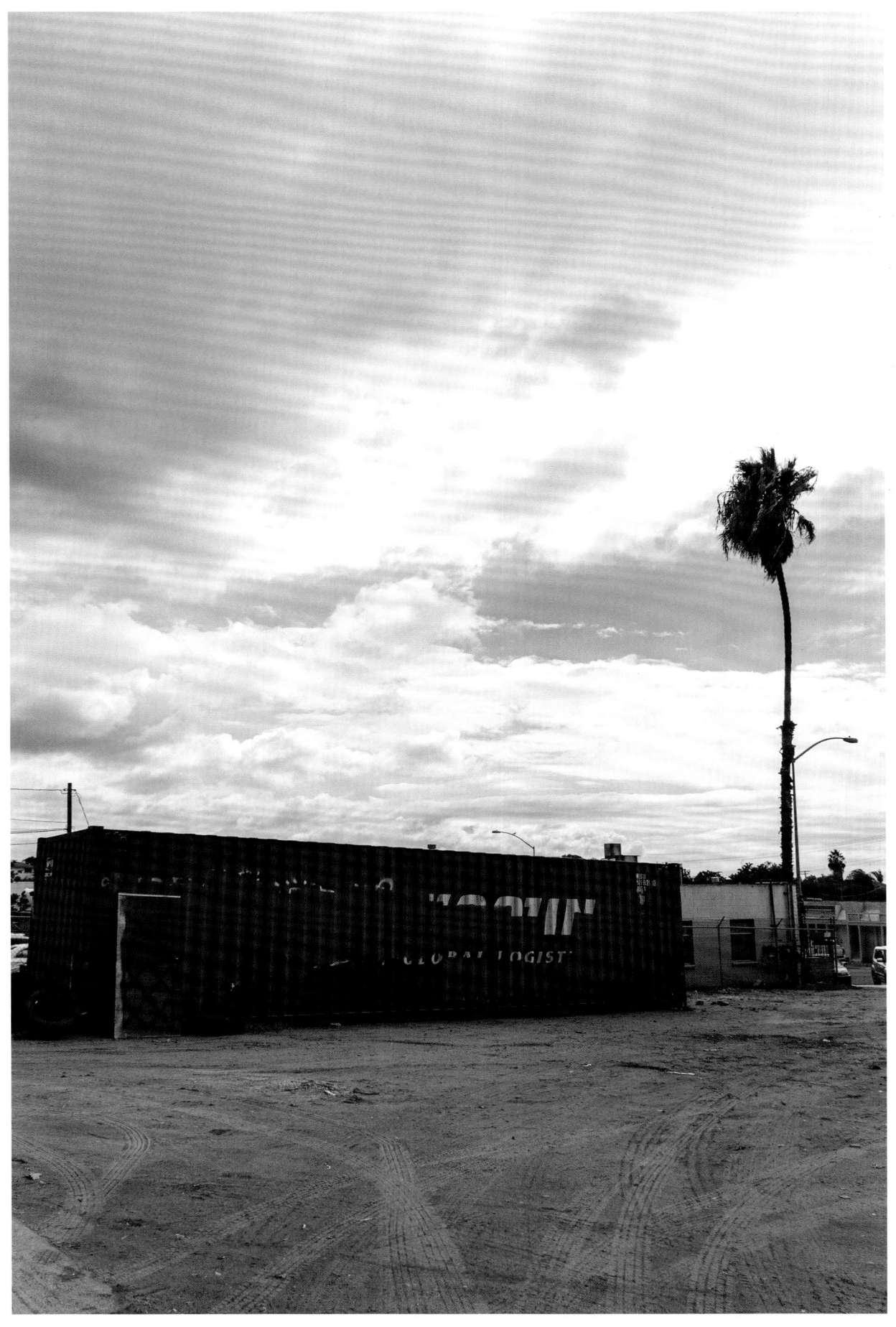

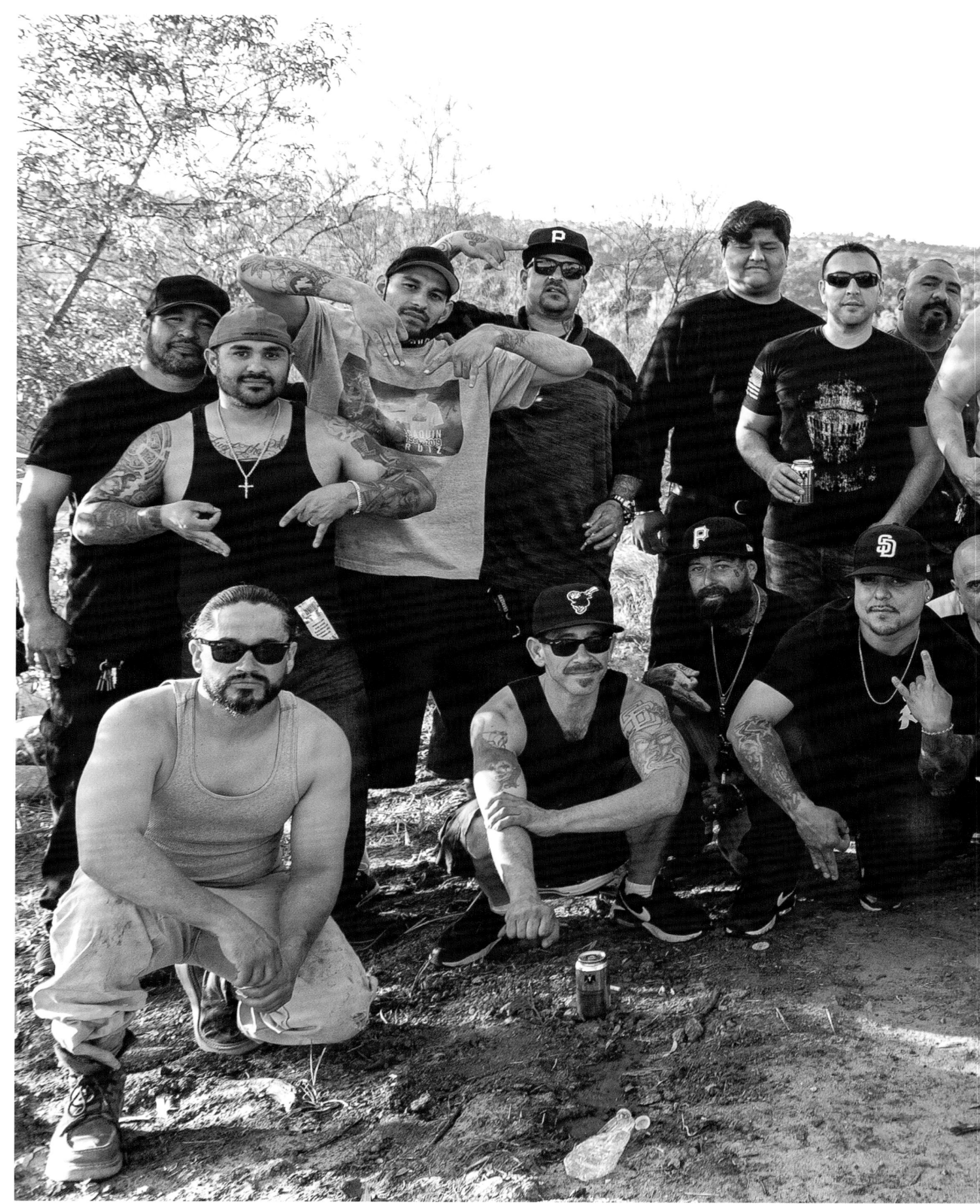

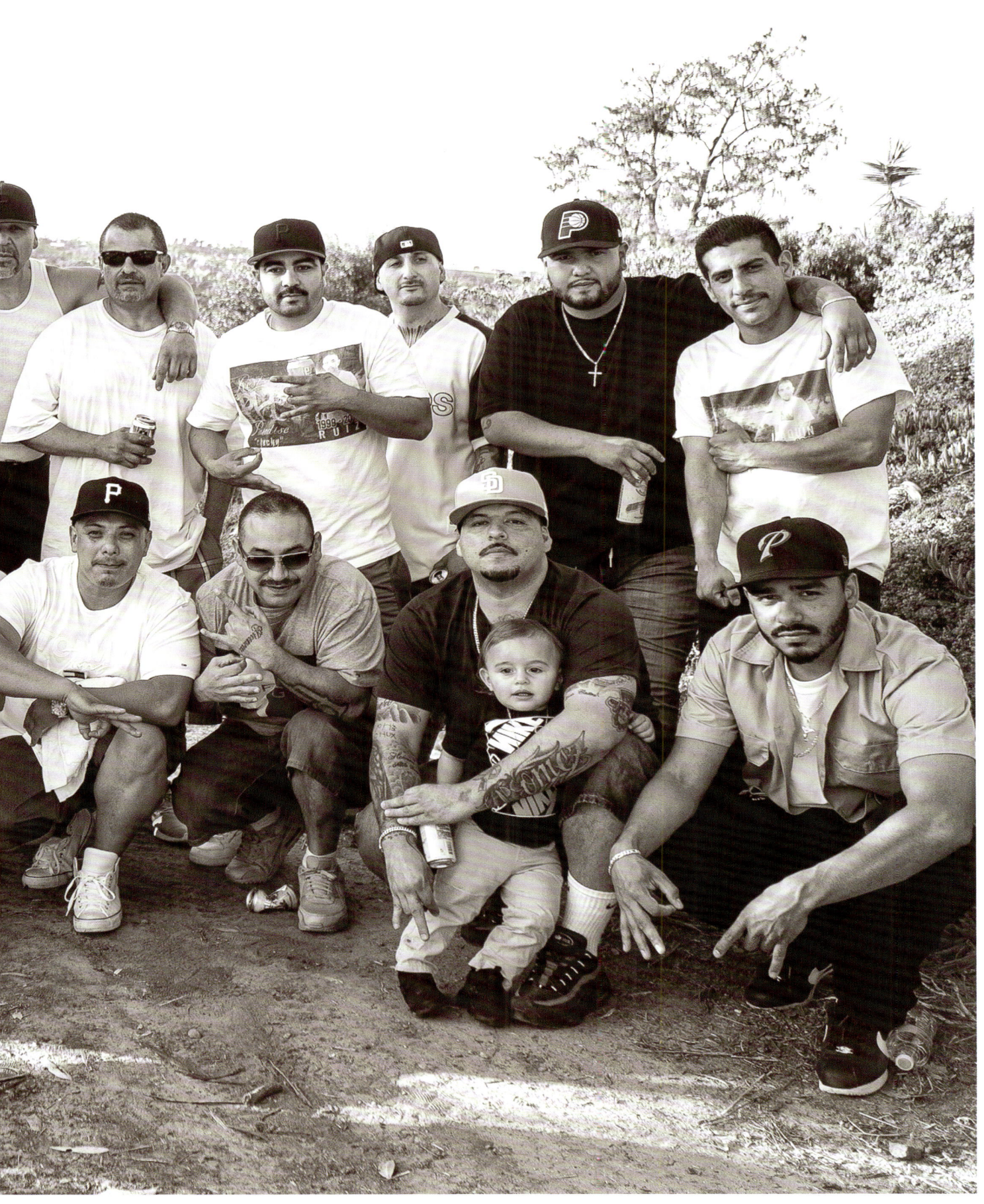

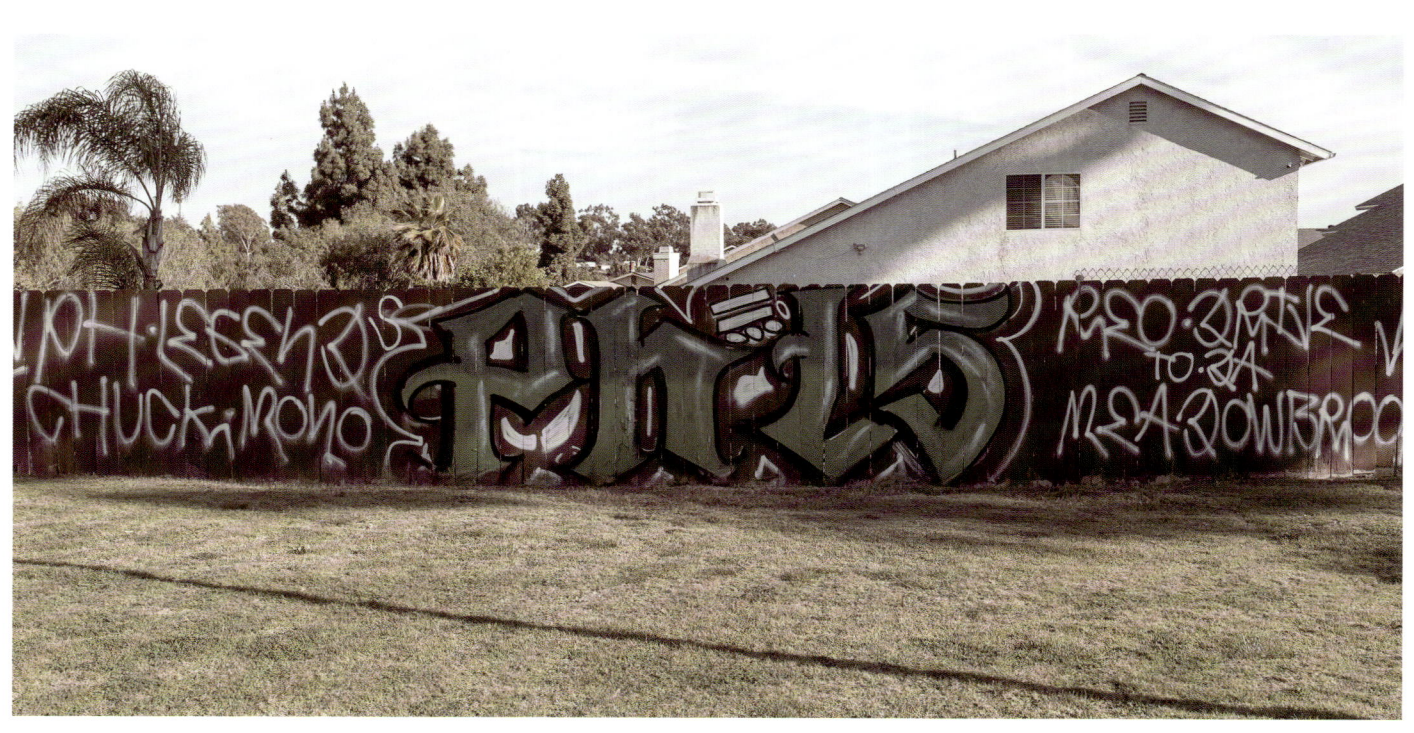

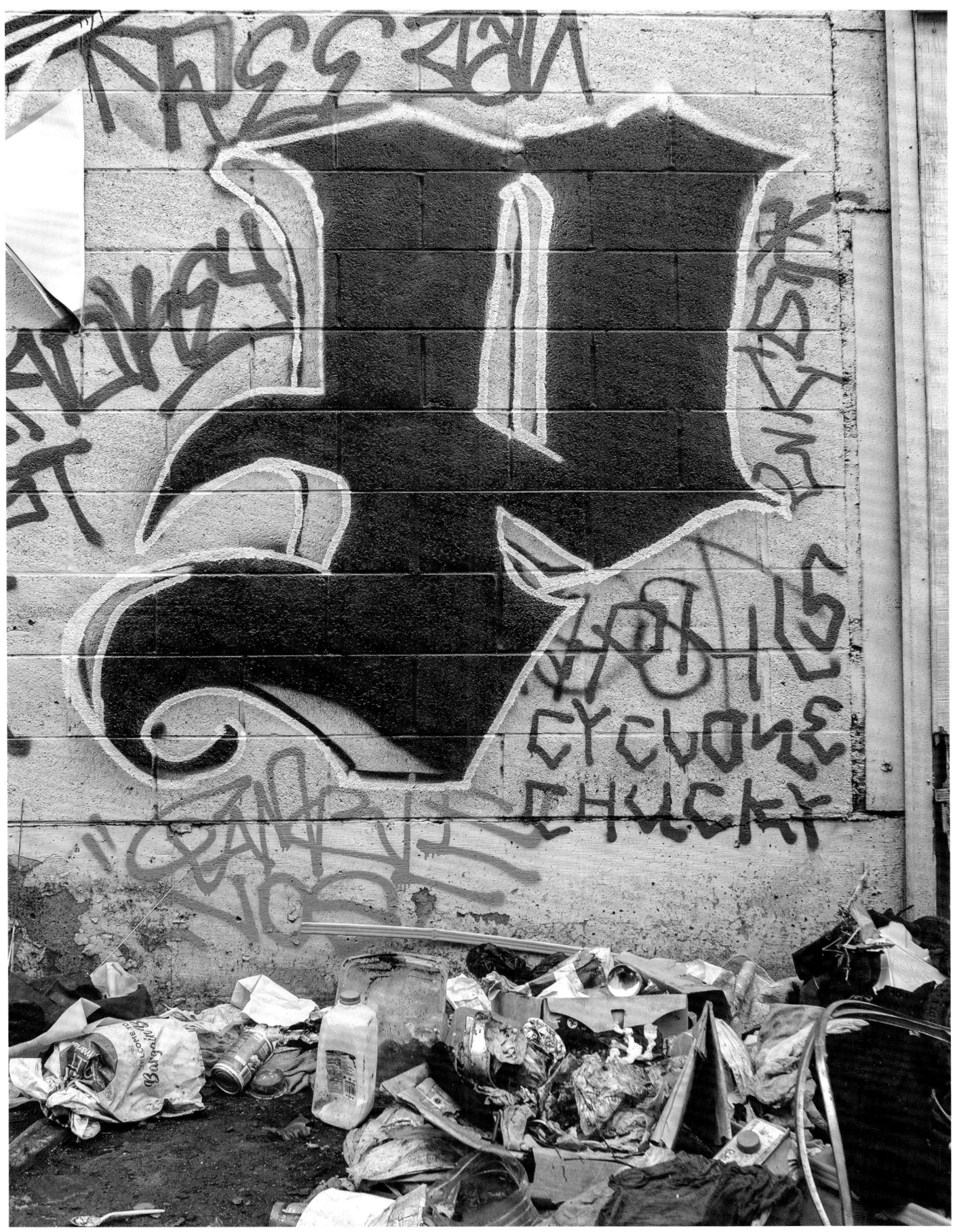

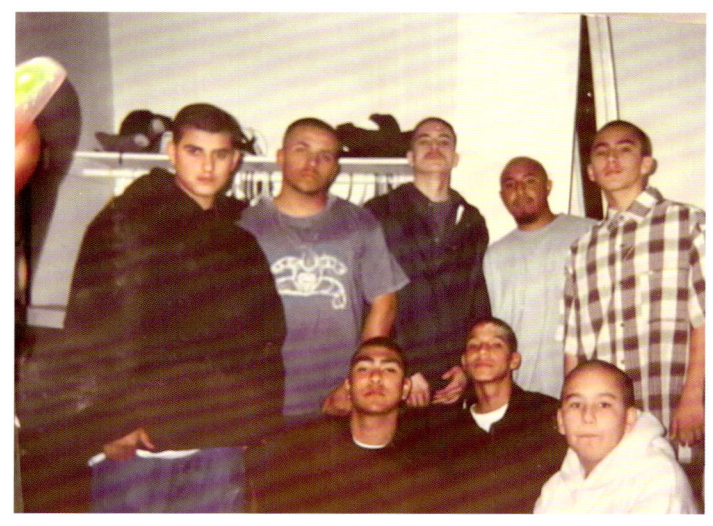

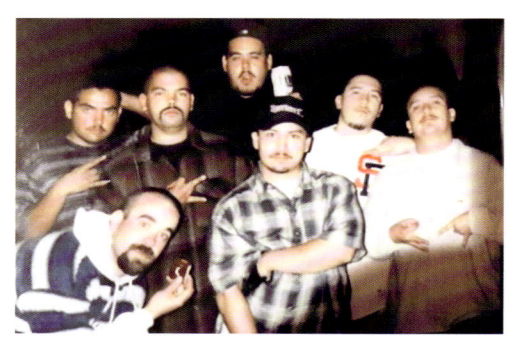

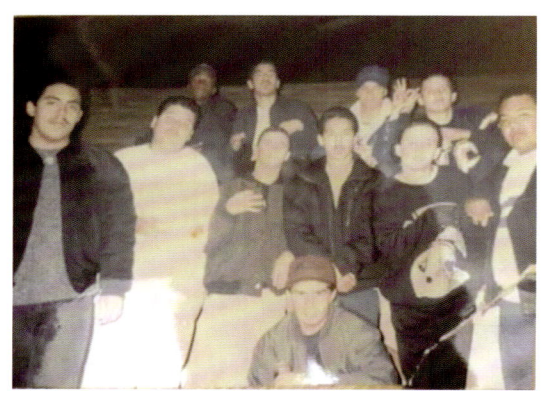

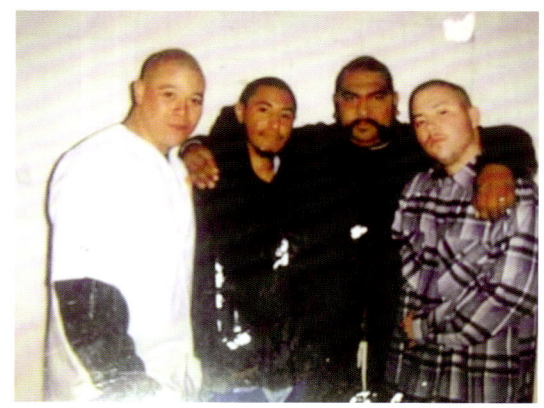

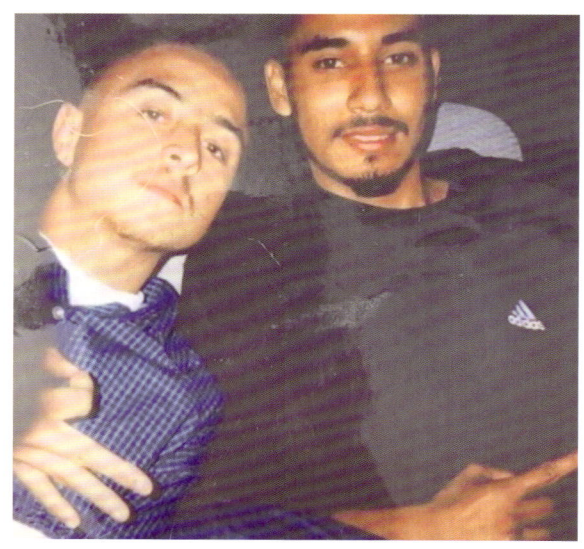

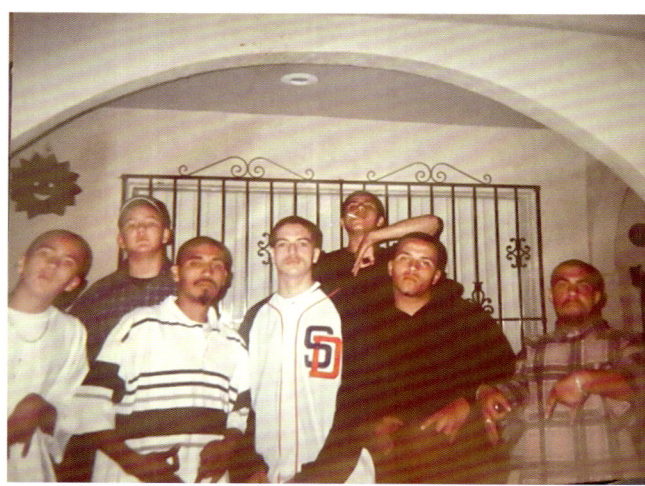

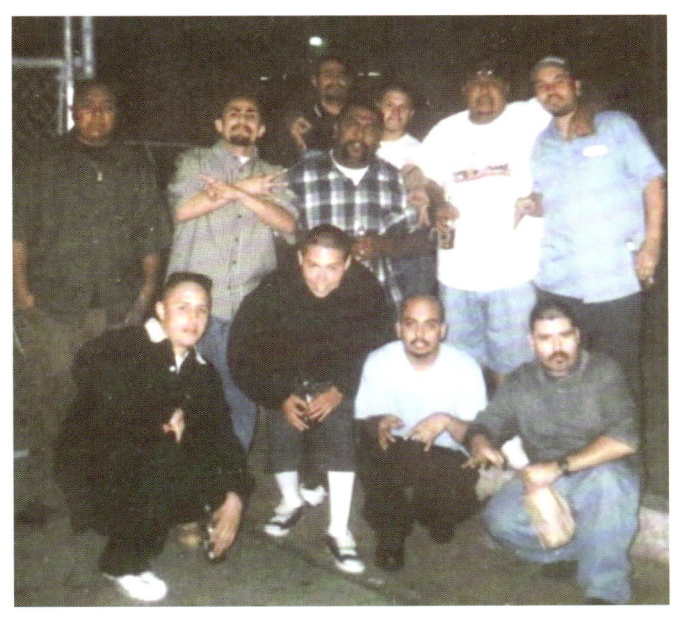

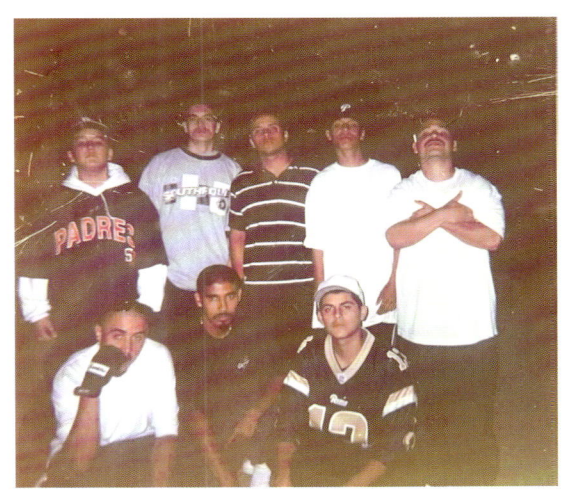

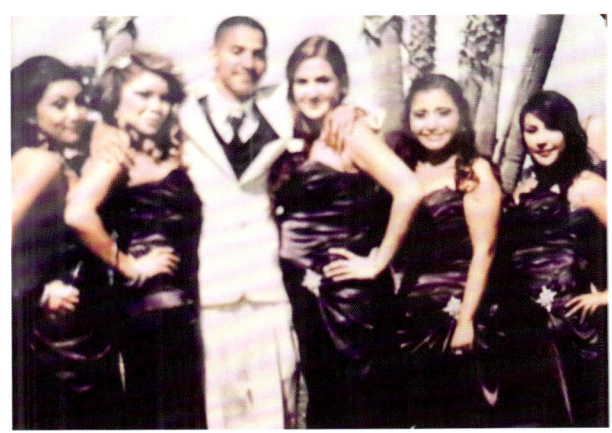

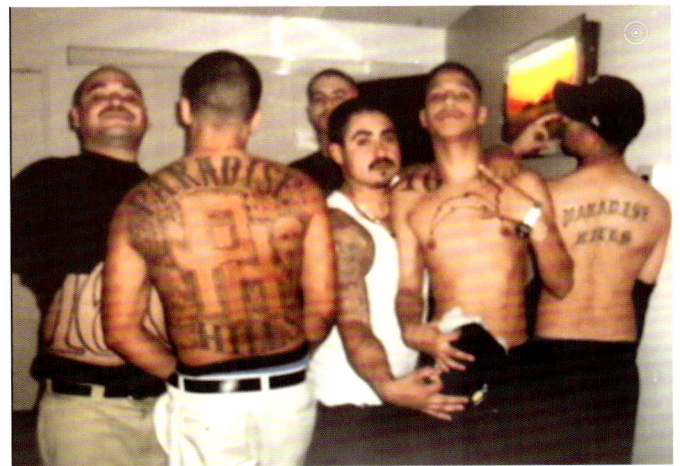

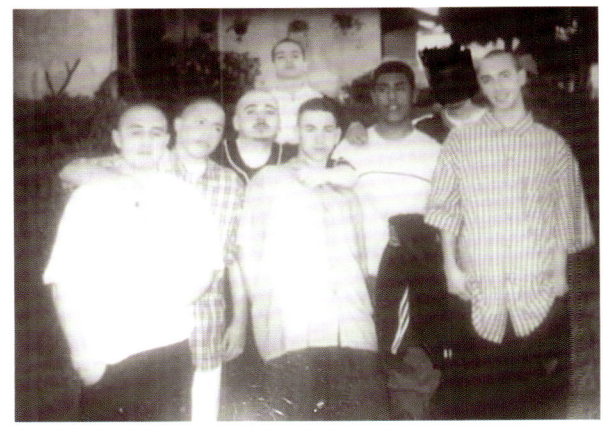

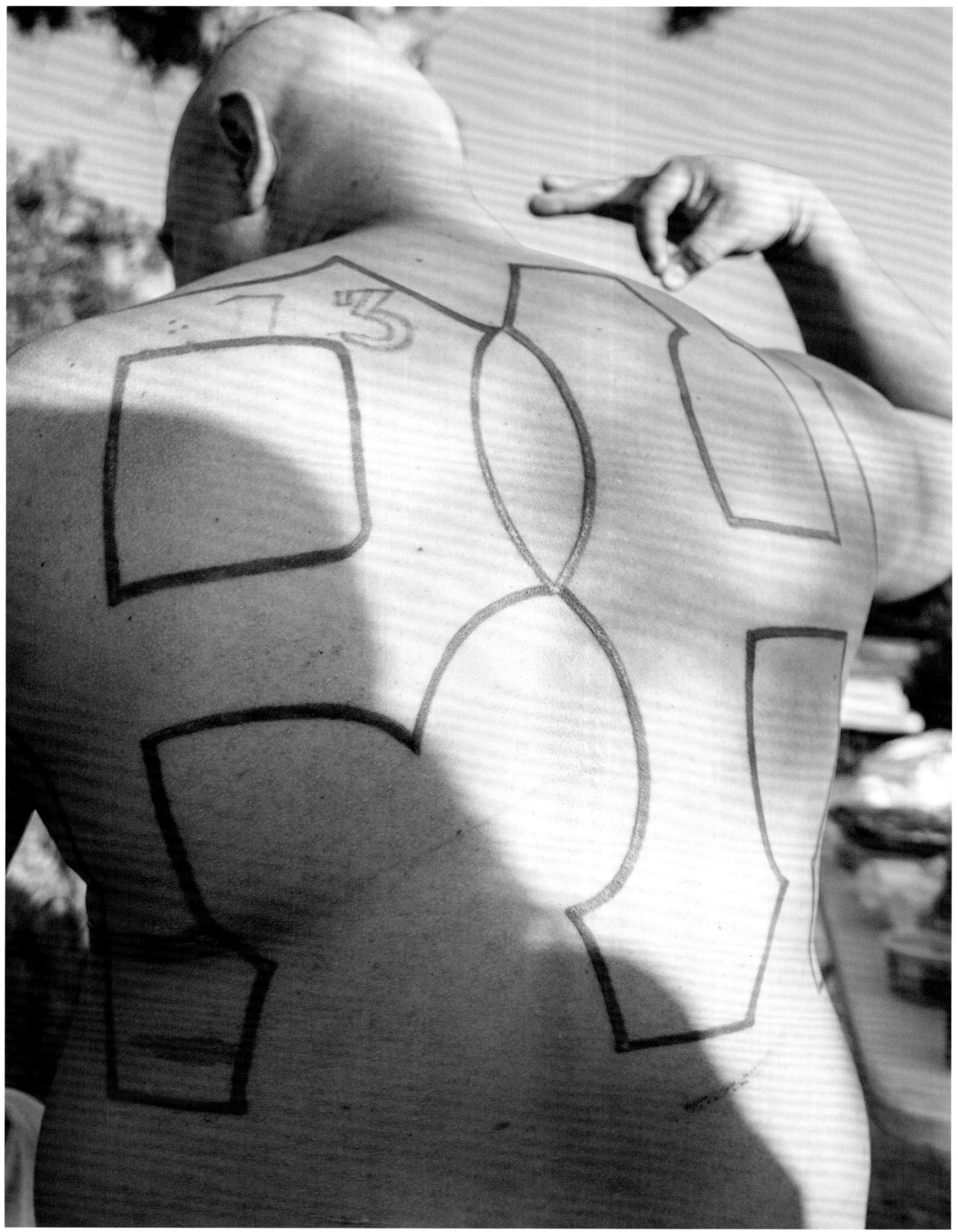

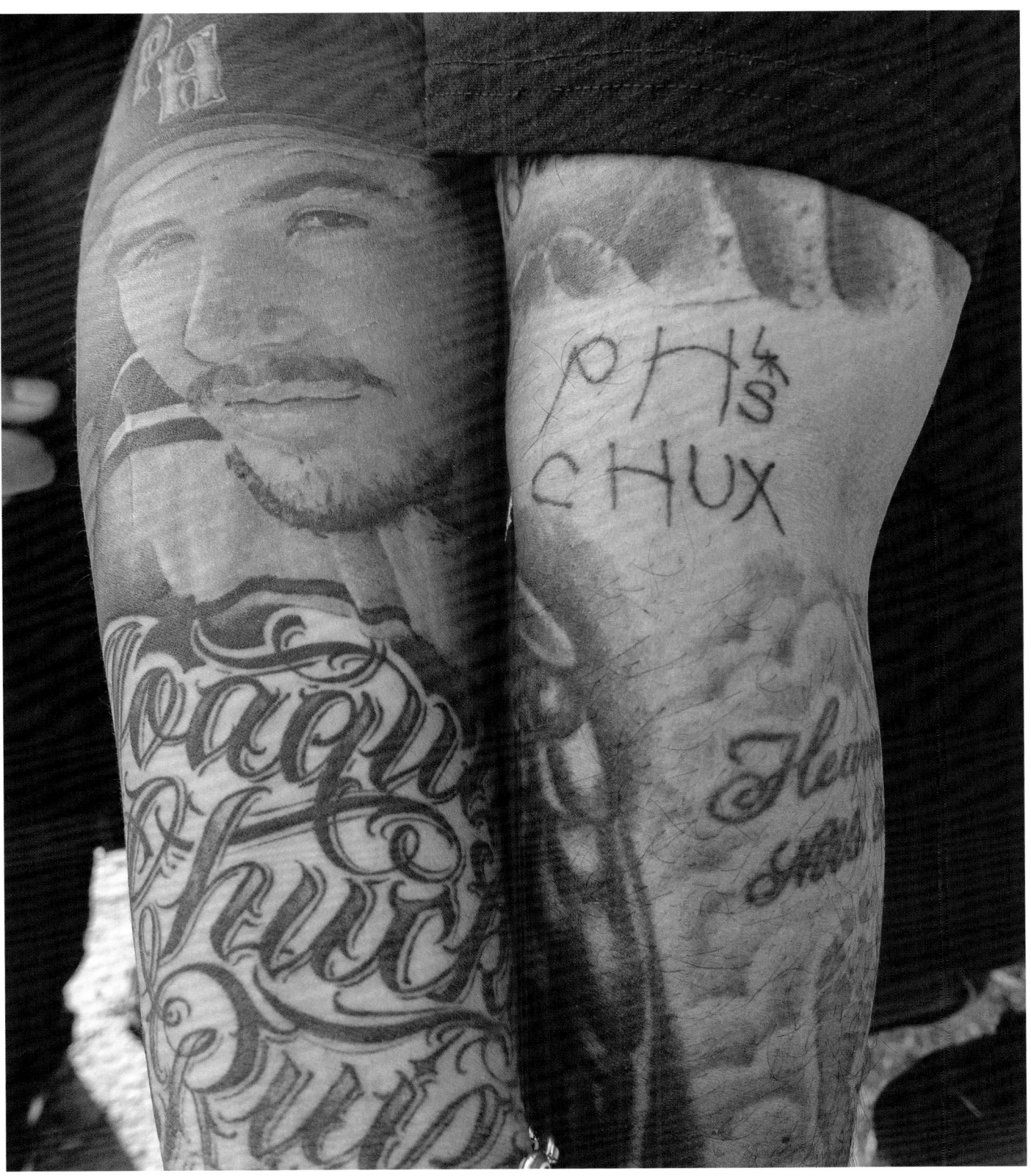

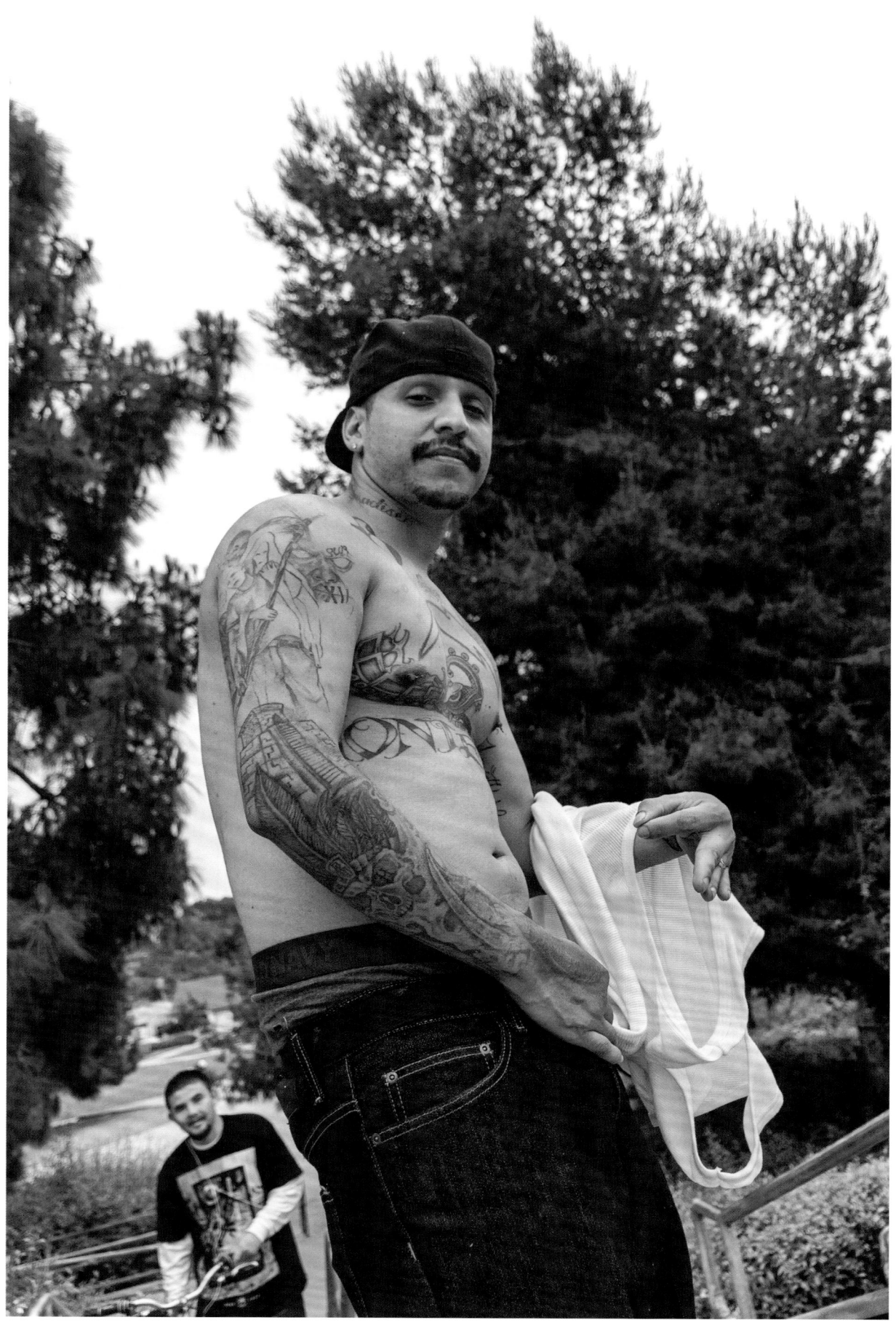

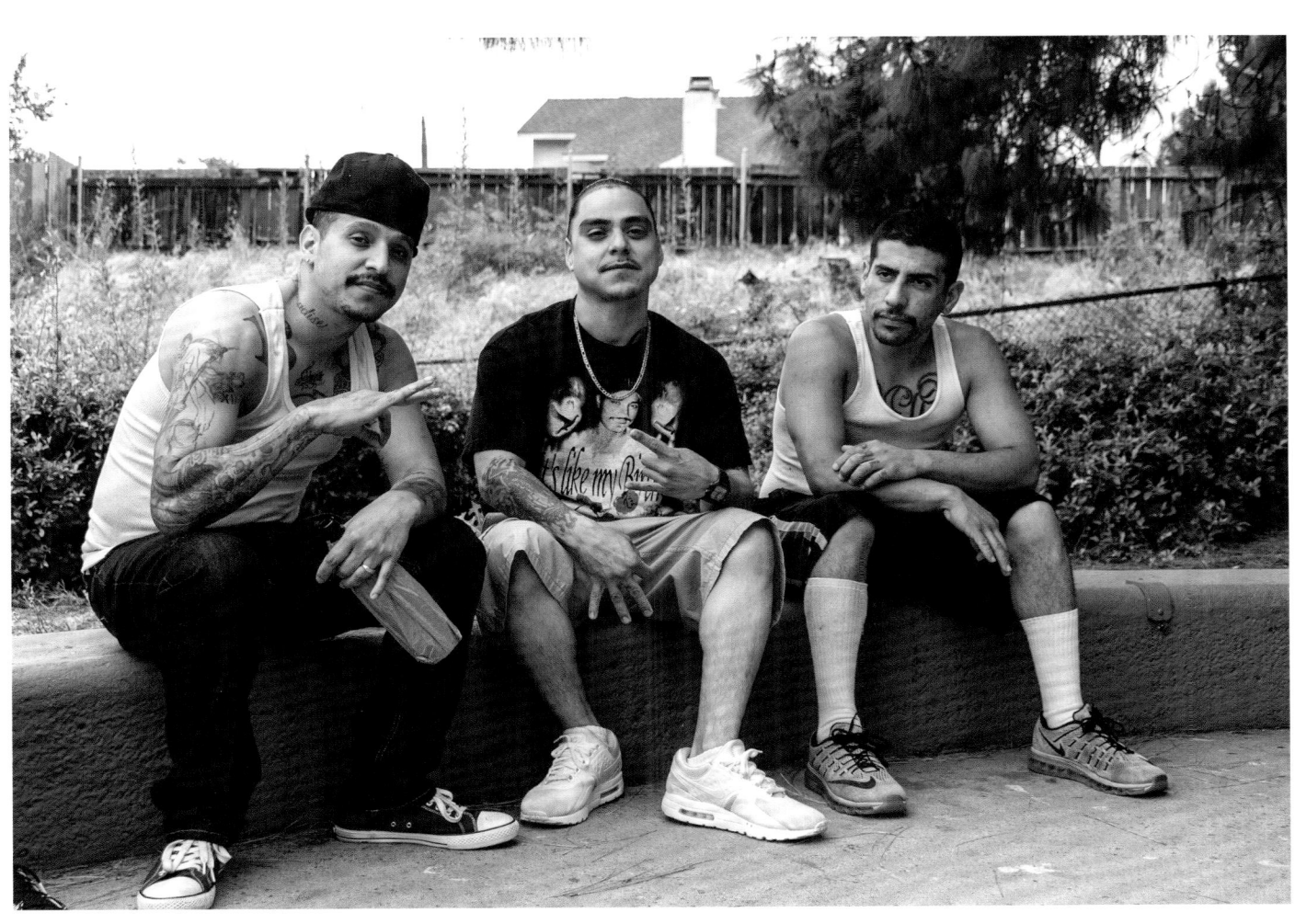

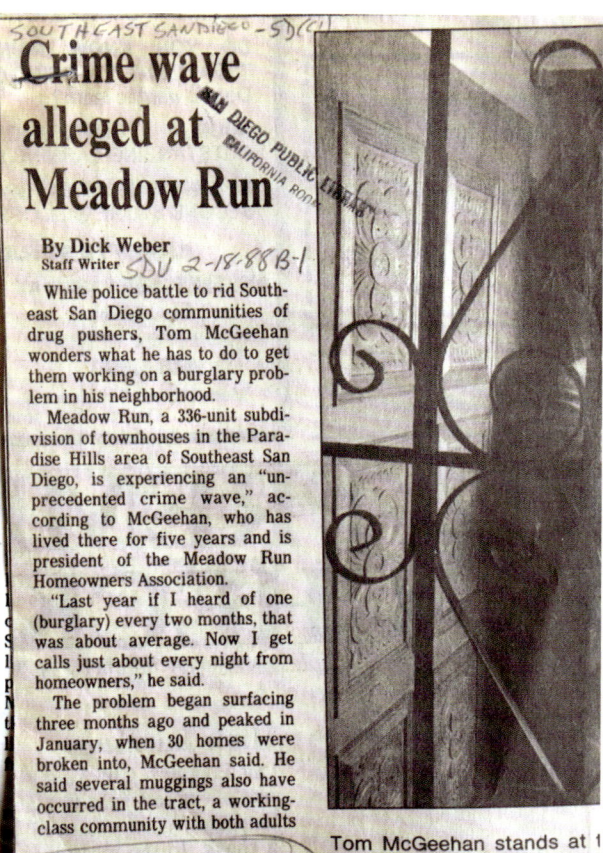

SOUTHEAST SANDIEGO - SD(1)

Crime wave alleged at Meadow Run

By Dick Weber
Staff Writer SDU 2-18-88 B-1

While police battle to rid Southeast San Diego communities of drug pushers, Tom McGeehan wonders what he has to do to get them working on a burglary problem in his neighborhood.

Meadow Run, a 336-unit subdivision of townhouses in the Paradise Hills area of Southeast San Diego, is experiencing an "unprecedented crime wave," according to McGeehan, who has lived there for five years and is president of the Meadow Run Homeowners Association.

"Last year if I heard of one (burglary) every two months, that was about average. Now I get calls just about every night from homeowners," he said.

The problem began surfacing three months ago and peaked in January, when 30 homes were broken into, McGeehan said. He said several muggings also have occurred in the tract, a working-class community with both adults

Tom McGeehan stands at t
Paradise Hills, an area that I

See **Meadow Run** on Page B-5

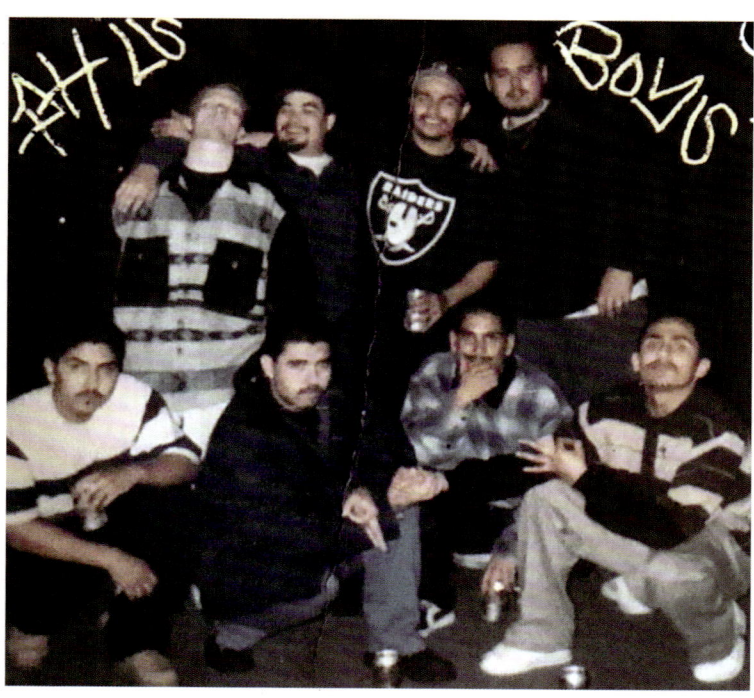

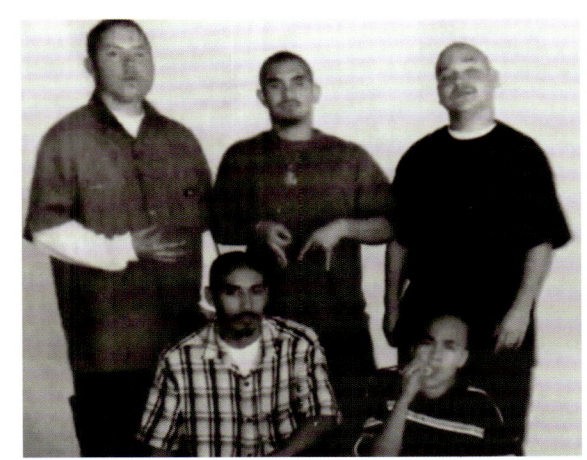

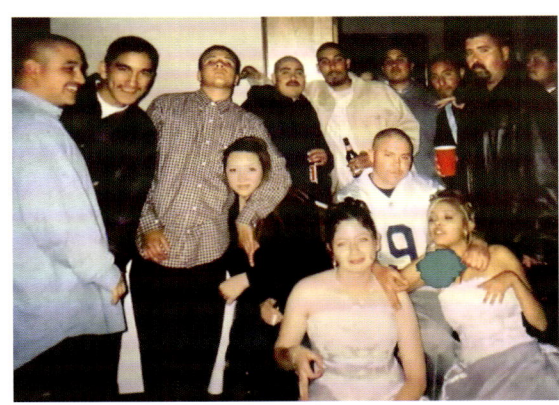

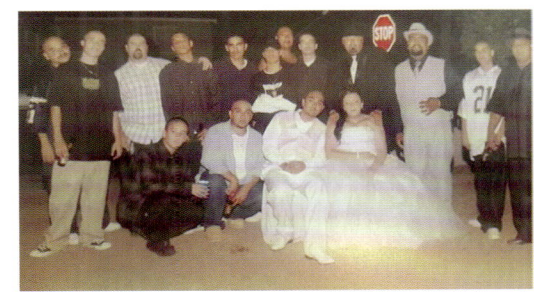

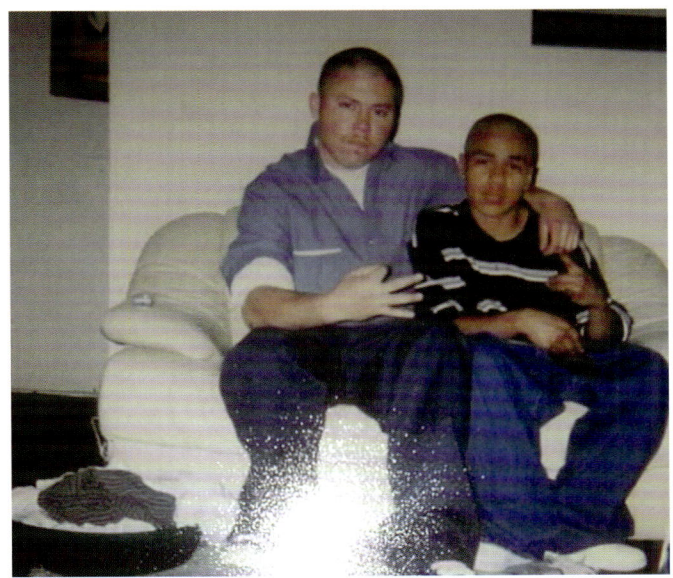

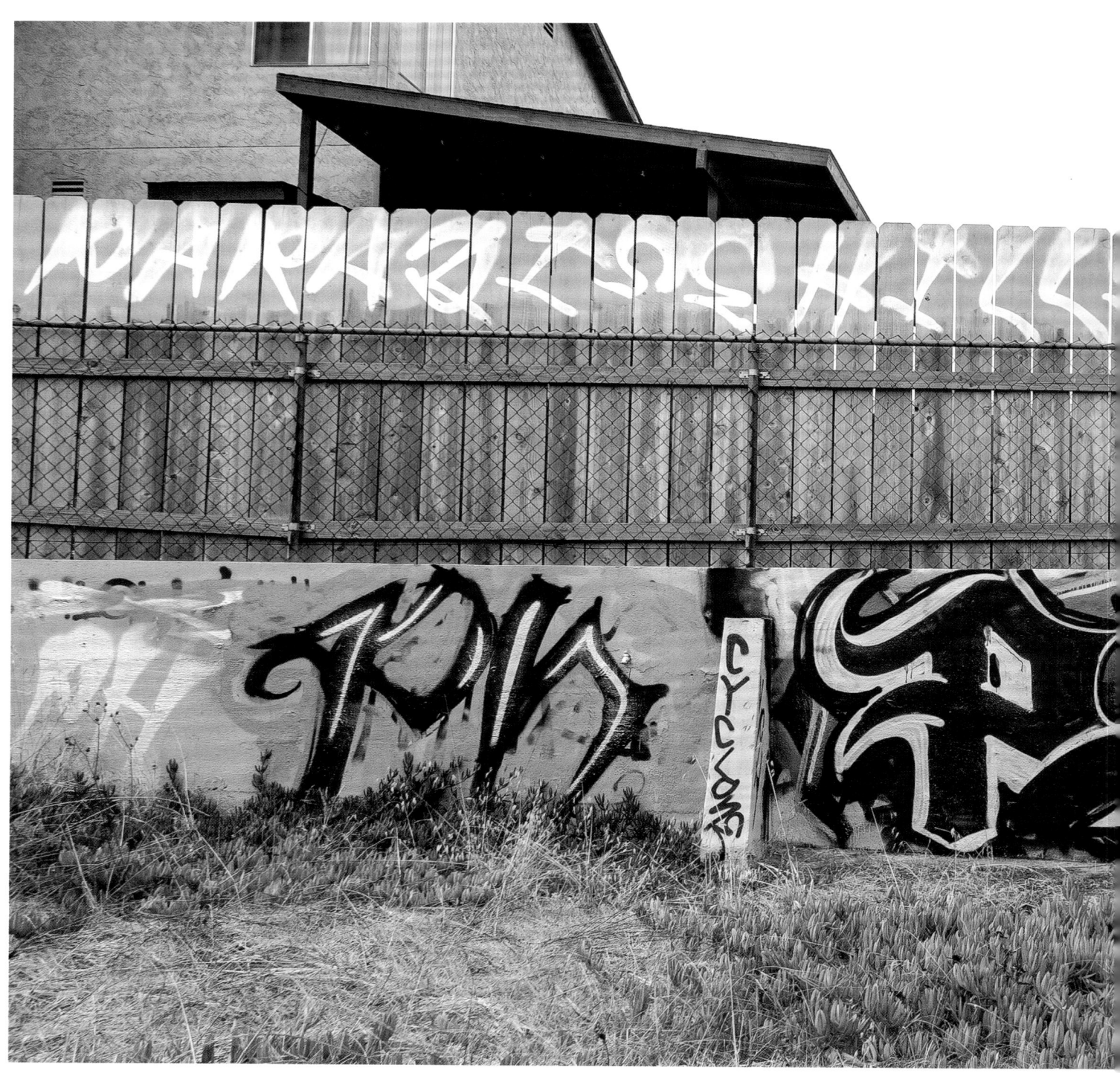

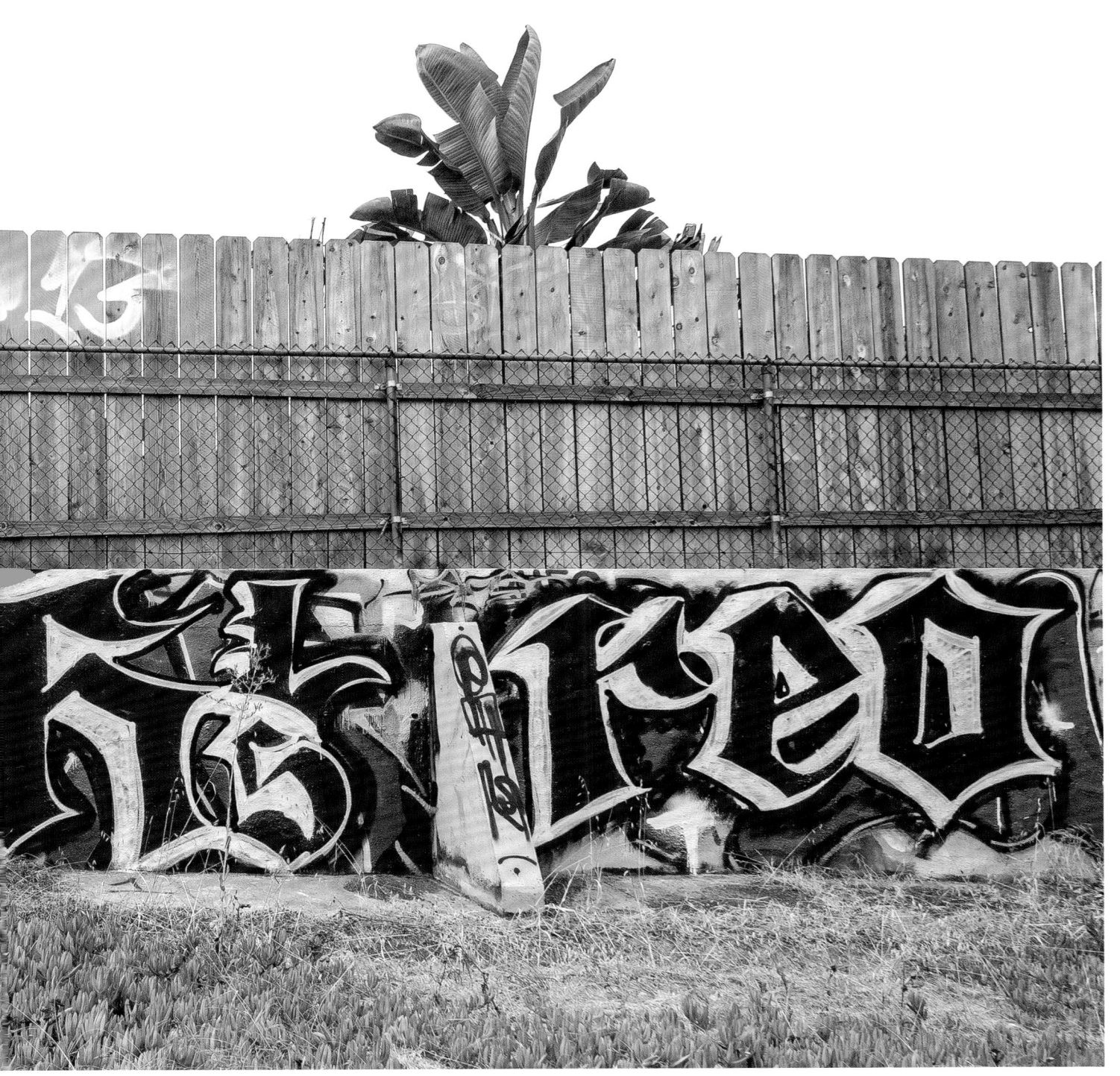

LOMITA

VILLAGE

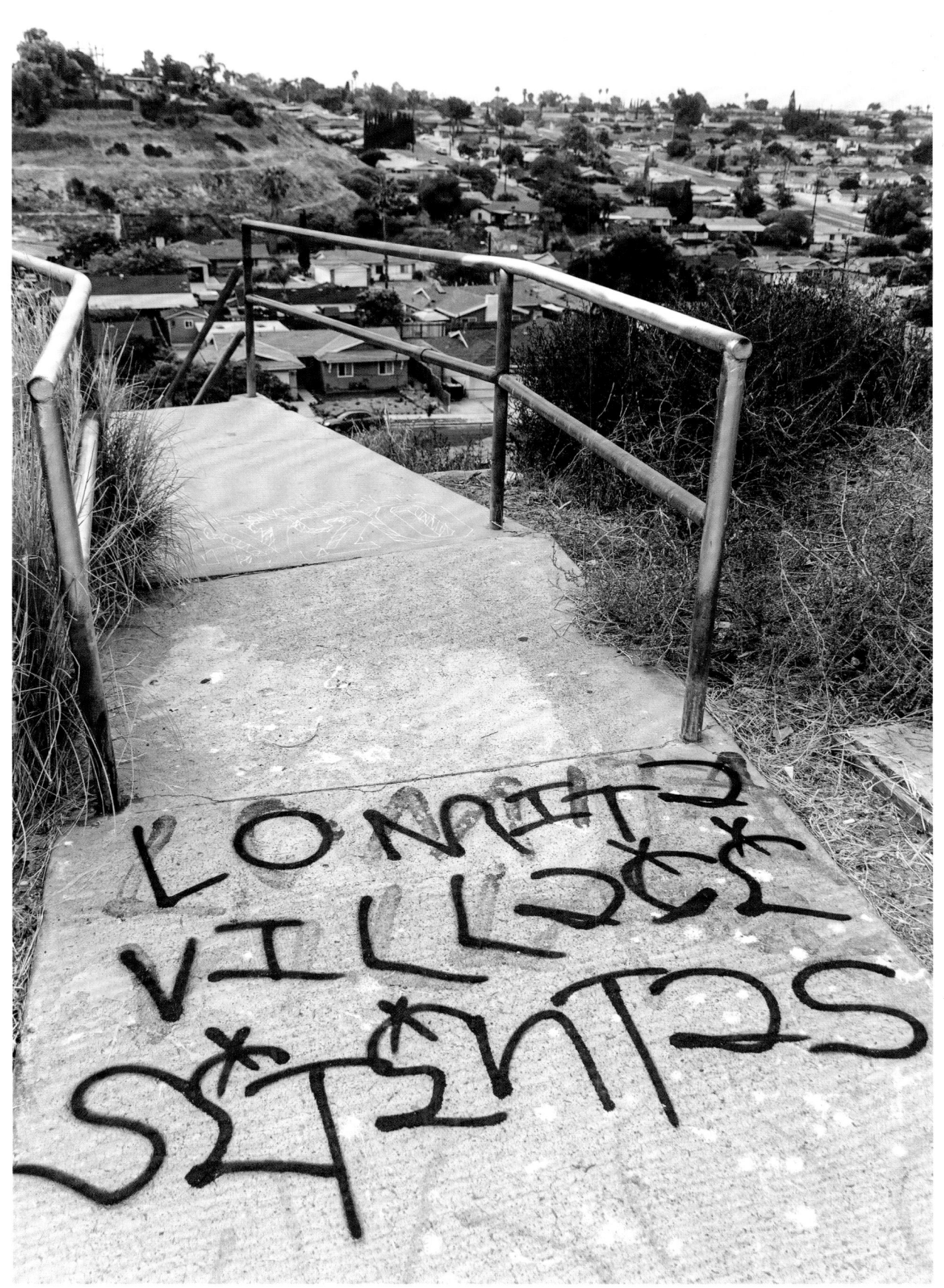

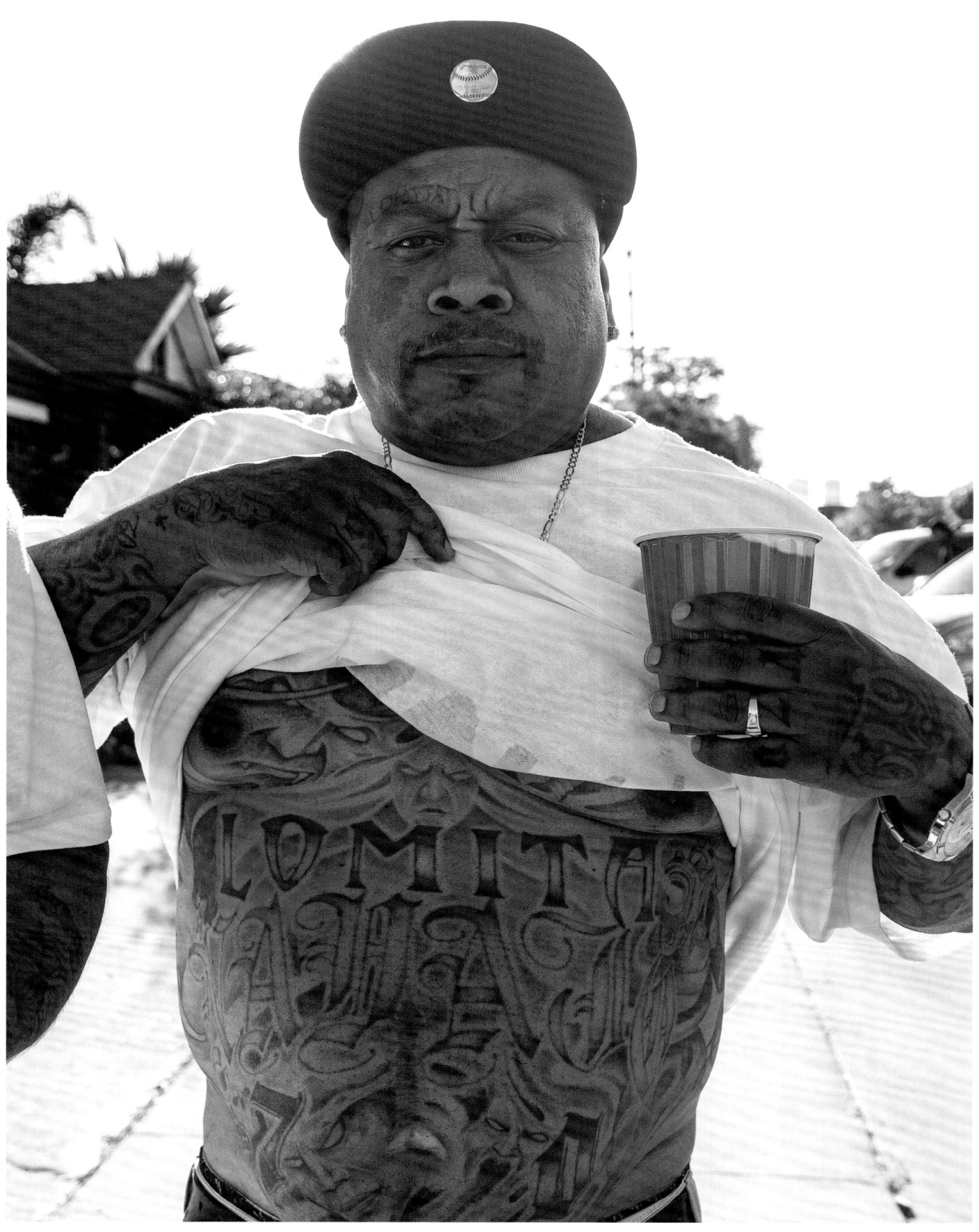

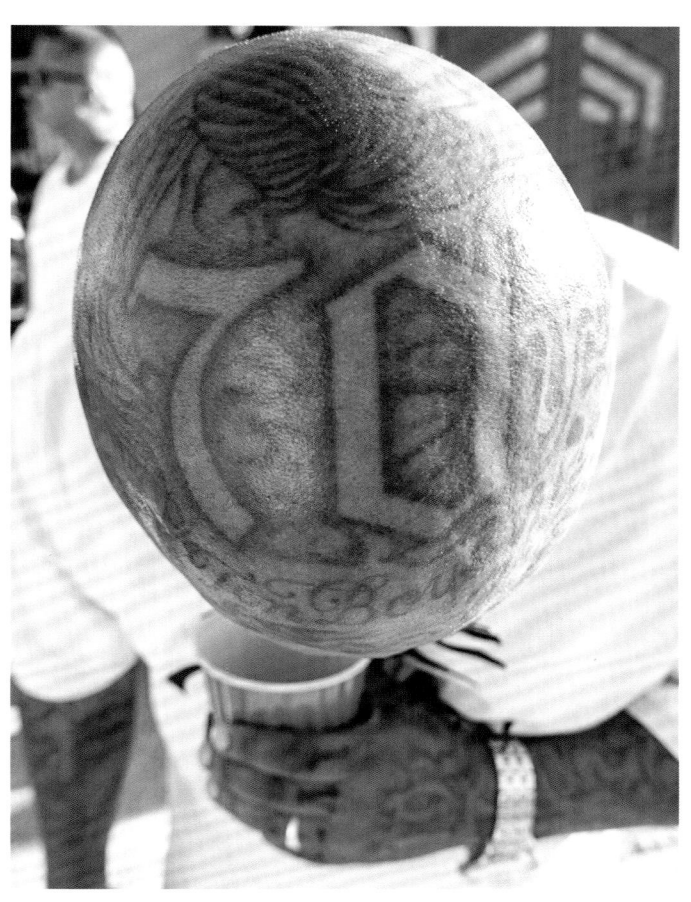
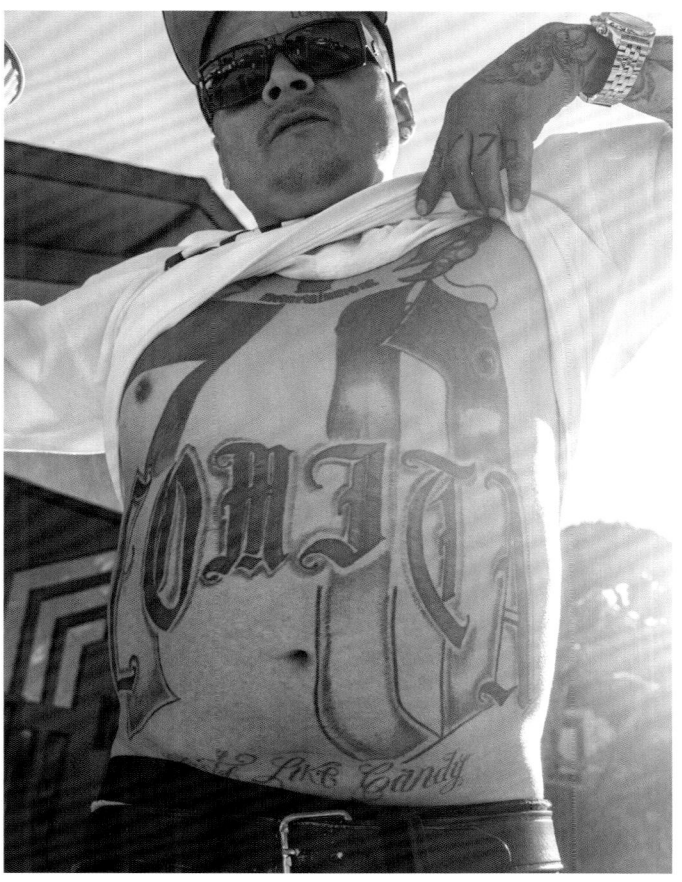

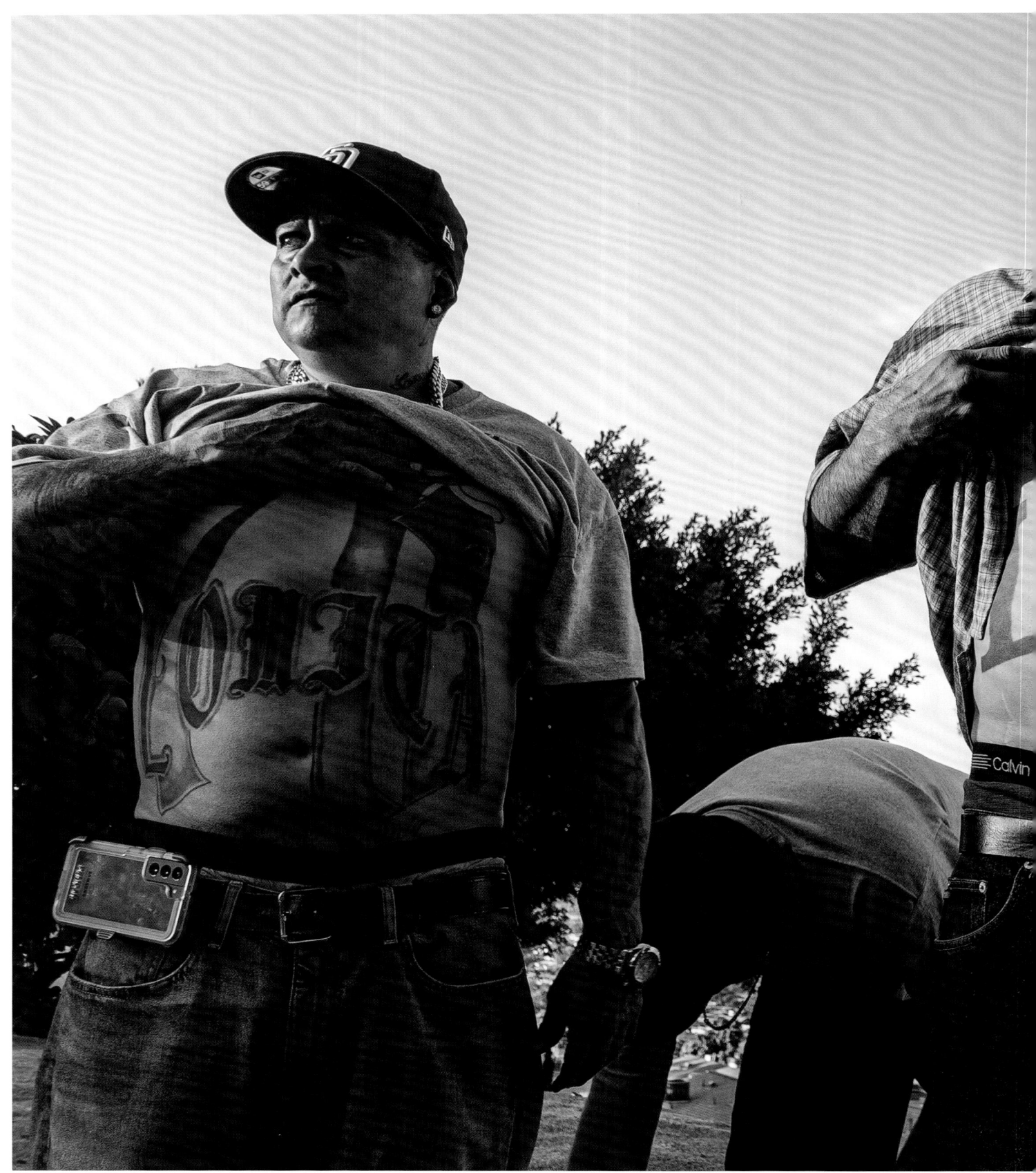

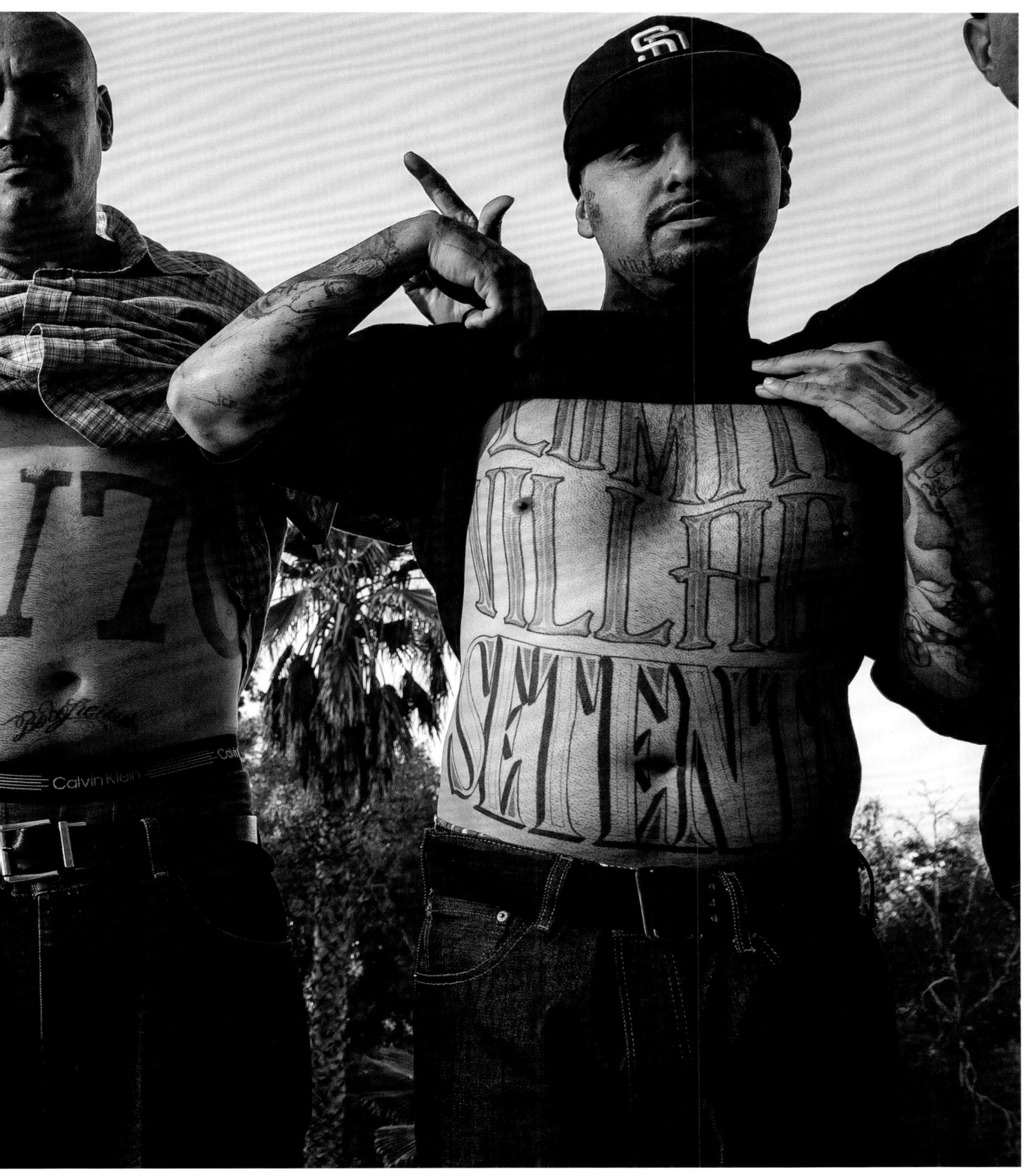

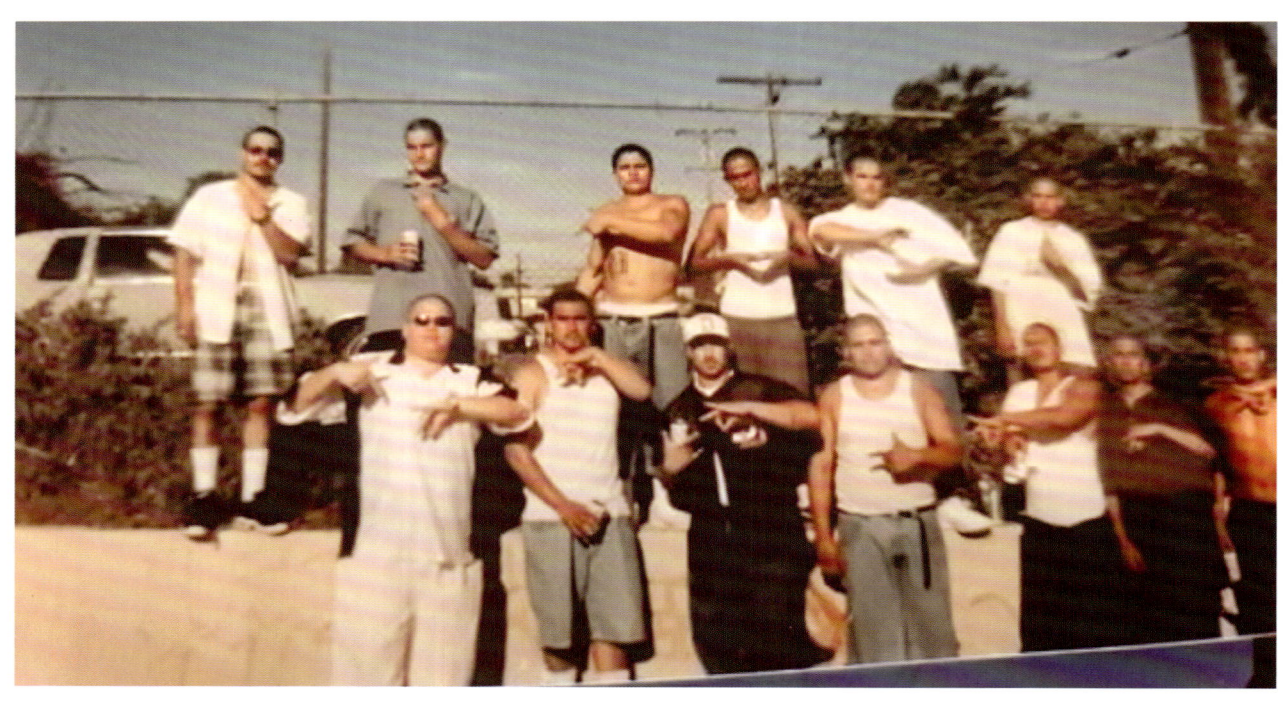

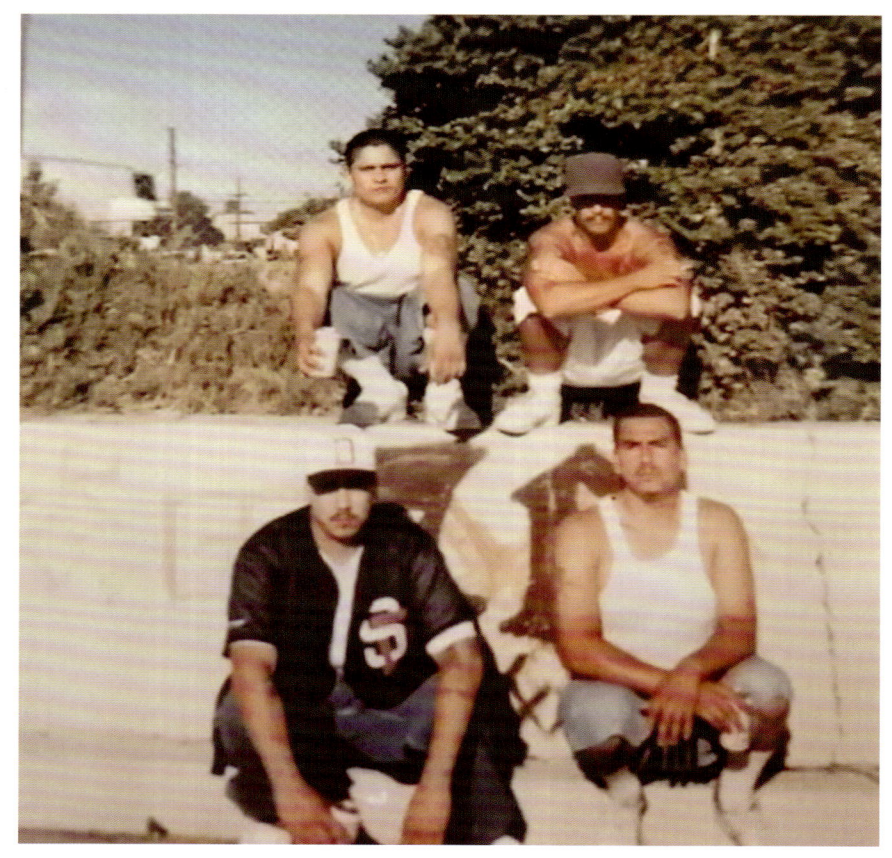

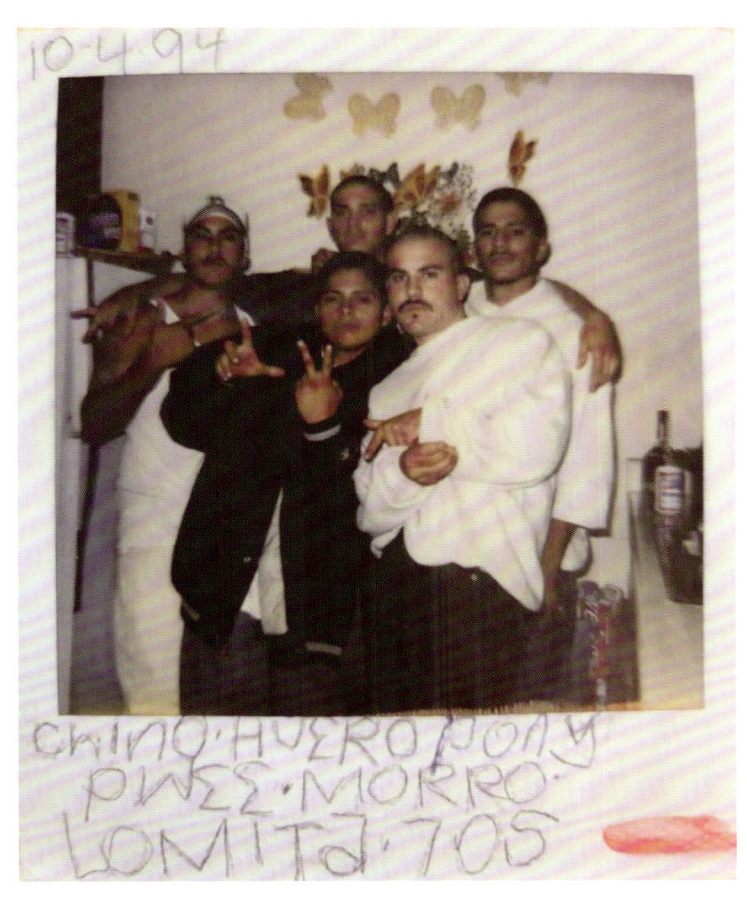

CITY

HEIGHTS

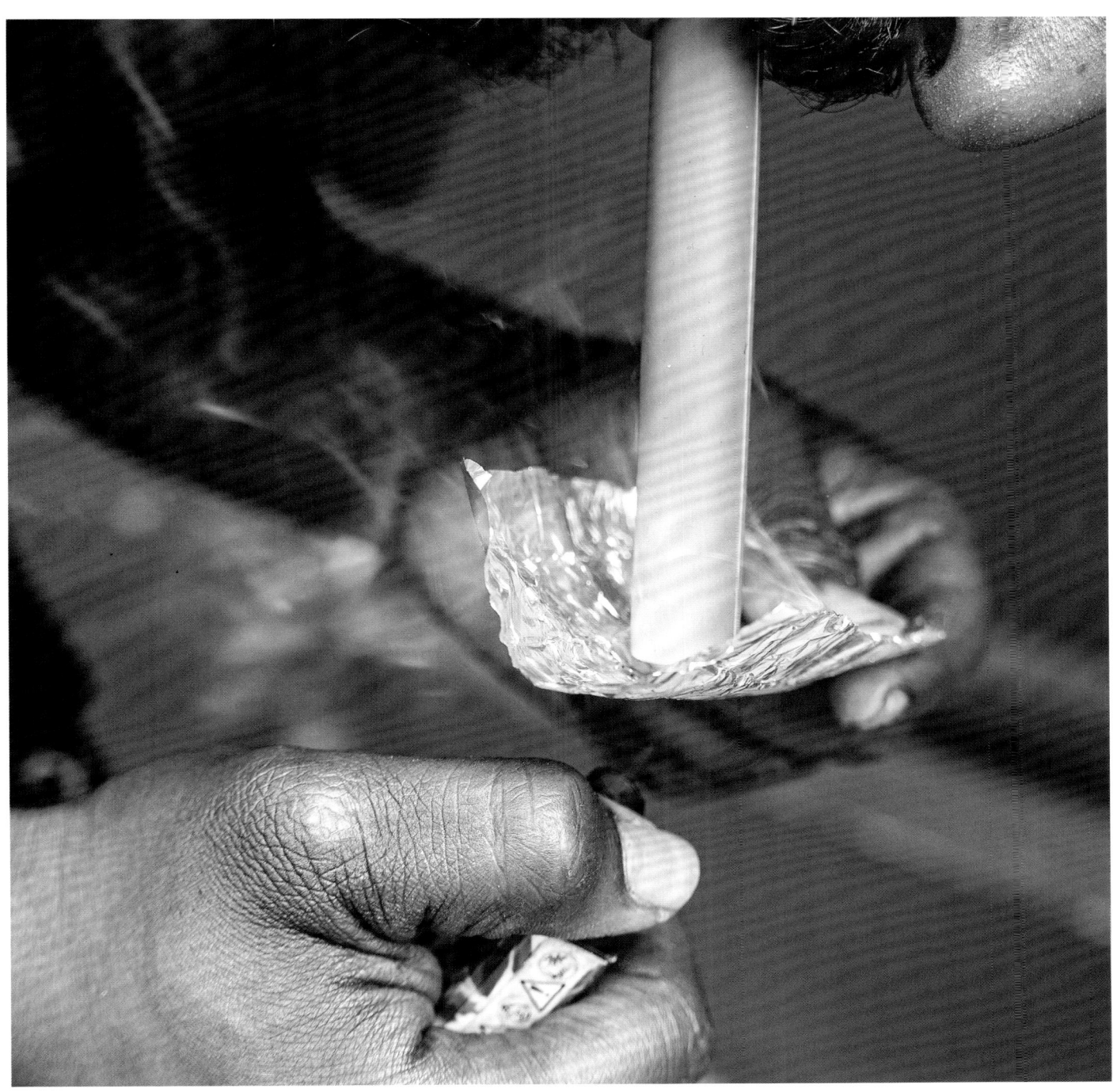

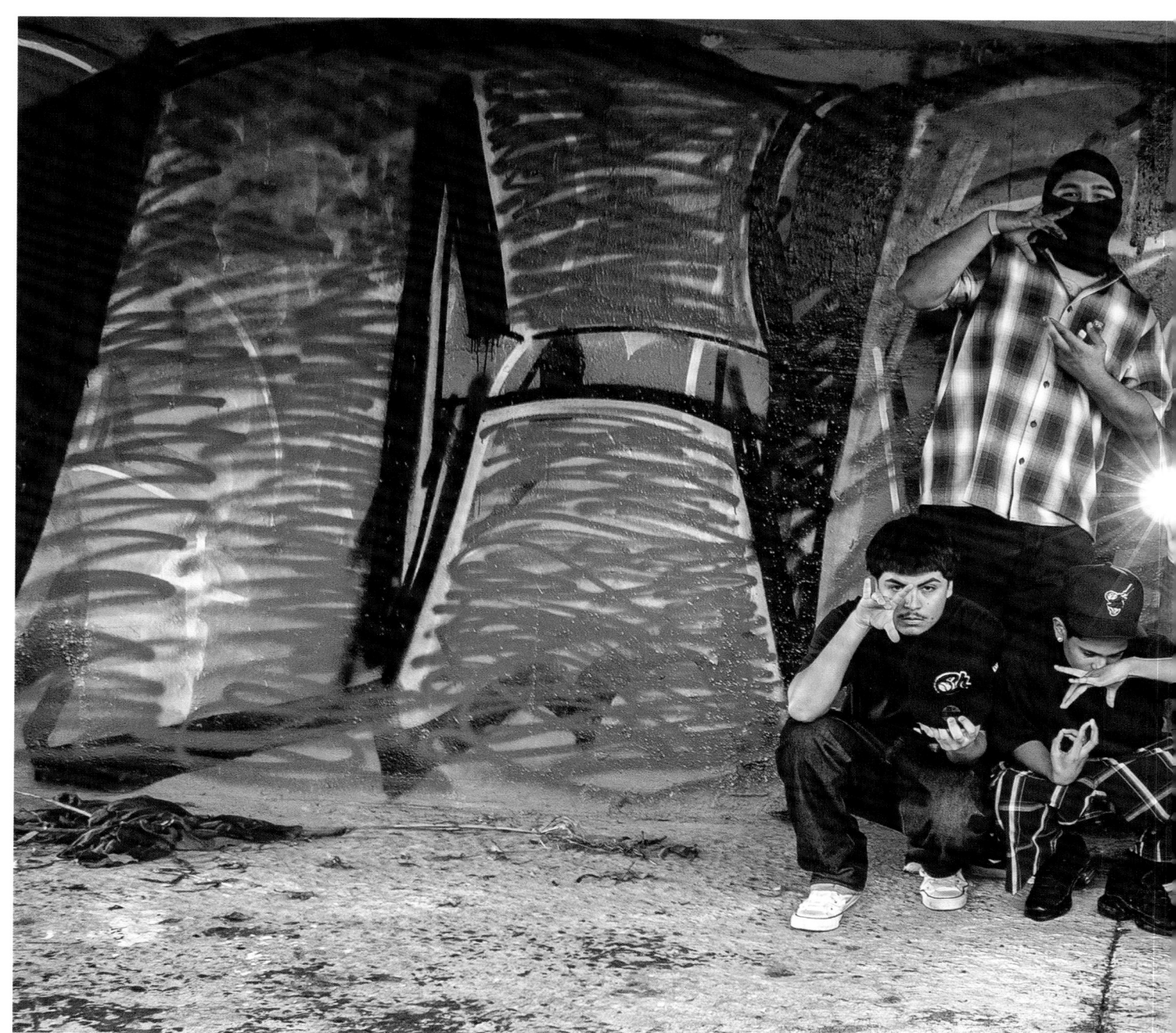

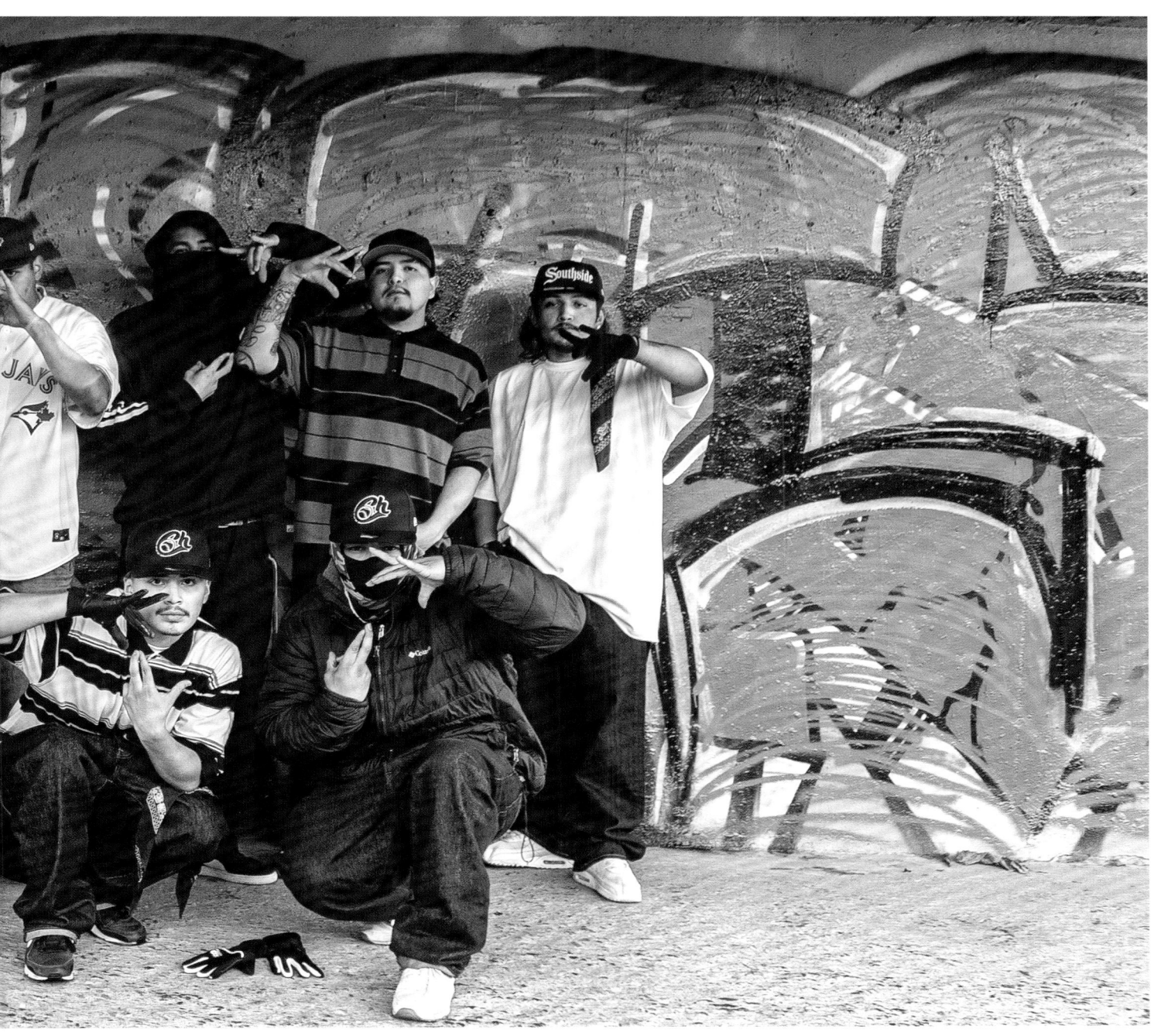

SAN

YSIDRO

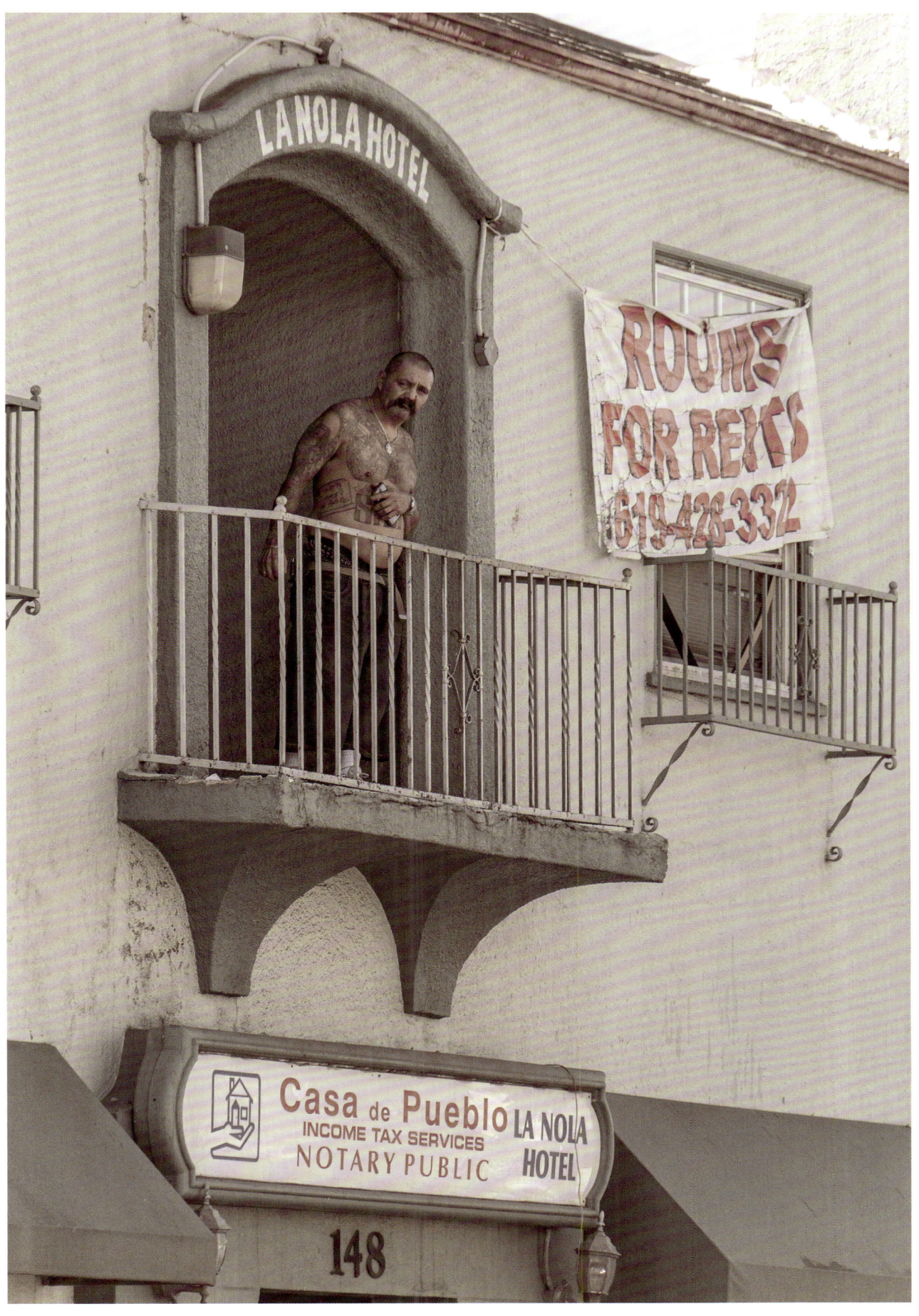

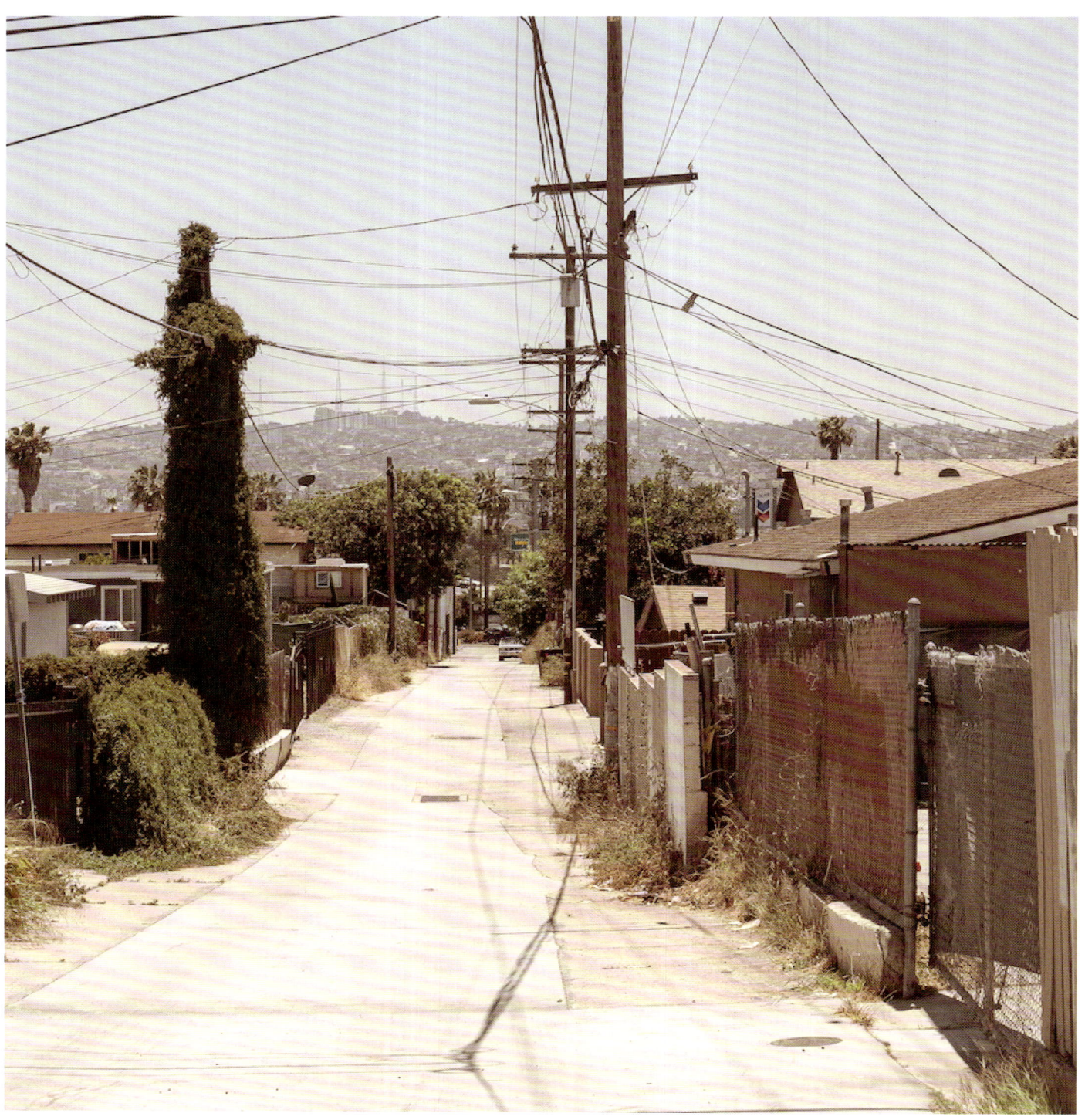

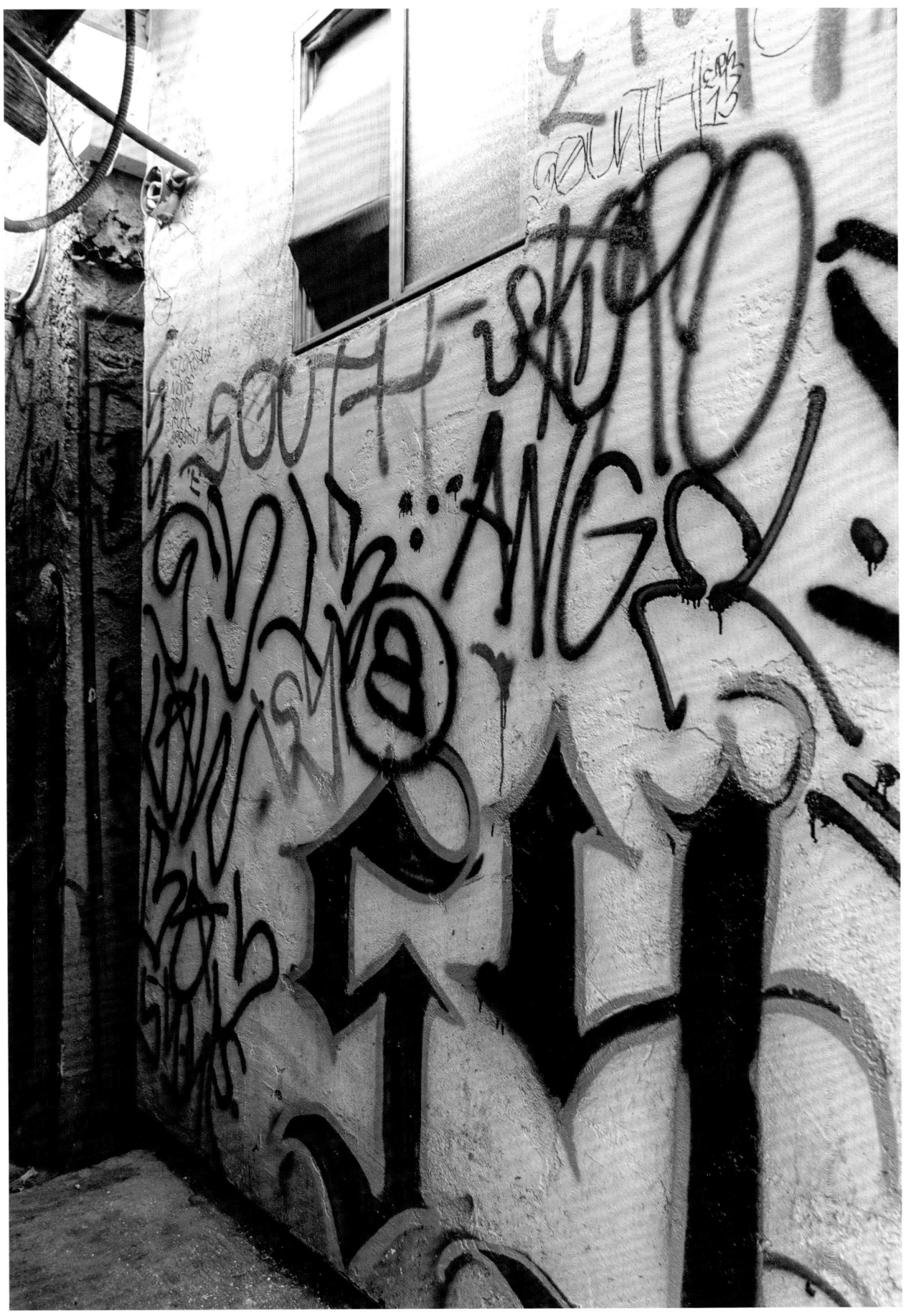

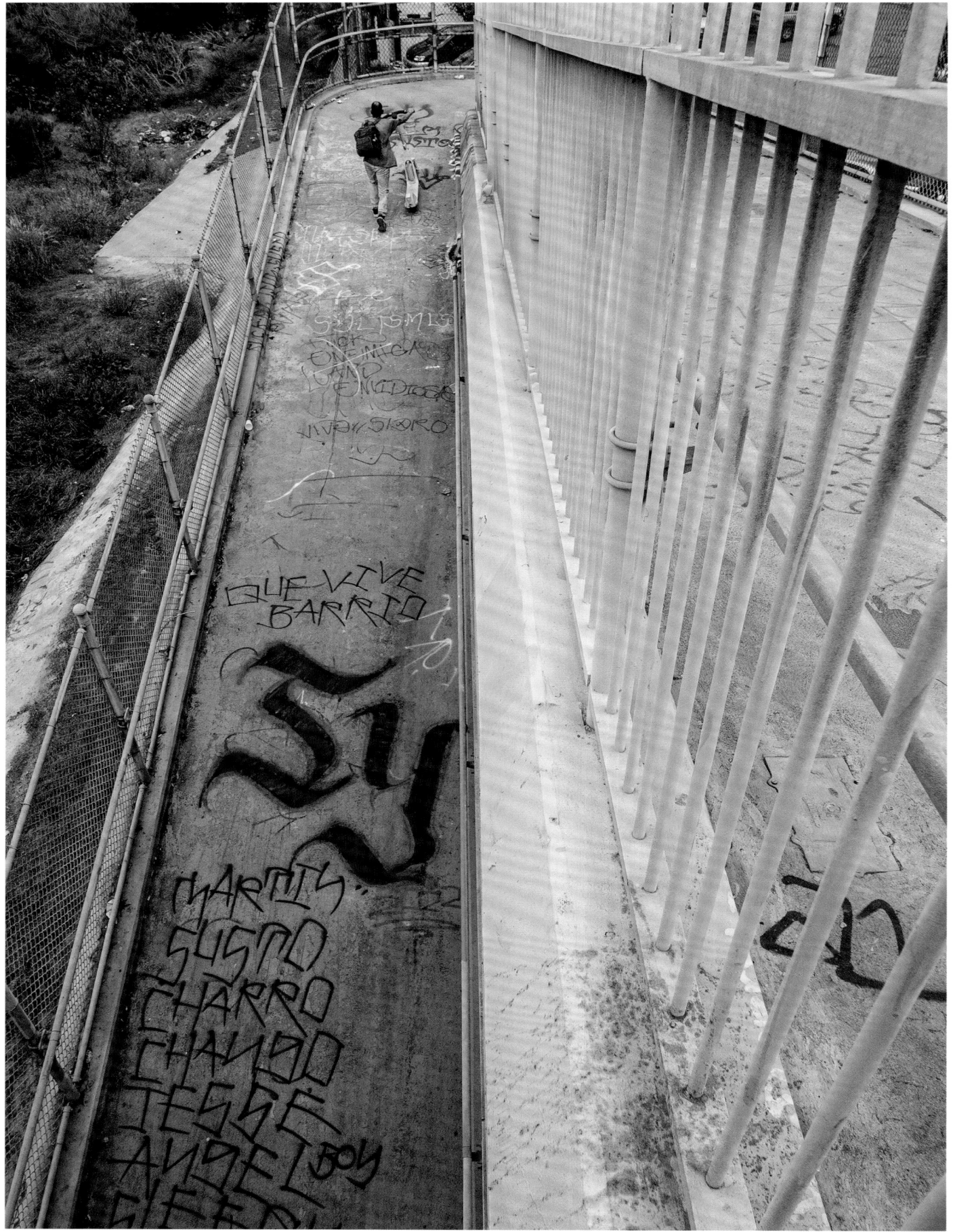

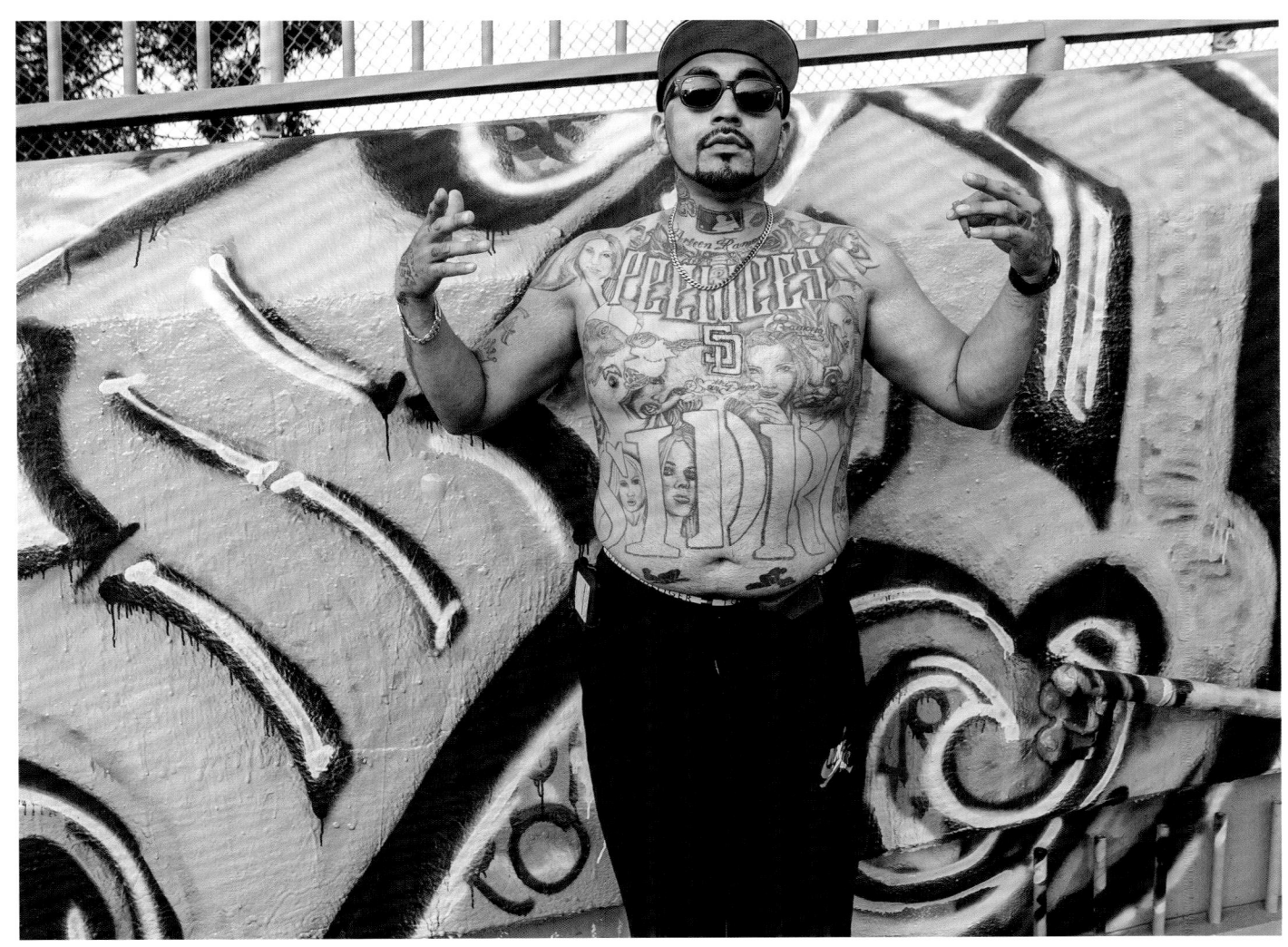

I fell in love with the streets at a young age and I am one of the
few survivors. I've seen it all, from homie love to betrayal and
then death. My city is now a ghost town ever since fentanyl hit the
streets. This is my city where you can't trust anyone, not even your
own. 'Border Town.' Just check my stats. We're familiar with the
struggles where I'm from.

I should have been dead thirty years ago, many times, and I'm still here. I don't know why I'm still here, alive. I've been through a lot of shit, gang shootings, gang stabbings, you name it. The bullets pass right over me, I'm not proud of my past. I hang around here and I try to help out the young people, this new generation, to teach them or try to, so that they can comprehend it's not about prison, it's about going to college, school. Because I had that opportunity and I messed up and I paid my consequences to society. Besides that, I was struggling to get my life together. It takes time but I'm doing it.

This lifestyle wasn't meant for me. I was a schoolboy, somebody coming from Tijuana at the age of four or five, not knowing English and going to school here and I didn't know what the fuck these people were talking.

This is San Ysidro, this is where I grew up. Everybody on this block—old people, young people—they know of me. My older brother was the one who used to take me with him when I was young. He would buy me clothes, like homie clothes, and dress me up like a homie. I didn't like it but it was my older brother so I had to kind of do it. That's how it started, and then one time, he knew I was doing bad things, he talked to me and said, 'You know what? Shut the fuck up!' I never disrespected my older brother, never! But that day after he gets me into all this. I said, 'You know what, you created a monster now. I'm doing what I want to do! And your name, I'm taking it away! And I'm taking over! Okay?' I say, 'You know what, I was doing good, you're the one that brought me into this state.' At the end, I say, 'Show some respect to the carnal! This conversation is over, ya estuvo!' I hardly talk to him anymore. He's doing good, I mean after what he's done, too, now he's doing good and I'm here and I'm doing good, been to prison . . . a few times and I survived prison and I'm out here now."

—MARIO "LIL PAYASO" SEVILLA (RIP)

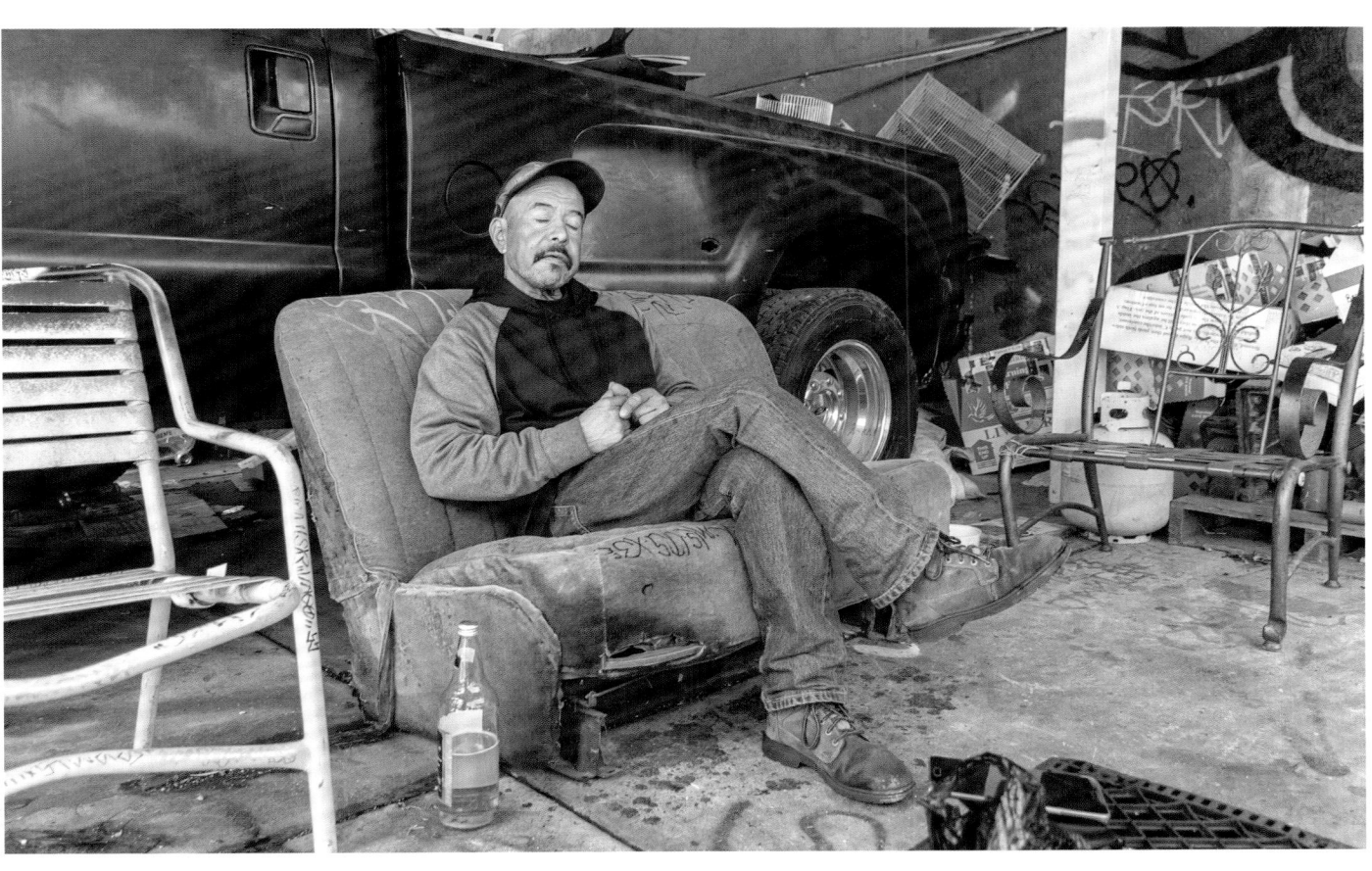

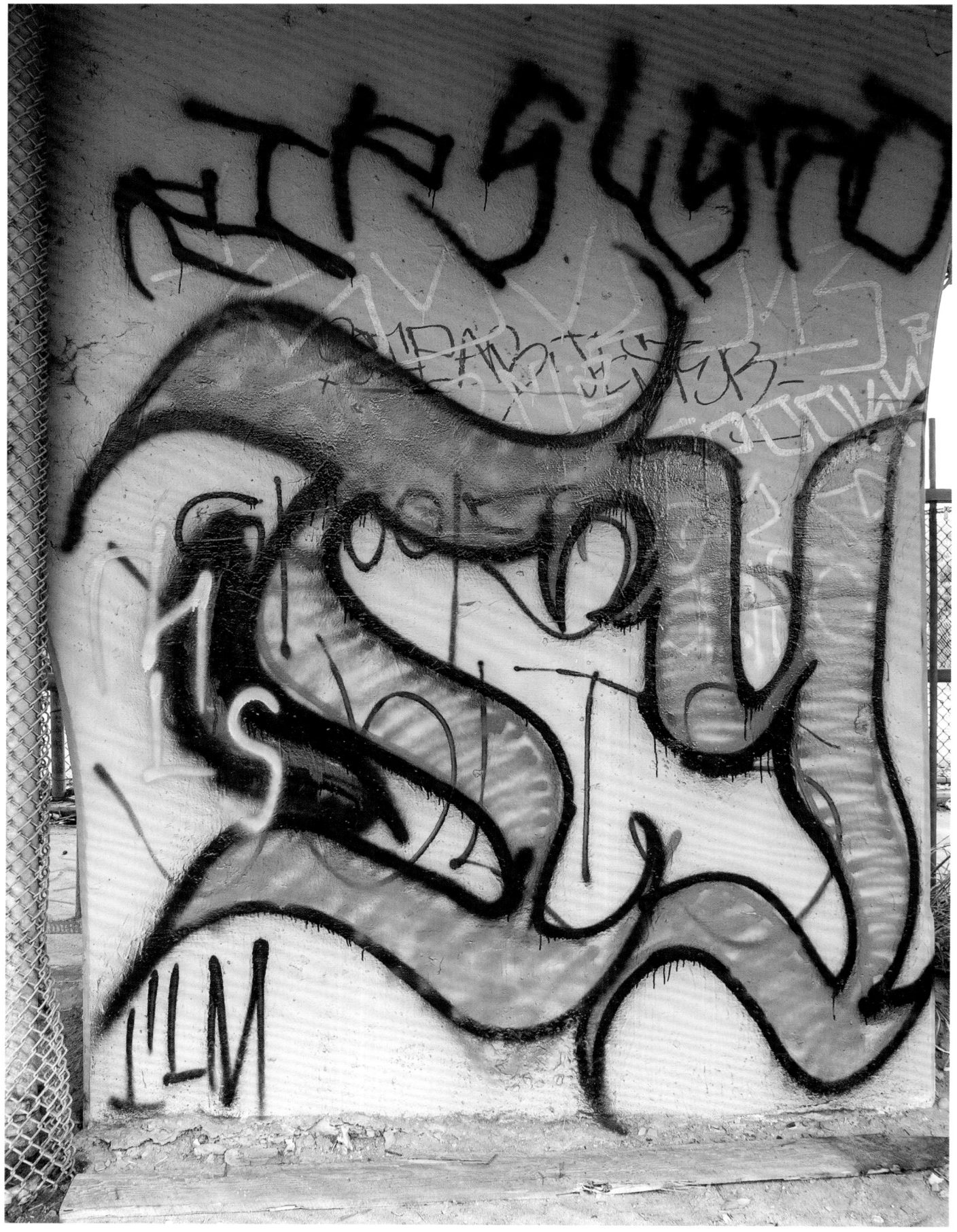

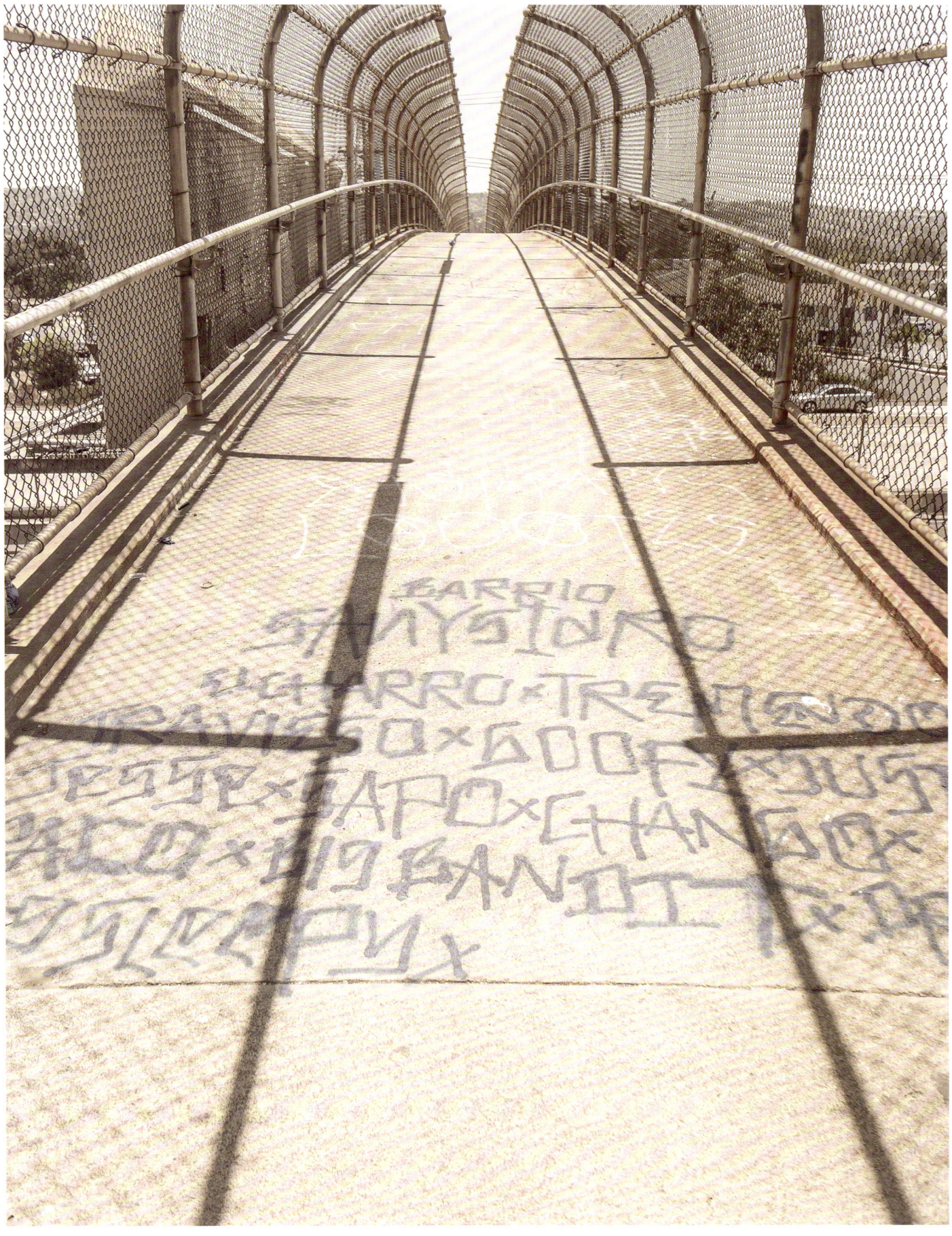

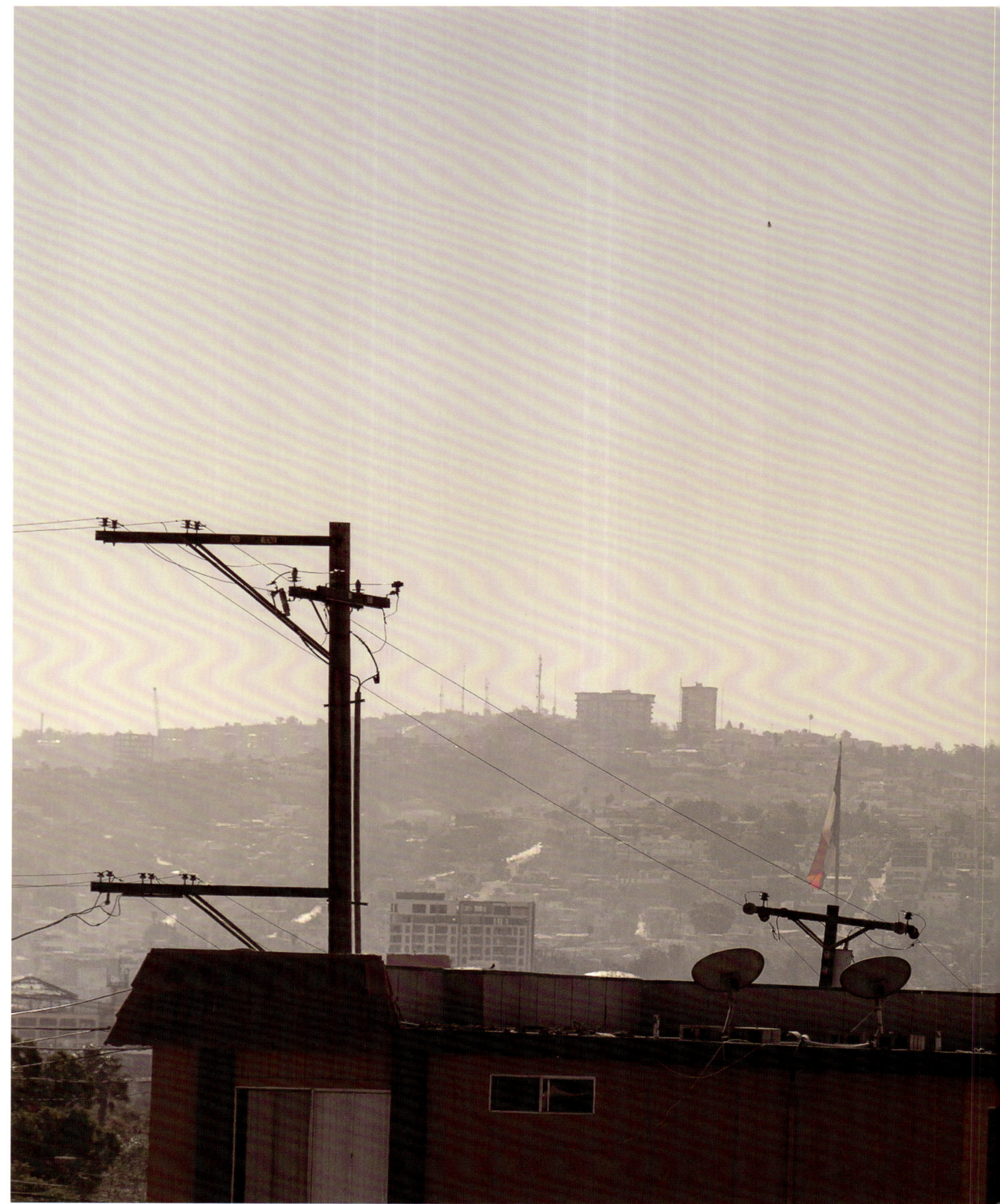

ESSAY BY MIGUEL VALENCIA

They want to know the thoughts that leap through my skull and what makes my brain tick. What makes someone go outside and fuck around the way I do. When I do something, I always have a purpose, a vision for it and I think that this is just the form of art I relish in. True stories from another human being yet, living beneath the shadows. Then there's something about being on the edge of life; it just feeds me. As intrigued as I am with them, I think they are just as fascinated with me as well for whatever reason, and then there's a lot I find that I have in common with many of them.

I am not perfect, I am not here to tell you that I am better or to say that I am anyone that you should follow as a form of inspiration to look up to. I keep a lot to myself, I hold a lot in and I am someone very much in the background, I don't like a lot of attention. I am who I am and if you know me then you know how I move.

I like to tell true stories visually. I always have and it is an intriguing way to get to know someone and what they have gone through in their lifetime—the neighborhood and the things that happen here and from those living that lifestyle. I think about how some of my own homeboys along with their girls gave up their lives to abandon their kids to become dope fiends, or when someone's parents passed away from an overdose when we were kids. The homies pops is doing life so his brothers are in gangs continuing to push for the neighborhood to make a name for themselves. Things of that nature that I grew up with would eventually push me to tell such stories or photograph such a unique moment later in my life.

I do also feel that San Diego is very fabricated if not very deceiving, so I felt that I needed to tell the truth about a lifestyle and the in-depth reality of those in the background. What they call 'the margins of San Diego' we say 'South Bay', 'South East', or 'North County'.

A lot of those kids out there want to meet me or ask their older homeboys for me to photograph them. I've met some of them and I like all those kids. They're really good kids, their personalities and the questions they ask me. It's one of the few things that could make me crack a smile. So it does affect me a little bit when the lifestyle they dress up as and don't yet comprehend has buried them too early.

Thoughts that enter my frame sometimes, "It's a part of the game Miguel and you know that! Isn't this what you set out to do? So do what you do best and remain emotionless and move on. Why let it affect you?"

What I want people to know is that I care about the caliber of my photographs. I am about the art within the performance of my shots and how these people are represented.

The hands I have shaken of those I have photographed, to the best of my capabilities, I interpret them through the frame of my lens. I felt them, I spoke with many of them and I got to be around very exclusive figures.

I partied with quite a few of those specific figures of famous names within the background and I got to know them very well as they would also become a part of my own personal life while advising my documentary. They shared their histories with me and how that cultivated their names and characters.

This would also inspire my way of thinking about how I could possibly shoot this body of work when I would step outside to shoot such photographs.

Some of them would eventually become incarcerated, putting it all on the line, and then some would eventually meet their demise. I remember what they were like and our interactions. I remember how I shot their pictures.

These are solid heads that I have come to know and they also have families and kids, yet they are a part of a lifestyle until the very end. A lifestyle that people don't understand unless you were there or brought up around.

I want people to see a true representation of an authentic San Diego from the background.

ACKNOWLEDGMENTS

I would like to take the time to thank the following neighborhoods and some very special names who I know very well or who have assisted me in some way. I would like to thank the following:

My homeboy, Bigg Solo from OTAY, for always being there when I needed anything. Thank you, player. Mr. Dopey from Logan Heights 30th and the Logan Heights family period and my boy Negro. Was always epic doing pictures for Logan! My ShellTown family, thank you Mr. TuTs for your advice and collaboration, and of course Big 'O' dogg and my boy Chato! We made history a few times. Shout out to the 38 family, what up Speedy! Thank you! To Lil Sapo and my primos from the OTNC Insane Boy family and 24th Park Apartments for National City, thank you. The homie Grumpy from Lomas 26th. It was a lot of fun to be around you and listen to your stories from the days of way back. Thank you! The Sherman 20th, 27th, and GHP family and to Big Sparky for fucken with me and believing in my work since day one, thank you, and to Mr. Clyde as well, thank you sir! Shout out to the legendary Prayers! The Paradise Hills family, my boy P. You know who you are, Thank you. My North County fam always for your hospitality and for welcoming me with a second home. Oceanside Posole Town, thank you! Thank you to the homeboys in Delsol. To the Market Street family, thank you for having me as well. To the lil homies from Juniors. Thank you to everyone that took the time to fuck with me on this. Also my condolences and RIP to the ones that I photographed that are not around. And to the ones I also photographed that are now doing a life sentence, thank you for that moment and memory. If I forgot anyone please don't take it personally, running out of time and page counts. This is off the top of my head. Thank you!

Miguel "Chromatic" Valencia
The Other Side of San Diego

Published by Blurring Books
BlurringBooks.com
@BlurringBooksNYC

Project management by Sean M. Johnson
Editorial Assistance by Anne McPeak and Elliott Rogers
Front cover script by Bigg Solo, OTAY

First Edition, First Printing

Library of Congress Control Number 2024952270
ISBN 978-1-963814-06-4
Printed in China

Book design by Francesca Richer